Region and Partition

Bengal, Punjab and the Partition
of the Subcontinent

Region and Partition

Bengal, Punjab and the Partition
of the Subcontinent

Edited by

Ian Talbot
and
Gurharpal Singh

OXFORD
UNIVERSITY PRESS

OXFORD

UNIVERSITY PRESS

Great Clarendon Street, Oxford OX2 6DP

Oxford University Press is a department of the University of Oxford.
It furthers the University's objective of excellence in research, scholarship,
and education by publishing worldwide in

Oxford New York

Athens Auckland Bangkok Bogotá Buenos Aires Calcutta
Cape Town Chennai Dar es Salaam Delhi Florence Hong Kong Istanbul
Karachi Kuala Lumpur Madrid Melbourne Mexico City Mumbai
Nairobi Paris São Paulo Singapore Taipei Tokyo Toronto Warsaw

with associated companies in Berlin Ibadan

Oxford is a registered trade mark of Oxford University Press
in the UK and in certain other countries

This edition in Oxford Pakistan Paperbacks 2000

ISBN 0 19 579378 1

Printed in Pakistan at
Mueid Packages, Karachi.
Published by
Ameena Saiyid, Oxford University Press
5-Bangalore Town, Sharae Faisal
PO Box 13033, Karachi-75350, Pakistan.

Contents

Preface

viii

Pakistan came into existence following the British transfer of power in India in August 1947. The division of the two major centres of Muslim population in Bengal and Punjab was integral to the redrawing of the political map of the subcontinent into the two successor states of the Raj. The partition was accompanied by a communal holocaust which sparked off totally unexpected mass migrations. The resulting transfers of population have indelibly marked the history of the subcontinent.

Most studies of the partition have centred around the causes of the Pakistan demand and the circumstances in which the Muslims emerged triumphant as the British dismantled their Indian empire. Much less has been written about its consequences for the regions which were split asunder in 1947. Even less interest has been evoked in the consequences of the partition for their populations. This volume maintains that fifty years after the transfer of power, it is appropriate to direct attention from the national to the regional level with respect to the impact of partition.

Many of the chapters in this volume took their initial shape as papers submitted to the 14th European Conference on Modern South Asian Studies. I would like to thank the hosts at Copenhagen University for facilitating the organization of the panel on the partition. I am also especially obliged to the panel's co-sponsor Gurharpal Singh.

I would also like to thank the International Journal of Punjab studies for permission to reproduce the articles by Mohammad Waseem, Yunas Samad, Gurharpal Singh and Shinder Thandi. My piece on 'Literature and the Human Drama of Partition' has been reproduced with permission by Sage. Finally, my thanks are due to the individual contributors for their good humour in responding to editorial promptings and for ensuring the expeditious completion of the manuscript.

Ian Talbot
Coventry, March 1998

Acknowledgements

We thank the following for permission to reproduce the material included in this volume:

International Journal of Punjab Studies for chapters by Mohammad Waseem, Yunas Samad, Shinder Singh Thandi, Gurharpal Singh which appeared in a special thematic issue on partition Vol 4 Number 1 January-June 1997; *South Asia* for Ian Talbot, 'Literature and the Human Drama of the 1947 Partition' *South Asia* XVIII, Special Issue (1995) pp. 37 - 56. This article was subsequently published in a Sage volume entitled *Freedom, Trauma, Continuities: Northern India and Independence*. Editors D.A. Low, H. Brasted.

Introduction

The partition of Punjab and Bengal which accompanied the British departure from India and the emergence of Pakistan was a historical event of immense magnitude. At the most conservative estimate[1] around two hundred thousand people were killed and twelve million were rendered homeless by the massacres and migrations which resulted from the communal holocaust of August 1947. Studies have focused however more on the causes of the partition[2] than on its human consequences. They have also neglected a comparative approach to the study of the two regions which were most affected by it. Ironically one of the few Pakistani works on Punjabi sacrifice in the partition event has been written in Urdu by Mohammad Hanif Ramay.[3] A purpose of this volume is to begin to extend a regional and human dimension to the study of the partition.

While the violence had spent itself in exhaustion by November 1947, the sufferings of refugees in makeshift camps dragged on for months and in some cases for years as is illustrated by Harihar Bhattacharyya's work on refugees in West Bengal. As late as 1960, the Indo-Pakistan Joint Partition Implementation Committee was attempting to resolve financial disputes relating to the pensions of the holocaust victims. In the sense that the Kashmir issue is part of the 'unfinished business' of partition,[4] five decades later there are still refugee victims in such camps as Ambore in Azad Kashmir. Their Hindu counterparts, the pandits who fled the valley after 1989 can be seen selling carpets in New Delhi's tourist areas. Patricia Ellis and Zafar Khan in their chapter argue for the voice of the Kashmiris themselves, the victims of the dispute between Pakistan and India to be heeded more than it has been in the past.

One of the most controversial elements of the machinery of partition was the Radcliffe Boundary Commission. While the

Award concerned itself only with the demarcation of boundaries in British India, its decisions with respect to the Gurdaspur district of Punjab were significant for the future evolution of the Kashmir dispute. The sense of grievance about its lack of impartiality has been fuelled in recent years by Christopher Beaumont's revelations concerning Lord Mountbatten's 'tampering' with the Award.[5] A number of the chapters in this volume reflect on these controversies. The Commission's findings concerning Bengal have tended to be ignored by historians because they have proved less contentious. This lacunae is remedied in the authoritative study by Joya Chatterji.

One consequence of the partition was to divide the Sikh community of the Punjab. The return to East Punjab of settlers from the Canal Colony areas which became part of Pakistan, as Shinder Thandi demonstrates, has exerted a profound influence on that region's economic development. The migration left not only the canal colony landholdings behind in Pakistan but such holy sites as Nankana Sahib. Singh and Fair in their joint chapter produce a pioneering examination of the psychological and cultural consequences of partition on Sikh sacred space.

It is not only in the disputes concerning Kashmir and the Boundary Commission that the partition's legacy has loomed large over South Asian politics. Pakistan began its history coloured by the disputes with India over the division of assets and the waters of the River Indus[6] as well as by the personal experiences of the millions of refugees and their descendants from East Punjab and north-western India. As Mohammad Waseem remarks in this volume, Pakistan is in a real sense a refugee state, although few academic studies of its political development have reflected on this. Punjabi attitudes to India and to the Kashmir dispute can only be fully understood for example in terms of the existence of not only a large Kashmiri exile community, but of five million migrants from East Punjab.

The partition paved the way for a Punjabi-Mohajir[7] domination of the machinery of the Pakistan state. This alienated the Sindhi population especially as it saw Urdu speaking refugee enclaves in Karachi and Hyderabad being carved out of its cultural region. From the time of Ayub onwards and especially in the post-Bangladesh era, the Punjabi power increased to the disadvantage of the mohajirs. This culminated in the establishment of a mohajir ethnic identity. Fifty years after independence, Pakistan still faces the problem of accommodating pluralism with the requirements of nation building. This immensely important theme forms the focus for Yunas Samad's reflection on partition and Pakistan's political dilemmas in this volume.

The historiographical debate on the causes of partition is particularly lively.[8] Unfortunately the majority of texts produce more heat than light. For in the words of Ayesha Jalal they tend to bear the imprint of 'made in India' or 'made in Pakistan'.[9] For many Indian writers, partition is still seen as an aberration in the unity of the subcontinent's history. Pakistani writers have countered by trumpeting the inevitability of partition because of the existence of two 'separate' nations in the subcontinent. The anniversary of the British departure from India has inevitably produced similar official histories from both sides of the 'great divide'.

This work is intended as a new departure which will avoid the reproduction of ideology as history.[10] One way it seeks to avoid this trap is to bring together the writings of leading historians from Pakistan, India and overseas in a single volume. More importantly it seeks to avoid polemics by focusing foremost on the human dimension of partition. This continues a trend in developing a 'history from beneath' which Ian Talbot called for in his recently published work *Freedom's Cry*.[11] In order to achieve this end, the volume builds on the growing academic interest in the regional history of South Asia by concentrating primarily on developments in Punjab and Bengal, the two Muslim majority regions of the subcontinent which were most affected by the partition. Finally, it introduces both new sources and methodological concepts. Thus the partition is understood for the first time for example in terms of Ian Lustick's theory of state contraction. Such new insights help to bridge the gulf between the studies of historians which tend to stop in 1947 and those of political scientists who write as if Pakistan politics were constructed on a *tabula rasa*, rather than being influenced by values, ideas and events from both partition and the earlier colonial era.

Many of the chapters in this volume were presented as papers at the fourteenth European Conference on Modern South Asian Studies held at Copenhagen in August 1996. The contributions complement each other. Joya Chatterji's chapter for example beautifully provides empirical evidence of the concept deployed by Gurharpal Singh of a 'war of manoeuvre' between politicians during the endgame of Empire about the nature and boundaries of the Indian state. The work offered in this volume represents the best in new thinking about the partition and its legacies. The authors come from a variety of academic backgrounds and disciplines. They are united in the belief that the partition should be rescued from the 'dead-hand' of official history and that a human dimension should be restored to this great event.

The first section moves on from an examination of the unexplored background to the partition of Punjab and Bengal in the chapters by Hashmi and Malik to the processes of boundary demarcation. Together the contributions on the Radcliffe Award by Ishtiaq Ahmed and Joya Chatterji provide one of the most comprehensive analyses yet to be published. The narrative history of this section of the book is supported by Gurharpal Singh's novel theoretical underpinning based on the ideas of Ian Lustick.

The final part of the book focuses on some of the legacies of partition for the contemporary subcontinent. The chapters draw on the varied disciplines of anthropology, sociology, economics and politics. The chapters contain both fresh methodological insights and empirical material. As in the opening section, the emphasis is placed on a comparative analysis and on listening to the voices of those whose lives have been disrupted by the partition event.

Ian Talbot
Coventry, March 1998.

NOTES

1.   The number of deaths has itself been controversial. The figure of 200,000 cited by P. Moon in *Divide and Quit* (London, Chatto & Windus 1962) has received support from Ziegler and Alan Campbell-Johnson. The latter

claims the massacres were of short duration, but Indian newspapers carry reports of violence as late as November in the Punjab region. Trouble continued in Ajmer until the end of that month, while riots in Karachi in January 1948 led to a belated departure of over eleven thousand Hindus from that city. The final figure for the massacres will never be known, the estimate of a death toll of half a million by Gopal Das Khosla, *Stern Reckoning; a survey of events leading up to and following the partition of India* (New Delhi, Oxford University Press 1989) is likely to be nearer the truth than Moon's figure. It is a great pity that the issue of the number of fatalities has become something of a political football between Mounbatten's supporters and his critics. This has obfuscated an issue which in any case would have been difficult to corroborate.

2. Many of the themes in the literature can be found in M. Hasan, (ed) *India's Partition. Process, Strategy and Mobilization* (Delhi, Oxford University Press 1994) p. 1-44.

3. M.H. Ramay, *Punjab Ka Muqadama* (The Case of Punjab) 4th ed. (Lahore, 1988).

4. For a variety of explanations of the origins of the Kashmir dispute, see P.S. Jha, *Kashmir 1947: Rival Versions of History* (Delhi, Oxford University Press 1996); A Lamb, *Kashmir: A Disputed Legacy, 1846-1990* (Hertingfordbury, Roxford, Books 1991); R.G.C. Thomas (ed) *Perspectives on Kashmir: The Roots of Conflict in South Asia* (Boulder, Oxford University Press 1992).

5. This charge was given wide publicity in the incandescent attack on the Mountbatten Viceroyalty in A. Roberts, *Eminent Churchillians* (London, Weidenfield & Nicolson 1994) Ch. 2.

6. A. A. Michel, *A Study of the Effects of Partition* (New Haven, 1967) p. 196.

7. See, Y. Samad, 'Pakistan or Punjabistan: Crisis of National Identity' *International Journal of Punjab Studies* 2, 1 (January-June 1995) pp. 23-43.

8. For a useful introduction to fictional representations of the 1947 partition see: John A. Hanson, 'Historical Perspectives in the Urdu Novel', in M. U. Memon, ed., *Studies in the Urdu Ghazal and Prose Fiction* (Madison, University of Wisconsin 1979), pp. 257-84; M. U. Memon, 'Partition Literature: A Study of Intizar Husain', *Modern Asian Studies,* 14, 3 (1980), pp. 377-410.

9. A. Jalal, 'Secularists, Subalterns and the Stigma of Communalism: partition Historiography Revisited' *Modern Asian Studies* 30, 3 (July 1996) pp. 681-9.

10. See, A. Jalal, 'Conjuring Pakistan: History as Official Imagining' *International Journal of Middle East Studies* 27, 1995 pp. 73-89.

11. I. Talbot, *Freedom's Cry. The Popular Dimension in the Pakistan Movement and Partition Experience in North-west India* (Karachi, Oxford University Press 1996).

Chapter One

Peasant Nationalism and the Politics of Partition: The Class-Communal Symbiosis in East Bengal 1940-1947

Taj-ul-Islam Hashmi

I

Despite Marx's portrayal of peasants as 'rural idiots' and 'sack of potatoes', representing 'barbarism within civilization' or 'the unchanging remnants of the past', Mao and some Latin American revolutionaries like Che Guevara and Fidel Castro considered peasants as active participants in revolutionary movements in the twentieth century. However, despite their decisive role in the revolutionary changes in China, Cuba, Nicaragua and Vietnam, peasants in general are perceived by scholars, 'development experts' and administrators as representatives of the 'subculture' of 'traditional mentality' promoting passivity, apathy and resistance to change.[1] So far as the region of this study is concerned, during the 1940s, peasants in certain sub-regions resorted to armed struggle with militant anti-*jotedar* (rich peasant and intermediary landholder between *zamindar* and lower peasants) and anti-*mahajan* (moneylender) movements. These movements, especially the famous Tebhaga movement of 1946-7, form a watershed in the history of peasant movement in South Asia.

Despite its failure the class-based Tebhaga movement (literally, 'three shares-movement' led by sharecroppers for two-thirds of crops from landholders) does not suggest that East Bengali peasants were politically inert and unwilling to change the oppressive systems. This is an attempt to show how and why peasants' political activities, motivated by conscious efforts to improve their lot led to the creation of a separate homeland called East Pakistan (which later became Bangladesh in 1971) for the Muslims of the region in 1947. This is also an attempt to show how religious kinship and factional ties cut across class alignments, leading to the communalization of class struggle between peasants and their exploiting classes, who in general, respectively represented the Muslim and Hindu communities in the region. Since other agents of exploitation, mainly the *jotedars,* were predominantly Muslim and were also perceived as their patrons-cum-kinsmen by the bulk of the Muslim peasantry, Hindu *zamindars, bhadralok* (professional elites) and *mahajans* emerged as the real and only enemies of the peasants.

It is interesting that while the bulk of the Muslim peasantry singled out the *zamindar-bhadralok-mahajan* triumvirate as *the agents of exploitation,* it simply turned a blind eye to the handful of Muslim *zamindars* and *bhadralok* and a large number of Muslim *mahajans.* While some leading Bengali Muslim leaders, Abul Hashim, for example, defended Muslim aristocrats and *zamindars* as 'pro-peasant', others, like (Poet) Mozammel Haq, declared that all Hindus, including Gandhi and Nehru, were 'the arch enemies of the Muslims'.[2] Consequently Muslim peasants in general followed Muslim non-peasant leaders, who were either their patrons or part of the agents of exploitation. Factional ties or patron-client relationship and peasants' inability to identify the enemy led to this type of mobilization on communal lines. This is, however, not confined to East Bengal peasants. Their counterparts elsewhere in Latin America and Asia also suffered from this sort of myopia.[3]

In view of the East Bengali Muslim peasants' spontaneous support for non-peasant Muslim leaders, one should not surmise that the former only acted in accordance with the guidance of the latter having no sense of direction and desire for *swaraj* or independence, as perceived by the illiterate or semi-literate masses everywhere. One may, in this regard, point out what an ordinary peasant in the region thought of *swaraj* during the India-wide anti-British Khilafat and Non-Cooperation movement in the early 1920s. To him *swaraj* stood for 'a golden age when

prices should fall, taxation should cease, and when the State
should refrain from interfering with the good pleasure of each
individual man'.[4] However, not long after the Non-Cooperation
movement, which was jointly led by prominent Indian leaders
(both Hindu and Muslim) like Gandhi, Maulana Muhammad Ali
and Maulana Azad, East Bengali Muslim peasants turned
'communal' or anti-Hindu for specific economic and cultural
reasons. This was for the first time after the militant peasant
movements of the nineteenth century (the 'Wahhabi' and Faraizi
movements) that East Bengali peasants were again mobilized by
local and regional Muslim theologians or *ulama,* under the aegis
of the central leaders like Gandhi, Ali and Azad in the name of
'restoring' the Caliphate of Turkey by non-cooperating with the
British, 'enemies' of the Caliph and Islam.

Consequently under the influence of the mullahs, the revival
of Islamic solidarity after a lapse of about fifty years brought
about communal solidarity among the bulk of peasants.
Afterwards they were, sort of, convinced that 'Islam comes first
and after that country; religion takes precedence over
motherland', and that they were 'first of all Muslims and only
after that ... Indian'.[5] Among several factors leading to this shift
in the attitude of the peasantry, besides the influence of the
mullah, were the land-and-credit systems and the nature of the
British Raj, which successfully distanced itself from the main
agents of exploitation — landlords and moneylenders — in this
predominantly rural region of the Indian subcontinent.

The land-system which prevailed in the region upto the 1940s
was created by the Permanent Settlement Act of the British in
1793. This act not only accorded proprietory rights on land to the
tax-collecting *zamindars* but also permanently fixed the amount
of revenue. The new landlords were also supposed to enjoy the
ownership of land through generations provided the revenue was
paid off regularly. The new system created several intermediaries
between the *zamindar* and the actual cultivators. Consequently
'farm within farm became the order of the day, each resembling a
screw upon a screw, the last coming down on the tenant with the
pressure of them all'.[6] The *zamindars,* in short, were the masters

and the tenants, nothing more than servants. They were often treated as untouchables and 'even as livestock'.[7]

It is, however, interesting that by the end of the period of this study the government had already protected the interest of the tenants by granting them occupancy rights and the right to transfer their holdings by circumscribing the power of the *zamindars*. Consequently a section of the well-to-do tenants or *jotedars* emerged as the 'real landlords' and 'actual masters' of the lower peasants in most places.[8] According to a government official, if any 'blood sucking' of the peasants was done at all, it was not the *zamindar* but the *jotedar* who was responsible for this.[9] It naturally prompts the question as to why East Bengali peasants in general were much more vocal against the *zamindars* (with whom they had hardly any score to settle) than against their immediate landlords, the different categories of rich peasants, *jotedars* and *taluqdars* (petty landlords). The answer lies in the fact that firstly, most *zamindars* were Hindus and so were the professional elites *(bhadralok)* and the moneylenders *(mahajans)*, while the bulk of the intermediary tenure-holders and *jotedars* shared the common faith of Islam with most peasants; and secondly, for the average Muslim cultivator, the *jotedars* were not only fellow-Muslims but were at times also related to him. Most importantly, *jotedars,* as tenants or *projas* of *zamindars* also belonged to the amorphous peasant community, albeit having tremendous power and influence over their tenants as their patrons and leaders.

One may also point out in this regard, how exacting the moneylenders were, charging 12 to 280 per cent interest from their clients:[10] Most moneylenders again, belonged to the Hindu community. On average, between 45 and 50 per cent of the peasants were indebted to the moneylenders. During the Great Depression of the 1930s and the Bengal Famine of 1943-44, a large number of occupancy tenants were turned into landless or semi-landless peasants, as they failed to repay their loans to the *mahajans*. There must have been many among them like the peasant from Mymensingh district who told a government officer in 1929: 'My father, sir, was born in debt, grew in debt and died in debt. I have inherited my father's debt and my son will inherit mine'.[11]

Along with this abysmal picture of exploitation and almost total helplessness of the lower peasantry in East Bengal emerges another picture, projecting almost the total polarization of the 'haves' and 'have nots', respectively, into Hindu and Muslim camps. Muslim *jotedars* and lower peasants had religious, factional and other affinities; so were Hindu *zamindars*, *bhadralok* and *mahajans*-cum-traders linked to each other. By the turn of the twentieth century a large section of this Hindu landed, professional and business elites, contrary to the expectations of the British government, had turned into nationalists. This precipitated the shift in the British policy from the 'pro-*zamindar*' and 'pro-Hindu' to the 'pro-peasant' and 'pro-Muslim' one. Not long after this shift in the government policy, several tenant and peasant associations were formed in Bengal with government encouragement. Leading Bengali Muslim professionals and elites were directly involved in such associations. The Calcutta Agricultural Association, formed in 1917 by Fazlul Huq (Bengali Muslim professional with *jotedar* background) and a group of lawyers and journalists, and the Bengal *jotedars'* and *Ryots'* (tenants) Association (1920), were important among such associations demanding the abolition of the *zamindari* system.[12]

Against this background, the introduction of the Union Boards (local self-government body), allegedly formed with 'anti-Permanent Settlement' objectives,[13] and the extension of the franchise by the Government of India Act 1919 granting 33 rural seats to the Muslims in the Bengal Legislative Council and increasing the number of voters from 9,000 to 1.5 million, the majority of whom were cultivators in the whole province, alarmed the Hindu *bhadralok* and *zamindars*.[14] These Acts created great enthusiasm among the well-to-do enfranchised peasants, who formed their own associations which were the precursors of the major Muslim peasant organization of the later days — the Proja Party, formed by Fazlul Huq in 1929.

Afterwards the high-caste well-to-do Hindus were sharply polarized from the Muslim peasant masses. Henceforth the peasants, especially the enfranchised section, defied the *zamindars* and Hindu *bhadralok* classes in different ways, depending on government support and expecting further 'boons' from it. The situation has been explained by a government report in 1918:

Our rule gave them [peasants] security from the violence of robbers and the exaction of landlords, regulated by amounts of revenue or rent that they had to pay, and assured to both proprietor and cultivator — in the latter case by the device of the occupancy right — a safe title in their hands. The change was so great that they sank into a condition of lethargic content; even yet they have barely realized that Government has any other gifts to offer; as for the idea of self-government, it is simply a planet that has not yet risen above their horizon.

But there are signs of awakening. They have already learnt an important lesson — that it is legitimate to bring their troubles to the notice of the Government and that a good Government will listen to them with sympathy...

Hitherto, they have regarded the official as their representative in the councils of Government; and now we have to tear up that faith by the roots, to teach them that in future they must bring their troubles to the notice of an elected representative — further, that they have the power to compel his attention.[15]

The report also predicted the future political code of conduct of the peasant: 'eventually it will dawn upon him ... that because he has a vote he has the means of protecting himself ... It will occur to him eventually that if landlords are oppressive and usurers grasping and subordinate officials corrupt he has at his command a better weapon than the *lathi* or the hatchet with which to redress his wrongs.'[16]

The above observations were almost prophetic as far as the political behaviour of the peasants in East Bengal in the subsequent period of this study is concerned. Different categories of landlords and tenants, under-tenants and landless labourers fought for their respective 'rights', which they believed they were entitled to. The *zamindars* wanted to get rid of the intermediaries for the loss of income from *abwab* (illegal cesses), as *jotedars* in their turn as landlords collected these from their tenants. This attitude is well reflected in various memoranda of the landlords' associations to the Land Revenue Commission in 1940.[17] The *jotedars* wanted the status of proprietors and called themselves *talukdars* to elevate their social position. The occupancy *ryots* wanted lower rates of rental and more assured rights over their holdings, while the non-occupancy *ryots* aspired to permanent occupancy rights, the sharecroppers to permanent rights and two-thirds of the crop, and the landless labourers to the status of *grihastas* or husbandmen to get a higher social position as well as permanent tenures.[18] The middle and rich peasants' aspiration to become *bhadralok*[19] was the dominant theme in the politics of the peasants throughout the region. By the 1940s, due to several government measures and rise of political consciousness among the well-to-do peasants, the *zamindars'* power was waning and the hopes of the occupancy *ryots* and *jotedars* were increasing. Both the *zamindars* and the dominant tenants looked on the other 'with considerable suspicion and jealousy'.[20] Some observers held that the prosperity of the rich and upper middle peasants 'awakened them to a sense of their inferiority'.[21]

The suspicion and rivalry between the *zamindars* and rich peasants, the latter's relative prosperity after the 'jute boom' (1914-18) and the sense of inferiority due to their low social status in relation to the *zamindars* and Hindu *bhadralok* were significant in arousing them politically. The prospect of making a better living in the event of abolishing the *zamindari* system, made all sections of the peasantry avowedly anti-*zamindar*. The prospect of getting better opportunities in all spheres of life in the 'promised land' of Pakistan — firmer rights over lands, higher social status, better deals from creditors and better job opportunities for their progeny — quickened the mobilization of the bulk of the peasantry against high-caste *zamindars, mahajans* and *bhadralok*. In short, the 'peasant utopias' of different categories of peasants were the driving force behind the politics of the peasants in the period under review.

Under the influence of the *ashraf* elites, *jotedars* and the newly emerging overambitious Muslim *bhadralok* classes, who had hardly any fascination for lower-class or peasant-oriented politics, the *zamindar-jotedar* and the Muslim-Hindu elite conflicts subsequently emerged as the most important and determining factors. While the class-based politics of the lower peasantry became irrelevant to the proponents and followers of the 'two-nation' theory on the eve of the partitions of India and Bengal in 1947.

II

Although peasant insurrections on class lines occupy but a short time in the history of modern Bengal, whereby the communal politics of 1947 eventually subsumed agrarian 'class struggle' as well, the Tebhaga movement of sharecropper peasants in the late 1940s had a long-lasting impact on the subsequent politics as well as on the historiography of the region. This is reflected in the militant 'Maoist' peasant insurrections of the 1960s and 1970s, commonly known as the Naxalite movement, to capture land (eventually political power) by members of the lower peasantry and also in the numerous historical writings in Bengali and English that cropped up in the wake of the movement. Most of these works are somewhat romantic accounts of peasant militancy. Historians with strong commitment to communism, including those belonging to the Maoist and the neo-Marxist 'Subaltern School', have mainly authored these works, either over-stretching the extent of the sharecroppers' movements and glorifying the role of the Communist Party of India (CPI) or exaggerating the potential of the poor peasants and their so-called 'autonomous domain' or culture to create an 'alternative order' by capturing state power through revolution. These writings either put the blame on the rightist communal forces for the failure of the movement or criticize the CPI leadership for its vacillating role.

The Tebhaga movement, though said to have engulfed almost the whole of Bengal, was more intense among the tribal sharecroppers of Dinajpur and Rangpur districts of East Bengal than among the non-tribal Muslim and Namasudra (low-caste Hindu) sharecroppers elsewhere. With J. Bhattacharyya it may be agreed that these revolts were probably the most extensive in the history of the East Bengal peasantry,[22] but the figure of six million peasants taking part in the movement, as suggested by communist activist, Abdullah Rasul, sounds too high to be true.[23]

Tebhaga, which literally means 'three-shares' in Bengali, was a movement by sharecroppers, commonly known as *bargadars* or *adhiars,* against their landlords *(jotedars),* demanding two-third instead of one-half of the yield. The availability of a substantial amount of primary and secondary sources has made the task of writing the history of the movement much easier. Again, as this is undoubtedly one of the most famous peasant movements of the modern times in South Asia,[24] it attracts the attention of many modern 'peasant authorities', although the movement itself does not connote the destruction of landlordism or cropsharing. However, the participation of a large number of landless and semi-landless agricultural labourers in the movement, who did not have any *bargadari* interests whatsoever, suggests the wider implications of the movement. By challenging the overlordship of petty landlords including *jotedars, mahajans,* the middle peasants who had sharecroppers as tenants and the *bhadralok* who had sublet their holdings to sharecroppers, the movement, in fact, was aiming at the eventual destruction of all intermediary interests in between the actual cultivator and the State. Contrary to the general belief that the movement was initiated and sustained by the CPI, there is evidence that in the early 1920s, before the inception of the party, there had been several attempts to elevate the position of the sharecroppers in the region by some 'pro-peasant' politicians. A section of the Proja Party that coalitioned in 1937 with the 'communal' Muslim League in Bengal, as well as the Government of Bengal, were considering measures to give better rights to the *bargadars.*[25] The Revenue Commission's criticism (also known as the Floud Commission) of the 1928 Tenancy (Amendment) Act might have emboldened the *bargadars* due to its failure to protect the *bargadars* and for its advocacy of *tebhaga.*[26] The pro-communist Bengal Kisan Sabha, which later took a leading role in mobilizing mass support for *tebhaga,* popularized the demand for better rights for *bargadars* and labourers. It did not, however, categorically demand the introduction of *tebhaga* before the publication of the Floud Report in March 1940. In its Memorandum to the Floud Commission, the Sabha demanded ten-sixteenths of the crop as the sharecroppers' share, which was slightly less than two-thirds, as stipulated by the demand for *tebhaga.*[27] For the first time the Kisan Sabha demanded two-thirds of the crop for the sharecroppers at its fourth annual conference on 9 June 1940 at Panjia, a village in Jessore district.[28]

Though the Kisan Sabha had repeated its demand for *tebhaga* at the Nalitabari Conference (in Mymensingh district) in May 1943, it did not take any bold decision regarding *tebhaga* at its next Conferences at Phulbari (Dinajpur) on 29 February to 2 March 1944 and at Hatgobindapur (Burdwan) on 13-14 March 1945. Being predominantly under CPI control, the Bengal Kisan Sabha at that time put greater stress on the post-Bengal Famine (1943) campaign of 'grow more food' along with their anti-Fascist campaigns.[29] While the central leaders of the Kisan Sabha were almost silent about the *tebhaga* demand, local leaders and cadres from the lower peasantry were more enthusiastic about achieving their goals with regard to their demand for *tebhaga.* At the Phulbari Conference of the Kisan Sabha in 1944, thousands of poor peasants shouted slogans in support of *tebhaga* and the abolition of illegal exactions by landlords and moneylenders. Their main demand was the transfer of proprietory rights over land to the tillers.[30] In the early 1940s, according to the police chief of Rangpur, the potential for violent insurgency had already existed among the district's *bargadars,* who only needed someone to spark the flame.[31] When the Kisan Sabha had a formal enrolment of 255,000 primary members in Bengal by early 1945,[32] it was no longer possible for the leaders to ignore their demands. It is reasonable to assume that the majority of the members were from East Bengal districts, especially from the tribal dominated tracts of Mymensingh, Rangpur and Dinajpur and from among the Namasudras of Jessore, Khulna, Faridpur and Bakarganj. Meanwhile, the 'leftist' Krishak Samity members of the Tippera-Noakhali sub-region, being predominantly Muslim, had succumbed to the communal propaganda of the Muslim League. Thus the pro-CPI Kisan Sabha was left with little alternative except to concentrate on the mobilization of the non-Muslim peasants, especially the tribals, who were not vulnerable to Muslim League propaganda. The Kisan Sabha's numerous rallies and conferences in the tribal-Namasudra tracts of Mymensingh, Jessore, Dinajpur and Rangpur during the period demanding the abolition of landlordism and the British Raj aroused great enthusiasm among the lower peasants of these districts. The *bargadars,* whose ranks were swollen by the mass impoverishment of the middle peasants after the Famine of 1943-4, found the Kisan Sabha's anti-hoarder, anti-black marketeer stand an attractive plank, as most of these exploiting people happened to be local *jotedars* and *mahajans.*

It is difficult to agree with Hamza Alavi that the post-Famine period fulfilled the objective condition of the *bargadar* revolt on account of a shortage of labour, since a large number of poor peasants had died in the Famine and many others had become unemployed after the War.[33] The post-War unemployment, again, does not support his hypothesis of a labour shortage in agriculture in the region. The figures of mass 'depeasantization' of occupancy tenants in the wake of the Famine,[34] on the other hand, suggest a tremendous rise in landlessness among poor peasants. In Nilphamari (Rangpur) alone, land alienation by subsistence peasants rose by 1,000 per cent during the Famine; 41 per cent of peasants in Rangpur, for instance, were mainly living as *bargadars* and about 66 per cent of them were below the subsistence level.[35]

The actual rebellion first started in September 1946 in parts of Dinajpur-Rangpur sub-region, mainly under local middle-peasant leaders, who had very little contact with the CPI. The rebellion was so sudden that the top leaders of the Bengal Kisan Sabha had failed to foresee it in May 1946, at the ninth annual conference of the party at Moubhog (Khulna). Soon the sharecroppers' rebellion engulfed 19 districts of the province.[36] The rebels in most places surrounded *jotedars'* houses and took two-thirds of the crop from their granaries to store in the Panchayat Khamars or people's granaries. In one single day in some villages of Domar in Rangpur district, several hundred *lathials* (clubmen) and volunteers were organized by the local peasant leaders having some links with the District Kisan Sabha leaders.[37] Initially the leadership came from the impoverished middle peasants, but the landless sharecroppers and wage labourers fought well beside the middle peasants.[38]

The breakdown of the percentages of landless labourers, *bargadars,* semi-landless peasants and of lands under the sharecropping system in the region reveals that the intensity of landlessness and cropsharing as a mode of production in an area and the *tebhaga* movement were hardly correlative. The following table substantiates the facts:

	Landless Labourers	*bargardar*	Semi-landless Peasant	Lands under Share Cropping System
Bakarganj	61.8	7.1	23.6	30.7
Bogra	34.5	13.4	25.6	39.0
Chittagong	60.3	1.8	11.6	13.4
Dhaka	62.4	6.9	22.2	29.1
Dinajpur	24.2	13.8	23.5	37.3
Faridpur	81.5	23.8	15.7	39.5
Jessore	28.5	4.2	7.9	12.1
Khulna	55.6	13.2	41.9	55.1
Mymensingh	34.1	7.3	20.0	27.3
Noakhali	65.3	2.2	17.9	20.1
Pabna	64.1	26.1	15.2	41.3
Rajshahi	31.8	13.0	23.8	36.8
Rangpur	26.6	19.1	12.9	32.0
Tippera	63.9	1.1	4.8	5.9

Source: Floud Report, Vol. II, Table VIII (b and d), pp. 114-17

What one would expect in the light of the table is higher intensity in *bargadar*-labourer unrest in districts like Khulna,

Pabna, Faridpur and Bogra with higher percentages of *bargadars*, labourers and semi-landless categories than in Dinajpur, Rangpur, Mymensingh and Jessore, the most volatile districts so far as the *tebhaga* movement is concerned. These data also indicate that relatively prosperous peasants with greater independence were more militant than their impoverished, dependent counterparts. When we take into account the nature and extent of the movement in the different tracts of East Bengal, the hypothesis propounding the predominance of the middle peasants and tribal elements as the main factors of the *tebhaga* movement becomes a viable proposition.

In areas where both the *jotedars* and *bargadars* were Muslims, despite greater economic hardship *jotedars* and *jotedar* exactions, the *bargadars* were more inert and dependent on outside communist agitators than in areas where the two classes belonged to two different faiths. Peasant inertness in the former and unrest in the latter may be attributed to the arousal of communal rather than class-consciousness among the peasants.

In most districts, the customary share of the *bargadars* was one-half of the crop, which was usually stocked in the *jotedars'* or lessors' farm houses by the *bargadars,* who did not get anything for carrying and threshing the crop. The patron-client relationship in most areas in the central and south-eastern sub-regions was so strong that all attempts by 'outsiders' to incite *bargadars* against their lessors failed as the tenants did not dare oppose their 'patrons'. Bakarganj is a glaring example where *bargadars* were apathetic to the movement even though in some cases they were left with only one-third of the crop. Jessore provides a unique example where, in spite of a very insignificant proportion of *bargadars* (4.2 per cent) and labourers (7.9 per cent), and where the number of semi-landless peasants was one of the lowest (28.5 per cent) in East Bengal, there was some *bargadar* unrest during the period. What explanation could there be for such a phenomenon? Upon closer obervation it becomes clear that firstly, the poor peasants in Jessore were stirred up by local communists. Secondly, parts of Narail sub-division in Jessore, where the *tebhaga* movement took a serious turn, were notorious for *jotedars'* exactions — in some places they took three-quarters of the crop if they provided implements and manures. Collecting two-thirds, in any case, was quite common in this district. In Magura sub-division in the same district, the movement was confined to Namasudra *bargadars,* who were easily mobilized against their Muslim *jotedars* by local and non-local communists. Jhenidah sub-division was the mirror image of Magura. Here leaders stirred Muslim *bargadars* against high-caste Hindu and Namasudra *jotedars.* Parts of Jessore and Khulna had the notoriety of having serious communal riots in the past. Bitter communal antagonism between the two communities in Sirajganj (Pabna) and Satkhira (Khulna) might have quickened the process of *bargadars'* mobilization against their *jotedars* representing rival faiths.[39]

The *tebhaga* demand was first raised by the sharecroppers Dinajpur after a lull of about six years in late 1946. The villages in the area of Atwari police station, especially Rampur, were a hotbed of agitation. Local Rajbansi peasant leaders, Ramlal Singh, Pathal Singh and Rajen Singh, became active communist organizers under the leadership of Sushil Sen, a high-caste Hindu *bhadralok.* When sharecroppers of Rampur village went to cut the paddy on the plot of a Rajbansi *bargadar* called Phuljhari, with a view to stocking the crop in the 'people's granary' instead of the *jotedar's,* the police came and arrested Sen, but only after clashing with the peasants. Soon the news of the clash spread throughout Thakurgaon sub-division of Dinajpur district. Such leaders as Haji Danesh, Kali Sarkar, Hrishikesh Bhattacharyya, Gurudas Talukdar and Sunil Sen started organizing the *bargadars.* Within a fortnight the movement engulfed twenty-two of the thirty-two areas under the police stations of Dinajpur. Thousands of peasants including wage labourers, middle peasants and a few rich peasants joined the Kisan Sabha. Rajbansi women also took an active part in the movement. Their main slogans were 'Inqilab Zindabad' ('Long Live Revolution') and *'tebhaga chai'* ('We want *tebhaga').*[40]

Most Kisan Sabha members were *bargadars* and labourers. Not all cadres and supporters of the Kisan Sabha were communists, but some of the active communist leaders of Dinajpur had a poor peasant background. Monglu Muhammad of Rampur village, Rup Narayan of Phulbari, who also became an MLA (Member of the Legislative Assembly, Government of Bengal) in 1946, Bachcha Muhammad, Chiar Shai Sheikh, Samiruddin, Bachcha Munshi, Lal Muhammad Munshi, Pradhan Majhee and Spasta Ram Singh were prominent among them. Some of them were totally illiterate.[41] The poor peasants of Dinajpur-Rangpur sub-region learnt from the communists that the exploiting interests should be overthrown by an *inqilab* or revolution. In most cases they lost faith in the law-enforcing bodies of the government.[42] Under the influence of the CPI, a section of the peasants learnt about the revolutionary activities of Chinese peasants under Mao Tse-tung. They became familiar with the names of Chiang Kai-shek and President Truman, as has been depicted in some songs composed by Khabir Sheikh, a poor peasant in Dinajpur (of Phulbari village).[43] The communists, who were mostly the non-local Hindu *bhadralok* from the south-eastern districts, were not initially accepted by the tribal and Muslim peasants of Dinajpur. It was only after the tribal chiefs and local Muslim peasant leaders had announced the *tebhaga* programme quite independently of the CPI in September 1946, that the CPI and Kisan Sabha leaders were successful in organizing the poor peasants in the sub-region. They taught them how to resist police excesses without foreseeing that the poor, unarmed peasants would consider waging an armed struggle against the government and *jotedars*. Some of the CPI directives were ludicrously simple, such as asking the women cadres and supporters of the *tebhaga* movement to face the armed police force with broom sticks and chilli powder sprays. Despite their limitations, the communists aroused mass enthusiasm for the movement by establishing training camps in the rural areas of Dinajpur and Rangpur.[44]

Between December 1946 and February 1947, the police and sharecroppers clashed on at least five major occasions and thirty-one peasants and a policeman were killed.[45] The clashes led to mass arrests of peasant participants and leaders, in some villages in the area of Atwari police station, after which the militant *adhiars* continued on their own initiative to stack paddy in their own granaries—and soon followed up by breaking into *jotedars'* granaries and looting the entire crop. This was done after the publication in the *Calcutta Gazette* on 22 January 1947 of the Bengal Bargadars Temporary Regulation Bill, which promised to introduce the *tebhaga* system shortly throughout the province.[46] Meanwhile, the Sub-Divisional Officer of Thakurgaon tried in vain to achieve a peaceful settlement of the dispute between the *adhiars* and *jotedars* while some peasants chanted slogans demanding the entire crop and *'langal jar jami tar'* ('Land to the Tiller') instead of the *tebhaga*. By early 1947, according to the government, a parallel government had been established in parts of rural Dinajpur and Rangpur. Attacks on police parties by armed *adhiars* and labourers were quite common in some areas of Dinajpur and Rangpur. The police firings at Chirir Bandar on 4 January, at Khanpur on 20 February and at Thumnia on 22 February resulted in the deaths of several *adhiars*. At Khanpur alone, between 22 and 26 peasants were killed. About 1,200 peasants were arrested and about 10,000 were wounded by police and *jotedars* in Dinajpur during December 1946 and February 1947.[47]

Police firing and *jotedars'* excesses led to mass mobilization of *adhiars* and all categories of poor peasants, fishermen, barbers, blacksmiths and other menial classes against the *jotedars* and the government. In Rangpur, for instance, after the brutal killing of a Kisan Sabha volunteer, Tag Narayan, of Khagakhari Bari village in the area of Dimla police station by Masihur Rahman (Jadu Mia) a local Muslim *jotedar,* in December 1946, thousands of *adhiars* and labourers organized protest meetings and rallies throughout the district. According to some observers, local Muslim *jotedars,* who had been totally boycotted by their *adhiars* after the killing of Tag Narayan, instigated communal riots in Syedpur town, not far from Khagakhari Bari village, to communalize the *adhiar-jotedar* conflict. However, the *adhiars* and agricultural labourers under communist leadership, showed tremendous restraint in abstaining from killing Muslim *jotedars* and their agents, which they were otherwise quite capable of.[48]

Somenath Hore, a Bengali journalist, who went to Rangpur villages in December 1946, has given a vivid account of the *tebhaga* movement in Nilphamari sub-division in his diary. His sketches depict *adhiars'* militancy and discipline, especially their marching with the Red Flag, *lathis* and sickles, indicating that the movement was well organized. From his accounts it appears that local *adhiars* and labourers were too articulate to be dismissed as a 'sack of potatoes'. They defied the League and Congress leaders, who quite unitedly were opposing the movement, telling them that it was unnecessary on the 'eve of the enactment of the *Tebhaga Bill'*. The poor peasants of the area are said to have understood the implications of communal provocations by *jotedars*. In some cases they even defied the authority of the government by declaring in public meetings that the *adhiars* would make their own laws to try the *jotedars* and all exploiting interests. Many poor peasants believed that they had become *swadhin* or independent. One elderly tribal peasant felt that the Congress had done nothing for them in the last sixty years and that the 'comrades' were their real friends. It also appears from the diary that, though some *jotedars* were prepared to concede *tebhaga,* they urged the CPI leaders not to destroy the *'raja-proja* (landlord-tenant) relationship'. The so-called *'projas'* or *adhiars,* according to the account, wanted the 'total destruction' of landlordism.[49] The above account smacks of pro-CPI bias. In some isolated cases sharecroppers might have challenged the legitimacy of the sharecropping system, but in general, they did not demand the total destruction of landlordism, despite CPI propaganda. One should not overlook the restraining impact of peasant 'moral economy', which does not legitimize the expropriation of landlords. Elsewhere, in Mymensingh, Khulna, Jessore and parts of Dhaka — *bargadars* fought *jotedars* and the police, mostly under local peasant leaders. Some of them even came from the ranks of *bargadars*. Farazatullah and Hiralal Bain (a former professional *lathial* of landlords) of Shobhana Union (an administrative unit under a Union Board) in Khulna district and Anima, Phulmati and Sarala Bala Pal, three leading women volunteers of the Kisan Sabha in Narail (Jessore), were some of the leaders who came from among illiterate poor peasants. In parts of rural Narail, the *bargadars* were so well-organized that even armed policemen hesitated to enter their villages.[50] On one occasion the *bargadars* and labourers encircled about fifty armed policemen and kept them as hostages for several hours in a football field at Raghunathpur village in Narail. Local *bargadar* leaders wanted to appropriate their rifles but the CPI leaders from the metropolis pacified them. According to Mudassar Munshi, a local militant *bargadar* leader: 'Our battle was lost that very day' [Kamal Siddiqui et al., p. 15670]. In Netrokona, Jamapur and some other areas of Mymensingh district the *tebhaga* movement was crushed by the combined efforts of Hindu *zamindars* and Muslim *jotedars* who helped the police and aroused anti-tribal feeling among Muslim *bargadars*.[51]

Besides communalism, other factors also contributed to the failure of the Tebhaga movement. Its main drawback was that unlike the *tanka* movement of tribals in Mymensingh, it antagonized a larger section of the landholding classes. This sectional movement of *bargadars* or *adhiars* was diametrically opposed to the economic interests of *jotedars*, other rich peasants and some middle peasants who had sharecroppers as tenants.

Instead of accepting the extreme views of Dhanagare, who thinks that the movement did not pose any threat to the prevalent socio-economic and political systems, although the government is said to have realized the urgency of it,[52] one can point out that the degree and extent of the movement were not as intensive as depicted in the writings of communist and Kisan Sabha leaders, activists and sympathizers. We may partially agree with Adrienne Cooper who thinks that: 'To portray [the] share-croppers' movement as 'partial struggles' aimed at obtaining limited economic gains for poor peasants is to present an unimaginative view of these events'.[53] Agricultural labourers and others, who had no connections with the cropsharing system, joined the movement probably because they believed that they would achieve '*tebhaga* today, land tomorrow'.[54] The labourers also shared with the *bargadars* 'a common hatred' for the *jotedars* for taking away their lands. The middle peasants supported the movement in the hope that this would culminate in an anti-*zamindar* movement, to their benefit.[55]

Though CPI leaders were partly successful in stopping communal riots in Rangpur villages after the Sydpur riots in the wake of the killing of Tag Narayan by *jotedar* Masihur Rahman, and at Hasnabad in Tippera district after the Noakhali riots of late 1946,[56] they could not do so in tracts without a communist following among peasants. Even in parts of Dinajpur-Rangpur sub-region, where the pro-CPI Kisan Sabha had grassroots organization, the Pakistan movement had gathered such momentum by early 1947 that many high-caste Hindu communist leaders had to hoist the green and white flag of the Muslim League (and Pakistan) along with the red flag of the CPI in public meetings in order to attract Muslim peasant support. The Hindu and Muslim communist leaders often joined their Muslim peasant supporters in congregational prayers with a view to showing that religion and communism had no contradictions. They selected Haji Danesh, a Congress leader of Dinajpur with a religious bent of mind, as a leader of the Kisan Sabha to counteract Muslim League propaganda that the protagonists of *tebhaga* were atheists.[57]

From the compromising attitude of most CPI leaders, it is most unlikely that they aroused 'a revolutionary rural democratic spirit' among the poor peasants of Dinajpur Rangpur sub-region, as claimed by some leaders.[58] The truth probably lies between such sweeping comments as, on the one hand, 'the Tebhaga movement reflects the highest level of political consciousness of the peasants, which was different from (pre-political stages of) 'social banditry',[59] and on the other, the 'politicization' of the peasants weakened their 'rebellious impulse'.[60] The prevalent socio-economic and political systems were not congenial to militant peasant movements in the region. Though there is no denying the fact that economic reasons were inherent in the spontaneity of the sharecroppers, landless labourers and marginal peasants who joined the Tebhaga movement, there was also a promise of impunity from the leaders which aroused mass support for the movement. The illiterate, poor peasants were hardly aware how powerful the government machinery, the *jotedars*, the *zamindars* and other agents of exploitation were. Above all, the bulk of them did not question the legitimacy of the sharecropping system. They simply wanted some relief — and what was the harm if the entire crop or the lands were to come to them as a bonus by doing certain things in accordance with the leaders' wishes? But as soon as their *lathis*, bows and arrows proved ineffective against police-rifles and *jotedar*-guns, they yielded to authority. The movement failed also because the bulk of the sharecroppers who were Muslims, regarded their immediate landlords or Muslim *jotedars* not only legitimate but also as their patrons and 'natural leaders'. The strong influence of the *ulama* (Muslim clerics) and the *ashraf* (Urdu-speaking Muslim landed and professional elite) on the *jotedars* as well as on the poor peasants soon revitalized the old demon, communalism, which hammered the last nail into the coffin of the Tebhaga movement. In short, the objective conditions of a peasant revolution in the region were lacking as the 'conservative forces' in the countryside had not weakened.[61]

The poor and middle peasants had another difficulty in mobilizing themselves against the rich peasants in most parts of Dhaka, Chittagong and Rajshahi divisions. The predominance of Hindu *zamindars, mahajans* and *bhadralok* in these districts pushed the *jotedars* as a dominant class into the background. So, the *jotedars* in most districts could hardly be differentiated from the broad 'subaltern' category of *projas*. These *projas* in most places in Dhaka and Chittagong divisions and parts of Jessore, Khulna, Pabna and Bogra in Rajshahi division had strong bands of private armies in their *lathials*, which was not so common in Dinajpur-Rangpur sub-region. Above all, besides blood and factional ties, the common bond of religion between the *jotedars* and the rest of the peasantry proved too strong to be snapped by the doctrines of class struggle.

III

The essence of the story is the ascendancy of communalism in rural East Bengal in the 1940s and the CPI's failure to comprehend what seemed nothing more than 'mass irrationality' to its leaders. The CPI simply underestimated communalism as a factor because it had a 'narrow social base', which it believed could be 'rapidly liquidated' by the progressive forces.[62] In tracts with high intensity of communist activities, communalism emerged as a potential — subsequently real — threat to the communist and non-communal peasant movement. The Tippera-Noakhali sub-region, which had been a strong base of the radical Krishak Samity, lost its pre-eminence as a centre of radicalism in the mid-1940s, and instead, on the eve of the partition of India, was the setting for some of the bitterest communal riots in the history of East Bengal. These riots indicated that the communist ideology had only touched the veneer of the peasant society. The movement on class lines being confined to a small section of the total population in Bengal (mainly tribals),[63] the rest of the peasantry was vulnerable to the arousal of communal sentiment by small incidents and simple provocations.

Meanwhile, prominent Muslim 'peasant' leaders like Maulana Abdullah al-Baki, Abul Mansur Ahmed, Nawabzada Hasan Ali Khan (a *zamindar* from Mymensingh district) and Shamsuddin Ahmed of Kustia had joined the Muslim League. The 'most useful and important section of the young, militant and intellectual members' of the Krishak Proja Party (KPP) joined the pro-partition East Pakistan Renaissance Society, which was an important platform for publicizing the Pakistan doctrine among the Muslims of Bengal.[64] The mass defection of important KPP members to the Muslim League by early 1946 led to the *de facto* liquidation of the KPP. The League made ample room for both the extreme right and 'progressive' KPP men. By 1944 the League meant 'everything to everybody'. On account of Jinnah's 'progressive' pronouncements against exploitation and theocracy, many 'radical' Muslims joined the League during the period. On the eve of the 1946 elections, radical slogans like 'land to the tiller', 'labourers are the owners of industries'; 'crush the vested interest groups', and 'Pakistan stands for the workers and peasants' were chanted from the Muslim League platform. The abolition of the *zamindari* system without giving any compensation to the landlords became an important objective of the party after the Gaffargaon Conference (in Mymensingh district) of the Bengal Muslim League, held on 12 January 1946 under the presidency of Liaquat Ali Khan, the right-hand man of Jinnah.[65]

The League's advocacy of fixed prices and better distribution of food and its successful portrayal of the Hindu *zamindars, mahajans* and merchants as the real causes of the Famine of 1943-4, tilted the balance in its favour.[66] This became easier as many Muslim leaders, in the wake of the Famine, had circulated stories throughout the region about the alleged opposition of some Hindu leaders to sending food grain to East Bengal 'to teach a lesson' to the Muslims who demanded Pakistan.[67] The elections gave further opportunities to the supporters of the ML to spread fictitious stories about the alleged oppression of Muslims by Hindus in Bengal and elsewhere in the sub-continent. The pro-ML Jamiat-ul-Ulama-i-Islam played an important role in popularizing the ML among the rural Muslims during the elections. Due to the avowedly communal appeals, the ML had the edge over the CPI, Congress and other groups in the countryside. In short, the ML's anti-Congress and anti-Hindu propaganda, along with its promises of radical land reforms after the achievement of Pakistan, further alienated the Muslim peasants from the Congress and the CPI. The voting pattern of the rural Muslims in the region tended to confirm Shila Sen's assertion that the demand for Pakistan had great appeal among the Bengali Muslims and that 'in Bengal the Pakistan movement was mass based and democratic'.[68]

The CPI, Congress and other leftist and nationalist groups lost ground also due to internal differences and mutual squabbles. In some places, due to Congress and ML opposition, the CPI could not openly campaign in support of its candidates in the 1946 elections.[69] The CPI's concentration of most leaders and workers

in the urban and industrial centres further weakened its grip on
the peasants, excepting a handful of tribal Hajongs and
Rajbansis. Paradoxically, the party was more concerned about
the impact of the proposed abolition of the *zamindari* system on
the non-peasant classes than putting an alternative programme to
that of the League to draw mass support after the War.[70]

While the CPI in Bengal under Hindu *bhadralok* leadership
failed to develop 'an authentic peasant organization',[71] the
League put forward programmes of radical land reforms. The
large influx of anti-*zamindar* and anti-*mahajan* KPP men into
the League also helped transform it into a 'workers' and
peasants' party'. Though the *ashraf* leaders (Muslim aristocrats)
of the party had some reservations about the proposed expropriation of the *zamindars,* it seems that, under the tremendous
pressure from the new members of the party, the League high-
command had to accommodate anti-*zamindar,* anti-*mahajan*
programmes, which were again mostly meant to circumscribe the
power of the Hindu *bhadralok* classes. League leaders of all
categories — *ashraf, ulama, jotedars* and *bhadralok* — however,
put greater emphasis on the attainment of Pakistan as the precondition for attaining an exploitation-free society or a 'peasant
utopia'. Soon the demand for Pakistan became an integral part of
the demands for the abolition of the *zamindari-mahajani* systems
and better job and educational opportunities for the Muslims of
the region. The Hindu opposition to the Pakistan demand, was
generally motivated by the fear of economic victimization
arising from anti-*zamindar,* anti-*mahajan* measures; it led to
serious communal disturbances throughout Bengal. The holding
of 'Pakistan Conferences' by the League in every district, where
the speakers harangued the masses about the need to achieve
Pakistan 'not by begging but by revolution', provoked the
Congress and Hindu Mahasabha to hold counter conferences to
oppose Pakistan in the 1940s. [72] Due to the fervent communal
propaganda on both sides — the ML promising the restoration of
the *Badshahi* or Muslim rule,[73] and the Congress-Mahasabha
leaders (quite often the same people belonging to both the
parties) promising the establishment of the *Ramarajya* or Hindu

domain — by mid-1940s, the differences between the economic and religious issues had been blurred in most places. The so-called 'communist belts' of Dinajpur-Rangpur, Jessore-Khulna, Tippera-Noakhali and northern Mymensingh were no longer immune to communal violence. Communal clashes were no more spasmodic conflicts between the rich and the poor. By mid-1940s these had degenerated into indiscriminate fighting between the two communities. The countryside, as well as the small towns of the region again witnessed inter-and intra-class conflicts between Hindus and Muslims, the main issues being desecration of temples and playing music near mosques. In parts of Faridpur, Jessore and Khulna, riots between Namasudra and Muslim peasants during the period were only smaller than the Noakhali riots of 1946-7. Things took a serious turn at Mollahat in Khulna on 25 May 1944 over a dispute between a Namasudra and a Muslim peasant about a piece of land. Looting and rioting in a few square miles of Khulna and neighbouring Jessore was also affected by serious riots between poor Namasudra and Muslim peasants.[74] It resulted in six deaths, five among Muslims, and in the burning of 521 houses at Narail (Jessore), an important centre of the Tebhaga movement. Some Namasudra peasants of Mollahat, who apologized to the District Magistrate of Khulna, told him that they had been misled by some 'interested persons'.[75] In March 1945, Muslim peasants attacked Hindu students of Carmichael College in Rangpur town at the instigation of some Muslim students and leaders of the town.[76] It was not always local grievances that caused disturbances. The reported alleged defilement of a mosque in Gwalior state in west India by Hindus for instance, led to serious rioting in parts of rural Jessore in May 1947.[77]

By August 1946, Muslim peasants in East Bengal had become so committed to the idea of Pakistan that it was no longer merely a political or economic issue, but now possessed an emotional and religious appeal. Especially after the great Calcutta riots in the wake of the Direct Action Day on 16 August observed by the Muslim League government of Bengal and which resulted in more than 4,000 deaths, the situation was 'highly inflammable' as the entire region came to the brink of a civil war.[78]

Soon after the Calcutta riots Noakhali followed suit. The riots in Noakhali were certainly part of the struggle between the 'haves' and the 'have nots',[79] primarily between Hindu landlords, moneylenders and Muslim peasants. These riots also reflected the 'different meaning' of Pakistan for the Muslim masses.[80] After the great Calcutta killings of 1946, most Muslims in the region felt that Pakistan was the 'only solution' to the constitutional problem.[81]

The Noakhali riots of October 1946, which were grossly exaggerated in the Hindu press,[82] undoubtedly provided specimens of the most gruesome acts of violence in the history of East Bengal villages. About 372 Hindu villages were destroyed, thousands of homesteads were looted and burnt down and about 220 Hindus, including some moneylenders, lost their lives in the district. According to a contemporary observer most of these rioters were committed to the establishment of a 'local Pakistan', which would be 'wholly Muslim in composition'. This led to the mass attack on Hindus. Though the disturbances had an 'agrarian tinge...their primary incentive was communal'.[83]

By early 1947, though there had been a decline in the incidents of looting and rioting in the Tippera-Noakhali sub-region mainly due to the peace missions by Gandhi and Suhrawardy (the Chief Minister of Bengal), but communal bitterness reached its height due to the League and Mahasabha compaigns on communal lines throughout East Bengal. The Hindu and Muslim press did the rest in widening the gulf between the two communities.[84] By April 1947, Noakhali could no longer be singled out as the 'lawless region', since the situation was not much better in the districts of Dhaka, Mymensingh, Faridpur, Jessore, Pabna, Bogra and Rangpur. Muslim peasants were in the forefront, defying law and order — in the names of Islam, Pakistan and Jinnah Sahib (Mr Jinnah). By then the cry 'Islam in danger' not only drew armed *lungi*-clad, drunk Muslims to the pavements of Park Street and Chowringhee in Calcutta or Islampur and Nawabpur in

Dhaka, it also reverberated along the bamboo-hedges of rural East Bengal.[85]

What appears from the Muslim peasant behaviour towards the Hindu landlords, moneylenders, the *bhadralok* and the lower classes is that the peasants became confident of their 'newly acquired power and belief that they had already become 'independent'. After the mass exodus of Hindus from most villages in riot-affected areas of Noakhali and parts of Tippera, an elderly poor Muslim peasant is said to have remarked that they had achieved Pakistan as the region between Feni and Chandpur had been 'liberated'.[86] Muslim peasants' spontaneity in forcibly converting Hindus and marrying their women reflects their desire to humiliate and belittle their class and communal enemies. These acts gratified their hidden desires, which they thought they could fulfil after Pakistan was attained.[87] This attitude reflects the typical peasant notion of his 'utopia'.[88]

The sub-regional variances in the socio-economic structures, agrarian relations, extent of landlessness, demographic pressure and in the levels of political consciousness of peasants, determined the degree and nature of peasant insurgency in different areas. The high intensity of economic distress in the post-Famine period in parts of the riot-affected areas of Noakhali and Tippera,[89] along with the relative independence of the Noakhali-Tippera peasants, turned them violent at the slightest provocation from their leaders. The general political culture of poor peasants in this sub-region had been moulded by the 'Bolsheviks' who showed them the way of violence for redressing their grievances long before the disturbances of 1946. The poor peasants in the Rangpur-Dinajpur, Pabna-Bogra, Jessore-Khulna and Dhaka-Mymensingh areas did not turn 'communal' to that extent when compared with their counterparts in the Noakhali-Tippera sub-region, because the immediate exploiting classes in Rangpur, Dinajpur and parts of Pabna, Bogra, Dhaka and elsewhere were Muslim *jotedars*. The poor peasants in Rangpur-Dinajpur were again mostly bonded labourers and sharecroppers.[90] By late 1946, the poor peasants in parts of Rangpur, Dinajpur, Jessore, Khulna and Mymensingh again, were under communist control, fighting for *tebhaga*. It is, however, not absolutely true that the *bargadars* under communist control were not moulded by communal issues. Their aspiration to get higher social status *vis-a-vis* the high-caste Hindu landlords in Mymensingh and Muslim *jotedars* in Rangpur and Dinajpur may be easily identified as a by-product of tribal and communal exclusivities. One can agree with Guha: 'This apparent spontaneity was nothing but a measure of the displacement of class solidarity by ethnic solidarity.'[91]

For the Muslim *bargadars* and other categories of poor peasants there was hardly any communal motivation to stick to the *tebhaga* or other anti-*jotedar* movements. As discussed earlier, the introduction of the Bargadar Bill, commonly known as the Tebhaga Bill, was an important factor in dissuading Muslim *bargadars* from the movement, although it was never considered for enactment by the Suhrawardy government. It was nothing but a carrot to draw poor Muslim peasants' support for the Pakistan movement.[92] It was followed by another radical bill, the State Acquisition and Tenancy Bill, designed to abolish the *zamindari* system, tabled on 21 April in the Assembly by the Muslim League government.[93] This Bill got wide publicity throughout the region through the government and Muslim League media. Most peasants and some of their leaders believed that the Bill was intended to translate the 'land to the tiller' slogan into action.

Leading KPP leaders, Syed Nausher Ali and Abu Hossain Sarkar, for example, who had sympathized with the Tebhaga movement, became inert and gradually withdrew their support from the CPI. Suhrawardy's anti-communist stand, which was very popular among most Muslims, especially among the rich and middle peasants, succeeded in neutralizing the effects of the CPI on Muslim mass groups.[94] Through various radical promises, which worked as stunts, the League virtually took the wind out of the CPI sails after April 1947. Meanwhile, the Congress and other predominantly Hindu groups had been thoroughly discredited among the bulk of the peasantry as 'enemies' of Islam and Pakistan and as the 'protectors' of the *zamindars* and *mahajans*.

Dhanagare has rightly pointed out the devouring impact of communal politics which led to the desertion of a large number of Muslim peasants from the Kisan Sabha, but he has understressed the implications of the demands for the abolition of the *zamindari-mahajani* systems,[95] which had a tremendous impact on the bulk of the peasants. The League's success in enlisting peasant support for Pakistan lay in these demands, which had both communal as well as class appeal. The successful marriage of convenience between the *ashraf* and Muslim *jotedars* enabled them to jointly mobilize the lower echelons of the peasantry. In the long run, this signalled the ascendancy of the *jotedars* as a dominant class in rural East Bengal, which later played a decisive role in the history of the region.[96]

One may agree with those who blame the vacillating and compromising communist leadership for the failure of the class-based peasant movements of the 1940s. There is some truth in the assertion that at times the communists were opportunistic, mainly interested in mobilizing the sharecroppers with a view to strengthening their urban-based movements of industrial workers and proletariats (said to have more revolutionary potential than the peasants), and that this was reflected in the total non-representation of poor peasants in the CPI or Bengal Kisan Sabha Central Committees during the period. One may further criticise the CPI for not hitting British imperialism when it was 'at its weakest' by mobilizing peasants for the 'Greater Bengal Move' in 1947, thereby defying the 'one nation' and 'two-nation' theories. The sharecroppers are also said to have been prepared to 'go any length despite their limited grasp of revolutionary theory'.[97] But this sort of reasoning only underestimates the impact of the 'two-nation theory', which propounding separate nationhood for all the Muslims of the subcontinent, cut across class, ethnic and other differences. Without contesting the view that the CPI leadership was vacillating, at times betraying the peasant cause, one feels that the main reason why these movements failed was their total dissociation with the broader nationalist or separatist movements, which divided the different categories of peasants and sharecroppers by capturing their imagination, promising them their respective 'peasant utopias'.

One may, in this regard, cite the famous Bengali communist leader, Moni Singh, who felt total helplessness in the 1940s with regard to the mobilization of Muslim peasants by the Communist Party of India. According to him: 'While we promised *tebhaga,* Muslim League (pro-Pakistan Muslim separatist) leaders like Ghyasuddin Pathan promised them *Chou-bhaga* (literally, four quarters) implying the total expropriation of the Hindu land-owners of East Bengal after achieving Pakistan.'[98] In view of the above, it is no exaggeration to suggest that the so-called glorious Tebhaga movement had very little impact on the Muslim sharecroppers and other sections of the Muslim peasantry.

The movement failed, because contrary to the Communist assertions, it was not a spontaneous movement from below but an artificially produced movement from the top. It was, in general confined to the minority tribal sharecroppers, who could be vertically mobilized through tribal chiefs and communist leaders, unlike the typical peasants, who lived in faction-ridden peasant communities with a strong sense of private ownership of land. Bengali peasant 'moral economy' also justified the prevalent cropsharing arrangement on the fifty-fifty basis. Last but not the least, rich and middle peasants and the sharecroppers had different 'utopias' and it seems, the Pakistan movement blurred their differences as they were politically mobilized by the superordinate *ashraf-ulama-jotedar* triumvirate which championed the cause of Muslim separatism by singling out the Hindu-Muslim conflict as the determining factor, setting aside the existing class conflict between the rich and poor among the Bengali Muslims. Thus the bulk of the Muslim *jotedars* and others having conflicting class interests with Hindu *zamindar bhadralok-mahajan* triumvirate successfully mobilized the support of Muslim peasants in their struggle for a 'Muslim homeland' by communalizing the nationalist and class politics in the region.

This, however, was not the only case of peasant mobilization by non-peasant leaders from outside to strengthen the nationalist movement. Gandhi and other leaders of the Congress party of India also integrated the peasant-cause with the national one before independence. Consequently, to some extent, like East Bengal, rich peasants in India flourished in the wake of independence as beneficiaries of the nationalist movement. Although poor peasants of India actively participated and suffered most in the nationalist movement, but since they were only 'poor followers and not real decision makers' in Gandhi's multi-class movement, they were simply 'kicked away after the goals of mobilization had been achieved.'[99] One may agree with the view that in mass movements non-peasant elite leaders *often* 'throw away the ladder on which they rise to success', and that 'the explanation for this does not lie in any conspiracy theory, but in the understanding of a proper correlation of forces and alliances in which various fractions of the peasantry participate.'[100]

However, all peasant movements under non-peasant leaders do not necessarily leave the poor peasants crest-fallen at the end of the day. In China, for example, Mao (and the Communist Party) mobilized poor peasants not only because he realized their revolutionary potential, but also because he wanted to install them to power along with the other proletariats. Hence the glorification of the Chinese revolution as *Peasant nationalism* by Chalmers Johnson and others.

Without being polemical over the issue whether nation states are only *Imagined Communities* (Anderson) or by-products of 'invented traditions',[101] one may argue that elites might invent the traditions to legitimize their power but, there is reciprocity between the elites' notions and mass culture, institutions and perceptions of right and wrong, justice and injustice, morality and immorality. East Bengali Muslim lower peasants' bitter experience of maltreatment in every sphere of life — social, political and economic — by Hindu *zamindars*, *bhadralok* and *mahajans* during the pre-partition days, is equally important in this regard. As Paul Brass has shown, Muslim elites in Uttar Pradesh (north India) manipulated Muslim cultural symbols to create separate political identities without ignoring the preexisting cultural values and Hindu-Muslim differences;[102] similarly *ashraf* and *ulama* politicians in East Bengal mobilized lower peasant support for the Pakistan movement. Non-peasant Muslim leaders' success in the transformation of the bulk of East Bengal peasants into 'Pakistanis' is not altogether different from the transformation of French peasants into 'Frenchmen' by non-peasant French leaders and institutions in the late nineteenth and early twentieth centuries.[103]

The reciprocity between peasants and non-peasant elites is vital in all nationalist movements in the present world. The reciprocity takes place on a give-and-take basis. As Migdal observes, 'politics for peasants starts at the level at which they can trust outsiders'; they know that 'outsiders are willing to fill certain needs, if there is something to be given to them in return'.[104] Peasant mobilization whether by locals or non-locals also depends on leaders 'who are able to voice and express clearly what most people more or less vaguely feel.'[105]

However, we cannot ignore the role of ideology as the most important factor in mobilizing peasants against their exploiters. Bhambhri may be cited in this regard: 'Localized and scattered peasantry cannot be mobilized without a powerful social ideology, a strong party and an effective leader ... A peasant has never made history, he can be mobilized to make history under proper leadership and with alliances.'[106] It is altogether a different matter if the ideology happens to be 'a wrong ideology' and the consciousness, a 'false' one. Then the process of mass mobilization, is a by-product of the 'cultural hegemony' of the elites — who successfully appropriate the so-called 'autonomous domain' of the 'subalterns', contrary to the views of Ranajit Guha and others of the 'Subaltern School'.[107]

In sum, one may argue that the study of nationalism in a peasant society like East Bengal, requires an understanding of the elite conflict between the newly emerging Muslim elite with the well-entrenched Hindu one, emanating from (and representing) Muslim upper peasantry and Hindu landed and professional classes, respectively. Elite conflict rather than 'peasant nationalism' had been the determinant factor both in the

partition of Bengal in 1947 to form East Pakistan as well as in
the creation of Bangladesh in 1971.

NOTES

1. G. Huizer Heath Lexington Books, 1972, The Revolutionary Potential of
   Peasants in Latin America (Lexington, 1972) p. 13.
2. Taj-ul-Islam Hashmi, Pakistan as a Peasant Utopia (Boulder, 1992) p. 206.
3. R.P. Misra a T.N. Dyng (eds) Third World Peasanty (New Westview Press
   Delhi, 1987) p. 5.
4. HPF, 395/1924 (1-3). Home Dept. Political Files Govt. of Bengal.
5. Hashmi, Ch. 3, 'Peasants in the Khilafat Movement'.
6. Baden-Powell, — B. H. Baden-Powell Land Systems of British-India
   vol. I. (Oxford, OUP 1892) p. 407.
7. N.C. Chaudhury, p. 230. — The Autobiography of an Unknown Indian
   (Hogarth 1987 London, p. 230).
8. BDG, Jessore, 1912 p. 114, Dinajpur, 1917 p. 95; Bengal District
   Gazetteer.
9. Bell, SSR, Dinajpur, pp. 21-6. – Calcutta, 1941 – (henceforth SSR
   abbreviation for Survey and Settlement Operation).
10. Simon Report, vol. XVIII, p. 197.
11. Islam, S., 'The Bengal Peasantry in Debt 1940-49' Dhaka University
    Studies 22 June 1974.
12. A. B. Ahmed, Amar Dekha Rijnitic Punchash Bachhar (Dhaka, 1970) – J.
    Broomfield, Elite Cornflict in a Plural Society (Berkeley 1968), pp. 95,
    155-9.
13. R.R. Kabeer, Change in Bengal Agrarian Society C. 1760-1850 (Delhi,
    1979) P. 46-7.
14. British Parliamentary Papers. (henceforth BPP), 1920, Cd 812,
    Vol. XXXVI, pp. 295-9.
15. BPP Cd 9109, 1918, pp. 120-1.
16. BPP Cd 9109, 1918, PP. 120-1
17. Floud Report, III & IV, passim.
18. Pabna-Bogra, SSR, pp. 67-8; Floud Report, I, p. 67.
19. BDG, Mymensingh, 1917, pp. 39 & 43.
20. BDG, Mymensingh, 1917, p. 107.
21. Pabna-Bogra, SSR, p. 73.
22. J. Bhattacharyya, 'An Examination of Leadership Entry in Bengal Peasant
    Revolts 1937-47' Journal of Asian Studies 36, 4 (Aug. 1978), p. 612.
23. A. Rasul, Krishak Sabhar Itihad (Calcutta, 1969), p. 154.
24. See, Das Gupta; The Naxalitc Movement (Calcutta, 1974); and Sunil Sen
    chs. V and VII. — Peasant Movement in India: Mid-Nineteenth and

Twentieth Centuries (Calcutta 1982)
25. *Pabna-Bogra SSR,* pp. 71 - 2; N.C. Sen, Director, Land Records and Survey to the Settlement Officer, Mymensingh; 29 July 1939, B.P. Singh Roy Papers, File No. 3 (I).
26. Floud Report, I, pp. 66-73; Huque; N.C. Sen to the Settlement Officer, Mymensingh, 29 July 1939, B.P. Singh Roy Papers, file No. 3(I).
27. See 'Memorandum by the Bengal Provincial Kisan Sabha', Floud Report, VI, pp. 44-52; *Bangiya Pradeshik Krishak Sabhar Ishtahar (BPKSI)* (The Bengal Provincial Krishak Sabha's Manifesto), Calcutta, Jan. 1940, Govt. Bengal Home Political Files, W-48/40.
28. Rasul, p. 104.
29. *BPKSI,* pp. 210-1, 131-8.
30. M. Kamal and A. Kamal, 'Dinajpur's Tebhaga Andolon 1946-8' Bichitra, Dhaka 25 February 1983.
31. SP Rangpur, W.A.B. Price to IGP, GB, A.D. Gordon, D.O. No. 1308, 6/7 April 1941, Dimla, Rangpur, HPF (File cover missing, available at the West Bengal State Archives, Calcutta).
32. Rasul, p. 278.
33. For the remote and immediate causes of the Tebhaga movement see H. Alavi, K. Gough O.P. Sharma Ledjj Imperialism a Revolution in South Asia (New York Monthly Press Renew 1973) (Peasants and Revolution) in pp. 321-3.
34. For details about land alienation in Bengal see Bhowani Sen, 'The Tebhaga Movement in Bengal', *Communist,* Sept. 1947, cited in Alavi, pp. 321-3; Bhattacharyya, p. 618.
35. Interview, Aboni Lahiri – New Delhi, 22 April 1983.
36. Rasul, pp. 147-50; Alavi, pp. 318-19.
37. Interview, Aboni Lahiri; M. Kamal and A. Kamal, p. 107.
38. Alavi, pp. 323, 334.
39. See the Sub-Divisional Officers' Reports to the Additional Secretary of Revenue, GB, 'Relation Between Bargadars and Their Landlords — Tebhaga Movement', GB, Dept. of Land and Land Revenue File, No. 6M-38/47, Proceedings 'B' of Dec. 1948, 15-107.
40. Sunil Sen (1972) pp. 36-41; Interview, Sunil Sen; Interview, Aboni Lahiri; M. Kamal and A. Kamal, pp. 113-16.
41. Satyen Sen, Gram Banglar Pathe Pathe (Dhaka, 1970), pp. 31-43, 52-109.
42. See confidential reports by SDOs of Dinajpur and Rangpur, GB, Land Revenue File No. 6M-38/47; 'Peasant Unrest in North Bengal', *Statesman,* 19 March 1947; Rasul, pp. 109-21, 132-51.
43. M. Kamal and A. Kamal, p. 111.
44. M. Kamal and A. Kamal, pp. 111-12.
45. 'Peasant Unrest in North Bengal', *Statesman,* 19 March, 1947.
46. Interviews, Sunil Sen and Aboni Lahiri Calcutta, 1 May 1983.
47. Ibid.; Rasul, pp. 156-8; Satyen Sen, pp. 98-109.

48. Umar, pp. 88-91; Sunil Sen B. Umar, Chirosthai Bondobosto O. Bangladesher Krishak (Dhaka, 1973) p. 43; Satyen Sen, pp. 13-30.
49. See for details – Hore, 'Tebhagar Diary' Ekhon (Calcutta, Oct. 1981), pp. 1-59.
50. Satyen Sen, pp. 124-59; Umar, 20 October 1982, Dhaka, pp. 94-103.
51. Home Fortnightly Report, 1st half, March 1947; P. Gupta, p. 104; Interviews, Moni Singh and Aboni Lahiri; Interviews, Noor Jalal and Mudasser Munshi (peasant leaders of Narail, Jessore), by Kamal Siddiqui et al., The nature of peasant resistance during the Tebhaga Movement (Hong Kong, 1987).
52. D. N. Dhanagare, Peasant Movements in India (Bombay, Oxford University Press 1983).
53. A. Cooper 'Share croppers' and Landlords in Bengal 1930-50' Journal of Peasant Studies 10 Jan. April 1983.
54. K. Siddiqui, et al., 'Tebhana Movement in Bengal (1946-7): An Assessment' Bangladesh Historical Studies 3, 1978, p. 153.
55. Sunil Sen, pp. 82-3.
56. Sunil Sen, pp. 41-1; Rasul, pp. 151-3; Satyen Sen, pp. 24-8.
57. Interviews, Sunil Sen and Aboni Lahiri.
58. Interviews, Sunil Sen and Aboni Lahiri.
59. M. Kamal and A. Kamal, p. 105.
60. Dhanagare, p. 175.
61. J. Broomfield, Elite Conflicts in a Plural Society (Berkeley, University California Press 1968), p. 229.
62. G. O. Overstreet and M. Windmiller, Communism in India (Berkeley, University of California Press 1959), p. 363.
63. Sunil Sen (1972) pp. 83-5.
64. J. De, 'Sreni Dwanda Krishak Andolon O Krishak Praja Dal, 1937-9' Bangla Alademy Patrika 2, 1972, Dhaka 22-3 May, 1983.
65. Interview, Maulana Tarkabagish; Gankovoskiy and Gordon Polonskaya, p. 94.
66. Yu. V. Gankovosky and L. R. Gordon – Polonskaya A Soviet History of Pakistan (Washington DC 1968).
67. A. M. Ahmed, p. 236; Umar, pp. 57-8.
68. Shila Sen, — Muslim Politics in Bengal 1937-1947 (New Delhi, Impex India 1976), pp. 196-7.
69. HFP, 2nd half, March 1946; Amrita Bazar Patrika (Calcutta) 22 March 1946; P. Gupta, Je Sangramer Sheshi nei (Calcutta 1971) pp. 93-4.
70. Rasul, pp. 149-50.
71. Sunil Sen, p. 85.
72. HFR, 2nd half, March-April and May 1944.
73. Interview, Moni Singh.
74. HFR, 1st half, May and Dec. 1943, 2nd halves, May and June 1944, 1945-47.

75. HFR, 2nd halves, July-Aug, and 1st half, Oct. 1944, 1945-47.
76. HFR, 2nd half, March 1945.
77. HFR, 1st half, May 1946.
78. *The Times,* 17-28 Aug. 1946.
79. *The Times,* 16 Oct. 1946.
80. Overstreet and Windmiller, p. 254.
81. HFR, May-Oct. 1946.
82. Governor F. Burrows to Lord Pethick Lawrence, 20 Oct. 1946, Wavell Papers, cited in N. Mansergh, Vol. VIII, pp. 753-4; *The Times,* 18 Oct. 1946; *Amrita Bazar Patrika* (Calcutta)12-30 Oct. 1946; 'Communal Trouble in Ramgang, Noakhali 1946'; HPF, No 40C-29/46.
83. *The Times,* 10 Feb. 1947.
84. HFR, Oct. 1946-April 1947.
85. Interview, Annada Sankar Ray Culcutta 15 January 1983; *The Times,* 24 April 1947; HFR, 2nd half, Dec. 1946 and March-April 1947.
86. Interview, Sirajul Haq Majumdar – Village Chhagalnaiya, Noakhali 29 October 1982.
87. 'The Elections', editorial *Amrita Bazar Patrika* (Calcutta) 28 March 1946.
88. E. Wolf, *Peasant wars of the twentieth century* (London Faber and Faber 1971) pp. 290-2.
89. See P. C. Mahalanobis 'A sample survey of the after-effects of the Bengal Famine of 1943' *Sankhya* 7, 4. 1946, p. 6.
90. *SZSR, Jessore,* pp. 71-2; *Dinajpur,* p. 25; *Dacca* pp. 47-8; *Pabna-Bogra,* p. 72; *Banking Enquiry Committee Report* (Bengal), II, pp. 543, 697.
91. R. Guha Elementary Aspects of peasant insurgency in Colonial India (Oxford 1983), pp. 169-70.
92. Sunil Sen, pp. 47-57; 'Extracts from the minutes of the meeting of the Council of Minister', 18 March 1947, Proceedings 'B', Dec. 1948, GB. Land and Land Revenue Dept., File No. 6M-38/47; HFR, 2nd half, Feb. and April 1947; Interview, Moni Singh.
93. Bengal Legislative Assembly Proceedings. See *BLAP,* 21 April 1947, vol. 72, no. 3. 1947; HFR, 2nd half, Feb. 1947.
94. P. Gupta, p. 105; Sunil Sen (1972) pp. 66-8; Interviews, Sunil Sen and Aboni Lahiri.
95. Dhanagare, pp. 172-3.
96. E. Stokes, the Peasant and the Raj (Cambridge, Cambridge University Press 1978) Stokes, p. 281; Gankovsky et al., p. 94.
97. K. Siddiqui, 'The nature of peasant resistance during the Tebhaga movement' in R. Ghose (ed.) *Protest movements in South and S.E. Asia* (Hong Kong University of Hong Kong Press 1987) pp. 63-6.
98. Interview, Moni Singh.
99. C.D. Bhambhri, 'Peasant Mobilization in China, India' in R.P. Misra Dung (eds) Third World Peasantry Vol. 2 (New Delhi 1987), 215.
100. Bhambhri, p. 215.

101. E. Hobsbawm. The Nation as Invented Tradition' in J. Hutchinson and A.D. Smith (eds) *Nationalism* (Oxford 1994) p. 76-7.
102. P. Brass, *Ethnicity a nationalism theory and comparison.* (New Delhi 1991), pp. 69-108.
103. Hobsbawm, p. 77.
104. J.S. Migdal *Peasants, Politics and Revolution Pressures Toward Political and Social Change in the Third World* (Princeton, Princeton University Press 1974) pp. 193-4, 212-16.
105. Huizer, pp. 22-3.
106. Bhambhri, p. 215.
107. Guha p. 4.

Chapter Two

Regionalism or Personality Cult?
Allama Mashriqi and the Tehreek-i-Khaksar
in pre-1947 Punjab.

Iftikhar H. Malik**

Most of the studies on pre-partition Punjab focus on a select-few parties or personalities ignoring several others deemed insignificant. Thanks to an exclusive emphasis on Pakistani nationalism and its complex relationship with the colonial state, with the Indian National Congress (INC) or with the regional forces, several 'grey areas' have remained unattended within the Pakistani historiography. By assuming the role of the flag-ship for the Pakistani nation-state, the Muslim Punjab seems to have peripheralized its own ethno-regionalism which, like in the pre-1947 years, at some juncture may have challenged the trans-regional nationalism espoused by the All-India Muslim League (AIML). Such a role sometimes called the Punjabization of the Pakistani state has never been tension-free leading to dissent from other constituent units.[1] Several political forces including the Khaksars and Ahrars in the pre-1947 Punjab and their counterparts elsewhere have not received the academic attention they deserved.[2] By categorizing the Ahrars and Khaksars merely as the pro-INC *nationalist* elements arrayed against the AIML the Pakistani establishment and several historians have tended to sideline their respective roles in the crucial decades before

** The research for this chapter is spread over a long span of time. However, acknowledge the cooperation and assistance of the Mashriqi family and several Khaksars all over the Punjab. My visits to Lahore, Rawalpindi and Faisalabad in 1996 have greatly benefited from the intellectual support provided by Arshad Malik, Aslam Malik, Sher Muhammad Garewal and Ahmed Saeed. Ishtiaq Ahmed at Stockholm University and Saleem Qureshi at the British Library, London, also deserve my special gratitude.

independence.³ Such a historiographical reductionism has only fed simplified interpretations of Muslim nationalism. Consequently, the Aligarh movement, evolution of the AIML, Iqbal's Allahabad address of 1930, the Lahore Resolution of 1940 and anti-Khizr movement become consensual markers in interpretations on Pakistan. Prominent leaders such as Fazl-i-Husain, Abdul Ghaffar Khan, H. S. Suhrawardy, G.M. Syed, A. K. Azad, Husain Ahmed Madani and Khizr Hayat have all received only marginal attention.⁴ Such narrow-based interpretations have equally deprived Muslim majority regions of the roles they played within the Pakistan movement. By apportioning exclusive credit to some provinces the vision of an integrative Pakistani nationalism is distorted.

In addition to reservations about regional studies a deep-seated suspicion of pluralism has disallowed any open debate on Punjabi identity, despite the province's preeminent role in national life. The separation of East Pakistan in 1971 followed by Zulfikar Ali Bhutto's problems with the Pashtun and Baloch leaders further discouraged any debate on regional histories and identities.⁵ It appeared that rather than internalizing the lessons from East Pakistan, Pakistani leaders still opted for superimposed centralization. Under General Zia, when Pakistan suffered under the longest martial law in its brief history, centralization of the state and perceptions about its being totally Punjab-Pashtun dominated became quite apparent, especially among the rural and urban Sindhis. Both the Sindhis and Muhajireen assumed violent stratagems to implement their ethno-nationalism which further augmented the centralist tendencies disallowing any serious intellectual debate on plurality. With Karachi being extremely restive in the 1990s and the Pakistani civil society becoming more vocal, it is now comparatively easier to discuss regional diversities and ethnic pluralism despite an obvious official nonchalance. It is largely through media or private think-tanks that an intellectual articulation for a redefinition of Pakistani nationalism from below has begun to emerge.⁶

The study of the Khaksar Movement and its leader, Allama

Inayatullah Khan Mashriqi, is not only essential for promoting interest in Punjab studies, but is equally vital for a number of other reasons. Pakistani official emphasis on ideology especially under military regimes has exposed numerous fissures within an imagined Islamic sameness. The sectarian violence like the afore-mentioned ethnic ferment underlines the need to study Islamic unity in reference to inherent diversity. It is this inherent reality of pluralism wanting intellectual expression plus the imposition of selective Islamic strictures from above, without any consensual arrangement at the societal level that produced inter-sectarian disorder of such proportions. It cannot simply be decried as chauvinism or fundamentalism, nor can it be attributed to obscurantist *mullahism* as it is linked with the undefined but exaggerated dependence of the polity upon ideology itself.[7] Shunning a Jinnahist model of equality and tolerance in tackling the mundane issues of nation-building and legitimacy, the official relapse into religious shelter has only added to strains on the society. Frequent drifts in national policies, spasmodic totalitarian phases, the weakening of the development sector and the rejection of religio-political parties in the elections have all contributed to the sectarian violence, further exacerbated by the Saudi-Iranian lobby-making competition in Pakistan amongst the Sunnis and Shias, respectively.[8] The Khaksar Tehreek, while espousing an Islamic model in the 1930s, volunteered to intervene in the UP to arbitrate between feuding Shias and Sunnis during the Muharram and in the process politicized (communalized!) itself. But lacking the intellectual and institutional wherewithal like several individual tolerant Muslim groups in present-day Pakistan,[9] it utterly failed and ended up confronting the provincial government. The Khaksars were predominantly Sunni but their lack of a composite, mutually acceptable Islamic creed offered no check on volatile sectarianism. Intellectually, the movement represented a rather ill-defined and largely rhetorical inter-mixing of religion with politics applying modernist symbols and reconstructing a glorious past.

At another crucial level, a study of the Khaksar movement and its rise and fall typify the personality-centred, cultist patterns of political parties in the developing world. Prioritization of so-called strong men over institutions in colonial and post-colonial societies only betrays the absence of programmic politics. It remains curiously unacknowledged that the movement tried to challenge the rural domination of the Punjab politics and reaffirmed the urban nature of revivalism and reformism that had remained quarantined at the behest of the colonial state and the co-optive Unionists for so long. Like the INC and AIML, the Khaksars were mostly townsmen with a considerable level of literacy, and unlike the land-owning or upper middle classes, belonged to *petite bourgeoisie* groups. It is not to say that the movement did not attract influential professionals or a sprinkling of landed elites or such other Muslim notables.[10] Like today's Muhajir Qaumi Movement (MQM) in Karachi, it began as a reform movement by promising vital changes, but ended up fighting on several fronts. The role of a charismatic leader like Mashriqi and his unchallengeable position only exhibited a preference for personalist and fascist strategies. Psychologically, the emphasis on marches, uniforms, holding of *bailchas* (spades) and organization of the entire movement on a semi-military pattern created a sense of identity, dignity and cohesion amongst the un-recognized bourgeois at a time when politics remained the monopoly of a few landed intermediaries. Such an assertion, in a powerful manner, also showed a popular trend among various contemporary South Asian parties seeking inspiration from Hitler and Mussolini. The rumours of Mashriqi's alleged meeting with Hitler in Germany created an aura of authenticity.[11] Concurrently, Mashriqi's own erratic life and idiosyncrasies played a major role in his downfall and eventual disintegration of the movement without achieving any tangible results. The Khaksars were initially used by the AIML against the INC in the NWFP to destabilize the Khan Brothers while in the mid-1940s they were surrogated by the INC to destabilize the AIML in its pursuit for Pakistan. Such opportunism only added to the Khaksars' isolation at a time when the colonial state had tightened its controls on the movement and its leadership. However, the movement must be given credit for pioneering the effective use of modern media and propaganda to reach a wide audience in the cities. Through producing a regular periodic literature meant for populist consumption, the Tehreek produced a fascinating and a massive amount of source-material on its organization and ideology.

Following a few introductory statements on the movement itself, our study aims first at surveying the serious commentaries on the movement so far, second it constructs a short biography and the philosophy of its founder, and third it investigates the political career of the party itself.

The Tehreek-i-Khaksar, was created in 1930-1[12] by a former educationist and a Cambridge graduate, Inayatullah Khan Mashriqi. It provides a unique case-study in the complex quest for identity. It vacillated between different and often contradictory constructs varying from Indian nationalism to Muslim trans-territoriality, and from Islamization to a critique of *mullahism*. It equally reflected a strange and often painful personality cult, practiced military-style drills, and engaged in copious pamphleting. Its followers carried spades and mostly came from Northern India with Punjab being their main centre. Initially, they concentrated on social work, but gradually turned more towards an ambiguous political programme irritating the colonial authorities. Their first show-down with the UP government in 1939 resulted in several deaths in Bulandshehr. It was followed by a bigger confrontation with the Unionist regime of Sikandar Hayat in Lahore on 19 March 1940. The latter happened soon after Mashriqi's offer to provide 50,000 volunteers for war, which was construed as one of his several idiosyncrasies. His own temperamental about turn, personal insecurity and nonchalance for any second-tier leadership created inherent problems for the movement. Mashriqi's bouts with the Ahrars, Unionists, INC and AIML further isolated him from the contemporary political forces. His emotional tirades against all the political leaders, left the movement in the doldrums, though there was never a dearth of volunteers from Punjab, NWFP, Sindh, Hyderabad and even from as far as Bihar and Bengal. The colonial administration, especially in Punjab, was able to easily crush the movement. Mashriqi was released in early 1943, but the movement had already plummeted. The vacillation between supra-communal politics to a more interventionist role within the Sunni-Shia conflict, an unmitigated attack on *mullahs* — the semi-literate Muslim clergy — and altercations with the INC, Khudai Khidmatgars, Unionists and the AIML betrayed a confrontational politicking. Such an oppositional politics only exhausted the resources and manpower resulting in a gradual decline of the movement itself. The periodic temperamental tirades of the Allama, his family problems, lack of a well-sustained ideology and strategy, and drain of resources everywhere on shadowy causes and unsustained rhetoric all led to the weakening of the movement. It is curious to note, however, that the Tehreek starting from Punjab remained the only organization to have strong India-wide contacts during its heydays but was soon confined to a few areas around Lahore. Its sudden decline mirrored its dramatic rise, and by the time of partition the party had already lost most of its appeal and vigour. Mashriqi, until his death in 1963, was a respectable freedom fighter, yet he had already turned into a 'has-been' in Pakistan politics where his former Unionist adversaries ruled the roost.

Source-material on the Khaksars

As mentioned above, the Khaksars have received only marginal scholarly attention. The few books on the Allama or the Khaksar troubles with the UP government and subsequently with Sikandar Hayat's ministry in Punjab have been largely written in Urdu by the former party members themselves. The disputation over the leadership of the party after the founder's death among his various claimants led to a dispersion of his papers and publications, which luckily have been preserved by a few Khaksars in Lahore besides those preserved in the official records in London. The contemporary official archives, mass of Urdu writings and the Khaksars' own willingness to talk about their political career — though often stained with exaggeration — provide a unique opportunity to study this misunderstood,

volatile, lower middle class, urban party, cashing in on the name
of its founder, who himself relished meeting Hitler according to
unverified accounts.

The earliest sketchy account of the Khaksar movement was by
W.C. Smith in his work *The Modern Muslim India: A Social
Analysis* (1943),[13] followed two decades later by a work by
Waheeduzzaman.[14] My own study on Sikander Hayat Khan
contained a chapter on the Khaksar Movement and its
relationship with the Unionists, which, with some updating, was
finally published as a political biography in 1985.[15] It is
noteworthy that until the submission of a full-fledged doctoral
dissertation[16] on the Khaksars at Multan University in 1996, no
substantial and interpretive research was ever undertaken on the
Allama, his views and the movement.[17] In the early 1970s, two
M.A. dissertations for history and Islamic studies at the Punjab
University[18] did devote themselves to the Khaksars but ended up
reproducing only abridged versions of books by Safdar
Saleemi.[19] In addition a few more works in the same decade on
the Khaksars largely displayed nostalgia but lacked any serious
analysis.[20] Saleemi's books, however, provide a wealth of
information on the Khaksars as they reproduce a massive amount
of the Tehreek's own literature. Shabbir Husain's important
studies, in recent years, aim at reconstructing the Tehreek besides
rehabilitating the Allama from a personal ideological
viewpoint.[21] Another category of contemporary writings on the
Tehreek was motivated by political expediency to win over
Allama's sympathy for some particular cause.[22] A few solitary
research papers have tried to study the movement with reference
to contemporary Muslim politics in India or within the context of
identity formation in Punjab.[23]

The doctoral dissertation by Aslam Malik must be
acknowledged as the most comprehensive and well-documented
study of the leadership, philosophy, strategy and political history
of the Khaksars to date. It is the result of several years of
painstaking study of diverse Urdu literature either produced by
the Khaksars themselves or about them at different levels.
Malik's earlier research on Allama Mashriqi and his interviews

with several leaders duly equipped him with a comprehensive data on the charismatic but often idiosyncratic personality of the Allama. The study, however, for all its contribution, falls short of conceptualization and needs to be linked up with other complex ideological and sociological undercurrents of South Asian Muslim societies.

Allama Mashriqi: A Profile

Inayatullah Khan, subsequently known as Allama Mashriqi, was born in a lower middle class Muslim family in Amritsar (now in Indian Punjab) on 25 August 1888. His father, Ata Muhammad, a petition writer in the local courts, had written a few books on Islamic interaction with Western thought besides a poetry collection. After graduating from Forman Christian College, Lahore, in 1906, with excellent results, he sought admission at Government College to pursue a Master's in mathematics.[24] In 1907, Inayatullah Khan reached Cambridge to spend the next five years at Christ Church. He obtained four Triposes in mathematics, natural sciences, Oriental languages and mechanical sciences–something which was considered extraordinary and was deeply lauded by the British and Indian press. Mashriqi's tryst with the civil service resulted in his qualification for the Indian Education Service (IES). It is not clear how he ended up as a vice-principal at Islamia College, Peshawar, in March 1913. The official sketch prepared by the intelligence agency gave its own version of the Allama's early life. He is mentioned to have been born in 1883 and not 1888, to pursue a 'brilliant scholastic career'. He proceeded to England after an MA from the University of Punjab and failed the ICS 'owing to ill health, but passed into the I.E.S'. It is noteworthy that his entire official service since 1907 had been in the NWFP. In the official report, he was characterized 'eccentric in his views (and) an ardent pan-Islamist'.[25] Since Mashriqi sought retirement in the early 1930s, he must have been part of the IES and after his return from Cambridge joined the Islamia College only for an interim period before his official appointment. After a short phase as an assistant secretary for education, he became the headmaster of Government High School at Peshawar, a puzzling development indeed. It is generally given out that as an Indian, he faced discrimination and despite a brilliant academic record was more often left out in the cold. In 1930, he sought medical leave prior to his retirement until his pensionability in October 1932.

While teaching in Peshawar, the Allama simultaneously took up writing and travelling, besides, planning for a future course of political action. It was here that he wrote his two famous works *Ishraat* and *Tazkirah*. While certain volumes in the former remain unpublished, the second work has proven to be the main embodiment of Mashriqi's views on Islamic reformism suggesting guidance on regeneration through a military-type discipline. It was first published in 1924 with a second edition appearing a year after the author's death in 1964. Written in a rather jargon-ridden and Arabicized Urdu, *Tazkirah* is a difficult book though its Introduction, written in Arabic itself, is the summation of the entire volume. The Allama, in his *magmum opus*, seems to be moving towards Islamic trans-regionalism. It is curious to note that despite such a high-profile lobbying for its recognition as an original work in Islamic studies the Allama did not think of translating his major work into English. Soon after its publication, *Tazkirah* became controversial and was condemned by the traditionalist *ulama* though modernist Muslims found it innovative. It appeared to be in line with the thinking of Sir Syed Ahmed Khan, the founder of the Aligarh movement in the nineteenth century and Mashriqi sent copies to numerous people including Muslim heads of states.[26] In 1926, he undertook a visit to Cairo to attend the Khilafat Conference, organized by Sheikhul Islam of Egypt. He opposed the proposal to designate the Sultan of Egypt as the new caliph 'on the grounds that a vassal ruler could not be a spiritual leader of the Islamic world.' Despite an avid canvassing among the delegates he did not receive any support for his scheme of a proposed *Baitul mal*—an Islamic fund — with £20,000. In Cairo he met several Muslim notables and especially the 'notorious' Maulana Ubaidullah Sindhi.[27] Mashriqi, in this visit abroad, is also rumoured to have met the Sultans of Morocco and Tunisia. It appears that Mashriqi was trying to establish his scholarly credentials in North Africa and Europe by hobnobbing with political and academic personalities as he harboured a desire for a greater role than being an ordinary teacher in a provincial town.[28]

In addition to *Tazkirah*, Mashriqi tried his pen on almost every subject including poetry, journalism and religious commentaries except for his own academic specialization—mathematics. During the heydays of the movement he issued a number of pamphlets aimed at popular readership and turned out to be the pioneer publicist using print media to reach a wider audience. It was from his books, pamphlets and articles in his weeklies like *Al-Islah* (Lahore) that one can sketch his religio-political ideology. The cornerstone of his ideology was to capture political power through military means by marshalling a community of well-disciplined believers. His ideas show a mixture of Darwinism, romanticism and hero-worship. He may not have qualified as an Indian nationalist since he kept fluctuating between an Indian (territorial) identity and Islamic (trans-regional) dispensation. Despite his early espousal for non-communalism, his Tehreek was mainly a Muslim movement applying Islamic symbols so as to forge historical consciousness and communitarian bonds. He appears to have been deeply influenced by European Philosophers, like Kant, Fitch and Nietzsche. But, rather than reconstructing a form of cultural nationalism, he became influenced by the fascist ideologies of the twentieth century and ends up combining Social Darwinism with National Socialism. An undefined mishmash of such conflictive ideologies centred around a powerful personality may have been a derivative from Carlyle or Weber, but in the Indian context, given the lack of nationalist ethos and the pre-industrial nature of the society itself torn by so many loyalties, such a construct was out moded. Such inherent ideological tensions in tandem with Mashriqi's own flamboyant and often erratic personality only hastened the downfall of the movement leaving

the Allama out in the cold.[29] His post-1947 stance on relations
with India or Islamization of Pakistan equally betrays a similar
form of erratic grasp of societal and ideological realities.

However, it is quite curious to note that despite his movement
being overwhelmingly from Punjab especially in post-1940
years, Mashriqi always tried to chart a wider and bigger role for
himself. There is no doubt that he was an ambitious scholar-
politician lacking the erudition and seasoning of a statesman and
suffering from temperamental vacillations. In the class
perspective, Mashriqi also represented a feeble Muslim middle
class still unable to carve out its own niche between the powerful
trajectories of the colonial state and the predominantly landed
intermediaries. Simultaneously, in a powerful way, the religious
elites—ulama and pirs—held sway over the rural Muslims and
Mashriqi had already annoyed them by his unconventional views
on religion. Even if Mashriqi had not alienated them ideologically, his very urban lower middle class moorings themselves
were adequate enough to isolate him from contemporary Muslim
power houses. An extremely weak civil society in the context of
an exceptionally low rate of literacy, and the rural and agrarian
nature of Muslim communities in the absence of a trans-regional
solidarity, meant that Mashriqi, like several other middle class
ideologues, failed to transmit a lasting imprint.

Building a religio-political party with cross-ideological
dimensions was no ordinary achievement, but to sustain it
without engaging in confrontation with several other competitive
and more well-entrenched forces proved an arduous task. Despite
several denials by the Allama,[30] the Khaksar movement was a
political movement since its ideology centred around the
acquisition of power. Its apolitical claims aimed to neutralize
official and other antagonisms; however, its disavowal of
militaristic designs in the face of the military-like training,
discipline and parades not only caused confusion but failed to
allay official and communalist criticism of the Khaksars.
According to Tazkirah, the Prophet (PBUH) was the ultimate ideal
who, in his person, had combined political, ideological and
pragmatic qualifications. Thus Islam was the only motivating

spirit underwriting the Muslim conquests in the past and it was only by reverting to the Koranic *ilm* (knowledge) and *hikmah* (wisdom) that the Muslims could retrieve their power. [31] Gaining power, to him, was true to the Islamic spirit. Mashriqi, emphatically, rejected both capitalism and socialism which, to him, were anchored on exploitation and sheer materialism. Both the systems, according to him, would not last long as they were devoid of spiritual and moral values. Good deeds and a powerful belief system as stipulated by Islam could assure Muslims a renewed global supremacy. Mashriqi rejected Gandhian pacifism and derided it as a traditional Hindu ploy. He lashed out at Muslim followers of Gandhi and, instead, considered his own idea of *askariyat* (militarism) to be rooted within the revolutionary Islam.

Mashriqi's views on political Islam and Muslim activism under a single titular leader are akin to those of Syed Abul Ala Maududi and Imam Khomeini. [32] (The famous poet-philosopher, Allama Muhammad Iqbal, also believed in Islamic activism of a democratic and egalitarian essentialism —a point differentiating and distancing him from the other radical Islamists.) Mashriqi, in his political ideology, vested all powers with an *amir* (leader) whose unchallenged authority lay in leading the revolution and in commanding an unquestioned obedience from the *raiyat* (subjects). He was to be faithfully followed and supported by a party (*jama'at*) of followers imbued with an extreme sense of sacrifice. In his reconstruction and reinterpretation of Islamic teachings and beliefs, Mashriqi saw an inherent strategy for the globalization of Islam. From beliefs to congregational prayers and from fasting to pilgrimage, all the practices, for him, aimed at developing a military-type discipline among the believers. [33] Thus, *jihad* (holy war) was both a virtue and an ideal for Muslims to be carried out collectively under the supreme leadership of an *amir.* Here, Mashriqi's idealization of strong men and his preference for unchallenged and unaccountable leadership is quite pronounced since it cannot be reprimanded by the community for deeds and decisions. Thus any revolt against the *amir* will be the gravest crime only inviting divine wrath. [34]

Mindful of the negative connotations of the word 'dictator', Mashriqi defined the *amir* as a Nietzschean character embodying divine authority and ultimate power. Despite accepting the institution of a *shoora* (consultative council), Mashriqi rendered it powerless by allocating instead all the powers to the leader, a source as well as a symbol of totality. To him, an *amir* was the viceregent of God and the Prophet (PBUH) and thus preceded the *shoora*, which itself was a later innovation. By assaulting upon such a major historical and juridical institution, the Allama deeply annoyed the *ulama*, whom he derided as *mullahs* (illiterate clergy). Unlike Maududi [35] and several other Islamists of the twentieth century, Mashriqi failed to differentiate between *khilafat* (caliphate) and *malukiyyat* (monarchy) which baffled several keen observers of Muslim history. The Allama, to the further annoyance of many Muslims and especially the *ulama*, rejected *ahadith* (the traditions of the Prophet (PBUH)), *ijma'a* (consensus) and *ijtiha'ad* (re-interpretation) and considered them the root-cause of Muslim disunity and downfall. He criticized Muslim logicians like Averroes, Ibn-i-Razi and Avicenna for synthesizing purist Islamic thought with those of the Greeks. To him the Koran itself was sufficient to guide the Muslims. He thus sounded like Ghulam Ahmed Pervaiz of Lahore who also held a similar Koran-centric approach. [36]

Mashriqi, like several adherents of a populist Islam, considered *maulvis* and *mullahism* to be the root-cause of Muslim sectarianism and educational underdevelopment. In a number of powerful pamphlets, called *Maulvi Ka Ghalat Madhab,* he abhorred the institutionalization of clergy in Islam. He considered most of these religious leaders ill-suited since they lacked proper scholarly training and had only been expounding localism and ritualism. Similarly, he annoyed several other Islamic activists by denouncing the demand for the restoration of the Caliphate because, to him, collective purification and regeneration amongst the Muslims should precede the restoration of an otherwise powerless institution in Arabia or elsewhere. [37] Mashriqi's tirades provoked an India-wide denunciation, with the Majlis-i-Ahrar, Jamiat-i-Ulema-i-Hind and Maulana Maududi spearheading the counter-campaign. His equation of *jihad* with militancy received a staunch rebuke from Maududi who went to the extent of calling Mashriqi a *munafiq* (hypocrite) dangerously poised against Islam.[38] Maulana Maududi doubted the sanity of the Allama, as he noted: 'The Khaksar menace is nothing but a symbolization of the misfortune of Muslims ... Allama Mashriqi's writings, speeches and activities prove that he is an unbalanced individual. The movement led by him can be likened to a vehicle driven by a drunk'.[39] When Maududi subsequently chose Punjab as the headquarters for his Jama'at-i-Islami, the Khaksars were obviously displeased. Syed Suleman Nadavi, a leading Muslim scholar of the early twentieth century criticized the Allama for advocating unbounded obedience to the *amir* which may even erode the sanctity of prayers and fasting. The Ahrars were equally critical of the movement largely out of ideological reasons and more so because of their jealousy with the rising popularity of the movement among the Punjabi Muslims. Mashriqi's attacks on clerical Islam were immensely resented by the Ahrars who critized the Tehreek-i-Khaksar because of 'its lack of a spiritual crusade and because of its revolt against the *sufi* and *maulvi.*'[40] However, he was defended by Ghulam Ahmed Pervaiz, the Lahore-based Koranist.[41] Mashriqi equally antagonized the *pirs* and *sufis* whom he considered to be the major reason for Muslim decline. 'He was disgusted by their pacifism, quietism, and universal toleration *(suleh kul).* He held them responsible for the decline and fall of Muslim empires because their creed turned the attention of Muslims away from power *(tamakkun)* and domination *(ghalba).*'[42]

Despite the centrality of Islam to his views and strategy, Mashriqi, to the extent of self-contradiction, yearned for human unity and considered religion to be a cause of discord. Here, he sought guidance from mathematics and desired a science-like role for a universal religion which should be acceptable to humankind otherwise the latter would remain divisive. He wrote an open letter to the world scientists imploring them to lead the world to a unified and equal partnership.[43] However, from the pedestal of a global unity he quickly reverted to the intra-Muslim unity as a model for the world, though he preferred the term *akhuwat* (fraternity) over Pan-Islamism. Eventually, it was trans-regional Islam within the sub-continental and then in Pakistani paradigms that retained his concentration. Such kind of activism was less Pan-Islamic and more of a territorial Muslim nationalism.

Akin to their conflictive relationship with the religious establishment, Mashriqi's followers retained an enigmatic relationship with other contemporary political parties which often hinged on outright opposition or a mutual rejection of each other. The AIML observed the evolution of the Tehreek in the Punjab and NWFP closely without offering any opposition. To the contemporary Leaguers, it was like several other post-Khilafat segmental, regional or emotional organizations that would eventually wither away. During the stormy days of the Khaksar-Unionist confrontation in March 1940, Jinnah tried to sound cautiously sympathetic which strengthened his own status as the India-wide Muslim leader. He avoided being judgemental on the issue but expressed his agony over the human loss. Similarly, even after an assassination attempt on him in 1943 by Rafiq Sabir, a Khaksar, Jinnah never turned hostile towards the movement. He rather tried to persuade Lord Linlithgow to lift the official ban on it. However, by the late 1940s, several Leaguers felt that the Tehreek had turned pro-INC.[44] In fact, Mashriqi, at one stage, had allowed his followers to join the AIML.[45] This led to the interpretation that the Khaksars were basically a pro-AIML faction.[46] As regards Mashriqi's own meeting with Hitler, it has caused various interpretations. Several Khaksars, in their interviews, used it to build up their self-importance and a global outreach. The official British sources occasionally did refer to his visit to Germany, but remained uncertain about the validity of his meeting with Hitler. In one of his own interviews, finally, Mashriqi observed: 'I never met Hitler except for three minutes. I do not require any money. Every Khaksar is expected to be self-supporting.'[47] His followers, even long after his death, tried to exaggerate the Mashriqi-Hitler connection to build up his posthumous image.[48]

The Organization of the Khaksar Movement

Allama Mashriqi, unhappy with his professional career and imbued with ambitions, decided to actualize his own ideology which, as mentioned above, was a mishmash of several cross-currents varying from militarism to regenerative Islam and romanticized collectivism. He was a Darwinist who believed in a Nietzschean super man and saw in himself a role which could synchronize Indian Muslim idealization of Caliphate and modern totalitarianism. He 'analyzed the Holy Koran and discovered a ten-point formula of *"baqa-i-asleh"*—the survival of the fittest. The early Muslim conquests were presented as proof of the truth of the formula. The formula focused on the acquisition of state power *(tamakkun fil arz)* and political domination *(ghalba)*. In accordance with this formula, the Muslims of India were exhorted to reestablish their domination over the whole subcontinent and revive the glory of General Mohammad Bin Qasim and Sultan Mahmud.'[49] Both the Allama and the movement became synonymous as he was the founder, ultimate *amir,* arbiter and *de jure* ideologue for all the Khaksars. The members were commanded to follow a specific code of conduct with an unquestioned subordination to the authority of the *amir,* also known as *Adara-i-Aliya,* the supreme designation. Each member, called sepoy, wore the khaki uniform and carried a *bailcha* (spade) which symbolized both religious and martial significance. The members were further divided into three groups on the basis of their commitment: *Mujahids* were regular participants in the daily *mohalla*-based activities; *Mahfooz* attended weekly meetings after receiving a three-month military training; *Janbaz* would sign in blood a pledge to obey the Allama to death; *Pakbaz* pledged their entire property to the Tehreek and, *Muavin* were the helpers also known as *Quaid.* In the Khaksar hierarchy each *mohalla* unit—the main nucleus of

the movement— was headed by a local *sala'ar* with the Allama
as the supreme commander *(sala'ar-i-A'la)*. There were ten
different departments under the control of the *Adara-i-Aliya*.
These included finance, politics, publicity organization, and
auditing. There was a full-fledged social services department and
a magistracy to punish the defaulting Khaksars whose schedule
otherwise kept them busy in daily and weekly parades. The
parades were held in the evenings, but each member was
required to engage in a two hour weekly social service like
cleaning the street and removing litter.[50]

As mentioned earlier, the movement, during its heyday in the
late-1930s was able to enlist the support of regional notables like
G.M. Syed of Sindh, Ghulam Sarwar Khan of the NWFP,
Habibullah Khan of the UP, Sarfaraz Khan of Punjab and Nawab
Bahadur Yar Jang of Hyderabad Deccan. In addition, a number
of middle class Muslim professionals and intellectuals in the
NWFP and Punjab offered their services to the Allama. They
included Barrister Ahmad Shah from the NWFP, and Ehsan
Danish, Hafeez Jullundhri, Sufi Ghulam Mustafa Tabassum,
Akhtar Chishti, Noon Meem Rashid, Waqar Anbalavi and Ibne-
Arabi from Punjab.[51] Akhtar Hameed Khan, a capable Muslim
ICS, was deeply impressed by the Allama and left the service to
join the Tehreek. He, subsequently, married the Allama's
daughter. In addition to weekly *Al-Islah* (lit. reformation)
published from Lahore, the Tehreek, before its confrontation
with the Unionist government in the Punjab, owned several Urdu
weeklies and monthlies. It professed to be a non-communal
organization, but despite its intent, turned out to be a
predominantly Muslim movement. However, it never encouraged
any communal tensions though the Allama's appeal[52] was mainly
directed at the Muslims. He wanted to forge a unity among
various Indian communities to dismantle colonialism, but
beyond that he generally remained ambiguous.[53] Initially, several
non-Muslims were attracted to the movement, but gradually it
became a *total* Muslim body: 'The ultimate aim of the Khaksars
is to create a condition in India in which the two major
communities, Hindus and Muslims, as well as others, can live

peacefully, contented and happy with one common idea and one common purpose.'[54]

From a Dramatic Rise to a Traumatic Fall

Allama Mashriqi established the Tehreek-i-Khaksar at a time while he was still on leave from his teaching position at Peshawar.[55] On 25 August 1931, the first regular Khaksar contingent held its parade at Panduki, a town 25 miles outside Lahore. The first regular parade in Lahore took place on 14 February 1932, which led some observers to believe that 1932 in effect was the year of its formation.[56] It appears that a concurrent contingent had come into being in Peshawar in 1931-2 on the patterns of the 'labour corps, armed with spades, the ostensible object being to perform social service of the more menial kind'. It seems to have been patterned on the model of the Boy Scouts movement and Seva Samiti. Within a year, it assumed a more aggressive drill style when it engaged itself in training for bayonet-style fighting. Alarmed at its growing popularity in a province already astir with political militancy, the deputy commissioner of Peshawar imposed some restrictions on the Khaksars in November 1932. Accordingly, their total gathering was not to exceed 250 and people from outside the city were not allowed to join the parades. Moreover, the uniforms were disallowed for the evening parades. Subsequently, the Frontier government externed Allama Mashriqi from the province in August 1933 following reports of the Tehreek's activities in the rural areas displaying 'some of the fascist tendencies'. The ban was not lifted until 1937, when Sahibzada Abdul Qayyum was able to prevail on a reluctant governor to rescind the restrictions.[57]

After the lifting of the ban, the efforts to revive the movement on the Frontier were officially seen as an anti-INC policy with an undeclared support from the Sahibzada. The communal character of the movement became obvious in a meeting in Abbottabad in 1937 which reprimanded Khan Abdul Ghaffar Khan for his pro-

INC persuasion.[58] The anti-INC postures by the Khaksars became more visible both in the NWFP and UP despite an apparent apolitical pretension of the Tehreek. By late 1937 it was described as 'the chief danger to the Congress party' and with the support from the land-based Khans it could potentially unnerve the INC–Red shirts alliance.[59] While the *mullahs* were still undecided, several residents of the Hazara and Peshawar districts had begun to support the movement by exhibiting a strong anti-INC attitude. Following the AIML session at Lucknow in October 1937, it appeared as if the Khans and the Khaksars were coming together as a pro-AIML bulwark against the INC-Red Shirts combine, who were being projected by the former as the protegees of the Hindu moneyed interests. Officially, it was estimated that the movement had swollen to 1000 members. Jinnah could have made a break-through in the INC-dominated province since the Khans believed 'that outside money and leaders of other Provinces have established the Congress in the position it now holds here.'[60] However, such a break-through, as officially expected, did not take place largely 'because of want of leadership and funds' with the INC continuing as the only real political force in the province. There were reports of Khaksar processions on the Eid Day in December 1937 and a display of power outside the residences of Sahibzada Abdul Qayyum and Dr Khan Sahib with the latter lamenting that 'he cannot control the Khaksars as he controls the Red Shirts.'[61]

During the ban in the NWFP, Allama Mashriqi concentrated his energies on establishing an organizational network in Punjab and UP. It appears that the Allama's main attention was focused on Punjab, a fertile ground for all kinds of political enterprises. The Unionist control of provincial politics guaranteed through official co-option had kept the urban lower-middle class largely disempowered. Consequently, both the INC and the AIML were kept at bay by the Unionists whereas communal and other parties remained divided and personality-centred. The Tehreek-i-Khaksar presumably could make major inroads by providing middle ground at least to the urban Muslims through a glorification of the Muslim past and by undertaking social work in inner-city areas where Muslims could be recruited. The early experimentation proved encouraging, but following the official restrictions by the NWFP government, the Allama became more cautious: 'He took considerable pains in the course of interviews with Government officials to persuade them that his movement was in no way antagonistic to Government, (The Governor of the Frontier noted in his report of 6 September 1937) but was merely an endeavour to organize Muhammadans for the purpose of social service and in order to prove their unity and self-efficiency to obtain the Swaraj in a shorter time than the methods employed by the Congress.' The official circles were quite watchful especially following his meetings with Abdul Ghaffar Khan, the frontier Gandhi, and Safi-ud-Din Kitchelew 'both of whom promised him the fullest support'. Such contacts with the nationalists only substantiated offical estimation of the movement as an anti-Raj project.

The contemporary secret official reports, now in the India Office Records, report growing Khaksar activity in central Punjab but not in Jullundar. Within a year of its establishment, the Tehreek, reportedly, had 600/700 members in Punjab. The Tehreek's most influential recruit from amongst the legislators was Mohammad Sarfaraz Khan, the MLA from Chakwal in the Jhelum district who had joined the movement in 1935. Mock war exercises were held in October 1935 with crackers instead of live cartridges. A similar mock exercise in Amritsar in 1935 attracted 10,000 spectators. In addition to Punjab, branches were established in Bangalore, Mardan and Sitapur with the Khaksars in Peshawar engaging themselves in *gatka bazi* (a muscle-building exercise). The Tehreek did not demand any subscription which was an additional incentive to would-be recruits, who through the uniform and hierarchical promotion attained a greater sense of social significance and recognition. The Tehreek, on the completion of the training programmes distributed 'promissory notes' of 5/10 rupee denominations to be redeemable 'on the attainment of independence'. The sub-divisional membership statistics for 1938-9 were reported as follows:

District	Number	
Lahore	200	
Amritsar	175	
Gujrat	55	(including a sword group as well)
Jallalpur Jattan	30	
Gujranwala	60	
Wazirabad	20	
Chakwal	not known	
Sialkot	25	
Ferozepore	20	
Dera Ghazi Khan	25	
Jullundur	not known	

The numbers of Khaksars had swollen especially during and after the 1935 Shahidganj agitation as it gave Mashriqi a head-start over the embattled Ahrars. Mashriqi had promised to buy parade grounds for training purposes in Lahore. The Khaksars did benefit from conflicting rumours, sometimes spread purposefully to attract new recruits. One popular rumour in the late 1930s suggested that King Ibn-e-Saud of Saudi Arabia was planning to invite 1,000 Khaksars for Haj as this guests. Another rumour suggested that the Nizam of Hyderabad would take the salute from a smart Khaksar contingent. Another rumour attributed to Pir Jammat Ali Shah, an influential Punjabi *pir*, exhorted Muslims to join the Khaksars in droves. All these rumours were subsequently denied but not without seriously compromising Inayatullah Mashriqi's own prestige.[62]

Just before the outbreak of the Second World War, some sections in the British press, began to display interest in the movement. *The News Chronicle* reported on a debate in the UP legislature regarding the Khaksars and their alleged funding from abroad. R.F. Mudie, the UP works minister, while referring to such speculation on a foreign connection, informed the legislators: 'It is said so; we have no information'. The British press report observed that according to several Khaksars, the movement 'claims to have 400,000 members and 4,000 centres in the country ... The Movement, it is stated in London, is not anti-British, and is mainly confined to the Frontier Province.' It was viewed as 'a counterblast to Abdul Ghaffar Khan's Red Shirts'.[63] The growing polarization in Europe and serious concerns about the existence of semi-military organizations in India deeply worried several officials in London who feared a possible connection between the Nazis and the Indian organizations. In a query from the Secretary of State,[64] Lord Linlithgow discounted any Nazi-Khaksar collaboration since..... 'there is no reason to believe the movement is financed from outside sources but further enquiries will be necessary before definite suggestions for an answer can be made'.[65] However, the provincial governments kept New Delhi informed of the Khaksar activities which were incorporated in the viceroy's reports to London.[66] The colonial administration maintained a close watch on Allama Mashriqi and his movement in the pre-War phase: 'Hitherto it has not developed dangerously and its workers are well-disciplined and unusually amenable to official authority. Further enquires confirm that there is no evidence whatsoever to support allegation that the movement is in receipt of foreign money.'[67]

Confrontation with the UP Government

The Shia-Sunni dissensions, especially during the month of mourning, have frequently led to violent clashes. To Mashriqi, these sectarian differences were not doctrinal but rather resulted from the nefarious objectives of the *mullahs* who had reduced Islam to a few rituals. In 1937, in his *Maulivi Ka Ghalat Madhab No 4,* he had denounced the sectarian *mullahs* for schism and had used an aeroplane to drop the leaflets on Delhi — itself an innovation in populist politics and pamphleting. He thought of arbitrating between the two Muslim sects in UP in 1939 and offered his services to the effect. In addition, he asked his followers from Punjab to gather in Lucknow as a 'third force' to separate the two feuding factions during the Muharram processions. Mashriqi, with the central Punjab as his base by now, appeared to be quite confident of his populist appeal. Such a mediatory role would give him a much-coveted All-India stature, besides exposing the weakness of the INC-led provincial administration. Such a high-profile suited his oppositional style of politicking and could prove useful in boosting his party support. However, the effort to resolve Shia-Sunni discord turned into a confrontation with the UP administration especially at a time when the government, due to its extreme sensitivity towards such military-type organizations, had decided to outlaw their parades.

While the Shias and Sunnis were strengthening their rank and file, Mashriqi, boasting of three thousand *janbaz* announced his arbitration plan. The UP-bound Khaksars, though predominantly from Punjab, had also small representations from the NWFP and Sindh. Tehreek's main organ, *Al-Islah,* unhappy with the ban, persistently rebuked the government. But the Allama, however, accepted the clamp-down on the parades and even reprimanded some local Khaksars for violations. *Al-Islah,* issued a death threat to sectarian *mullahs* in case they persisted with their tirades against one another. Mashriqi believed that a few hundred *mullahs* from both sides could be expended for greater fraternity and peace amongst the Muslims. In a rather naive manner, he forgot the complex and sustained forces underpinning the Shia-Sunni conflict, which had intensified in recent years especially in the UP. He kept on issuing threats and deadlines to undertake his 'cleansing operation'.[68] The doctrinal differences could be resolved however only through negotiations among the sectarian leaders and not by bellicosity. Mashriqi's arrival in Lucknow, the centre of sectarian conflict in 1939, was viewed with great concern by the Congress ministry.

Following his warnings to both the sects to suspend mutual denunciation, Mashriqi reached Lucknow on 25 August 1939. He was arrested on the first of September, but was released three days later after submitting an undertaking. It appears that he did not accept the secular credentials of the Congress leaders and took upon himself to resolve the intra-Muslim differences. Since Mashriqi could not mitigate the age-old differences and equally could not, eliminate feuding *mullahs*, his mission in August-

September appeared to have failed. For the government, the presence of the Allama and several hundred of his followers mainly from Punjab posed a threat much more serious than the Shia-Sunni riots. Consequently, several of Mashriqi's followers were arrested and deported, leaving him immensely dejected. The governor of the province viewed it as the 'collapse of the Khaksar movement in Lucknow' since a rather perplexed Allama was allowed to proceed to Delhi only after promising not to return. The ministers were cautioned by the governor 'to remove the menace to the peace in Lucknow and not to embark on an attempt to break the Khaksar movement altogether.' The governor appeared very jubilant over the Khaksar retreat from the UP.[69] But, his exultation proved premature, as Mashriqi, on his return was ridiculed by his critics for surrendering to the official authority without gaining anything. To counter such criticism, he returned to the UP on 12 September to defy the restrictions and was consequently put behind bars for a month besides incurring a fine of Rs. 50.

Even after his release, the Allama did not end his tirades against the UP government which kept pressurizing both the Central and Punjab governments for further restrictions on the Khaksars. In the meantime, Khaksar activity in Bulandshehr, Muzzaffarpur and Meerut in October 1939 resulted in clashes with the police and the military. Some official reports linked such clashes with the AIML's manoeuvres to browbeat the ruling Congress in the province. When five Khaksars died in a police shoot-out on 8 October inside the city jail, Sikandar Hayat, the Punjab Premier, asked the Allama to relent his campaign against the UP government, though the Muslim press kept supporting the Khaksars.[70] The dead Khaksars came from North-western Punjab and the NWFP and their funerals were paraded through the streets of Lahore creating a strong anti-British sentiment, as was noted by the Punjab governor: 'I fear, however, that this Khaksar affair is likely to increase communal bitterness generally throughout northern India for some time to come.'[71] On 4 November 1939, a six-point agreement was signed between Mian Ahmad Shah, representing the Khaksars and R.F. Mudie, representing the UP government. Accordingly, the Khaksars agreed not to interfere any further in the Shia-Sunni conflict; The government agreed to investigate any unjust action on its part; and not pursue any campaign against the movement; *Al-Islah* agreed to avoid misreporting; while all the Khaksar internees were to be released and the outsiders were to leave the province. Ahmad Shah, a barrister from the NWFP, had taken up the command of the Khaksars in the negotiations and was reputed to have 'always taken a reasonable line'.[72] Following the agreement and dissolution of the Congress ministries the Khaksars 'practically disappeared from the news altogether...'[73] In the meantime, the Governor decided to supress the inquiry report of the Bulandshehr shooting as 'it would be most undesirable to publish the report, and my present intention'. The Governor opined is to do nothing to call attention to it and in the meantime to pursue at our leisure the various matters which clearly require attention. The less we say about it publicly, the better.' Even, the Allama, ironically, seems to have lost interest in the matter!

Confrontation with the Unionist Ministry in the Punjab

The clash between the Khaksars and the Unionist government had its roots in the tense relationship between the two from December 1937 when the Allama confronted Sikandar Hayat with the following three demands:
1) A *zakat* organization should be created and the administration of *baitul mal* should be carried out on an all-India basis.
2) The Punjab government should correspond with the central government for the permission of a radio station in the province.
3) Government officials should not be barred from joining the movement and all such restrictions should be withdrawn.

When Sikandar Hayat invited a Khaksar delegation for negotiation, the Allama appreciated his gesture.[74] Bahadur Yar Jang, in a letter on 7 February 1938, also requested Sikandar Hayat to be considerate towards their demands. However, the pro-government daily *Inquilab* found the demands impractical.[75] Following a number of letters, the Allama emphatically asked the Unionist premier to hasten his decision from the deadline of 19 November 1938. On the last day, Sikandar invited the Allama for negotiations and tentatively accepted his demands. The rapprochement with Sikandar Hayat greatly enhanced Mashriqi's profile in the province. This was followed in 1939 by an offer of 50,000 volunteers to fight for Britain, an offer politely turned down by the central government. Soon, the Khaksars became suspicious of the Punjab Government which, presumably, had sent a secret circular published by the chief secretary disallowing employees from joining the movement.[76]

Following the showdown between the UP government and the Khaksars, the Punjab government had become equally suspicious of the Tehreek at a time when the province was the centre of the Imperial war effort. The UP government had kept Lahore abreast of its handling of the 'new problem in India' since most of *jathas* had come from that province. At one stage Lahore was advised to freeze their funds to cripple the movement: 'It is a curious thing the Khaksars belonging to the UP are giving practically no trouble, and remain quiet.'[77] The concentration of the Khaksars in Punjab was a growing concern for Sikandar Hayat's ministry which, to neutralize the Allama's hostility, maintained contact with him. A contemporary confidential and exhaustive report on the movement presented the following figures on the movement:

Province	Number of members
Punjab	5,000
UP	4,771
NWFP	2,500-3,000
Bengal	1,400
CP	1,200
Bihar	210
Balochistan	119
Bombay	215
Sindh	830

Delhi	80
Madras	nil
Assam	nil
Orissa	nil

In the state of Hyderabad there were 60 Khaksars led by Nawab Bahadur Yan Jang while a similar activity had been initiated in the Bahawalpur state by Malik Muhammad Akram of Rawalpindi. Mysore had 47 members, Indore had 300, Bhopal reportedly 1,600; Khaksar figures for Gwalior and Junagarh were 70 and 30, respectively. Kashmir did not have its own contingent but efforts were being organized by the Khaksars in Sialkot to build up a local chapter. The Khaksars in Ajmer and Merwar mostly comprised apolitical Muslim artisans; in Sindh they were led by an influential *wadera,* Mir Nur Hussain Talpur. The branches in Nagpur, Amrauti and a few other towns in the CP mostly included lawyers and middle class professionals, who avoided agitational activities. The branches in Bombay and Balochistan had been organized by individuals from North-western Punjab. Branches in Burma, Egypt, Aden and Bahrain were reported to have existed while an emigrant from Rawalpindi had begun some organizational work in Kenya. The total figures were estimated to be around 17,000. Many Hindus were reportedly concerned with the predominantly Muslim character of the movement and, in some cases, exaggerated the Allama's German connection. The Khaksar Movement's appeal to the Muslims was perceived mainly as a 'communal' response to similar other non-Muslim outfits. A few non-Muslims did join the movement but 'Inayatullah's claim that a large number of Hindus and Sikhs belong to his movement is a gross exaggeration.' Official reports estimated the total number of such members around fifty and especially during the parades no Hindu or Sikh was reportedly ever noticed. In a sense, its hyped-up image amongst the Muslims was equally misplaced.[78]

Following such reports, amidst growing war-related activities, the Punjab government imposed a ban on drills, uniforms and assembly of more than ten people, publicized through a press note on 28 January 1940, though religious and school gatherings were exempted.[79] In the meantime, *Al-Islah* published a pamphlet written by the Allama, *Aksaraiyat Ya Khoon* (Majority or Blood) claiming that during the last two centuries on average 125 Muslims had sacrificed their lives for India's defence for every Hindu life. The pamphlet also carried his offer of 50,000 volunteers.[80] The Allama, in a telegram to the Viceroy, while seeking an interview reiterated his offer of volunteers to fight for the Raj. On 28 February 1940, the government proscribed the pamphlet and other Khaksar literature followed by a police raid on the Mohammadi Press in Lahore.

Mashriqi possessed an influential friend in the person of Justice S.M. Sulaiman, the former vice-chancellor of Muslim University Aligarh. He wrote to J.G. Laithwaite, the private secretary to the viceroy interceding on his behalf. To Sir Sulaiman, who had known the Allama for more than thirty years since their days in Cambridge, the Khaksar movement was not anti-British. He requested Laithwaite to hold an interview either with Mashriqi or with Bahadur Yar Jang. [81] An interview did take place between Mashriqi and Laithwaite in which the former expressed his complete loyalty to the British government. He repeated his offer to the government and complained against Sikander Hayat for not forwarding his letters to New Delhi out of jealousy since Mashriqi 'had stolen a march upon him'. To Mashriqi, the INC embodied *baniya* mentality and was unreliable. During the interview, the Allama expressed his desire to meet the Viceroy otherwise the clash between the Khaksars and the government may take place or the Allama may join the INC. To Laithwaite's mind, Mashriqi had 'all the qualities of a popular leader' as he exuded humour, persuasion and emotions.[82]

On the same day, minutes of a conversation between J.G. Laithwaite and J.D. Penny, the Chief Secretary of Punjab, described Mashriqi as 'almost mad' because UP successes had given him 'a swollen head'. He was identified as a communalist. Both the civil servants had brooded over the possible ramifications of Mashriqi's meeting with the Viceroy which they found unnecessary as it might further inflate the Allama. [83] In the wake of the dramatic events, *Al-Islah* was also banned by the

Punjab government with its offices being shifted to Delhi by the movement. The Allama was in Delhi when he heard of the ban on his organization and issued a denunciatory statement. [84] In a letter to Laithwaite, Mashriqi maintained that the official ban on parade and uniform was not applicable to the Khaksar movement as it was, basically a social movement and had not participated in any communal disturbances since its creation in 1930. Other communities had rather followed its suit because the 'peoples of all communities, irrespective of caste or creed, have remained as members in the Movement and are now joining in large numbers'. He told the private secretary to the Viceroy that he would wait for official clarification until 16 March otherwise he would continue with the usual activities. He also informed Laithwaite that his followers had been 'arriving in Lahore from distant places in a mood of uneasiness, as well as those Khaksars who belong to Lahore are hereby ordered to continue their programme of social service and night prayers outside the Mochi Gate and inside their local mosques. Further orders in connection with the Khaksars of the Punjab will be published shortly in the El-Islam'. [85] A few days later, Mashriqi in another letter to Laithwaite challenged the ban by implicating Sikandar Hayat for the move: 'The Punjab ban is purely Sir Sikandar Hayat Khan's creation who had thought of crushing us out of rivalry', following the Allama's unconditional offer of the Khaksar volunteers. He also warned: 'If in the meanwhile, Government bodily injures any Khaksar for the performance of his normal action we shall resist this to the last drop of our blood.'[86] Jinnah tried to resolve the stalemate during Sikandar Hayat's visit to Delhi, but the battle appeared to have become more personal between the Allama and Punjab Premier.[87]

In a state of despair and emotionalism, Mashriqi sent out a clarion call to his followers all over India to send a total contingent of 30,000 members to Lahore within the shortest possible time. It was quite obvious that he wanted to pursue a showdown with Sikandar Hayat. [88]

The tensions between the Khaksars and the Punjab government were running very high at a time when the AIML was to hold its annual meeting in Lahore. Sixteen years had elapsed since the League convened its last major rally in Lahore.The AIML's meeting was intended for the fourth week of March 1940 and was purported to chalk out a clear strategy for the Indian Muslims. Sikandar Hayat was worried because he needed to safeguard his domain by keeping the Unionist coalition intact. Sikandar Hayat's opponents from various parties including Punjabi Leaguers like Malik Barkat Ali could see that the Punjab Premier was in a precarious position. Any armed confrontation with the Khaksars could potentially compromise his affiliation with the League which represented the Muslim interests in the entire subcontinent. Simultaneously, Hayat did not want to appear too soft towards the banned organization and aimed at vigorously pursuing his pro-war, loyalist policies. Sikandar Hayat, who, during the Lucknow session of the AIML in 1937, had accepted Jinnah as the unchallenged leader of the Indian Muslims could not himself muster enough courage to ask Jinnah for the postponement of the session and rather sought help from Nawab Quli Khan, the Pashtun notable. The mission failed as Jinnah remained resolved to hold the annual session in Lahore in March. During this impasse the Allama remained in Delhi leaving the local Khaksar commanders to make their own decisions. This eventually led to an unnecessary clash on 19 March resulting in numerous Khaksar casualties at the hands of the trigger-happy Punjab police.

Defying the official ban, a 313-strong Khaksar contingent led by Khushal Khan Jadoon of the NWFP began its preparations to march through the streets of the old city in Lahore. In the meantime, the Punjab government, apprehensive of a clash, requested the Allama to hasten to Lahore with a similar appeal being published by the Urdu daily, *Inquilab*. [89] Sikandar Hayat sought to avoid an armed confrontation, but according to the Punjab governor 'Inayatullah is one of the most unreasonable of men and possibly not wholly sane. But Sikandar says he is a coward and has not the slightest intention of risking imprisonment, and for this reason will probably not come to Lahore himself.' [90] The Allama for some incomprehensible reason did not return to Lahore, which left the movement on its own. There are different interpretations of the march proposed by Jadoon, who, to some, was a dubious character and was used as a surrogate to precipitate the clash.[91] On 18 March 1940, Jadoon made a fiery speech and the following day led the marching 313 Khaksars with spades on their shoulders towards the Badshahi Mosque. Near the Shahi Mohalla, he was confronted by the police. Here one comes across three different versions of the train of events which followed. According to the first the police opened fire on the Khaksars, while the second version considers the Khaksars responsible for initiating the clash. The third, put forward by Khadim Hussain Batalvi, the head of the police facing the Khaksars, maintained that the firing started abruptly, without any orders to shoot. Sikandar Hayat, a week later, in a parliamentary statement, produced a similar version.[92] As a result of the firing, more than fifty Khaksars were killed. Earlier accounts put the estimate between twenty-three and thirty-two.

Sikandar Hayat's popularity hit an all-time low while the masses in Lahore rallied around the Khaksars in a wave of sympathy. Sikandar Hayat approached Jinnah for permission to explain the case before the AIML Working Committee which was meeting at the residence of the Nawab of Mamdot. He delivered a long speech and, to a great extent, was able to vindicate himself. Jinnah visited the hospitalized Khaksar victims and while speaking to the League session demanded an impartial inquiry into the incident and urged the lifting of restrictions against the movement. Despite his open sympathies with the bereaved Khaksar families, Jinnah resisted the pressure to expel Sikandar Hayat from the AIML, something that annoyed several Khaksars.[93] Nawab Bahadur Yar Jang, a Khaksar and also a Leaguer, came under a strong scrutiny for his alleged 'dual role in politics'.[94]

In the Punjab assembly, Sikandar Hayat was confronted with a joint motion sponsored by Khalid Latif Gauba duly supported by Gopi Chand, the leader of the opposition. The Khaksars blamed the British and Sikandar Hayat for the provocative action presumably to distrupt the League session,[95] whereas several contemporaries held that the Punjab Premier was quite sincere in holding the session.[96] But the fact remains that the Allama himself by agitating his followers endlessly and then absenting himself from Lahore was equally responsible for the clash and the loss of innocent lives. In his absence, an inept leadership took matters to a disastrous and illogical extreme. In view of the unavailability of the Young Inquiry report on the clash, it is rather difficult to reconstruct the events sufficiently enough to apportion blame. However, contemporary official correspondence between Lahore, New Delhi and London throws some light on the course of events.

Sir Henry Craik, in a letter to the Viceroy on 18 March—a day before the fateful clash—reaffirmed Sikandar Hayat's resolve to avoid the clash and identified Mashriqi as 'an insane individual'.[97] The next day, in a telegram, the governor informed Linlithgow and London of a clash 'between the police and a body of Khaksars mainly drawn from the North-west Frontier Province who endeavoured to hold a procession in military formation in defiance of the ban recently imposed...' Both the senior superintendent of police and his deputy (SSP and DSP) were reported to be in critical condition with two constables killed and twelve others injured. According to the preliminary report submitted by the district magistrate, twenty-three Khaksars had been killed with forty injured followed by extensive arrests. The Khaksar headquarters in Ichhra, Lahore were also raided with the inmates being teargassed.[98] The same day the movement, was declared unlawful and steps were taken to arrest Mashriqi in Delhi. On 20 March, another telegram from Lahore identified the injured senior police officials as D. Gainsford (SSP) and P.C.D. Beaty (DSP) while F.C. Bourne, the district magistrate, had been slightly injured. It was further reported that the funerals of the dead Khaksars had 'passed off without incident' with the revised figures of twenty-six Khaksar dead and fifty admitted to hospital.[99]

In another letter to Lord Linlithgow with an accompanying report from the district magistrate, F.C. Bourne, the governor regretted the clash and provided further details. Bourne was reported to be 'one of our most senior and most reliable District Officers, in whose character and capacity I have the highest confidence. He is the last man in the world to lose either his wits or his temper'. Bourne's five-page report referred to a Pathan city magistrate—'a stout-hearted officer—to whom the Khaksars 'came on like wolves'. The home department of the Indian government had informed London of the imposition of the ban on the Khaksars in Punjab, NWFP, Sindh and Delhi: 'The decision to declare the Khaksars an unlawful association under the criminal Law Amendment Act was taken by Sikandar himself and I was not consulted, but I confide that the order was entirely correct and indeed inevitable.'

According to the agitated governor, the total 'responsibility for this lamentable business rests on him (Mashriqi). He is not only a most dangerous fanatic, but also a coward and a liar. He himself remained at a safe distance at Delhi and from there issued secret orders to his followers to defy the ban and published articles ... He urged them, for example, to "surround the cot of Sikander with a bed of corpses".' To him, the movement's 'claims that it is a non-communal organization for social service is the merest nonsense that has now been proved twice, in Lucknow and here, that its methods are those of the Nazi storm troopers on the model of which it is founded.'[100] Despite provocation by *Al-Islah,* the Khaksars elsewhere had not shown any retaliation against the killings in Lahore.[101] Despite the wide-scale official annoyance with the Khaksar movement, several provincial governments did not support a total ban on the Tehreek. Their reluctance emerged either from the weakened nature of the movement itself or out of concern for wider Muslim public opinion.

After the bloodshed and funeral processions, several Khaksars from other districts sought shelter in Lahore's mosques, where they were fed by the local Muslim community but the city itself remained calm. On Jinnah's arrival in Lahore a small demonstration raised slogans against Sikandar Hayat but no untoward incident occurred. The Punjab Premier, already under pressure from Jinnah and other Muslim leaders, desired a full-fledged inquiry into the matter to forestall any major repercussions but Henry Craik wanted to keep it a low-key affair. Finally, on the latter's prerogative, amidst press censorship a rather tame reference was issued for the committee 'to enquire into the circumstances in which certain officers were killed and injured and the police opened fire on the morning of March 19'. In the meantime, the forthcoming League session was posing a serious problem for the administration. By censoring the Unionist ministry and by denouncing the Craik administration, it could prove a grave embarrassment and could thus agitate Muslim public opinion against the British during the crucial phase in the war. It could also give a new lease of life to the Khaksars. Thus, efforts were made by Sikandar Hayat, Henry Craik and Lord Linlithgow to indirectly influence Jinnah through Khan Bahadur Quli Khan and Zafrullah Khan. It appears that Sikandar Hayat's opinion on holding the session in Lahore radically changed after the clash and the resultant criticism by various Muslim opinion groups. The session was viewed as the 'most embarrassing complication' and Sikandar Hayat could not outlaw the session since it would have brought the League and the Khaksars together, adding to his worries. Several Leaguers in Punjab were not happy with him though the governor felt that it was only 'the lower classes in the city and goonda element' who felt that the Khaksars had been brutalized. The governor appreciated the viceroy's effort through Zafrullah: 'I need hardly say that I fully appreciate the difficulty you felt in regard to any attempt to influence Jinnah yourself, and I am most grateful to you for asking Zafrullah to speak to him. I gather, however, that Jinnah is not responsive and that the Session will have to go forward'. [102]

It is quite revealing to piece together the story of the League session during this charged atmosphere. The British government did not appreciate Jinnah's holding of the session at Lahore although, ironically, several authors have alleged the League received official support to counterbalance the INC. [103] If the government had any influence on Jinnah, it would have succeeded in postponing the League's session. Sikandar Hayat planned to attend the meeting of the League's Executive Committee to deter any resolution of condemnation being passed against him. In such an eventuality, he had resolved that 'he and his followers would immediately resign from the League'.[104] The Viceroy, in his response, appreciated the courage shown by the Punjab administration in dealing with 'a most unlucky affair'. He informed the Punjab governor of his meeting with Jinnah whom he found firmly against the idea of postponing the League session: 'We have reason to be very grateful to Zafrullah who handled a difficult interview with much tact and without raising any suspicion in Jinnah's mind that Zafrullah's intervention was in any way actuated by pressure or suggestion from outside.'[105] Z.H. Lari tried to move a resolution against Sikandar Hayat in the Muslim League Council on 21 March, but Jinnah suggested it be discussed in the meeting of the Subjects Committee. However, the said meeting went peacefully with Sikandar Hayat making a moving speech for seventy-five minutes which received applause from a number of the Leaguers including Bahadur Yar Jang.[106] Jinnah's handling of the meetings and open session prevented any further polarization. Without taking any side, he avoided arbitrary statements and equally withstood pressures to postpone the Lahore session. This session proved to be a historic landmark as it allowed the South Asian Muslims to chart out their own political future within the context of Muslim nationalism and the resolution passed in Lahore on 23 March 1940 came to be known as the Pakistan Resolution. In hindsight, the Punjab governor also commended Jinnah's decision to go ahead with the meeting: 'I realize now on looking back that it was almost impossible for Jinnah to postpone at a moment when he must himself have been on the point of starting for Lahore. On the whole, this attitude has been quite correct and impartial and he has not said a word, in public at any rate, to which my ministers can take exception.'[107]

The Viceroy's report to London repeated the Punjab official view of the Khaksar fiasco calling it a 'lamentable outbreak' unleashed by 'this dangerous volunteer organization'. Lord Zetland was informed that Craik had asked the Viceroy to indirectly dissuade Jinnah[108] from holding the League's session in Lahore 'though I made it clear at the same time to Zafrullah that I was fully alive to the delicacy of the decision from Jinnah's own point of view, given the extent to which he was committed to holding the meeting, and the fact that a very large number of delegates had already arrived in Lahore.' Linlithgow reflected on the impact on the Muslims and its possible exploitation by the INC.[109] Jinnah's demand for lifting the ban on the Khaksar movement was resisted by Sikandar Hayat who feared the possibility of another clash. *Al-Islah*, in the course of time, had been shifted to Sindh and there were plans to make Aligarh the next headquarters for the movement. Sikandar Hayat worried that amidst conflicting news of the ban removal, the Khaksars in Lahore's mosques might again head for another confrontation. The governor felt that the ban could be lifted only after the removal of the Allama from the command of the movement, and the cessation of drills and wearing of uniform.[110] To allay Craik's worries, Sikandar Hayat reaffirmed the embargo on the movement and informed the governor of his parleys with Bahadur Yar Jang in Delhi. However, he felt uneasy in justifying the restrictions on uniform but defended his own loyalty by observing: 'If no longer enjoying the confidence, I may be relieved of my office.'[111] The governor, on his return from North-western Punjab, met the Punjab premier and the misunderstanding was eradicated. In a report to the Viceroy, he mentioned a visit by Raja Narendra Nath, an important Hindu leader, who brought a collection of the Allama's writings 'to show that the whole basis of Khaksar organization is the cult of violence and that its object is securing by force Muslim domination over the whole of India.' According to Nath, the collection had been secretly compiled by Deshbandhu Gupta, editor of the Delhi-based *Tej*.[112]

Following the bloodshed, other provincial governments were alerted to any possible reaction from the Khaksar organizations. Lancelot Graham, reporting from Sindh, observed: 'I endeavour to keep in touch with the movement through one of my Ministers, Mr G. M. Syed, who, though not actually a Khaksar is

intimate with the organizers and has influence with them. I have
impressed him to ask them to maintain law and order. He shares
the Viceroy's views. Khaksars didn't participate in the
Manzilgah affair.'[113] Craik himself wrote to J.
Cunningham at Peshawar to forestall supplies to the Khaksars sheltering in
Lahore's mosques. He asked him to ban the movement in the
NWFP as the '...position here is becoming more and more
embarrassing'. Still about 100 Khaksars sheltered in the mosques
were resisting and any further bloodshed could have enhanced
the ill-will.[114] A CID report mentioned 109 arrests in Peshawar
and 7 in the UP on 19 March, while three weeks later, the
numbers stood at 181 and 46, respectively. The new leaders of
the Tehreek were identified as Bashir Ahmed Siddiqui,
Dr Mohammad Ismail Nami and Mian Ahmad Shah. Mian
Ahmad Shah, a barrister from Charsadda, had already played a
crucial role during the UP episode and was to become active
once again for reconciliation between the Allama and the
government.

Sikandar Hayat wanted other provincial governments to ban
the Khaksars to demoralize their counterparts in Lahore
otherwise it would be impossible to extricate them from the
mosques. While there were daily demonstrations in Lahore by
Muslim men and women in the support of the Khaksars amidst a
growing Khaksar activity in Aligarh, Sikandar Hayat kept
persuading the 120 Khaksars in the three mosques of Lahore to
surrender.[115] In the meantime, Jinnah, in a press statement,
offered to arbitrate between the Khaksars and the government.[116]
In fact, Mashriqi had sent a letter and a telegram to Jinnah
applauding his efforts to bring about a rapprochement between
the Punjab government and the Khaksars.[117] Subsequently, Mian
Ahmad Shah met Jinnah on 29 April 1940. Dr Nami delegated
powers to Jinnah for reconciliation and on 5 July Jinnah asked
the latter to suspend their defiance against the government,
which was confirmed the following day.[118] Jinnah gave a press
statement to the effect in late June[119] and approached the Viceroy
to initiate the dialogue.[120] In fact, on approaching the Viceroy,
Jinnah was told by the former that it was a provincial matter and

could be dealt only by Sikandar Hayat.[121] Sikandar Hayat, who was earnestly involved in the war effort, felt as if the Khaksars had been used by anti-war and anti-Muslim forces to thwart his own war efforts and thus vacillated between sympathy and sheer antagonism. After meeting Jinnah, Ahmed Shah had visited Sikandar Hayat in Lahore on 5 May 1940 and put before him the following five demands:

1) Release of Allama Mashriqi,
2) Lifting of restrictions on the movement,
3) Compensation to the dependents of the killed Khaksars,
4) Release of all the imprisoned Khaksars, and,
5) Return of the transferred/non-transferred property to the Khaksar movement.

Sikandar Hayat rejected the demands right away, but hinted towards the possibility of lifting the ban in the future. Ahmad Shah persisted with the demands in a letter suggesting a compromise but nothing came of it.[122] Jinnah approached Linlithgow in early August for reconciliation between the Khaksars and the government but could not break the ice. The Punjab administration, intent upon suppressing the movement, misread Jinnah's arbitration and found fault with his intentions.[123] Jinnah's press statements on the failure of his mission *vis-a-vis* the government were viewed as the 'most inopportune and, I suspect, were deliberately made to create mischief in order to give a fillip to the movement, which had practically died out. There is of course no intention of making departure from the conditions already laid down for rescinding the order of the 19th of March.' Henry Craik had already made crystal clear his personal preference to Sikandar Hayat to maintain the ban and to defy Jinnah's efforts for reconciliation.[124]

Following the failure of the reconciliatory mission undertaken by Jinnah and Ahmad Shah, [125] the Khaksars resumed their activities and on 19 March 1941, solemn ceremonies were held to commemorate the first anniversary of the massacre. In the meantime, the Central government asked the Punjab administration to provide an assessment report on the Khaksars and their future prospects. It was feared that the Allama and his followers might, on their release, join the Congress-led Quit India Movement.[126] With the Allama still in prison, Ahmad Shah formally assumed the leadership of the movement and informed Sikandar Hayat of the development in a letter on 24 March 1941. In another letter, he once again pleaded with Sikandar Hayat to use his offices in the release of the Allama.[127] Sikandar Hayat came under strong pressure from his British superiors not to relent on the issue. On 2 May 1941, a Mashriqi day was observed in many parts of India but without any impact on official policy. The government was deeply concerned about the possible resumption of the Khaksar defiance. It feared large-scale demonstrations for the release of the Allama followed by occupation of mosques once again.[128] The total strength of the Khaksars, according to a Reuters' report, was estimated to be 30,000, which, in hindsight appears to be exaggerated.[129] In the summer of 1941, as reported by the British residents, a number of princely states like Mysore and Hyderabad banned the movement within their jurisdiction.

Ahmad Shah persevered in his efforts to persuade the Viceroy[130] and the Punjab administration to release the Khaksars and lift all restrictions.[131] In November 1941, when the Allama was reported to be gravely ill in prison by Sitaramya Pattbhi, demonstrations across the subcontinent took place against his continued incarceration with a number of political parties pledging their support for his release. The official assessment in late 1941 confirmed the vociferous Khaksar demand, as articulated by Ahmad Shah, for the release of their leader. However, it was felt that Shah did not want the Khaksars to join the League so as to preserve their own separate identity.[132] The Allama, earlier, appreciative of Jinnah's role had by now gradually turned against him, despite the fact that the AIML in 1942 passed a resolution demanding the lifting of restrictions on the Khaksars and the release of the dentenues.[133] The Allama was finally released on 28 December 1942—three days after Sikandar Hayat's sudden death—but by then the Khaksars had ceased to be a focal point.[134] A press statement by Mashriqi accepted the official restrictions in exchange for his release.

Following the Quit India Movement, when most of the Congress leaders and workers were in jail, the Khaksars started sending telegrams and letters to Jinnah asking him to seek a compromise with Gandhi. The Viceroy, advised all the provincial governors to be watchful of any possible rapprochement between Jinnah and the Khaksars—'the most dangerous organization'. He asked them to be on their guard since the AIML was gaining in strength: 'It is true that Jinnah has not so far betrayed any special interest in the Khaksars and it is possible that the Allama may regard himself as a rival to, rather than a willing colleague of, the Muslim League leader. But there have been signs, both in the Muslim League volunteers, as well as among the Khaksars, of the kind of sabre-rattling which I am sure we should do well to suppress at the outset and which will only become more difficult to deal with the longer we leave it alone.'[135] In June, the Khaksars were reportedly organizing their parades sometimes in violation of the restrictions accepted by the Allama.[136] Linlithgow was unhappy with their parades and feared a compromise between the League and the movement.[137] However, there soon followed an assassination attempt on Jinnah by a Khaksar. Rafiq Sabir unsuccessfully tried to kill Jinnah in his Bombay office on 26 July 1943. Jinnah received minor injuries and Sabir was imprisoned for five years.[138] Despite the attempt and Mashriqi's frequent denunciations of Jinnah, the AIML and its leadership avoided adopting any anti-Khaksar posture.

Henry Craik's successor in the Punjab, Bertrand J. Glancy, shared his views on keeping the movement under strict control. He found the Allama 'unreliable' who, in violation of an agreement with the government, had reverted to donning uniforms and badges. To Glancy, Mashriqi was losing popularity among the Muslim Leaguers for admitting Hindus and Sikhs into his organization, but if faced with a total isolation he might join the League so as to suit his own interests.[139] A report from the NWFP, seeing an affinity between the Khaksars and the AIML, showed slackening of the movement after a warning by the deputy commissioner: 'The Khaksar Movement has always potentially been the militant side of the Muslim League, and might be a valuable weapon in their hands. But I think Aurengzeb Khan would feel bound to take action if there were any flagrant challenge to Government'.[140]

It appears that following the Allama's conditional release [141] and by his doing 'what Government required' the movement had plummeted. [142] Moreover, as the main initiative for political action now rested with the India-wide parties like the INC and AIML, the government felt confident in localizing and neutralizing the movement. The Allama, in a last-ditch effort, tried to bring in religion by asking his adherents to carry the Koran instead of spades so that the police might not touch them, but the official annoyance and his own temperamental about-turn deterred him from continuing this innovation. [143] An intelligence report prepared in 1944-5, quantified Khaksar numbers at 20,000 in 1944 compared to 23,000 a year earlier. Mashriqi was characterized as totally 'unreliable' heading an entirely Muslim movement: 'In theory the Khaksar movement is open to all communities, but in practice, it is entirely Muslim and its appeal is purely communal. This appeal and the militant aspect of the movement, combined with his dictatorial methods, make the Khaksar organization extremely dangerous.' As a future course of action, it was opined that Mashriqi might be emboldened by lenient policies but with the fresh powers under the Defence of India Rules of 23 September 1944, his activities would be further restricted. It was revealed that the Allama had already opened a department of politics (Babal-i-Siyasat) in Bombay to work for 'immediate and right sort of independence for India'. In his latest overtures, he planned to bring both the INC and AIML together. This department was reportedly headed by Syed Allah Bakhsh Shah, who was earlier entrusted with promoting Hindu-Muslim unity. In this context, Mashriqi had been unsuccessfully trying to meet Gandhi and had also advised Muslims to avoid cow-killing, which, again was a tremendous demand. [144]

After the creation of Pakistan, Mashriqi established a new Islamic party and made news from time to time on issues like

Islamization, relations with India and a more belligerent stance on Kashmir. His was personal life interspersed with various unsuccessful marriages and litigation. After his demise in 1963, his papers, property and, most of all, the leadership of the movement caused a rift amongst his family members and followers. Mashriqi has remained a charismatic figure to the dwindling number of his followers who pay him an occasional tribute on special days like 19 March by organizing parades in the major cities of Pakistani Punjab. To the new generation of Pakistanis and for that matter, Indians and several historians of the British Punjab, Mashriqi is already forgotten figure.

NOTES

1. Several studies have been built upon the premise of monopolization of politics and economy by Punjab at the expense of others. For instance see, Yunas Samad, *A Nation in Turmoil,* (New Delhi, Sage 1995). Samad does not see any benefit accruing to Punjabis as such except for specific sections. See his 'Pakistan or Punjabistan: Crisis of National Identity' in Gurharpal Singh and Ian Talbot, (eds.) *Punjabi Identity: Continuity and Change,* New Delhi, Sage 1996. Earlier works equally saw Punjab synonymous with the entire country. The problems of governance were also interpreted with reference to the Punjab-dominated bureaucratic-military axis. See Hasan Gardezi and J. Rashid (eds) *Pakistan: The Roots of Dictatorship,* (London, Zed 1983). Fifty years on, there have been new alliances and equations with greater mobility and economic integration which necessitate a new analysis. See Iftikhar H. Malik, 'The State and Civil Society in Pakistan', *Asian Survey,* XXXVI, 7 July 1996.

2. One finds more studies on the Red Shirts of the NWFP and on Sindhi ethnicity as such but Muslim politics in the Punjab in the twentieth century has been largely confined to the League and its relationship with the Unionists.

3. One may allude to several such studies by known Pakistani historians including K.K. Aziz, Ishtiaq Husain Qureshi, A.H. Dani and Abdul Hamid. K.K. Aziz, however, published a volume on Chaudhary Rahmat Ali, but that was again not in his role as a South Asian Islamist. See his *Rahmat Ali: A Biography,* Lahore, 1987. Another similar and useful study is by Rafique Afzal on Malik Barkat Ali, the Lahore-based leader of the Muslim League and a critic of Sikandar Hayat. See M. Rafique Afzal, *Malik Barkat Ali: His Life and Times,* (Lahore, Research Society of Pakistan 1969.

84 REGION AND PARTITION

4. Biographical and regional studies are recent additions to scholarship. Studies by David Gilmartin, Ian Talbot, Craig Baxter and Imran Ali have set the stage for Punjab studies, though within Pakistan the field still has to go a long way to establish its disciplinary position.

5. Since all the historians and political scientists in Pakistan work for the public sector universities and graduate colleges, they avoid writing on those subjects which may have challenged the mainstream historical interpretations centred around the League and Jinnah. The opening up of the Punjabi Department in the Punjab University's Oriental College heralded a much-needed development but the focus has been more on literary aspects rather than on broadening the debate in comparative and historical studies. The efforts by a few urban intellectuals like Hanif Ramay and Fakhar Zaman proved temporary ripples as they wrote on Punjabi identity when they were out of government. In 1993 following the second PPP administration they assumed ministerial positions and reverted to a country-wide espousal. M. Zaigham, Afzal Rindhawa or Abdullah Malik and a few others did carry on serious work on the recognition of Punjabi culture and identity yet their works like a few on Punjabi identity have suffered fissures due to national, religious and regional counter-claims. While the Sikhs may try to debate a Punjabi identity with greater academic zeal, the Punjabi Hindus like the Punjabi Muslims would end up siding with trans-regional espousals. The Pothowari and Siraiki challenges to Punjabi identity and, more recently, the salience of Kashmiri identity by deemphasizing the commonalities with the Punjabis by the Azad Kashmiris, in particular, have only added to the ideological and communitarian splits.

6. The discipline of history and its simplification to meet the nationalist and selective prerogatives is being challenged from different quarters though any rectification in the near future is still a hope.

7. For further details see, Iftikhar H. Malik, *State and Civil Society in Pakistan: Politics of Authority, ideology and Ethnicity in Pakistan*, (London, Macmillan 1997).

8. Afak Haydar, 'The Politicization of the Shias and the Development of the Tehrik-e-Nifaz-e-Fiqh-e-Ja'afria in Pakistan,' in Charles H. Kennedy, (ed.,) *Pakistan: 1992*, (Boulder, Westview 1993).

9. There are two religio-political forces in the country today organized on a sectarian basis: The Anjuman-e-Sipah-e-Sahaba of Pakistan (ASSP) with its demand for the country to be declared a Sunni state by official designation of the Shias as a minority. Its armed wings have been engaged in selective killings of the Shia *ulama* across Pakistan including bomb blasts at Shia *imambaras*. On the other hand, Tehreek-e-Nifaz-e-Fiqh-e-Ja'afria (TNFJ), representing Shias, demands the parallel implementation of Ja'afria jurisprudence for its followers. Its armed wing, Sipah-i-Muhammadi, has been equally engaged in the selective killings of the

Sunni *ulama*. The recent sectarian violence has been systematic, country-wide and is mostly perpetrated in cities and towns and cuts across ethno-regional loyalties.

10. Some of the most prominent names include Dr. Akhtar Hameed Khan, the well-known expert on rural development and a leading NGO, whose major social welfare projects like Comilla Rural Development Project (in former East Pakistan) and the Orangi Pilot Project (OPP) in Karachi are globally acknowledged. A former Cambridge graduate and a member of an Agra-based family, Khan left the much-coveted ICS to join the Khaksars and in the process became one of the closest disciples of the Allama. In fact, he married the Allama's daughter and was deeply influenced by his Darwinist ideology of reestablishing the Muslim Raj through power. For his own views see, Akhtar Hameed Khan, *Orangi Pilot Project: Reminiscences and Reflections,* (Karachi, OUP 1996), pp. 1-31.

Another noted Muslim was Nawab Bahadur Yar Jang, a close relative of the Nizam of Hyderabad state. Barrister Ahmed Shah and a few other such professionals from Sindh, Bihar, Bombay and the UP joined the movement in the 1930s though several of them left in the 1940s while the movement suffered from drift and the Allama remained incarcerated in British jails.

11. It was given out by the Khaksars that the Allama had deeply influenced Hitler in his ideas and schemes for Nazi Germany. The British also used this emphatically to justify their witch-hunt of the Khaksars in the 1940s, it is safe to assume that the meeting between Mashriqi and Hitler, despite various claims to the effect, never took place.

12. In a letter to the private secretary to the Viceroy, Mashriqi identified 1930 as the year of its establishment. See note 82.

13. W. C. Smith, *The Modern Muslim India: A Social Analysis,* (London, Victor Golleniz 1946), 1943.

14. Waheeduzzaman, *Towards Pakistan,* (Lahore, Publishers United) 1969.

15. Iftikhar H. Malik, *Sikandar Hayat Khan: A Political Biography,* (Islamabad National Institute of Historical & Cultural Research 1989) Islam 1985.

16. There are a few references to the Tehreek-i-Khaksar in a Ph.D. dissertation completed in the early 1990s. See Muhammad Khurshid, 'The Role of the Unionist Party in the Punjab Politics 1923-36', unpublished doctoral dissertation at Islamia University, Bahawalpur, 1992, pp. 270-1.

17. Muhammad Aslam Malik, 'Allama Inayatullah Khan Mashriqi (1888-1963): A Political Biography', an unpublished doctoral thesis at Bahauddin Zakariya University, Multan, 1996.

18. Abdullah Kaleem, 'Khaksar Tehreek', M.A. thesis, Punjab University, 1970; Abussalam, 'Khaksar Tehreek', unpublished M.A. dissertation, Punjab University, Lahore, 1972; and Muhammad Iqbal, 'Allama

Inayatullah Khan Mashraqi ka Nazariya-i-Mazhab', M.A. thesis, Punjab University, 1978.

19. Safdar Saleemi, *Khaksar-i-Azam aur Khaksar Tehreek,* (Lahore, 1967); and *Khaksar Tehreek Ki Sola Sala Jiddo-Juhd,* Lahore, n.d.

20. Shan Muhammad, *Khaksar Movement in India,* (Delhi, Meenakshi Prakashan 1973). Also, Aga Bashar, *Moscow Say Makkah Tak,* Lahore, 1969.

21. Syed Shabir Hussain, *Al-Mashraqi: The Disowned Genius,* (Lahore, 1991): *Allama Mashraqi: Man's destiny,* (Rawalpindi, 1972) and *Sirat-Mustaqeem,* (Rawlapindi, 1966).

22. A case study in point in Hera Lal Seith's *The Khaksar Movement Under Searchlight,* (Delhi, 1943), which aimed at winning over the Tehreek's sympathy for the INC.

23. See Y.B. Mathur, 'Khaksar Movement' in the *Studies of Islam,* VI, 1, 1969; and, *Growth of Muslim Politics in India,* Delhi, 1972; Iftikhar H. Malik, 'Identity Formation and the Muslim Politics in the Punjab, 1897-1936', *Modern Asian Studies,* XXX11, May 1995; also 'Muslim Nationalism and Ethno-regional Postulations; Sir Fazl-i-Husain and Party Politics in the Punjab' in Pritam Singh and Shinder S. Thandi (eds) *Globalization and the Region: Explorations in Punjabi Identity,* Coventry, 1996.

24. Allama Mashriqi to Habibullah Saddi, 4 February 1938 in the Mashriqi Papers organized by Chaudhary Abdul Ghafoor, Lahore in Aslam Malik, op.cit., pp.20-22.

25. J. A. Thorne, Home Department, Government of India, New Delhi, to A. Dibdin, India Office, London, 15 March 1939, L/P and J/868, India Office Records and Library (IOR and L), London, hereafter Khaksar collection.

26. It is also haughtily opined that Mashriqi held a meeting with Hitler and presented him a copy of his book. Such a claim, neither rejected nor affirmed by Mashriqi, was used against him by the official sleuths to link his movement with the fascists especially in post-1939 period. But, it appears that despite his visit to Germany after the Cairo conference, the Allama did not have a meeting with the Fürher. It appears that the ambiguity surrounding the supposed meeting with Hitler served everybody's purpose.

27. Thorne to Dibdin, op.cit.

28. It is also opined in some of his Urdu biographies that *Tazkirah* was recommended to the Nobel committee by noted Indian Muslims like Sir Fazal-Husain, the founder of the Punjab Unionist Party, Sir Abdul Qadir, an Influential Punjabi Muslim and Sahibzada Aftab Ahmed Khan, the vice-chancellor of Aligarh University. In *Khaksar* there is ample correspondence between Mashriqi and these personalities on the subject.

29. Like his political career, Mashriqi's life seems to be both dramatic and traumatic. He was married five times and almost every marriage ended in

controversy if not in tragedy. Marrying young women in his later years, especially when he was already a spent political force, only added to his suspicions of them. The court cases dragged on even after his death.

30. Allama Mashriqi, *Isharaat,* Lahore, 1931 p. 6. During his bouts with the UP government and subsequently during his incarceration in the early 1940s, he made such observations quite frequently.
31. Allama Mashriqi, *Tazkirah,* Lahore, 1964, p. 66.
32. For useful commentaries see, Syed Vali Reza Nasr, *Mawdudi and The Making of Islamic Revivalism,* (London, I.B. Tauris 1996; and, Ervand Abrahamian, *Khomeinism,* (Berkeley, University of California Press 1993).
33. Ibid., pp. 121-2.
34. Ibid., p. 172.
35. For details, see Syed Abul'alla Maududi, *Islami Riyasat,* (Lahore, Islamic Publications 1962).
36. Chaudhary Ghulam Ahmad's followers are known as Pervaizies in Pakistan. A contemporary of Iqbal and Mashriqi, Pervaiz was equally resentful of Muslim sectarianism and obscurantism.
37. *Tazkirah,* p. 129.
38. Syed Maududi, 'Khaksar Tehreek aur Allama Mashriqi', *Al-Furqan* (Delhi), Vol. 1, 3, p. 10.
39. *Al-Furquan* (Delhi), VI, 1358 A. H.
40. Chaudhary Afzal Haq, 'Presidential Address, April 1939', in Janbaz Mirza, ed., *Aaab-i-Rafta,* (Lahore, Tabsarra 1960, p. 32.
41. Ghulam A. Pervaiz, 'Lumhaat', *Tulu-i-Islam* (Urdu monthly), III, 3, 1940, p. 16.
42. Akhtar Hameed Khan, *Orangi Pilot Project: Reminiscences and Reflections,* (Karachi, OUP 1996), p. 24.
43. Allama Mashriqi, *Human Problem: A Letter to Scientists,* (Lahore, 1954), as quoted in Aslam Malik, op.cit., pp. 103-4.
44. Building on such a view, the early biographer of Jinnah declared the movement to be 'anti-Jinnah, anti-Muslim League and led by a malcontent educated at Cambridge'. Hector Bolitho, *Jinnah: Creator of Pakistan,* (London, OUP 1954), p. 128.
45. W.C. Smith, *Modern Islam in India,* (Lahore, Muhammad Ashraf 1943), p. 280.
46. Humayun Kabir, *Muslim Politics: 1906-1942,* (Calcutta, 1943), pp. 40-3.
47. Quoted in the *The Times of India,* 8 August 1939.
48. During my interviews in the early 1980s such views were emphatically aired in Lahore and elsewhere by the contemporay Khaksar leadership. A story of Hitler's emissary visiting the Allama in Lahore in 1943 was printed in a newspaper in 1983. See *The Daily Jang* (Lahore) 13 May 1983. His own son, Hameed-ud-Din Ahmad, confirmed Mashriqi's meeting with Hitler's emissary in 1934. (My interview with Mr Ahmad

was held in Lahore on 14 May 1983.) However, according to Aslam
Malik's research Mashriqi had a fling with a German woman and they
exchanged love letters. His study of such personal letters shows intimacy
between the Allama and Berth Prokauer. The former met her in Germany
in 1926 and she visited him in 1927 and stayed with him in their house.
For details see, Aslam Malik, op. cit., pp. 53-55.

49. Akhtar Hameed Khan, op. cit.

50. 'It is a volunteer organization based on brotherhood, simplicity of life and
special emphasis on religious dignity of manual labour and service to
every man and woman without the slightest distinction of caste, creed or
party, and without the motive of material gain or money. Services to all
and service purely for God's sake and unity and brotherhood grounded on
equality and communion in manual labour is the cardinal principle of the
movement. "Silence" and freedom from sectarianism is their great
virtue...In fact the movement is entirely non-political; non-communal and
non-sectarian. It is mainly a Muslim body, but counts Hindus and Sikhs as
its members and supporters and has so far attained a golden opinion for
social service.' Editorial in *The Star of India* (Calcutta), 5 October 1939.

51. See *Al-Islah* (Lahore), 24 March 1939.

52. For Allama Mashriqi's personal view on communalism, see *Isharaat*,
Lahore, 1931, p. 123 and A. Chakravarty, 'Mysteries of the Khaksars',
Asia (New York, 1939).

53. Allama Mashriqi, *Qual-i-Faisal*, (Lahore, 1935), p. 16 ad pp. 72-4.

54. *The Star of India*, 19 October 1939.

55. Some pro-Khaksar authors have maintained that the Allama had left the
government service during the Khilafat Movement in 1919. See Safdar
Saleemi, op.cit., pp. 23; Shaheed Farabi, *Khaksar Tehreek and Pakistan*,
Lahore, 1966 and Waqar Ambalvi in the Weekly *Chittan* (Lahore),
20 March 1967.

56. Identified as the Anjuman-i-Khaksaran, an official report emanating from
Peshawar described the Allama as 'a pensioned officer of the Indian
Educational Service who was formerly Headmaster of the Government
High School, Peshawar'. Extracts from the Notes on the NWFP
Governor's Report, 6 September 1937, L/P&J/8/680 (The Khaksar
Collection) at IOL&R.

57. Ibid. The report described the movement as an 'exclusively Muslim'
organization.

58. While the Khaksar rally characterized the Red Shirts leader 'as a 'Kafir',
the official agencies feared the emergence of a rival tradition of private
military outfits. The NWFP Governors's Fortnightly Report, 4 September
1937, *The Khaksar Collection*.

59. The NWFP Governor's Report, 24 September 1937.

60. The NWFP Governor's Fortnightly Report, 9 November 1937.

61. The NWFP Governor's Report, 27 December 1937.

62. This portion is based on the 8-page report prepared by the Punjab CID for official perusal both in India and London. For details see, Home Department, Government of India to A. Dibdin, The India Office, 15 March 1939 in L/P&J/8/680, *The Khaksar Collection.*

63. *The News Chronicle* (London), 19 April 1939. Also see, *The Daily Telegraph,* 19 April 1939.

64. It preceded a point raised in Parliament by MP Sorenson on 24 April 1939 which evinced a non-committal response from Lord Amery.

65. Lord Linlithgow to Leopold Amery, 23 April 1939.

66. The Governor of Bengal in his report expressed his worry on its growth in the province and observed: 'Their spades, at present only symbolic would be very effective if they were ever put to use as weapons.' Fortnightly Report (No. 11) of the Governor of Bengal of Lord Linlithgow, 6 June 1939.

    In a similar periodic report from Bombay, the Governor informed the Viceroy of an official fine of one rupee each on two Khaksars in addition to one-day imprisonment for demonstrating in Ahmedabad. It was reported that they had received an order from Lahore to defy the rules and it was noted: 'The question of allowing them to carry spades, which can easily be converted into weapons of offence, is under consideration.' Home Department (Bombay) to Home Department, Government of India (New Delhi), 3 August 1939.

    During June 1939, an official source put the total number of the Khaksars throughout India at 7,400.

67. Linlithgow to Amery, 19 May 1939.

68. The magazine was reported to have 'been publishing the most mischievous and sensational instructions to his followers.' The UP Governor's Report to the Viceroy, 22 August 1939.

    In a follow-up report, the Governor of the UP rather prematurely felt happy over the discrediting of the Allama since he was not taken so seriously by the UP Muslim leaders. He observed in his letter: 'Another very satisfactory development is the collapse of the Khaksar movement in Lucknow'. UP Governor's Report, 6 September 1939.

69. UP Governor's Fortnightly Report, 6 September 1939. A day earlier, the Governor, in his report to the Viceroy, had noted: 'He left Lucknow for the Punjab that very night as did practically all his followers who had come from other provinces, although the departure was by no means smooth'.

70. H.C. Haig (the UP Governor) to Lord Linlithgow, 8 October 1939. A secret official inquiry report suggested that the Khaksars from the Punjab had agreed to surrender their spades inside the jail. Lack of communication between the police superintendent and district magistrate led to confusion resulting in police shooting. The report confirmed that the

Khaksars did not shoot first. See Private Secretary to the Viceroy to the Private Secretary to the Secretary of State, 13 October 1939.

71. Governor of Punjab to Viceroy, 13 October 1939. Also Fort Fightly report of 29 October 1939.
72. Chief Secretary (UP) to Government of India, Delhi, 9 November 1939; and the UP Governor to Viceroy, 8 November 1939.
73. Henry Craik (UP Governor) to Lord Linlithgow, 16 November 1939.
74. For the text of the letter from Mashriqi to the Punjab Premier, see Saleemi, op.cit., pp. 72-80.
75. *Inquilab* (Lahore), 22 February 1938.
76. See Saleemi, op.cit., p. 203.
77. H.G. Haig to Henry Craik, 18 October 1939.
78. Secretary to Viceroy to the Under Secretary of State, 8 January 1940.
79. See Lord Linlithgow to Lord Zetland 30 January 1940; and, Fortnightly Report from Punjab, March (second half) 1940.
80. The 12-page pamphlet written in a typical emotional style was published in *Al-Islah* on 20 October 1939.
81. Justice S.M. Sulaiman to J.G. Laithwaite, 28 February 1940.
82. Note of a conversation between the private secretary to the Viceroy and Dr Inyatullah Khan, New Delhi, 29 February 1940.
83. Record of conversation between private secretary to the Viceroy and J.D. Penny, 29 February 1940.
84. *Al-Islah*, 8-15 March 1940.
85. Mashriqi to Laithwaite, 6 March 1940. The letter was originally written the previous evening.
86. Mashriqi to Laithwaite, 12 March 1940.
87. See Saleemi, op.cit., p. 206.
88. Abdullah Malik, *Punjab Ki Siyasi Tehreekain*, Lahore, 1971, p. 290.
89. *Inquilab*, 17 March 1940.
90. Craik to Linlithgow, 18 March 1940.
91. Some Khaksar leaders in 1983-4, in their interviews with the present author, doubted his Khaksar credentials. To them, he was a close relative of Mahmooda Saleem, Sikandar Hayat's sister married into the Jadoons of Abbotabad and was used as a scapegoat. To them he never wore the Khaksar uniform and was able to capture the command of this particular contingent. This was stated by Ashraf Khan, the Khaksar leader in the 1980s in Lahore. However, Shaukat Hayat, interviewed in Islamabad, refused to accept this conspiracy thesis. Muhammad Shafi (Meem Sheen), a Lahore-based journalist and politician, during an interview in Lahore in 1983, claimed that Sikandar Hayat himself was not present in Lahore preceding the clash and the city administration was left to decide for itself. The claim could not be verified.
92. 'No order was given by any responsible officer', he observed. *The Indian Annual Register*, Vol. 2, 1940, p. 189.

93. M. H. Saiyid, *Mohammad Ali Jinnah,* M. Ashraf 1953) Lahore, 1553, pp. 434-5.
94. Ibid.
95. See Shaukat Siddiqui, 'Sir Sikandar Angrezon Ki Nazar Mein', in *Al-Fatah* (Karachi), 14-21 May 1976; *the Daily Musawaat* (Lahore), 21 March 1971 and Sir Mohammad Yameen Khan, *Nama-i-Ahwaal,* as quoted in Mohammad Ali Fariq, ed., *Angrez, Sir Sikandar Aur Khaksar Tehreek,* (Lahore, 1979), pp. 88-9.
96. Both Meem Sheen and Abdus Salam Khurshid, the contemporary authors and Lahore Muslim notables, in their interviews with the present author in 1983, rejected the Khaksar denigration of Sikandar Hayat. However, in an early article, Professor Khurshid did support the Khaksar view. See his article in *The Daily Mashriq* (Lahore) 19 March 1972.
97. Craik to Linlithgow, 18 March 1940.
98. Craik to the Secretary of State, 19 March 1940.
99. Henry Craik to the Secretary of State, 20 March 1940.
100. Craik to Linlithgow 20 March 1940.
101. Home Department Government of India to Secretary of State, 21 March 1940. Interestingly, in a similar report six days later, the Home Department informed London of the NWFP and UP government viewing the ban as 'unnecessary', The central government had accepted their reservations.
102. Craik to Linlithgow, 20 March 1940.
103. Such an interpretation shows Jinnah and the AIML being built up as a bulwark against the INC-led defiance. See Ayesha Jalal, *The Sole Spokesman,* (Cambridge, Cambridge University 1985; and, Yunas Samad, *A Nation in Turmoil,* Delhi, Sage 1995). Not only is such a view premised on a conspiracy theory, it equally denies Jinnah autonomy in pursuing his own strategy.
104. Craik to Linlithgow, 21 March 1940. In a similar report sent the next day, Craik told the Viceroy that he would advise Sikandar Hayat to resign from the League in case it tried to censure him over the Khaksar affair.
105. Linlithgow to Craik, 21 March 1940. This is a serious indictment of Zafrullah Khan who, subsequently, came very close to Jinnah and after 1947, rose to be the first and effective foreign minister of Pakistan. The Viceroy's overture seemingly had the support from the Punjab Governor but Jinnah's own decision foreclosed any possibility of his being *used* without his knowledge.
106. Craik to Linlithgow, 24 March 1940.
107. Craik to Linlithgow, 23 March 1940.
108. Craik, once again, praised Jinnah's handling of the situation: 'I think it must be admitted that Jinnah handled a difficult situation with greater skill. His primary objective was, of course, to preserve unity in the League, and I do not suppose that he was actuated by any particular

consideration for Sikander or his Ministry. But the general result has been better than that at one time seemed likely.' Craik to Linlithgow, 25 March 1940.
Jinnah's handling of the situation obliged Sikandar Hayat to the former. *Ibid.*, 31 March 1940.

109. Lord Linlithgow to Lord Zetland, 21 March 1940.

110. He was perturbed by the reports in *Civil and Military Gazette, Tribune, Milaup, Inquilab* and *Ihsan:* 'The situation is in my judgement clearly one that attracts my special responsibility under section 52(1) (a) of Government of India Act for the prevention of any grave menace to the peace or tranquillity of the province.' Craik to Sikandar Hayat, 6 April 1940.

111. Sikandar Hayat to Craik, 7 April 1940.

112. Craik to Viceroy, 8 April 1940. In his response, the Viceroy acknowledged the 'damaging' nature of Nath's compilation on the Khaksars. Viceroy to the Punjab Governor, 13 April 1940.

113. L. Graham (Karachi) to Linlithgow, 13 April 1940.

114. He also referred to some reports in *The Tribune* emanating from Peshawar that around 600 Khaksars were preparing to march into Punjab to relieve the pressure on their colleagues in Lahore. Craik to Cunningham, 23 April 1940.
Cunningham, while concurring with Craik, informed him of Arbab Sher Akbar Khan as the Khaksar Leader and proposed to arrest him and other leaders. Cunningham to Craik, 15 April 1940.

115. See Craik to Cunningham, 5 May 1940. Craik sent him the translation of a booklet by one Dr Kazmi denouncing Sikandar Hayat as a traitor. The booklet had been intercepted by the Punjab CID. Also, Craik to Viceroy, 30 April and 5 May 1940. In another letter, the Sindh governor confirmed G. M. Syed's role in collecting information on the Khaksars. See Governor of Sindh to the Viceroy, 9 and 24 April 1940. Zetland also sympathized with Sikandar Hayat for being left out in the cold and expressed his concern over Aligarh University becoming the next focal point for the Khaksars. See Zetland to Linlithgow, 9 May 1940.

116. *The Statesman* (New Delhi) 10 May 1940. Linlithgow, while writing to Leopold Amery, the new Secretary of State, praised Sikandar Hayat and accused Mashriqi of seeking legitimacy through violence. See his letter to Amery, 30 May 1940. This is the time when Dr Nami, on behalf of the Khaksars renewed Mashriqi's offer of 50,000 volunteers to fight on the side of the Allies. See M. Ismail Nami's telegram to Lord Linlithgow 18 May 1940.

117. The telegram was dated 19 April 1940 but the letter bears no date.

118. Correspondence between M.A. Jinnah and Ismail Nami in *The Khaksar Collection.*

119. See *The Hindustan Times,* 29 June 1940.

120. Jinnah to Viceroy, 16 July 1940.
121. See Linlithgow to Jinnah, 24 July 1940.
122. See Saleemi, op.cit., 227-9. Ahmad Shah wrote further letters to Henry Craik and Sikandar Hayat requesting for further negotiations but without much result. See Ahmad Shah to Henry Craik and Sikandar Hayat, 27 and 28 August 1940. During the same week, he had given a press statement confirming the Khaksars' willingness to hold parades without spades. To him, this concession had been personally sanctioned by the Allama whom he had met recently. See *The Hindustan Times,* 23 August 1940.
123. Many of Jinnah's own colleagues were disheartened by the cold shoulder that the Muslim leader received from the government. Some of them turned extremely critical of Sikandar Hayat. See M.A.H. Ispahani to Jinnah, 20 July 1940 in Malik, *Sikandar Hayat Khan: A Political Biography,* p. 137.
124. Craik to Linlithgow, 29 August 1940.
125. Ahmad Shah wrote letters to the central government pleading the case for a review. In a letter he reaffirmed the Khasksar willingness to cooperate with the government in lieu of a general amnesty for the Khaksars including the Allama. He described the economic hardships being faced by the Mashriqi family following his arrest and impounding of his property and accounts. To him, Mashriqi's dependents were virtually 'starving'. See Ahmad Shah to R.F. Mudie, 17 October 1940. Maurice Hallett forwarded Shah's letter to the Viceroy with his commendation of the latter's conciliatory role during the UP crisis. See Hallett to Linlinthgow, 31 October 1940.
126. Sir Richard Tottenham, Additional Secretary to the Government of India to Chief Secretary, Government fo Punjab, 7 March 1941.
127. Ahmad Shah to Sikandar Hayat, 15 April 1941.
128. Government of India to the Secretary of State and the Governor of Punjab, 5 June 1941. However, London advised a conciliatory and low-key response by suggesting to Sikandar Hayat and other friendly Muslim notables to issue friendly statements. See Secretary of State to the Viceroy, 6 June 1941.
129. See the Khaksar: A Reuters' Message, 7 June 1941, in *The Khaksar Collection.*
130. He reminded the Viceroy that it was only the Khaksar movement—a Muslim body—which suffered under the ban and other restrictions whereas other organizations like INC went on with their activities largely unreprimanded. See Ahmad Shah to Linlithgow, 24 August 1941.
131. Ahmad Shah to Henry Craik and Sikandar Hayat, 27 August 1940.
132. The Department of Intelligence (DIB) Report, 24 December 1941.
133. See Linlithgow to Amery, 7 April 1942, in Nicholas Mansergh and E.W.R. Lumby, eds., *The Transfer of Power,* Vol. 1, (London, 1970,

p. 685. The AIML resolution called for the release of the Alama, all the Khaksar prisoners and lifting of the ban on the movement itself.
134. *The Daily Telegraph,* 29 December 1941.
135. Linlithgow to Provincial Governors, 25 May 1943. It is quite clear that the colonial administration strictly desired to keep all the political forces isolated from one another to disallow a common front. However, many provinces reported absence of any notable Khaksar activity. See H.D. Dow (Sindh's Governor) to Linlithgow 2 June 1943. Similar reports were submitted by the governors of Orissa and Bengal in June 1943.
136. In fact, the Allama had resumed a high-key political activity soon after his release. On 3 January 1943, he addressed a rally in Lahore and asked his followers to be vigilant. To celebrate his release, the Khaksars had organized the special meeting in the Badshahi Mosque. He announced the expulsion of Mian Ahmad Shah, Agha Ghazanfar Ali Shah and of Nawab Bahadur Yar Jang from the Tehreek for pursuing reconciliatory policies *viz-a-vis* the government. (The Allama never bothered about his own written commitment). Extract from Addendum to the Note on the Khaksar Movement prepared by the CID Punjab in 1941, dated 3 January 1943. Also, Tottenham to Provincial Governments, 8 May 1943.
137. Linlithgow to Amery 6-5 July 1943. He also complained of Governor Cunningham, who 'true to Type' would not take any action.
138. For a contemporary account, see *A barrister-at-Law, Jinnah Faces an Assassin,* Bombay, 1943. This volume has a collection of Khaksar letters in its appendix., i.e., pp. 118-22.
139. While reporting on the Khaksars' renewed activity in the province, the Punjab Governor argued for a new warning to be given to the leadership. Glancy to Linlithgow, 8 June and 3 July 1943. In a similar report M.G. Hallet from the UP informed the Viceroy of general Muslim preference of Jinnah over Mashriqi. Hallet to Linlithgow, 15 June 1943.,
140. Cunningham to Viceroy, 29 June 1943. Sir Tottenham, in his directive to the provincial governments felt no need for a new ban on the movement, but advised for vigilance. It was suggested that restrictions might be reimposed on drills, spades following a warning to Mashriqi. Sir Richard Tottenham to Provincial Governments, 19 July 1943.
141. The Allama, in a statement, expressed his willingness to obey official restrictions and agreed to end the parades and carrying of spades. His statement, dated 22 July 1943 is preserved in *The Khaksar Collection.*
142. Note on the Khaksars at the India Office, 19 August, 1943.
143. Tottenham to Provincial Governments, 29 November 1943.
144. Extract from Addendum to the Note of the Khaksar Movement (1943-45), Document No. 5285, 15 February 1945.

Chapter Three

The Partition of India in a Comparative Perspective: A Long-term View

Gurharpal Singh

Introduction

The fiftieth anniversary of the partition of India has been accompanied by renewed calls for a more detailed examination of the causes and consequences of the most significant event in the modern history of the subcontinent. Coming as it did soon after the end of the Cold War, the collapse of the USSR and its European satellites, the reunification of Germany and the implosion of Yugoslavia, the anniversary provided a sober moment for thoughtful reflection in a world where conventional assumptions have been turned upside down. The old world order of imperialism and the Cold War is a distant memory and the political elites who were bloodied in the partition no longer hold sway. As sub-national problems rooted in the partition refuse to go away and South Asia faces the economic challenge of the ASEAN countries, there is growing realism among leading politicians for an open discussion of the previously unmentionable.[1]

In many ways these issues have been thoroughly examined by historians. With more and more evidence becoming available every year since 1947, the role of key actors and institutions has been put under intense scrutiny. Although historians have been sensitive enough to undertake this work within the context of developments within the discipline — the shift in history from above to below for example — it has been virtually impossible for those of subcontinental and British origin not to be labelled as partisan. To some extent the nationalist schools of historiography generated by 1947 were always beholden to the ideology of nation building. What is more lamentable however, as Jalal[2] has recently pointed out, is the failure of self-proclaimed radicals, subaltern or otherwise, to ask the right questions and indulge in polemical attacks on scholarship they dislike. Historians, it would appear, are ideological animals and especially insofar as the partition is concerned.

Some of the difficulties encountered by historians of the partition might be better overcome if we examine the event in a comparative as well as a historical context. Post-1947 history, and especially post-1989 history, has much to offer in reworking old questions. State collapse, contraction and expansion are no longer uncommon; non-majoritarian modes of governance function relatively peacefully within ethnically plural and democratic societies; and some of the most intractable political problems (South Africa, the Palestinian-Israel conflict and Northern Ireland) have begun to be unravelled. A few scholars have recognized the significance of these developments in the language of 'Back to the Future?' and the relevance of reworking the partition to understand unmanageable ethnic conflicts both in the periphery and the core.[3] More systematic and comparative work is also being done on ethnicity, state secularism and nation and state-building.[4] In short, the areas of comparative analyses today are so varied, complex and, potentially rewarding, it is difficult to sustain the insularity so far evident in the historiography of the partition.

The aim of this paper is to review the partition with reference to Ian Lustick's theory of state expansion and contraction.[5] Lustick's work, it will be argued, offers new insights into the process of partition and its post-1947 consequences, particularly the politics of the 'disputed lands' which it created.

Lustick's Theory of State Expansion and Contraction

Lustick's work derives from his study of what he calls 'unsettled states' and 'disputed lands' with reference to three case studies: Britain and Ireland, France and Algeria, and Israel and the West Bank-Gaza. His primary concern is to examine the causes of state expansion and contraction in a context in which the status of state boundaries is a part of the political competition that constitutes them. This intertwining is best understood as a process of political institutionalization and deinstitutionalization which occurs as a result of changes in the geographical size of the state. Such change is often non-linear, sudden and discontinuous.[6] Any contraction or expansion in the size of the state, insists Lustick

can be expected to trigger shifts in the distribution of power within a state by changing the resources available to different groups and, ultimately, by changing the prevailing norms and legal arrangements to correspond with the interests of newly dominant groups. Substantial change in the shape and size of the state thus has long-term implications for the relative power position of different groups within it. Accordingly, unless the border of the state is accepted as an immutable given, we can expect that different groups within the state will align their own perceptions of the proper border in the light of the implications that different borders, or different principles of inclusion and exclusion, may have for their chances to achieve and/or maintain power.[7]

But borders, as Lustick continues, are also

institutional constraints, subject to change in time of crisis, which advantage certain groups and rival elites within the state at the expense of others. Substantial changes in the territorial shape of a state represent institution-transforming episodes. Struggles over the size and shape of the state must accordingly be understood as struggles over the 'rules of the game.' Boundaries specify who and what are potential participants of objects of the political game and who and what are not. Different borders have different demographic implications and different political myths associated with them. The territorial shape of the state thus helps determine what interests are legitimate, what resources are mobilizable, what will be relevant, what cleavages could become significant, and what political allies might be available.[8]

To understand the political outcome of such developments Lustick offers 'a theory of punctuated institutional transformation' [9] to the problem of territorial change. The theory contends that there are three distinct stages of state expansion or contraction related to the type of conflict they generate. The first type of conflict (incumbency stage) is associated with incumbency, a struggle for rule among the governing elites. At this stage the political future of governing elites is at stake. The outcome of this conflict is determined by the nature of political competition and if 'competition is limited to political bargaining, threat to bolt from the ruling coalition, electoral campaigns and, so forth, it is easily contained within the political institutions of a developed polity.' [10] However, if the political institutions for regulating conflict among elites are inadequately developed, such conflict may rapidly pass to the second stage (regime stage) where there is 'the real possibility of violent opposition and the mounting of extra-legal challenges to the authority of state institution.' [11] Regime level conflict often involves' 'illegal' competition over the rules themselves in a game treated at least in part as an 'end of the world' contestation'. [12] The third and final stage (ideological hegemony stage) involves conflict among governing elites, over the regime, and hegemonically established beliefs about the political nature of the state and the community. The relationship between these three stages, Lustick notes, can be examined in terms of institutionalization and dislocation caused, for example, by state contraction from a particular region and the implications this may have for the governing elites (incumbency), the regime (the legal order), and the hegemonic political beliefs. This relationship is depicted in Figure 1.

Figure 1. Territorial State-building and State Contraction

The Changing Shape of States		
Incumbency Stage	Regime Stage	Ideological Hegemony Stage
Disengagement means struggle over incumbency	Disengagement means struggle over regime integrity	Disengagement means struggle over ideological hegemony
(Decolonization)		(Secession)

regime   ideological
threshold   hegemony threshold

◄———————— state contraction ————————
————— state expansion/state-building ————►

(Source: Ian Lustick *Unsettled States,* p. 42.)

The three stages identified in Figure 1 are separated from each other by asymmetric thresholds with zones of transition. State expansion or contraction can be seen as a movement across the thresholds determined largely by the degree of insti-tutionalization and development of a particular polity. In the case of contested state contraction from a particular region, the movement will be backwards across the ideological hegemony threshold and may cross over to the regime threshold. The process of movement across and between the thresholds in either direction (state expansion or contraction) as depicted in Figure 1 can be analyzed in terms of Gramscian 'wars of position'(over the terms of political discourse) and 'wars of manoeuvre' (over the struggle for the control of instruments of state authority).[13]

Lustick maintains that his theory adequately explains the changing shape of the British and French states over a period of many centuries and Israel since the 1940s. In addition it can be applied to understanding the collapse of the USSR, the implosion

of the Ottoman and Austro-Hungarian Empires, the retreat of
colonial empires, and separatist movements as diverse as the
Québecois and Basques nationalists. The theory has also
considerable value, Lustick insists, in explaining the tensions
around the new institutionalization of the European Union as a
United States of Europe and the declining importance of nation
states.[14]

Lustick's Theory: Partition and After

At first glance it would appear Lustick's theory is of little
relevance in enhancing our understanding of the partition and the
events that led to it. If anything it is clearly more applicable to
the post-partition period in which Pakistan witnessed serious
state contraction with the creation of Bangladesh. Before 1945,
moreover, the national political structures under the colonial
state were poorly institutionalized. Not until the decisive
elections of 1945-6 did there emerge a clear move towards
establishing an interim regime of a sort. Indeed, this regime was
beset by difficulties from the outset and remained a weak
structure, incapable of effecting its own will let alone establish
hegemonic beliefs. Political power rested above all at the
provincial level where most of the key battles were fought and
lost. Large areas of the country, furthermore, remained outside
the formal structure of the colonial state as princely autarkies,
nominally independent but strictly regulated. In fact it is difficult
to ignore the strength of the argument that the colonial state was
not an impartial arbiter but an instrument for structuring the
choices, opportunities and outcomes made by the principal actors
and parties in the events that led upto the partition. In sum the
uniqueness of the partition, it could be argued, precludes it from
being compressed into a case study for the kind of theory Lustick
has to offer.

Despite these potential objections, it is still possible to
operationalize Lustick's theory in a number of areas. First, we
can examine why the colonial state did not adequately

institutionalize national political structures long before the partition. Had such effective structures existed institutionaliz-ation at the regime level might have been possible. Second, the movement back across the ideological hegemonic and regime thresholds might be better examined at the provincial level, especially in Punjab and Bengal where the, 'ratcheting effect' was to produce chaotic conditions. Third, from 1945 onwards the debate between the Congress and the Muslim League about the future size, nature and boundaries of the Indian state can be seen as a shift from a 'war of position' to a 'war of manoeuvre' in which the objectives of political elites with reference to future career calculations in terms of territory, mobilizable resources, demographic strength, and ideological formulas becomes explicit, ultimately climaxing in the decision to accept partition. Of particular concern is the need to understand political interests which precluded a non-partitionable solution. Fourth, following partition we can look at how India and Pakistan structured ideological hegemonic beliefs about the size of the state against the backdrop of partition and the international and domestic environment confronting them. What coalition of politically significant elites, for example, stood to gain from the new borders? Finally, as a legacy of the partition, how have India and Pakistan dealt with those separatist movements that claim to be the unresolved business of partition? Why was state contraction successful in the case of Pakistan over East Pakistan/Bangladesh but is proving more difficult for Kashmiri, Sikh and Assamese separatists in India?

   Most of these issues require an extended discussion and there is sufficient secondary literature to undertake this more systematically. In the rest of this Chapter I will provide a summary of these points as a way of illustrating the relevance of Lustick's work in five areas: (i) institutionalization of national political structures before 1947; (ii) state contraction and provincial level politics; (iii) the national 'war of manoeuvre', 1945-7; (iv) post-partition state size and hegemonic beliefs; and (v), post-1947 separatist movements and the potential for 'rightsizing the state' in India and Pakistan. Taken together these five areas provide a comprehensive research agenda for a detailed examination of the application of Lustick's theory.

(i) Institutionalization of National Political Structures before 1947

Lustick has noted that one of the ways to review the collapse of colonial empires is to examine their shortcomings in intitutionalizing governance in respective countries.[15] In the case of the British Empire, the contrast between the older (white) and the new (black and brown) commonwealth could hardly be more striking.[16] But what is perhaps more relevant to the Indian case is the failure to evolve effective national political institutions that could have begun the process of institutionalization. To suggest that this was impossible is to fall into a teleological trap which sees the partition as predetermined. Some historians have argued that if the 'federal provisions [of the Government of India Act (1935)] had become effective before the war... the partition could have been avoided.'[17] To assert that these provisions provided an unworkable framework for resolving the question of Indian unity is to negate the proposition that if such an effort had been made the formal structures could have arisen which could have encouraged institutionalization. Of course these structures could have become unworkable, especially if the colonial state was reluctant to facilitate 'coercive power-sharing' because of its own short-term interests, but the experience of colonial institution-building in India suggested that local politicians could construct cross-communal alliances, work within the 'rules of the game' and establish harmonious governance. The absence of mediating federal structures certainly encouraged the process of communal polarization in which the Congress and the Muslim League became the embodiments of the majoritarian options. By 1946 when the interim government was established it was clearly too late to resurrect the federal provisions which had become redundant as a result of the escalating demands of Congress and the Muslim League.

(ii) State Contraction and Provincial Level Politics

If national level structures were poorly institutionalized, at the provincial level the Government of India Act 1935 had encouraged the establishment of 'quasi-regime' politics. After 1935 provincial level politics became the primary domain around which the main contenders for national political power eventually structured their strategies. However, before this development became pre-eminent, provincial level politics provided a fascinating site for the emergency of power-sharing and consociational arrangements. Recent research has drawn attention to how these arrangements resembled Lijphart's consociational model and were often founded upon similar structures at the level of the district and municipality.[18] In Punjab the Unionist Party was able to build a cross-communal alliance of agriculturalists that incorporated elements of power-sharing, proportionality, segmentational autonomy and the mutual veto.[19] These arrangements commanded sufficient political support in the province from the 1920s to the mid-1940s to marginalize the challenge of the Muslim League and the Congress. Indeed, Unionist hegemony in Punjab was well established and the fact that it was undermined was a very close run thing. Given this, how did the Unionist 'quasi-regime' respond to the Pakistan demand and the state contraction that it ultimately implied?

Although the Unionist Party had an ambiguous relationship with the Muslim League — a relationship that could be seen as twin-tracking — the official ideology of the party was committed to the integrity and unity of Punjab. The Sikandar-Jinnah pact (1937) was as much a basis for autonomy of the party in Muslim affairs as a blank cheque for Jinnah. Following the Pakistan Resolution of 1940, however, there began a 'war of position' between the Muslim League and the Unionist Party in which the hegemonic beliefs of the latter were fundamentally challenged. Initially the Unionist response to the Pakistan resolution was to reassert faith in a united Punjab with complete autonomy from the centre. But the erosion of the Unionists' hegemonic position was hastened when the collapse of the Sikandar-Jinnah Pact

(1944) signalled the emergence of the Punjab Muslim League as the alternative to the Unionists. This collapse, as Talbot[20] has chronicled, was further underscored by the difficulties of managing a wartime economy which had inflationary consequences for the Unionists' natural supporters, the death of two leading Unionists, and the increasing uncertainty about the post-war nature of colonial rule. After the Simla Conference (1945), the hegemonic threshold was rapidly crossed as the 'war of position' became a 'war of manoeuvre' in which the local Muslim elites opted for the alternative ideological vision, power, patronage and career opportunities offered by the programme of the Muslim League. Unionist efforts to cling to power following the 1946 provincial elections were accompanied by extra-constitutional mobilization of communal violence that moved state contraction to the zone of incumbency. Ironically, the 'ratchet effect' of movement across the hegemonic and regime thresholds was so profound that the parties which had previously insisted upon a united Punjab — Akalis and Congress — now demanded its immediate partition.

Thus the Punjab case clearly illustrates the asymmetrical nature of the transition zones. The movement from a challenge to the hegemonic position of the Unionists to a fight over incumbency was so rapid and bitter that the 'quasi- regime' had little opportunity to manage the contraction as an orderly policy question at the regime level. Political uncertainty over the borders of possible contraction reinforced the sense of impending doom in which the mobilization of resources, particularly demographic, became an alternative to traditional institutionalized politics.

In Bengal, though there was no parallel to the Unionist Party as an inter-communal coalition, a sense of regional cultural unity did appear to transcend religious divisions. The provincial 'quasi-regime' was indeed buffeted by all-India developments but (unlike Punjab) when the possibility of state contraction reached the regime threshold in 1946, it was able to generate a counter proposal to regime collapse by proposing a united independent Bengal. This proposal was opposed most vociferously by the Bengali Hindu elite whose demand for partition was influenced by the political opportunities which a united Bengal potentially foreclosed to them. 'It was the veto of the Congress High Command', as Sugata Bose concludes, 'that wrecked the possibility of preserving the unity of Bengal as a political entity. The partition of Bengal and Punjab had become a necessity for those who were anxious for a quick transfer of the centralized state apparatus from their colonial masters.'[21] In the light of this it could be conjectured that the 'quasi-regimes' in Punjab and Bengal might have fared better in maintaining and constructing new rules of the game had the absence of federal or confederal structures and the suddenness of colonial withdrawal not imposed the rapid crossing of hegemonic thresholds that quickly moved the debate to positions of state contraction.

(iii) The National 'War of Manoeuvre', 1945-7

The existence of 'quasi-regimes' at the provincial level and weak institutionalization at the national level created a national 'war of manoeuvre' between 1945-7 that was in essence a fight over incumbency. Traditionally this 'war' has been presented as an ideological struggle between two nations. Yet underlying this struggle were interest calculations of political elites that were often in conflict with the proclaimed ideological position. In Bengal, Kashmir and the princely states both the Congress and the Muslim League leadership sought a quick transfer of power that was strongly contested, opposed and resented by regional elites.

After the Simla Conference the national 'war of manoeuvre' became focused around the Muslim League's demand for and the Congress's opposition to Pakistan. The acceptance by the Muslim League of the Cabinet Mission's proposals in May 1946 appeared to mark a decisive breakthrough, but the Congress's decision to impose its own interpretation on the proposal scuttled it. This historic decision, which was followed by the removal of Azad as Congress President, was deeply influenced by the political implications for Congress if such an arrangement were accepted. The rejection marked a turning point after which 'direct action' and communal killings rather than negotiations began to dictate policy outcomes. Paradoxically, by the end of 1946, leading Congressmen rapidly moved to the position of privately accepting the need for partition which they had so consistently opposed.[22]

That partition rather than a dual federation or a confederation was in the strategic interest of Congress became evident in early 1947. Congress organizations in Punjab and Bengal were activated to support the idea. Nehru vehemently opposed the May 1947 plan which gave the provinces ('quasi-regimes') the right to determine their future but soon accepted the 3 June plan which transferred power to two successor states on the basis of dominion status. The third option, preferred by regional elites in provinces like Kashmir, Bengal and some princely states, was undermined by a combination of threats, bribes and appeals to demographic and strategic realities. Even Gandhi's symbolic gesture to propose Jinnah as alternative leader of the interim government in an effort to prevent partition, resulted in his withdrawing from the negotiations process because of opposition within Congress.

The absence of federal level institutionalization might explain why majoritarian fears leading to the 'war of manoeuvre' rapidly became a fight for incumbency. The weight of revisionist historical scholarship appears to suggest that it was the intransigence of Congress sustained by its strategic political interests that frustrated the development of national regime level rules fleetingly entertained by the Muslim League's acceptance of the Cabinet Mission proposals.[23] It has been persuasively argued that the demand for Pakistan was always a contingent bargaining counter for developing wider links with the Muslims in non-majority provinces. The argument that the partition was necessary to prevent bloodshed, civil-war and balkanization would now appear to be hollow given the consequences that ultimately resulted.[24] As Penderel Moon has noted: 'The Congress passionately desired to preserve the unity of India. They consistently acted so as to make its partition certain.'[25]

(iv) Post-partition State Size and Hegemonic Beliefs

In a way the partition of India strengthened the sanctity of the borders of the newly created states. The clashing visions that had led to the partition were now established as hegemonic beliefs supported by a coalition of interests that had most to gain from state contraction. As the new ideologies of state and nation-building were forged, the cathartic experience of partition, in both India and Pakistan created, as Lustick's theory predicts, a momentum across the thresholds for state expansion over 'disputed lands'. Kashmir became the main site of this contest though India's border with China and Burma also provided a number of complex borderland struggles.

In Pakistan this momentum for state expansion became regularized in the struggle for Kashmir, a Muslim majority princely state that had failed to accede to Pakistan but whose Hindu ruler opted for the India Union. Pakistan's ruling coalition of Punjabi landlords, bureaucrats and big business houses not only embarked on an ambitious programme of national integration that included the imposition of Urdu as a national language, but also made the acquisition of Kashmir as a necessary precondition of this process which had been set in motion by the 'two-nation theory'. That many Kashmiris did not wish to be part of a Pakistani (or Indian) state was a proposition which was foreclosed by the salience of hegemonic beliefs so assiduously cultivated after 1947. Two wars (1948 and 1965) and continuing support for Kashmiri insurgent groups advocating accession to Pakistan, demonstrate the success of all Pakistani regimes in embedding the Kashmir question beyond the hegemonic threshold. One could speculate [see below] that unlike the case of East Pakistan/Bangladesh, any 'war of position' towards the idea of an independent Kashmir would be unsustainable in Pakistani politics and may also precipitate a movement back across the regime threshold that could lead to a 'war of manoeuvre' and state collapse rather than contraction.

In India the ideology of the predominantly Hindu Congress became synonymous with 'secular' impulses towards state expansion. 'Disputed lands' — Kashmir, the princely states and the undemarcated colonial border with China and Burma — became the sacred territory of new 'secular' Bharat. Legitimizing the Indian presence in Kashmir the Congress fanned a curious double-speak which held that India's secularism would be threatened if Kashmir left the Indian Union. The obverse, that if India's secularism was so strong, the right of provinces to self-determination should be entertained, was insidiously made a politic non-issue, supporting the inference that the forced inclusion of Kashmir symbolized a tokenist secularism and an instrumentalist ideology. Such instrumentalist realism was also apparent in the Congress's opposition to borderland movements for the linguistic reorganization of states, for example in Punjab, which invoked Congress's secularism for their own strategic reconstruction of internal borders in line with what was proclaimed to be the unfinished business of partition. In these states the traditional support base of the Congress which had so enthusiastically supported the clamour for partition in 1947, was mobilized to resist the new demands on the grounds of the 'threats' they posed to the 'unity and integrity of the country'. After the Indo-China war (1962), the advocacy of secession from the Indian Union was made a criminal offence punishable with several years of imprisonment.

Post-partition hegemonic beliefs about state size were further reinforced by the compulsions of the Cold War. State integrity in South Asia was underwritten by a complex system of external alliances and, when the Bangladesh movement emerged, it produced one of the most complex episodes of the Cold War and the Nixon Presidency. Until recently Bangladesh was a rare example of a new state in a world where state boundaries had been placed in deep freeze by the Cold War. With hindsight, it is perhaps safe to conjecture that without the Cold War pressures for state expansion might have produced greater confrontations between India and Pakistan.

(v) Post-1947 separatist movements and rightsizing the state

An awareness of the dynamics of state contraction and expansion in India and Pakistan before and after the partition enables us to better appreciate the dynamics of some of the contemporary movements for secession from these states. All too often such movements are viewed in isolation, as the product of external agents and conspiracies imputed with a malicious intent or as *sui generis* cases explicable in terms of specific factors.[26] If we apply Lustick's theory, however, and see such movements — and the efforts of states to control them — as part and process of political competition over the size of the state instead of a reopening of a 'settled question', we will be closer to a more realistic political analysis than perpetuating the political mythology created by hegemonic elites. The real question about secessionist movements in India and Pakistan — and South Asia generally — is not what factors and conditions will enable them to succeed, but rather whether the state structures are sufficiently institutionalized to withstand the turbulence of movement across the hegemonic and regime thresholds without state collapse, and whether this institutionalization is adequately developed 'to destroy or deflect these movements so effectively that the image of united India (and Pakistan) whether Hindu (or Muslim) or secular nationalist, can itself become hegemonic.'[27]

In the case of Pakistan, the creation of Bangladesh provides a perfect fit with Lustick's theory. There was a prolonged 'war of position' dating almost from the pre-partition days. The persistent refusal of the West Pakistan elites to institutionalize the politics of the demographically majoritarian Bengal province eventually climaxed in a 'war of manoeuvre' and quick secession aided by external intervention led by India. That these rapid movements across the two thresholds produced only a regime rather than a state collapse in West Pakistan can perhaps be understood in terms of this state contraction benefiting traditional and new elites in the smaller (West Pakistan) state *a la* Bhuttoism and the Pakistan People's Party. But the post-1971 Pakistani state has continued to suffer from a weak political institutionalization as a result of populism under Z.A. Bhutto, military rule under Zia, and weak democratization since 1988 which has seen the presidential dismissal of three elected governments 1990, 1993 and 1996 and constant ethnic strife, especially in Sindh. It is possible therefore to appreciate why state expansion, for example over Kashmir, is pursued often in response to perceived dangers of state contraction, for example in Sindh. The compulsions of these two processes may lock the Pakistani regime, democratic or military, into a nuclear South Asian Cold War in which the contradictions of state size are explicated in the rhetoric of defence of the Islamic republic.

In contrast, India's aggressive state expansion articulated in the language of nation and state-building has not precipitated state contraction. The extension of the sphere of influence over Sikkim (1975) caused hardly a murmur among enlightened political opinion. The regional insurgencies in Kashmir, Punjab, Assam and the north-east have not eroded the ideological hegemonic beliefs about state size, and if anything, reinforced them over the last decade and a half, particularly as these insurgencies have been portrayed in popular political discourse as foreign inspired. Another explanation for why this erosion has been stalled could be found in the demographic size of these provinces and their inability to play the role of Ulster Unionists in New Delhi, even at times of minority and coalition national governments.[28] In other words, the political constituency of these provinces in national Indian politics is too insignificant for ambitious elites, regional or national to propose the restructuring of borders in a way that would challenge hegemonic beliefs. But an alternative argument, that the institutionalization of Indian democracy in the peripheral regions has crossed a threshold where it can act as an effective bar to secessionist movements, however, requires more critical evaluation.

Some political scientists like Kohli and Mitra insist that the rise and fall of some of India's secessionist movements need to be seen in the context of the rational and participatory opportunities afforded by India's democracy.[29] Kohli has argued that there is a bell-curve pattern of such movements which arise, accumulate momentum and then dissipate as their demands are coopted, deflected or incorporated through participatory mechanisms.[30] In essence the Indian state can continuously restructure the political demands of these movements. But this interpretation fails to appreciate the continuity in secessionist demands, the instrumentality of democratic structures in the regions where they arise, and the regular absence of political legitimacy of rule-bound behaviour that commands majority consent freely given and underpinned by 'normative agreement' on how rules are constructed.[31] Elsewhere I have suggested that a better approach to the issue of such regional movements is to view Indian democracy in ethnic terms in which non-Hindu areas are subject to hegemonic and violent control. Hegemonic control provides scope for the kind of accommodation that Mitra and Kohli describe but when such accommodation is challenged, contested and questioned, violent control is regularly imposed, undermining the structures of institutionalization.[32]

The constant imposition of violent control in the peripheral regions encourages deinstitutionalization within them and among the wider polity. An aggressive policy in Kashmir and Punjab, for instance, jeopardizes the kind of institutional regime strength that could also manage orderly state contraction or better integration through new structures. In fact, such is the suspicion with which peripheral movements are held, that their support for demands short of secession are treated as non-negotiable by governments at the centre — whatever their complexion — even through such demands are often readily conceded to areas within the fold of the ethnic democracy. Like Pakistan, the Indian state's response to movements of secession is aggressive state building and an enthusiastic espousal of a nuclear Cold War in South Asia as a guarantor of state integrity. The main paradox regarding state size and political competition in India in the mid-1990s, almost half a century after partition, is that after partition the Congress was so successful in establishing state expansion as a hegemonic belief that today, as at partition, although state contraction offers enormous opportunities for new political elites, it is becoming increasingly difficult to escape from the trap of ideology that the Congress has constructed. The new emerging discourse on the realities of partition is perhaps the beginning of the effort to escape from this predicament.

Conclusion

The five aspects that have tentatively been examined suggest that the reservations about the applicability of Lustick's theory to the partition and after are unjustified. The theory provides a good explanatory account of the difficulties associated with state contraction and the political factors that sustained the process. Its assumption about the rapid and chaotic movement across the hegemonic and regime thresholds in the absence of appropriate institutionalization is validated. It provides continuity between state contraction at partition, the subsequent drives for state expansion in India and Pakistan and resistance to this process in the 'disputed lands' which had contested the accession to either India or Pakistan. It also highlights the 'other' neglected dimension of separatist movements—whether it be Pakistan, Bangladesh, or the pursuit of independent Kashmir: that is, once the hegemonic threshold is crossed in a situation of weak institutionalization, state contraction can be rapid, decisive and irreversible. Much of contemporary scholarship on South Asia focuses on reinstitutionalizing the politics of separatist movements within *existing* state boundaries. This emphasis is both ideologically prescriptive and stands in opposition to global tendencies of 'rightsizing the state'. Unless, as Lustick urges us to believe, we see state boundaries as part-and-parcel of the political competition that constitutes them and recognize the significance and strength of political institutionalization to sustain their expansion and contraction in a peaceful way, the dangers of a partition-like contraction cannot be ruled out. Lustick's comparative agenda suggests clearly that it is time to refocus political analyses on the state rather than the imagined demon of the separatist who is popularly projected as the arch culprit of political decay, violence and instability.

NOTES

1. Mulayam Singh Yadev, the new Defence Minister in the United Front Government, has openly called for a new federation in South Asia, see *The Sunday Tribune* (Chandigarh), 21 July 1996. Nirmal Mukarji in another article, 'Strengthening Indian Democracy', *Economic and Political Weekly* (11 May 1996), (Bombay), pp. 1129-34, calls for a reconsideration of the Cabinet Mission (1946) proposals for regenerating Indian democracy.

2. See Ayesha Jalal, 'Secularists, Subalterns and the Stigma of 'Communalism': Partition Historiography Revisited', *Modern Asian Studies* 30 (3) (1996), pp. 681-689.

3. See for example, Ian Talbot's "Back to the Future?" The Punjab Unionist Model of Consociational Democracy for Contemporary India and Pakistan', *International Journal of Punjab Studies* 3(1) (1996), pp. 65-73, and Yunas Samad *A Nation in Turmoil: Nationalism and Ethnicity in Pakistan, 1937-1958* (New Delhi; Sage Publications, 1995).

4. See Ishtiaq Ahmed, *State, Nation and Ethnicity in Contemporary South Asia* (London, Pinter Press, 1996); S. Mahmud Ali, *The Fearful State: Power, People and Internal Wars in South Asia* (London: Zed Books, 1993); Subrata Mitra, 'What is Happening to the Political Science of Ethnic Conflict?', *International Journal of Punjab Studies*, 3(1) pp. 75-91; and Gurharpal Singh, 'What is Happening to the Political Science of Ethnic Conflict? (II)', *International Journal of Punjab Studies* 3(2), pp. 229-42.

5. Ian Lustick, *Unsettled States, Disputed Lands: Britain and Ireland, France and Algeria, Israel and the West Bank-Gaza* (London, Cornell University Press, 1993).

6. Space precludes a more extended discussion of the term institutionalization as operationalized by Lustick. For him 'An institution is a framework for social action which elicits from those who act within it expectations of regularity, continuity, and propriety. Such a framework is institutionalized to the extent that those expectations are reliably reproduced. Institutionalization is a process by which change in the rules of political competition becomes increasingly disruptive and decreasingly likely to be part of the strategic calculus of competitors within the institutional arena.' *Unsettled States*, p. 37.

7. Ibid., pp. 38-39.

8. Ibid., p. 41.

9. Ibid., p. 439.

10. Ibid., pp. 41-42.

11. Ibid., p. 42.

12. Ibid., p. 42.

13. See Ibid., ch. 2 for a detailed discussion of the theory.

14. Ibid., ch. 11.
15. Ibid., ch. 11.
16. For an interesting aside into the differing political cultures and institutional development of these two entities of the British empire, see. P.N.S. Mansergh, 'Some Reflection on the Transfer of Power in Plural Societies', in C.H. Philips and M.D. Wainwright eds., *The Partition of India: Policies and Perspectives* (London, George Allen and and Unwin, 1970), pp. 43-53.
17. R.J. Moore, 'The Making of India's Paper Federation', in Philips and Wainwright, *The Partition,* p. 54.
18. See Talbot, 'Back to the Future'? For a recent examination of the application of consociation theory to India see Arend Lijphart, 'The Puzzle of Indian Democracy: A Consociational Interpretation', *American Political Science Review,* vol. 90, no. 2 (June 1996), pp. 258-68.
19. Ibid.
20. Ian Talbot, 'The Unionist Party and Punjab Politics', in D.A. Low ed., *The Political Inheritance of Pakistan* (London: Macmillan, 1991), pp. 86-105.
21. Sugata Bose, 'A Doubtful Inheritance: The Partition of Bengal', in Low, *The Political Inheritance of Pakistan,* p. 131.
22. See V.P. Menon's discussions with Vallabhbai Patel, in Philips and Wainwright, *The Partition,* p. 577.
23. See Jalal, 'Secularists, Subalterns....'
24. This of course is the pro-Congress perspective. S.R. Mehrotra, writing on 'The Congress and the Partition of India', in Philips and Wainwright, *The Partition,* concludes that 'Continued slavery, civil war, chaos and the fragmentation of India — these were the only alternatives to partition in 1947. Nor was partition, in the judgement of many Congress leaders, an unmixed evil. *India was at long last free. The unity of at least two-thirds of India had been preserved',* [emphasis added], p. 220.
25. Quoted in Mansergh, 'Transfer of Power in Plural Societies', in Philips and Wainwright, *The Partition,* p. 47.
26. For a survey of the literature on Punjab see Gurharpal Singh, 'Understanding the Punjab Problem', *Asian Survey* vol. 27 (12), (Dec. 1987), pp. 1268-77.
27. Lustick, *Unsettled States,* pp. 443-4.
28. On the contrary, the Machiavellianism of regimes in New Delhi in first precipitating a boycott from the mainstream regionalist parties and then holding elections in these regions has largely been intended to benefit the ruling national party in an emerging situation of minorityism or coalition politics. Punjab 1992 and Kashmir 1996 provide ideal examples.
29. See Atul Kohli, 'Can Democracies Accommodate Ethnic Nationalism? Rise and Decline of Self-Determination Movements in India', *The Journal of Asian Studies,* 56(2); pp. 325-344. Subrata K. Mitra, 'Rational Politics of Cultural Nationalism: Sub-national Movements in South Asia', *The*

British Journal of Political Science, 25 (1995), pp. 57-78; and Subrata K. Mitra and R. Alison Lewis eds., *Subnational Movement in South Asia* (Oxford, Westview, 1996).

30. Kohli, op.cit.

31. For a discussion of the problems of constructing legitimacy in South Asia's peripheral regions, see Gurharpal Singh, 'Punjab Since 1984: Disorder, Order and Legitimacy', *Asian Survey* 34 (4) (Apr. 1996), pp. 410-21.

32. This argument is further developed in Gurharpal Singh, 'The Punjab Crisis Since 1984: A Reassessment', *Ethnic and Racial Studies,* 18 (3), (1995), pp. 476-93.

Chapter Four

The 1947 Partition of Punjab: Arguments put Forth before the Punjab Boundary Commission by the Parties Involved

Ishtiaq Ahmed

Introduction

Following Jawaharlal Nehru's press conference of 10 July 1945 in which he declared that Congress would enter the Constituent Assembly 'completely unfettered by agreements and free to meet all situations as they arise'[1] the leader of the Muslim League, Mohammed Ali Jinnah, gave the call for 'direct action' to protest because allegedly the future of minorities in a united India dominated by Congress had been made uncertain. On 16 August communal massacres took place in Calcutta which left thousands of people, mostly Hindus, dead and homeless. At that time Bengal was under a Muslim League ministry led by Husain Shaheed Suhrawardy.

The Calcutta killings triggered communal riots in many parts of India, but surprisingly Punjab maintained an uneasy peace until the beginning of 1947. In the third week of January the Muslim League started its 'direct action' in Punjab against the Unionist Ministry led by Sir Khizar Hayat Khan Tiwana. Although initially the demonstrations were non-violent, armed clashes soon followed between Muslim and Hindu-Sikh rioters. By early March, communal attacks against innocent men, women and children were being reported mainly from different parts of western Punjab.[2] In response to the demands of Sikh leaders, the All-India National Congress Committee passed a resolution during 6-8 March demanding the division of Punjab into two provinces so that 'the predominantly Muslim part may be separated from the predominantly non-Muslim part.'[3] Similarly the partition of Bengal was also demanded by Congress. The Muslim League had, of course, been agitating with great vigour, after the failure of the Cabinet Mission Plan, for the partition of India and the creation of a separate Muslim state. The partitions of India, Bengal and Punjab were conceded by the British Government in the announcement of 3 June 1947.

The partition of Punjab in mid-August 1947 was negotiated by the India National Congress, the Muslim League, representatives of the Sikhs and the various other minor religious and caste groups before the Punjab Boundary Commission. The deliberations served as the formal basis for the Radcliffe Award of 17 August (it was ready on 16 August), which demarcated the boundaries between India and Pakistan on the Punjab border. The Radcliffe Award, however, did not satisfy any of the major contestants, and has subsequently been criticized and even condemned by various disgruntled commentators. Especially in Pakistan the Award has been described as a conspiracy against it.[4] This outcome should not be surprising, because the purpose of the Award was to divide and separate a people who had through the centuries learned to live together. In central Punjab especially, Hindus, Muslims and Sikhs were found to be living side by side in substantial numbers in various towns and villages. The purpose of this chapter is to bring out the main arguments put forth by the actors involved in the negotiation process which began with the discussions before the Punjab Boundary Commission and culminated with the Radcliffe Award. The main research material used are documents published in a four-volume compilation of official documents, *The Partition of the Punjab 1947*.[5] There is no reason to doubt that the compilation is very thorough and authoritative, but it opens the doors to a great variety of research strategies.

While the Punjab Boundary Commission was in session, hectic political activities and initiatives relating to the question of partition were under way in the wider political arena. In the present study, the events and happenings taking place outside are not included: only the proceedings of the Punjab Boundary

Commission are presented and analysed. After a careful reading of the memorandums and statements submitted before the Boundary Commission by the various parties, it was decided that the distinct cluster of arguments put forth by the various actors should be identified. It is however the arguments espoused by the main contestants — the Congress Party, the Sikhs and the Muslim League (and in that order, because the cases were presented in the order) — which are dealt with in some detail. It is quite impossible to cover the whole range of arguments. The aim has been to select such arguments and examples which appear to be the most relevant. The arguments made in the memoranda and in the statements are more or less identical. Both have been used in the present investigation. The oral presentations, however, provide greater insight and clarifications and are therefore, referred to in most cases.

The different arguments have been grouped and subsumed under various common themes addressed by the parties concerned. In some cases emphasis shifts or new themes are introduced. New headings have been given to these. The positions of the various minor parties are reported very briefly because they appeared as allies of either the Congress-Sikh alliance or of the Muslim League. The concluding statements made by the members of the Boundary Commission and the Radcliffe Award are also included in the analysis. Finally, the chapter considers the cultural and political implications of the religion-based division of Punjab between India and Pakistan for post-independence South Asia.

The Politico-legal Context of the Boundary Commission

The plan to partition India was announced in a radio broadcast on 3 March 1947 by the Viceroy Lord Mountbatten. Among other things he observed:

> For more than a hundred years 400 millions of your people have lived together and this country has been administered as a single

entity. This has resulted in unified communications, defence, postal services and currency; an absence of tariffs and customs barriers, and the basis for an integrated political economy. My great hope was that communal differences would not destroy all this.

My first course, in all my discussions, was therefore to urge the political leaders to accept unreservedly the Cabinet Mission Plan of 16th May, 1946. In my opinion that Plan provides the best arrangement that can be devised to meet the interests of all the communities of India.

To my great regret it has been impossible to obtain agreement either on the Cabinet Mission Plan, or to any other plan that would preserve the unity of India. But there can be no question of coercing any large areas in which one community has a majority, to live against their will under a Government in which another community has a majority and the only alternative to coercion is partition.

But when the Muslim League demanded the partition of India, the Congress used the same arguments for demanding in the event, the partition of certain Provinces. To my mind this argument is unassailable. In fact, neither side proves willing to leave a substantial area in which their community have a majority under the Government of the other, I am, of course, opposed to the partition of the Provinces as I am to the partition of India herself and for the same basic reason.

For just as I felt there is an Indian consciousness which should transcend communal differences so I feel there is a Punjabi and Bengali consciousness which has evoked a loyalty to their Provinces.

And so I felt it was essential that the people of India themselves should decide this question of partition....

We have given careful consideration to the position of the Sikhs. This valiant community forms about an eighth of the population of the Punjab, but they are so distributed that any partition of this Province will inevitably divide them. All of us who have the good of the Sikh Community at heart are very sorry to think that the partition of the Punjab, which they themselves desire, cannot avoid splitting them to a greater or lesser extent. The exact degree of the split will be left to the Boundary Commission on which they will of course be represented...[6]

The statement of the Viceroy was followed by the statement of the British Government. Referring to the question of partitioning Punjab and Bengal, it was observed:

5. The provincial Legislative Assemblies of Bengal and the Punjab (excluding European Members) will, therefore, each be asked to meet in two parts, one representing the Muslim majority districts and the other the rest of the Province. For the purpose of determining the population of districts, the 1941 census figures will be taken as authoritative. The Muslim majority districts are set out in the Appendix to this Announcement.

6. The Members of the two parts of each Legislative Assembly sitting separately will be empowered to vote whether or not the Province should be partitioned. If a simple majority of either part decides in favour of partition, division will take place and arrangements will be made accordingly...

9. For the immediate purpose of deciding on the issue of partition, the members of the Legislative Assemblies of Bengal and the Punjab will sit in two parts according to Muslim majority districts (as laid down in the Appendix) and non-Muslim majority districts. This is only a preliminary step of a purely temporary nature as it is evident that for the purposes of a final partition of these provinces a detailed investigation of the boundary question will be needed and, as soon as a decision involving partition has been taken for either provinces, a boundary Commission will be set up by the Governor-General, the membership and terms of reference of which will be settled in consultation with those concerned. It will be instructed to demarcate the boundaries of the two parts of the Punjab on the basis of ascertaining the contiguous majority areas of Muslims and non-Muslims. It will also be instructed to take into account other factors...[7]

The Appendix was based on district-wise majorities as reported in the 1941 census. It showed that Muslims were in the majority in the following parts of Punjab:

Lahore Division: Gujranwala, Gurdaspur, Lahore, Sheikhupura, Sialkot.

Rawalpindi Division: Attock, Gujrat, Jhelum, Mianwali, Rawalpindi, Shahpur.

Multan Division: Dera Ghazi Khan, Jhang, Lyallpur, Montgomery, Multan, Muzaffargarh.

It is to be noted that Amritsar district, which belonged to Lahore division was a non-Muslim majority district.

On the other hand, Jullundur and Ambala divisions had non-Muslim majorities. The districts included in them were as follows:

Ambala Division: Gurgoan, Rothak, Hissar, Karnal, Ambala, Simla.
Jullundur Division: Ludhiana, Ferozepore, Jullundur, Hoshiarpur, Kangra.

On 4 June, Lord Mountbatten gave a press conference in which he made the following observations regarding the Sikhs:

...There are two main parties to this plan, the Congress and the Muslim League, but another community much less numerous but of great importance — the Sikh community — has of course to be considered. I found that it was mainly at the request of the Sikh community that Congress had put forward the Resolution on the partition of the Punjab, and you will remember that in the words of that Resolution they wished the Punjab to be divided between predominantly Muslim and non-Muslim areas. It was, therefore, on that Resolution, which the Sikhs themselves sponsored, that this division has been provided for. I was not aware of all the details when this suggestion was made but when I sent for the map and studied the distribution of the Sikh population under this proposal, I must say that I was astounded to find that the plan which they had produced divided their community into two almost equal parts. I have spent a great deal of time both out here and in England in seeing whether there was any solution which would keep the Sikh community more together without departing from the broad and easily understood principle, the principle which was demanded on the one side and was conceded on the other. I am not a miracle worker and I have not found that solution....[8]

The Punjab Assembly split into an eastern and a western entity on the basis of notional majority (that is numerical majority district-wise according to 1941 census). The West Punjab Assembly voted against partition by 99 votes to 27, while the East Punjab Assembly voted in favour of partition of the Province by 50 votes to 22.

There were several different suggestions as to how the Boundary Commission should be constituted. It was finally agreed that the Commission would include an independent chairman and four other persons. Of these four, two were to be nominated by the Congress (of which one was to be a Sikh) and two by the Muslim League. If possible, all the four nominated members were to be of high judicial standing. The Congress nominated Justice Mehr Chand Mahajan and Justice Teja Singh while the Muslim League nominated Justice Din Muhammad and Justice Muhammad Munir. Justice Mehr Chand Mahajan's proposal that Justice Din Muhammad, who was the senior most among them, should preside over the sessions of the Commission was adopted by the other members. On 27 June, it was agreed that Sir Cyril Radcliffe, a member of the Bar from England, should be the chairman of the Commission. Radcliffe arrived in Delhi on 8 July. It is important to note that he had never been to India before. The proceedings of the Punjab Commission were held at Lahore for ten days between 21 July and 31 July 1947 (no proceedings were held on Sunday, the 27 of July) but the Chairman did not attend any session. Arrangements were made to have the record of the proceedings flown to his office in Delhi for his perusal.

The leading counsel who represented the main parties were Sir Muhammad Zafrullah Khan for the Muslim League, Mr M. C. Setalvad for the Congress and Sardar Harnam Singh for the Sikhs (Sikh Assembly Party). Sir Zafrullah was assisted by Sahibzada Nawazish Ali, Sheikh Nisar Ahmad, Syed Muhammad Shah and Choudhri Ali Akbar; Mr Setalvad was assisted by Mr Tek Chand, a former Judge of the Lahore High Court and Mr Narotam Singh. In addition the following counsels presented the cases of the minor communities or interests:

1) Mr Bannerji, Secretary, Punjab Nationalist Christian Association.
2) Rai Bahadur Badri Dass, representing the Scheduled Castes.
3) Sardar Darbara Singh, representing the Mazhabi and Ramdasia Sikhs.

4) Mr R. C. Soni, for Bikaner State.
5) Dewan Bahadur S. P. Singha, on behalf of the Christians (Joint Christian Board).
6) Mr C. E. Gibbon, representing the Anglo-Indian community.
7) Sheikh Bashir Ahmad, representing the Ahmadiyya community.
8) Mr Salig Ram, representing the Scheduled Castes and Mazhabi Sikhs.
9) Sir Muhammad Zafrullah Khan, represented Bahawalpur State (also represented the Muslim League).

Although the major consideration in the demarcation of the boundaries was to be the contiguity of Muslim areas and of non-Muslim areas, the inclusion of 'other factors' in the Commission's terms of reference considerably broadened the scope of the debate. Thus inevitably historical, religious, geographical, social and economic aspects were brought into the discussions. That the Muslim-majority Rawalpindi Division should go to Pakistan and the non-Muslim majority Ambala Division should be allotted to India was not disputed by the parties concerned. On the other hand, conflicting claims were staked by both sides to parts and portions of Lahore, Multan and Jullundur divisions.

The All-India National Congress (Mr Setalvad and Memorandum)

Terms of Reference

Setalvad opened his brief by emphasizing that the terms of reference upon which the Boundary Commission was to ascertain the claims of the various parties appearing before it consisted of two sets of instructions. One, to demarcate boundaries according to the principle of contiguous majority areas and two, 'to take into account other factors'. As regards other factors, these could not be ascertained in a general manner;

these could differ from area to area and between parts of the boundary. Further, that there was 'no warrant for stating that *'other factors'* had a subsidiary place, nor any for stating that the *'other factors'* were such as might result in what was being termed as 'local deviations only'.[9] He remarked:

> It stands very much to reason that if it is a matter merely of ascertaining the contiguous majority areas, the work need not have been assigned to a Commission of this weight and importance, in that case a map could have been drawn by having the census figures on the one hand and any Deputy Commissioner could have drawn the line on the basis of contiguous majority areas.[10]

1941 Census Figures Unreliable

The Congress' counsel contested the reliability of the 1941 census figures. According to the 1941 census there was an overall Muslim majority of 57.1 per cent in Punjab. Non-Muslims of which the bulk were Hindus and Sikhs, constituted 42.9 per cent. However, Census Commissioner Yeatts and another officer, Khan Bahadur Sheikh Fazal-i-Illahi, had suggested that political considerations made people greatly exaggerate their numbers in 1941. Fazal-i-Illahi called it a 'Census War'.[11] It started as early as 1911 after separate electorates were introduced in 1909: each community exaggerating its numbers to secure more seats, which by 1941 turned into a complete farce.

Setalvad argued that in 1931 the Congress had boycotted the census. According to Yeatts '1940-41 saw also political influences on the census but in the opposite direction, since whereas the difficulty in 1931 had been to defeat a boycott, the difficulty in 1941 was to defeat an excess of zeal.'[12] However, the Congress' counsel admitted that the fault lay with both sides and it was not Muslims alone who had exaggerated their numbers.[13]

Security

Setalvad asserted that the Commission should take into consideration the rivers, the canal system built upon their water resources and the colonies developed by those irrigation systems. Together the rivers, canals and the colonies constituted the natural wealth of the province and were meant for the benefit of the whole of it. Moreover these formerly desert areas were developed mainly by the people of the eastern and central parts of the province. Sikhs and Hindus migrated in large numbers from these over-populated areas to the canal colonies. Through enormous sacrifices, hard work, perseverance and sheer stubbornness the Sikh Jats converted former deserts into the most productive areas of Punjab. Further, most of the land in Punjab, especially in the canal colonies, was owned by Jat peasant-proprietors and not by big landowners or capitalist-farmers.[14]

If the colonies in the Lyallpur-Sargodha and Montgomery districts of the Lower Bari Doab were awarded to West Punjab many of the Sikhs and Hindus would emigrate to India because anti-Hindu and Sikh riots in NWFP and northern Punjab had created great insecurity among them. Thus it was important to consider whether the demarcation of boundaries would not lead to their uprooting. On the other hand, Muslims who might leave from these areas for western Punjab could be settled in the Thal Canal area which was being developed.[15] In the absence of an obvious boundary such as a mountain range or a hill tract that could be used to demarcate international boundaries in Punjab, the best boundary would be a large river bed. The boundary should be one which could preserve peace between two states and prevent unnecessary conflict.[16]

Economic Stability

Setalvad argued that if the notional basis of division of Punjab were to be accepted, the eastern part would receive only 26,442 acres of waste land as against 3,64,164 acres going to the western part: 4,85,862 acres of unclassed forests as against 11,44,000 being given to western Punjab, (Later, Setalvad corrected this figure, informing that it referred to the total area of unclassed forests, and therefore western Punjab's share would be 6,58,138 acres).[17] Further, that the most important were the Crown lands in the colony areas which yielded over a sixth of the total revenue of Punjab. In the colonies the temporarily leased and unallotted Crown lands made up 16,22,655 acres. Under the notional system they fell into western Punjab. 'The eastern part is clearly entitled to a substantial portion of these Crown lands. This substantial share can be awarded to the eastern part by so demarcating the boundaries as to include in them a substantial portion of the temporarily leased and unallotted Crown lands in the colony areas.'[18]

It was claimed further that a non-Muslim majority was to be found in a contiguous belt extending over rural and urban parts of the Lyallpur colony. In the case of the Upper Bari Doab it was the same situation.[19] The peasant was the tiller of the soil and thus tied to the land. Setalvad admitted that the cultivators were not only non-Muslims, but insisted that in the Lyallpur district and Upper Bari Doab colony non-Muslims were in a majority in contiguous areas. He remarked 'also in an area extending right from the Gurdaspur district passing through Amritsar and extending to Lahore, known commonly as the Majha tract. All that tract is populated by a non-Muslim majority in whom all these economic interests are concentrated.[20] Further:

If you find... the Muslim majority to be 5 or 7 per cent in a certain tract, but if you find in the landholders, who till the soil, a majority of non-Muslim peasant proprietors, the question for your consideration would be, putting it as a point by itself, whether in that area the economic factor would not override the population factor. The question will be whether you will give weight to excess of 5 to 7 per cent of the Muslim population or to the 60 or 65 per cent of the peasant-proprietors who are non-Muslims.[21]

Lahore

Setalvad emphasized non-Muslims had deep cultural roots in Lahore. They had built colleges and libraries and also had outstanding economic interests in the district. Lahore district, although the 1941 census figures (disputed by Congress) showed a 60.62 per cent Muslim and 39.38 per cent non-Muslim population strength. Muslims paid only Rs. 5,81,235 as land revenue while non-Muslims paid Rs. 12,63,830. Moreover, Mulsims owned only 5,11,867 acres while non-Muslims owned 11,50,450 acres.[22] Thus economic aspects of the division of Punjab must also be taken into consideration. As to the city of Lahore:

> I will now take the city of Lahore. You will remember that so far as this city is concerned, the population ratio of Muslims and non-Muslims according to the census of 1941 is higher still; not 61 and 39 as in the district but 64 and 36. But... you will find that definitely a larger proportion of the land is in the hands of the non-Muslims.... Another factor, which is an allied factor, is in regard to urban areas and also in some districts rural areas. Here again you will find that in certain areas which are Muslim majority areas, the position is that the trade, industry, and the factories and so on and so forth are almost entirely in the hands of non-Muslims.[23]

Another thing to consider would be the transport and road system. No division could be acceptable which cuts up the railway and the road transport into unworkable portions. Moreover, the facilities for repairs and maintenance of the railway line for the eastern part of Punjab require that the 'Moghalpura Workshops [Located on the outskirts of Lahore] should be available to the Eastern part in order that the railway in the part should be able to function.[24]

Special Rights of the Sikh Community and Nankana Sahib

Commenting on the Sikh community, Setalvad emphasized that their rights in the province should be evaluated in terms of their historical services to Punjab. They were a martial race who had prior to British conquest been the ruling community in the province. Later after British annexation the Sikhs supplied large numbers of soldiers to the Indian army and contributed outstandingly to the development of the province. Accordingly 'Efforts must be made by those who are demarcating the boundaries, as far as it is possible and consistent with other considerations and interests, to preserve the solidarity and culture of the Sikh community and its religious freedom.'[25] Muslim-Sikh history was one of antagonism between the two communities. Therefore splitting up the Sikhs into two parts would be very wrong; they should be placed in eastern Punjab.[26] More importantly, according to the notional principle Nankana Sahib, which was the birthplace of the founder of the Sikh faith, fell in West Punjab. This was unacceptable. Therefore necessary adjustments should be made in the demarcation of boundaries so that Sikh history and culture were not split up into two separate states.[27] Moreover, the Upper Bari Doab canal [which passes through the Majha tract] had been constructed by the British primarily to settle the disbanded soldiers, mainly Jats, of the defeated Sikh armies of 1849 to a livelihood based on agriculture. This area should therefore be given to East Punjab.[28]

'Substantial area': Proper Unit for Demarcation of Contiguity

Regarding the question of demarcation of contiguous Muslim and non-Muslim areas, Setalvad argued that the term 'area' could not mean any infinitesimally small area, but must mean a substantial area.[29] What constituted a break in the contiguity must also be a substantial area. As to the word 'contiguity', it meant, according to the Oxford Dictionary, in a literal sense: touching; in actual contact; next in space; meeting at a common point; bordering, and adjoining. In the loose sense it meant neighbouring; situated in close proximity though not in contact. However, it was only in the strict literal sense, that contiguity should be understood in the context of boundary demarcation.

As for Ambala and Jullundur divisions (as well as in the smaller form of districts) they were not only non-Muslim majority areas but also showed that economic interests and social and cultural factors were predominantly of non-Muslim character. However, the map of the Muslim League based on the smaller unit of a *tehsil* or less had tried to connect some areas together to present a Muslim majority contiguity in them. This was inadmissible.[30]

Gurdaspur District

Coming to the crucial Gurdaspur district, Setalvad informed that it consisted of an area of 1,827 square miles. Up till 1921 it had a non-Muslim majority. In 1931, however, Muslims were reported to be in a majority of 15,534 while in 1941 that majority had been recorded as 26,435. Thus according to the 1941 census figures there were 5,89,923 Muslims as against 5,63,588 non-Muslims and therefore on the basis of notional division it had been placed in western Punjab. As pointed out earlier, Congress did not accept the 1941 census as reliable.[31]

Arguing further Setalvad said that the districts of Amritsar and Gurdaspur were united by very close trade relations. Amritsar was the clearing house for exports and imports of Gurdaspur. Further, the rail and road connection was such that it came up from Lahore to Amritsar and then went on to Gurdaspur and it linked Kangra Valley and district with Amritsar and Lahore. Therefore Amritsar and Gurdaspur should be taken as one unit rather than be divided into two separate districts. They together formed a non-Muslim majority and therefore should be awarded to eastern Punjab. Another major consideration for placing Gurdaspur in the eastern part was its intimate relationship with Sikh history. Many famous Sikh shrines were located in it.[32]

Gujranwala and Sialkot Districts

It was also argued that the Gujranwala district's importance for Sikhs should not be forgotten. It was here that Maharaja Ranjit

Singh was born. As for Sialkot district, its north-eastern part was for centuries part of Jammu State. This part was populated by Dogras who had linguistic and cultural links with the Dogras of Kangra and Gurdaspur and with those of Jammu. Moreover both in the Gujranwala and Sialkot districts non-Muslims owned more property and paid more revenue. Therefore they should also go to eastern Punjab.[33]

Extent of Area Claimed for Eastern Punjab

Proceeding on the assumption that partition of Punjab would involve massive population movement, the Congress memorandum[34] claimed altogether the following areas for eastern Punjab:

1) The whole of Ambala division.
2) The whole of Jullundur division.
3) The whole of Lahore division.
4) Lyallpur district.
5) Montgomery district.
6) Such other adjoining areas as may be necessary from considerations of canal and colony needs. Such a division of Punjab would consolidate some 34 lakh Sikhs out of their total population of 37,57,401 in East Punjab.

The Sikhs
(Sardar Harnam Singh and Memorandum)

Terms of Reference

Agreeing with Setalvad's interpretation of the terms of reference, Sardar Harnam Singh chose to comment on the Muslim League's memorandum in order to show that the importance of 'other factors' was admitted by it even when its main stress was on contiguous Muslim and non-Muslim areas. Thus it had asserted that the boundary should be a workable and practicable one and should be capable of fulfilling the functions of a boundary between two neighbouring states. Further, 'It should not be a crazy line running backwards and forwards over the areas of several districts and in and out of every village....'[35] Another point emphasized by the Muslim League was that there must be some rationalization of the canal system: the headworks of an irrigation system should be in the same part as the canals emanating from it.[36] Reasoning thus, it was pointed out, the Muslim League had claimed portions of the non-Muslim majority Pathankot *tehsil* because Madhopur waterworks are located there. However, if that were granted Muslims would be 45.4 per cent while non-Muslims would be 54.6 per cent of the population there.[37] Similarly, like the Congress the Muslim League also laid great stress on economic stability. It even alleged that judicial notice be taken of the source of non-Muslim wealth: 'They say that the non-Muslim property has been purchased from the proceeds of money-lending which have gone into the coffers of the Hindus and Sikhs.'[38]

Transfer of 'Floating' Population and Rights of the Tillers

Harnam Singh argued that the commission had to consider how the demarcation of boundaries would affect, on the one hand, the transfer of people from one part of Punjab to the other, and on the other hand, how the consolidation of the Sikh community could be realized in eastern Punjab. As to the question of transfer of people, the predicament of those who were rooted in the soil was different from those who followed a profession such as that of a lawyer or doctor or the various other rootless menial classes who could easily be moved.[39] In the Lahore district, out of the total paid land revenue of about 18 lakhs approximately 13 lakhs was paid by non-Muslims of which Sikhs alone paid 12 lakhs. Lahore was not an area of big landlordism. Here were to be found mostly peasant-proprietors, the majority of whom were Sikhs. It was virtually impossible to transfer people who were rooted in the soil. On the other hand, according to the 1931 census which included information on races, tribes and castes etc. , in the Lahore district out of the total Muslim population of 1,49,29,896 some 46,95,957 consisted of fakirs, beggars, weavers, herdsmen, cobblers, *khumars* or potters, *musallis,* carpenters, oilmen, bards, barbers, blacksmiths, washermen, butchers and *mirasis,* people who are described in the settlement reports as landless people and menials.[40] These were a 'floating people' and could therefore be transferred easily.

Moreover the question of 'one man, one vote' should apply only to the basis of legitimate government, not to the division of a country. Other factors such as relationship to the land, ownership of property and economic viability should be given proper consideration rather than just mere numbers. The Muslim League wanted the partition of India because it could not accept the principle of 'one man one vote', which it feared would place Muslims in a minority situation. However, it insisted that the division of Punjab should proceed purely on the basis of numerical strength. Thus it was exploiting an apparently democratic device to achieve an undemocratic political end.[41]

The Special Religio-cultural Claims of the Sikh Community over Punjab

Coming to the theme of special position of the Sikh community in Punjab, Harnam Singh asserted that even the Muslim League in its memorandum admitted that Sikhs deserved special consideration, but alleged that since Sikhs had aligned themselves with Hindus they had forfeited the right to special consideration.

Commenting on the Muslim League's demand for a separate state he said:

> Provide by all means the Muslim community with a new homeland that has been their demand, but when you provide them with a new national homeland you have also to keep in mind that the ancestral

home of the Sikhs is not destroyed, I submit that the central divisions of Punjab from time immemorial constitute the national home of the Sikhs. The question whether they are fewer in number or very numerous is quite irrelevant from the point of view whether a particular region or a particular tract is their homeland.[42]

Now if India was the homeland of the Hindus and Pakistan was the homeland of the Muslims, then Harnam Singh insisted, the area between Chenab and Beas was the homeland of the Sikhs (here the counsel referred to several books and official documents in which the Majha region of Punjab with Amritsar as its centre has been described as Sikh Country). Thus when a certain territory was recognized as the homeland of a community its rights to it could not be denied merely on the basis of another community being in greater numbers in it. For instance the Balfour Declaration described Palestine as the homeland of the Jews even when they were a minority in it in 1917.[43]

As regards the transfer of people, in his statement of May 1947 Jinnah opined that Hindus could leave Pakistan and go to their homeland in Hindustan and Muslims could migrate to their homeland, Pakistan. Later he changed his position and extended his hand of friendship to all communities, provided they accepted Pakistan as the national home of Muslims.[44] Harnam Singh remarked:

Therefore I submit that when you are considering this question, the special features of the Sikh community should be taken into account. I have the greatest possible respect for all religious denominations and for everybody's sentiments. But for the past two decades I have several times heard Muslim boys singing 'Ya Rab Mecca Madina le chal mujhe'. They have been looking westwards. They say, we are living in a strange country, in an alien country, we have no national home. Our national home is in Arabia. I am not hurting the feelings of my Hindu brethren when I say that they look to Hardwar and Benaras for their pilgrimage and the Muslims look to Mecca and Madina. But for the Sikhs, the city of Amritsar, the city of Nankana Sahib in Sheikhupura district, the city of Kartarpur in Shakargarh tehsil of Gurdaspur district, are their Mecca and Madina and their Hardwar and Benaras.[45]

Harnam Singh asserted that Sikh apprehensions about being persecuted by Muslims once again were based on historical experience. He cited a number of works, including a quotation from the *Tuzk-i-Jahangiri,* written by Emperor Jahangir, to prove that persecution had been sanctioned against Guru Arjun. The pith of his argument was that Muslim rulers generally followed an intolerant policy towards the Sikhs.[46] Proceeding further Harnam Singh stressed that Sikhs had clearly expressed a desire not to live in Pakistan. These facts had been set forth in detail in the Sikh Memorandum, which had been signed by 32 out of 33 members of the Punjab Assembly and the thirty-third had also later joined the group.

The Question of Language

The Sikh counsel asserted that the whole of Punjab province did not speak Punjabi. People in Karnal, Rothak, Hissar did not speak Punjabi. Similarly people in Dera Ghazi Khan, Isakhel, Mianwali did not speak Punjabi. Even in Multan they did not speak Punjabi but Multani [currently called Saraiki]. Similarly in Kangra a different language was spoken. Punjabi was spoken in the central regions of the province — that is in Lahore and Jullundur divisions and in the colony area.

The tract consisting of the Jhang, and Multan districts and the trans-Jhelum area was acquired by conquest by Maharaja Ranjit Singh and retained by the British for the sake of administrative convenience. Punjab proper extended to the banks of the Jhelum, excluding Jhang and Multan districts and the trans-Jhelum area. Thus from the boundary of Delhi to the banks of the Jhelum, excluding the districts of Jhang and Multan, the population was as follows:

Muslims	10,761,560
Sikhs and others	11,184,886

From the boundary of Delhi to the banks of Chenab river, excluding Multan and Jhang districts, the population was as follows:

Muslims	9,191,618
Sikhs and others	11,885,834[47]

In Rawalpindi and Multan divisions, out of a total population of 90,17,766 those who returned Punjabi as their mother tongue were 24,98,016. Others return Lehnda as their language. British records show Lehnda as a separate language.[48] Harnam Singh asserted:

> Now the figures disclose that these 24 lakhs are mainly concentrated in the colony areas of Montgomery, Lyallpur, and Khanewal and Mailsi tehsils of Multan district. The result is that Punjabi which is one of the main languages of India, is the spoken language of the Jullundur division of this province minus the Kangra division, the whole of Lahore division and parts of Multan division, namely the colony areas of Lyallpur and Montgomery districts and part of the Multan district. It is this area that we have claimed.[49]

Protection of Punjabi in East Punjab

The counsel for the Sikhs argued further that the census reports pointed out that Muslims had increasingly been recording Urdu as their mother tongue while Hindus had been recording Hindi: only Sikhs had remained steadfast to Punjabi, 'Therefore I say that if you are going to protect the language and culture of the people, you cannot do that by incorporating them in Pakistan where people are out to destroy that culture. It is not a matter of recent happenings in March, 1947. This thing has been going on for the past two decades.'[50] Further, in eastern Punjab 'the predominantly Hindu areas may be amalgamated with Hindustani speaking areas. A division and a further division will be my argument.'[51]

Lahore

Harnam Singh made a special effort to claim Lahore for the Sikhs. He pointed out that not only the districts of Amritsar and Gurdaspur contained many sacred places and shrines of the Sikhs, but also Lahore district was intrinsic to Sikh religious and cultural history. 'The fourth Guru Ramdas, the ancestor of all the succeeding Gurus, was born and brought up in Lahore.' [52] The remains of the fifth Guru Arjun lay also in Lahore. Lahore was famous as the Gurus' Cradle. [53] As regards Nankana Sahib in Sheikhupura district, the Sikh counsel insisted that it should go to the eastern part of Punjab, because here the founder of the Sikh faith had been born and it was the holiest Sikh shrine. The only solution for maintaining their communal unity and cultural continuity would be to amass the Sikhs in eastern Punjab.[54]

Claims to Parts of Lyallpur, Sheikhupura, Gujranwala and Sialkot Districts

Basing his calculation on the *zail* as the principle territorial unit Harnam Singh asserted that a contiguous non-Muslim majority area was to be found in the *Shahidi Bar*. The colonization policy in the canal areas of Lyallpur was such that Sikhs and Hindus were allotted land in one zone of Lyallpur district and Muslims in another zone. Thus in Lyallpur district the Sikhs held about 75 per cent of the land holdings in one compact area, paid about 80 per cent of the land revenue and constituted 40 per cent of the population.[55] The non-Muslim majority *zails* in the *Shahidi Bar* comprised parts of Lyallpur. Sheikhupura and Gujranwala districts. Thus a major portion of Lyallpur *tehsil,* a major portion of Jaranwala and parts of Samundri and Toba Tek Singh *Tehsils* of the Lyallpur district constituted a non-Muslim majority area. These were connected to the non-Muslim majority parts of Sheikhupura *tehsil* and a part of Gujranwala *tehsil* and included the Nankana Sahib Town and the estate of Nankana Sahib.[56] A look at the map would show that this was one contiguous solid block of territory within the Rachna Doab. Further, Head Baloki was shown on the map in Chunian *tehsil*. That portion of Chunian *tehsil* was predominantly a Sikh area. It was located in Lahore district which was a part of the Upper Bari Doab Canal. The entire Lahore district was contiguous to the non-Muslim majority areas and should go to the eastern Punjab.[57] As for Sialkot district, it was claimed in the Sikh memorandum that it held a significant place in Sikh sacred history. For economic reasons especially the *tehsil* of Narowal in Sialkot was claimed for eastern Punjab. It was claimed that that 'the boundary of eastern Punjab must extend up to the Chenab.'[58]

Montgomery District and the *Tehsils* of Khanewal and Mailsi in Multan District

The Sikh memorandum states that the district of Montgomery and the *tehsils* of Khanewal and Mailsi in Multan division were irrigated by the Lower Bari Doab Canal and the Pakpattan Canal. The colonists numbering 1,70,000 consisted mainly of hard-working peasant-proprietors whose families had originally migrated from central and eastern Punjab. Further it was stated, 'The trade, commerce and industry of Montgomery district and Khanewal and Mailsi sub-districts of Multan district are almost entirely in the hands of non-Muslims.'[59]

Extent of areas claimed by the Sikhs for eastern Punjab

The Sikh memorandum also stresses the inevitability of population movement and the need to consolidate the Sikh community in East Punjab. It claimed the following areas for eastern Punjab:[60]

1) Ambala division
2) Jullundur Division
3) Lahore division

4) Lyallpur district of Multan division
5) Montgomery district and Khanewal, Vehari and Mailsi *tehsils* of Multan division

Such a division would mean the consolidation of 34 lakh Sikhs out of a total population of 37,57,401 in eastern Punjab.

The Muslim League (Sir Muhammad Zafrullah Khan and Memorandum)

Terms of Reference

Zafrullah Khan took issue with the Congress-Sikh position on equating 'other factors' with the principle of contiguous Muslim and non-Muslim majority areas. Had religious sentiments, vested interests, ownership of acres, ownership of banking and insurance companies, of capital invested in factories been the argument for dividing India partition would not be possible. Further, there were Muslim shrines all over India, but it was impossible to measure how much sentiment Muslims attached to them. Likewise it was impossible to gauge the religious sentiments which non-Muslims attached to their shrines. The Muslim League demanded the division of India on the sole basis of Muslim majority in some regions of the subcontinent. [61] The legitimacy of such demand was conceded by the Viceroy when he said, '...there can be no question of coercing any large areas in which one community has a majority to live against their will under a Government in which another community has majority and the only alternative to coercion is partition.' [62]

Because Muslims were in a majority in some regions the British government could be persuaded to grant partition, remarked Zafrullah. The same arguments were then put forth by Congress and the Sikhs to demand the partition of Punjab and Bengal because in those otherwise Muslim majority provinces there were some parts in which non-Muslims were in a majority. Hence the Viceroy's remark: 'When the Muslim League demanded partition of India, Congress used the same arguments for demanding in that event the partition of certain Provinces. To my mind this argument is unassailable.'[63]

Zafrullah asserted that the operative part of the statement of the British Government which defined the functions of the Boundary Commission referred to ascertaining the contiguous majority areas of Muslims and non-Muslims.[64] As for the 'other factors' it referred only to local factors. In some exceptional cases the majority principle could be bent so as to accommodate local peculiarities.[65]

Claims to Ajnala, Jullundur, Nakodar, Zira and Ferozepore *Tehsils*

Zafrullah argued that the unit for determining Muslim and non-Muslim areas should be the *tehsil* because it had existed consistently as the fundamental administrative and revenue unit in Punjab's hsitory. On the other hand, new districts had been created and old ones dissolved. Anything smaller than a *tehsil* such as a village or cluster of villages called the *zail,* or police *thana* would not be useful, because they tended to overlap and were also more prone to periodic adjustments.[66] Thus if the *tehsil* was adopted as the unit for ascertaining contiguity, it would be found that in the Gurdaspur district only Pathankot *tehsil* had a non-Muslim majority. On the other hand, in the other three *tehsils* of Shakargarh, Gurdaspur and Batala Muslims were in the majority. Similarly in the Ajnala *tehsil* of Amritsar district Muslims were in a majority. In the Jullundur district, Muslims were in a majority in Jullundur and Nakodar *tehsils*. In Ferozepore district, Ferozepore and Zira *tehsils* were Muslim majority *tehsils*. Together these *tehsils* formed a contiguous area connecting them to western Punjab.[67]

The Question of Security

Commenting on the question of security, Zafrullah observed that the cut-off point of the international boundary between India and Pakistan proposed by Congress and the Sikhs was at the Chenab, although both had different interpretations of how this boundary should actually be demarcated. But such a boundary would make Pakistan easily vulnerable to Indian agression. Pakistan's defence required that its main communication lines and cities were protected from easy attack by the other side. For the protection of the Muslim majority area of western Punjab it was essential that the boundary be fixed at the Sutlej. Except for some *tehsils*, the area up to Bahawalpur or Rajputhana on both sides of Sutlej was that of Muslim majority.[68]

The Sikh Demand for Partition of Punjab

Responding to the Sikh demand for special treatment, the counsel for the Muslim League asserted that two main reasons had been submitted by them for it. One, the allegation that during the Mughul period Sikhs and their religious leaders had been tortured and persecuted by the Muslims, and that if they were again subjected to Muslim rule they feared that history might be repeated. Two, the contemporary killings of Sikhs allegedly at the hands of Muslims in Punjab.[69]

Zafrullah proceeded to refute both these charges. Referring to several authoritative Sikh and other publications he asserted that the Mughuls had actually been benefactors of the Sikh Gurus. Muslim rulers had bestowed grants in land and respected and protected the Sikh religion. Many holy Sikh shrines including Darbar Sahib and Nankana Sahib were built upon endowments made by Muslims.[70] The reason why Guru Arjun was punished by Emperor Jahangir was the former's help to his son Prince Khusro who had rebelled against him. In some other cases when Sikh Gurus were persecuted by the Mughuls it was the Hindus who instigated the rulers to mete out severe punishment to them.

On the other hand, during the time of Guru Gobind Singh, Sikhs preached hatred against Muslims and fomented rebellions against them.[71]

As regards the contemporary killings, although communal riots had broken out in 1946 in Bombay, Ahmadabad, Calcutta, Noakhali and Bihar, Punjab remained relatively calm. Beginning with the end of January 1947 there was a five-week agitation in Punjab organized by the Muslim League against the Unionist ministry. It was largely an orderly agitation. It came to an end on 28 February. The ministry resigned late on 2 March but that became known publicly on 3 March. On 4 March the first incident occurred in Lahore. Zafrullah referred to a government communique which alleged that Hindu and Sikh agitators provoked the violent clashes in Lahore, Gujranwala and Rawalpindi on 4 and 5 March.[72]

In order to strengthen his assertion that the Sikh leaders had only lately changed their perceptions of Muslim-Sikh relations, Zafrullah quoted a number of statements of Sikh leader Master Tara Singh. In *Sant Sipahi* of August 1946 Tara Singh wrote:

In respect of religious principles Sikhs are nearer to Muslims than to Hindus but their social connections are stronger with the Hindus. Among the Hindus there is a section which wants to put an end to our separate identity. Our ties with the Muslim are not strong but for that reason we have less to fear from them. I am in favour of an understanding with the Muslims and of promoting better relations with them. There are Hindus who through intrigue and diplomacy want to devour Sikhs. Our policy with regard to Hindus should be this: we should not be so far from them that we should be permanently estranged and we should not be so near to them that we should lose our entity. The Hindus should realize this position. If they give up the desire and attempt to absorb us we shall not be afraid to strengthen our bonds. But the past record and history inspires no confidence in us. We shall have to remain alert.

Congress is bound to seek our sympathy and assistance but has also been trying in the past to scatter our organization and shall do so in future. It does not accept our separate political existence because we are opposed to it on principle. It should thus be borne in mind that the Congress and Hindus will try to destroy our separate political existence. During the last election utmost effort was made to this end but we saved ourselves. If the Sikhs who got elected to the Punjab Legislative Assembly had all been elected on the Congress ticket, we should have died as a community.[73]

Zafrullah asserted that on 4 March 1947, however, Master Tara Singh came out of the Punjab Assembly and shouted, 'Pakistan Murdabad, Sat Sri Akal.'[74] Further, he brandished his *kirpan* declaring that the time had come when the might of the sword alone would rule and that the Sikhs were ready and they had to bring the Muslims to their senses. Then again on 4 March he had said:

O, Hindus and Sikhs! Your trial awaits you. Be ready for self-destruction like the Japs and the Nazis. Our mother land is calling for blood and we shall satiate the thirst of our mother with blood. We crushed Mughlistan and we shall trample Pakistan.... The world has always been ruled by minorities. The Muslims snatched the kingdom from the Hindus, and Sikhs grabbed it out of the hands of the Muslims and the Sikhs ruled over the Muslims with their might and the Sikhs shall even now rule them. We shall rule them and shall get the government fighting. I have sounded the bugle, finish the Muslim League.[75]

The Muslim League's counsel also referred to many other provocative speeches and newspaper articles of Sikh leaders which inflamed feelings on both sides.[76] In such communally charged circumstances riots, violence and bloodshed broke out in Lahore and the rest of Punjab.

The Census of 1941

Zafrullah argued that the Commission has no choice but to rely on the 1941 census figures. It was not only Muslims who were guilty of such manipulation. In many parts of Punjab the opposite was true. This was borne out by the 3 January 1946 statement of Bryant, the private secretary of the Punjab chief minister:

If a census is to be challenged merely because in a particular area one community has increased more rapidly than the others, then every census could be challenged on that basis. Moreover, although in Lahore the Muslims according to the census increased far more greatly in the decade 1931-41 than the other communities this was not true everywhere. In the Rawalpindi municipality area... the rate of increase of Hindus... was very much greater than of Muslims, and this in spite of the fact that the Rawalpindi Municipal area had been extended by the inclusion of villages with a predominantly Muslim population.[77]

Zafrullah also alleged that Sikh landowners had used their influence to make their menial classes return to Sikhism as their religion even if they belonged to other religions and sects such as the Ad-Dharmis.[78]

The Economic Basis of Partition

Zafrullah presented the Muslim League's standpoint that the real reason for the the partition of India, and by implication of Punjab, was the economic disparity and inequality prevailing between, on the one hand, rich Hindus and Sikhs, and on the other hand, destitute Muslims. Economic exploitation during the British period by Hindus and Sikhs of Muslims had caused widespread poverty among the latter. Even though the 1900 Punjab Land Alienation Act had slowed down the acquisition of Muslim agricultural property by Hindu and Sikh moneylenders there were various other devices available through which debt-ridden Muslims continued to be alienated from their holdings by the non-Muslims.[79] Zafrullah conceded that Muslims were generally poor. This applied also to Punjab where large-scale industrial production, banks and industrial companies were mostly in the hands of non-Muslims.

However, as to the question of land to the tiller and their rootedness in the soil, Zafrullah argued that Muslim peasant-proprietors and tenant farmers far exceeded non-Muslims and were as much rooted in the land, even though Sikhs who undoubtedly had made a valuable contribution to development in Punjab, owned agricultural property in much greater proportion to their percentage in the total population of Punjab. Muslims were generally owners of smaller holdings as compared to the Sikhs, but they were more numerous in absolute numbers.[80]

The Canal Colonies

Commenting on the canal colonies, the Muslim League's counsel asserted that the land was originally the homeland of Muslim nomadic and pastoral peoples. More importantly, the area allotted by the Crown in the canal colonies also showed that Muslims constituted a majority. Thus in the Lyallpur, Montgomery, Multan, Sheikhupura, Jhang, Shahpur and Gujrat colony areas all together 42,99,663 acres had been allotted. Out of these, Muslims cultivated 27,40,814 acres; Hindus 3,79,001; Sikhs 11,46,432; Christians 22,786 and others 10,635 acres. The percentages come to: Muslims 64; Hindus 9; Sikhs 26; and Christians and others.[81]

Regarding the crucial Lyallpur district to whose development the contribution of Sikhs had been emphasized so much by the opposite side, Zafrullah noted that in that district Muslims were 62.8 per cent of the population; they owned 62 per cent of the area; paid 57 percent of the land revenue and formed 69 per cent of the owners in the district. Further, Muslim Arains had too made contributions to agricultural production and not just the Sikh Jats. Moreover, in Lyallpur, Samundari, Sheikhupura *tehsils* Muslims constituted a majority of the population and owned more land than other communities. In Nankana Sahib and Montgomery *tehsils* and Multan district also Muslims were in the majority and owned more land than non-Muslims.[82] In Gujranwala, Hafizabad and Wazirabad *tehsils* also Muslims were the majority population.[83]

Lahore, Amritsar and Gurdaspur Districts

Commenting on the situation of the Lahore, Amritsar and Gurdaspur districts Zafrullah argued that those districts together had a population of 42,62,762. Of these Muslims were 22,75,390, which meant a Muslim majority of 2,88,018.[84] In the memorandum it was argued that although there were non-Muslim majority *tehsils* of Amritsar and Taran Taran in the Amritsar district they were surrounded by Muslim majority areas. On the other hand, Ferozepore Jhirka and Nuh *tehsils* were Muslim majority *tehsils* in the non-Muslim majority Gurgaon district of Ambala, but they were blocked from joining western Punjab because they were not contiguous to Muslim majority areas. The Muslims must therefore reconcile themselves to Ferozepore Jhirka and Nuh *tehsils* being left in eastern Punjab and non-Muslims must reconcile themselves to Amritsar and Taran Taran *tehsils* being left in western Punjab.[85]

Claim to Portions of Pathankot *Tehsil*

A deviation from the Muslim League's stand that *tehsil* be the unit of territory on which claims should be based was made when it was argued that:

> The Canal Headworks of the Upper Bari Doab system are situated at Madhopur in the Pathankot Tehsil (non-Muslim majority, *author's remark),* of the Gurdaspur District.... The whole of the Irrigation system of the Upper Bari Doab serves areas which would be comprised within West Punjab, the Headworks and a stretch of a few miles of the canal alone being within East Punjab.... It is submitted therefore... to include within West Punjab the portion of the Pathankot Tehsil of the Gurdaspur District which lies to the West of a line drawn from a point two miles above Madhopur and running to the East of the Upper Bari Doab Canal up to the point where the Pathankot *Tehsil* joins the Gurdaspur *Tehsil.*[86]

Extent of Areas Claimed by the Muslim League for Western Punjab

Unlike the claims of Congress and Sikhs which had been clearly stated at the end of their respective memorandums in the form of a list, the Muslim League neither in the memorandum nor in the oral presentation followed such an approach. Instead several paragraphs were devoted to present its claim. Zafrullah pointed out that of the seventeen districts of western Punjab based on the notional division of the province into two parts Muslims had a majority in all the *tehsils* except Pathankot. They should therefore come to Pakistan. Parts of Pathankot were claimed under 'other factors'. In addition Muslims were in a majority in the *tehsils* of Ajnala, Ferozepore, Zira, Nakodar and Jullundur which were contiguous to the Muslim majority *tehsils* of western Punjab. The non-Muslim majority Dasuya *tehsil* in the Hoshiarpur district was claimed on the basis of a Muslim-Christian majority; Zafrullah claiming that the Christians would prefer to live in Pakistan. Further the Muslim majority parts of Fazilka and Muktsar, Hoshiarpur, Jagraon, Ludhiana, Samrala, Rupar, Una, Moga, Garh Shankar, Nawan Sahr and Philaur were claimed from the non-Muslim districts of eastern Punjab because they were contiguous to the Muslim majority areas of Gurdaspur, Lahore and Montgomery. Proceeding thus the Muslim League claim came up to the valley of the Sutlej. Zafrullah rejected the Congress-Sikh thesis that partition would necessarily involve large scale movement of population across the Punjab borders. Even if that were to happen, more Muslims would have to leave the eastern part than the Hindus and Sikhs moving over to eastern Punjab. [87] In the memorandum it was asserted that a division of Punjab on the lines suggested by the Muslim League would mean that in West Punjab out of a total population of 20,427,946 there would be 69.86 per cent Muslims; 12.75 per cent Sikhs; 12.24 per cent caste Hindus; 2.68 per cent scheduled caste and Ad-Dharmis; and 2.47 per cent Christians and others.[88]

Arguments of the Minor Groups

Bannerji, representing the Nationalist Christian Association (his credentials were challenged in a letter by S.G. Dutta who claimed to be leader of the Punjab Christian League), argued that the bulk of Christians in Punjab lived in Multan, Montgomery, Lyallpur, Gujranwala, Sialkot, Gurdaspur, Sheikhupura, Lahore, Amritsar and Ferozepore. According to the notional division, most Christians would be placed in West Punjab. But since Christians were organized on an all-India level, they would like such areas to be included in India. Badri Dass (representing the scheduled castes), claiming to have the support of all the eight scheduled caste members of the Punjab Assembly and two members of the Constituent Assembly, asserted that scheduled castes considered themselves a part of Hindu society and would like to express their support for union with India. Darbara Singh (representing the Mazhabi and Ramdasia Sikhs), argued that the Mazhabi and Ramdasia Sikhs were an integral part of Sikh society. They resided mostly in Ambala, Hoshiarpur, Ferozepore, Amritsar, Lahore, Lyallpur, Sheikhupura and Montgomery districts. Therefore such areas should be included in eastern Punjab.[89]

S. P. Singha (representing the Joint Christian Board), asserted that there was no such thing as the Nationalist Christian Association and therefore Bannerji had no right to represent Christians. Naming a long list of Christian notables and claiming to represent the real Christian organizations he argued that Christians would rather have a united country according to the Cabinet Mission Plan, but if Punjab were to be divided they could expect better treatment in Pakistan than in a Hindu-dominated caste-ridden India.[90] Gibbon (representing Anglo-Indians), informed the Commission that the Anglo-Indians were happy to be in Pakistan. They regarded Lahore and West Punjab as their homeland.

Bashir Ahmad (representing the Ahmadiya Community), argued that Qadian in Batala *tehsil* of the Gurdaspur district should be included in Pakistan, because it was contiguous with the Muslim-majority *tehsils* of Ajnala and Narowal. The Sikhs, he said, were making a great deal of their holy shrines at Amritsar and Nankana Sahib. By the same token it could be asserted that the founder of the Ahmadiya community was buried at Qadian. That holy shrine should therefore be in Pakistan. [91] The Ahmadiya counsel claimed that altogether there were one million followers of the Ahmadiya community in the whole world of which half a million were in Punjab.[92] Moreover, out of their 745 branches as many as 547 branches lay in Pakistan (according to the notional division). Three-fourth's of the entire people who contributed to the Ahmadiya treasury lived in territories which belonged to Pakistan. Further, 'The economic stability of the community also requires that Qadian should fall within the area of Pakistan.'[93] Furthermore, it was not only the Sikhs who had rendered meritorious services to the British empire. The Ahmadiya community had been foremost in serving it. Both in the First and Second World Wars, the Ahmadis served in the army. Thus '...even in the last Great War about 199 members of this community held the King's Commission and they held very high and responsible positions.'[94]

Salig Ram (representing the scheduled castes and Mazhabi Sikhs of the Pakistan Scheduled Castes Federation; his credentials were challenged by other members of those communities, apparently because he himself did not originate from them), argued that the eight MLAs who voted for scheduled caste areas going to India did not represent the interests of those depressed classes and castes. Moreover, because untouchability was not known to Islam, the scheduled castes had experience of better treatment in the Muslim villages. Therefore their interest lay in the fact that they should be put together with the Muslims.[95] Further, 'So far as Mazhabi Sikh untouchables are concerned they have separate gurdwaras, if they have any; they get a different kind of *amrit* and they have nothing in common with the rest of the Sikhs.'[96] R. C. Soni, representing Bikaner State and Sir Zafrullah representing Bahawalpur State, disputed sharing of waters of the rivers and canals passing through those states and the waterworks connected to them.

Reports of the Indian Members of the Commission

The four nominated members of the Punjab Boundary Commission could not reach a unanimous decision and therefore submitted separate reports.

Justice Din Muhammad

Din Muhammad described the Sikh demand for special rights as 'most ridiculous, most unjustifiable and most unreasoned.'[97] The maps produced by the Hindu-Sikh side were declared misleading. He accepted numerical majority and contiguity as the main criteria for allocation of territory, but dismissed ownership of property as an invalid basis for such a claim. On the other hand, security and economic stability, including allocation of waterworks, were considered by him as important 'other factors'. [98] However, in contrast to the Hindu-Sikh demand, he found the Muslim demand, 'to have been framed reasonably and moderately and not with a view to bargaining. It was properly related to the population factor.'[99]

Justice Muhammad Munir

According to Munir, the Sikh claim to special rights by virtue of their shrines had no direct force. Muslims also had shrines all over Punjab. Nor was the stand on language a valid one because Lehnda was only a dialect of Punjabi. He also sought to refute that Muslim rulers had persecuted Sikhs and quoted instead several Sikh sources urging hatred and strife against Muslims.[100] The claim to hard work and exclusive contribution to the development of the canal colonies by the Sikhs was also dismissed as wrong. Muslim peasants had also made equal contribution to development. In Lyallpur not only the Sikh Jats but also Muslim Arains had played a great role in development.[101] The economic exploitation of Muslims by

Hindus and Sikhs was the real reason for demanding a separate Muslim state. Therefore, invoking greater property ownership in Punjab could not be an admissible factor for the allocation of areas.[102] Looking at the question of security, Munir opined that the Muslim League's proposal was the correct one. As the measure of contiguity only the *tehsil* could be employed fruitfully. Therefore '...the frontier between the two States should be that suggested by the Muslim League.'[103] He assured the non-Muslims that they had nothing to fear in Pakistan because Islam treated all citizens alike.[104]

Justice Teja Singh

Teja Singh laid great emphasis on the fears of the Sikhs to live under a Muslim communal government. While reiterating the Sikh counsel's version of the Muslim-Sikh animosity during the Mughal period he went on to discuss contemporaneous events in great detail. Commenting on the Muslim League agitation against the Unionist ministry, Justice Teja Singh asserted that it was not only violent but also proclaimed patently hostile slogans against non-Muslims such as:

> *Assey lengey Pakistan* (We will take Pakistan)
> *Jaise liya tha Hindustan* (The same way we took India).[10]

According to Teja Singh, the authorities did not move a finger when the agitation was on, but when the Sikh and Hindu students took out a procession on 4 March 1947 they were *lathi*-charged. Troubles spread from Lahore to other parts of Punjab. There were serious communal riots in the districts of Campbellpur, Rawalpindi, Jhelum, Amritsar, Multan and later on in Gurgaon. In the rural areas of Rawalpindi, Jhelum and to a lesser extent in Multan districts, Sikhs were raided by Muslim mobs.[106] Further:

> In some places the rioters numbered five to ten thousand, and almost the entire Sikh population including the old and infirm, women and

children were either killed or burnt alive. A large number of people were forcibly converted, children were kidnapped and young women were abducted and openly raped.[107]

According to Teja Singh, although the Hindu and Sikh version placed the number of victims at a very high figure the official figures mentioned as follows:

	Killed or burnt alive	Injured
Rawalpindi district	2,263	397
Multan district	189	183 [108]

Official estimates were that property worth two million rupees was destroyed in Multan and one hundred million rupees in Rawalpindi district. 'It is alleged that the whole thing was organized.'[109] Comparing the Muslim League's demand for the partitioning of India with the Sikh demand for the partitioning of Punjab, he observed:

The Muslim League depended solely upon the fact that they (Muslims) formed the majority of the population of the provinces which they desired to be made into an independent state. The Sikhs, on the other hand, not being in majority in any district of the Punjab demanded that part of it in which the bulk of them lived and which they claimed to be their homeland, be separated from the rest of the province so that they might escape communal rule of the Muslims. They knew that unlike the Muslims they could not have a state of their own but they preferred to live in that part of the Punjab which would join the Indian Union rather than Pakistan. They never relied upon their numerical strength, but stressed that because of certain factors they occupied a special position in the province and were consequently entitled to a special consideration on that account.[110]

Teja Singh pointed out that the Ahmadiya community who supported the stand taken by the Muslim League and to which community Sir Muhammad Zafrullah Khan belonged had also stressed the necessity of preserving the solidarity of their community.[111] Further, he reiterated that because many holy shrines and historical sites of the Sikhs were located in Lahore. Amritsar, Gurdaspur, Gujranwala and Sheikhupura districts they should go to eastern Punjab. In conclusion, he recommended a division of Punjab which largely though not entirely followed the position of the Sikhs. He observed, 'I have not calculated the figures but I believe that it would raise the number of the Sikhs in the eastern Punjab to about 31 lakhs [the Congress and Sikh plans placed 34 lakh in eastern Punjab] out of their total population of about 37 lakhs in the whole of the British Punjab.'[112]

Justice Mehr Chand Mahajan

Acknowledging that contiguous Muslim and non-Muslim areas should be separated and allocated to Pakistan and India respectively, Mahajan observed that 'other factors' were left to be determined at the discretion of the Commission. He made this interesting observation:

> I am convinced that it is possible for an ingenious Muslim to make the whole Punjab a contiguous Muslim majority area by adopting a certain line and, similarly, it is possible for an ingenious non-Muslim to make the province of the Punjab right up to the River Jhelum a non-Muslim area by adopting another line. He may go up even to the city of Rawalpindi.[113]

Proceeding in a relatively neutral and independent vein, Mahajan rejected the Congress and Sikh suggestion that the Chenab river should be the frontier between India and Pakistan. He said:

> This suggestion would seriously prejudice the claim of the Muslim League on the basis of the population factor and would also clash with the main principle of partition as it would include within the Eastern Punjab a huge majority of Muslims residing in areas which are predominantly Muslim. There are no such factors in this area which can override the population factor.[114]

Regarding the Muslim League's suggestion to fix the border on the Sutlej river, Justice Mahajan found that it had been worked out on the basis of *tehsil* as the unit for demarcation of contiguous areas. It could easily be reversed and then non-Muslim parts of *tehsils* could be put together to create non-Muslim majority contiguous areas and this could extend well into western Punjab.[115]

On the other hand, in the distribution of the two major canal systems and the colonies of Lyallpur and Montgomery, Mahajan sought to compensate both sides. Therefore while most of Lyallpur including substantial portions of the Shahidi Bar were to be awarded to western Punjab, Montgomery was to go to eastern Punjab.[116] As regards Lahore, according to his scheme it went to India but Mahajan acknowledged the common claims of all the communities and preferred an arrangement under which it could be made a 'free city' jointly supervised by India and Pakistan.[117] On the other hand Nankana Sahib was to go to India.

He said in conclusion: 'In my view the frontier of India and Pakistan should be demarcated on the west of the Ravi and in the neighbourhood of that river, as strategically speaking this is the only workable frontier that can be laid down between these two states which are being divided on religious basis.'[118]

The Radcliffe Award

In the report containing the territorial award Sir Cyril Radcliffe wrote that the divergence of opinion 'between my colleagues was so wide that an agreed solution of the boundary problem was not to be obtained.'[119] He said further:

> ... in my judgement the truly debatable ground in the end proved to lie in and around the area between the Beas and Sutlej rivers on the one hand, and the river Ravi on the other. The fixing of a boundary in this area was further complicated by the existence of canal systems, so vital to the life of the Punjab but developed only under the conception of a single administration, and of systems of road and rail communication, which have been planned in the same way.

10. I have hesitated long over those not inconsiderable areas east of the Sutlej River and in the angle of the Beas and Sutlej Rivers in which Muslim majorities are found. But on the whole I have come to the conclusion that it would be in the true interests of neither State to extend the territories of West Punjab to a strip on the far side of the Sutlej and that there are factors such as the disruption of railway communications and water systems that ought in this instance to displace the primary claims of contiguous majorities...

11. I have not found it possible to preserve undivided the irrigation system of the Upper Bari Doab Canal, which extends from Madhopur in the Pathankot *Tehsil* to the western border of the district of Lahore, although I have made small adjustments of the Lahore—Amritsar district boundary to mitigate some of the consequences of this severance.[120]

The Radcliffe Award deviated from the provisional list of districts (i.e., the notional division of districts) placed in western Punjab, by awarding three of the four *tehsils* of the Muslim majority Gurdaspur district — the Muslim-majority *tehsils* of Batala and Gurdaspur as well as the Hindu majority *tehsil* of Pathankot — to eastern Punjab. The fourth *tehsil* of Shakargarh, which had a Muslim majority, was awarded to Pakistan, apparently because it was situated on the western bank of the Ravi, unlike the other three *tehsils*. Additionally, the Muslim majority *tehsils* of Ajnala, Jullundur, Nakodar, Ferozepore, Zira and parts of Kasur *tehsil* were given to eastern Punjab. No non-Muslim majority *tehsil* was given to Pakistan.[121]

Analysis

The three main parties negotiating the partition of Punjab — Congress, Sikh and Muslim League — adopted maximalist strategies which apparently were purported to facilitate bargaining. Each side could argue plausibly that its demarcation of boundaries was consistent with the main terms of reference. Thus, for example, by excluding Jhang and Multan from Punjab proper, on the grounds that these were allegedly not Punjabi-speaking areas, the Sikhs could show a Hindu-Sikh majority extending from Delhi to Chenab. The Sikh counsel quoted official reports in which Lehnda had been recorded as a separate language. Similarly the Muslim League, by relying on the *tehsil* as the proper unit for demarcation of Muslim and non-Muslim contiguous areas could reach up to the Sutlej in the east. It could claim the non-Muslim majority *tehsils* of Amritsar and Taran Taran on the plea that they were not contiguous to non-Muslim majority *tehsils.* Proceeding thus, the whole of Amritsar district was claimed for Pakistan. On the other hand, the Congress and Sikhs strove to claim large chunks of Muslim majority areas including the city of Lahore on the basis of their ownership of property.

1) Terms of Reference

There is no doubt that the population factor was the overriding consideration which the three main parties had to contend with. The objections to the reliability of the 1941 census by Congress seem to have been dismissed out of hand by the Chairman of the Commission. However, the 'other factors' aspect of the terms of reference was indicative of an awareness that deviations from it under some circumstances were unavoidable. This tension can be identified in their arguments: while the Muslim League stood to gain from the fact that Muslims constituted an overall majority in the province and had majorities in seventeen districts of Punjab they emphasized this fact upon which partition should proceed, the Congress and Sikhs were compelled to rely on the weight of 'other factors'.

2) Unit for Demarcation of Boundaries

It can be asserted that neither the Congress-Sikh nor the Muslim League's way of interpreting contiguous Muslim and non-Muslim majority areas was accepted as authoritative. Had the district been chosen as the only valid basis of determining contiguity, the Amritsar and Jullundur districts blocked the way the Muslim League connected the Muslim majority *tehsils* as contiguous areas — a strategy whereby such contiguity could go up to the Sutlej. On the other hand, by the same token Gurdaspur would have gone to Pakistan. But if the *tehsil* were to be chosen consistently as the unit of territorial demarcation then Pathankot would have gone to India and the Muslim League's demand for parts of Pathankot *tehsil* where the Madhopur Waterworks were situated could not have been admitted. The adoption of the *zail* would surely have created many problems for Sikh claims as it provided even greater scope for manipulation. In their actual claims,therefore, all parties deviated from the unit of demarcation proposed by them, and invoked 'other factors' including security, economic stability, historical claims and so on.

3) Economic Arguments

The Hindu-Sikh positions were strongly based on claims to property ownership and rights of peasant-proprietors. Sir Zafrullah however tried to turn these arguments against them by arguing that Muslim poverty, allegedly the result of Hindu-Sikh exploitation, was the main reason why partition of India had been demanded by the Muslim League. He could also argue that Muslims were more numerous among peasant-proprietors but that they possessed smaller holdings. Further, that they were therefore equally rooted in the soil. There was an implicit suggestion in Sir Zafrullah's stress on economic justice that it would be realized in the future Muslim state. This rhetoric was not countered effectively by the Congress-Sikh counsels. In the final round of arguments an effort was made to rebut such a charge but it was based on academic economic theory rather than comparable rhetoric.[122]

4) Religion and Culture

The Sikhs were the only group which demanded concessions on the basis of what they called their special claims on Punjab. The actual argument was a mixture of religious, cultural and political factors. In this regard past history was invoked to prove, on the one hand, that Sikhs were the most legitimate claimants to Punjab, and that, on the other hand, living under Muslim rule was a threat to their identity and interest. From such a position while the division of Punjab was demanded it was urged that it should lead to the Sikhs being amassed in the future Indian East Punjab. It required necessary concessions in central Punjab where although the Sikhs were not in a majority they were to be found in substantial numbers. The Congress naturally supported such special considerations. Surprisingly Congress did not invoke any religious rights of Hindus in western Punjab. On the other hand, the Muslim League could point out that even Muslim shrines would be left in eastern Punjab as a result of partition.

5) Fear and Violence

The Sikh counsel and Justice Teja Singh took up historical as well as contemporaneous Muslim-Sikh animosity to urge a favourable consideration of their community's need for being consolidated in eastern Punjab. Many examples were given of mob attacks in Rawalpindi and Multan against Hindus and Sikhs. Zafrullah blamed Sikh and Hindu leaders and demonstrators for fomenting tension which led to the unfortunate urban clashes in different parts of Punjab. However, he did not mention any mob attacks against Muslims in the non-Muslim majority areas of central and eastern Punjab at that particular time. The infamous massacres of Muslims which occurred in Amritsar and other parts of eastern Punjab seem to have taken place mostly after the announcement of the Radcliffe Award. Many years later Justice Muhammad Munir confirmed in his book, *From Jinnah to Zia*, that communal riots first broke out in Rawalpindi and that the aggressors were Muslims.[123] Therefore Paul Brass' assertion that during partition Sikhs in eastern Punjab were the first to initiate communal attacks and violence against Muslims does not have support in the statements and observations of leading Muslims who were personally involved in the negotiations on the division of Punjab.[124]

6) Security and Economic Stability and 'Other Factors'

The question of the security of India and Pakistan did pose a perplexing problem for the three parties because there was no natural frontier existing in Punjab. Therefore rivers or river-beds were proposed as cut-off points; the Congress-Sikh counsels demanded fixing the border as far west as possible and therefore at Chenab while the Muslim League strove east to reach the banks of the Sutlej.

The most frustrating fact that rallied against any rational division of Punjab was the various developmental inputs — canals, waterworks, colonies — of the government that had benefited Punjab during the British period. These facilities had been planned for a united Punjab and could not therefore be divided in a neat manner. Here the emphasis on 'other factors' became unavoidable. While the Hindu-Sikh alliance tried to make the most of it by emphasizing the contributions of the Sikh peasants to the development of the province, the Muslim League invoked it only to claim parts of Pathankot *tehsil*. In the main the developmental schemes and areas were awarded to Pakistan.

7) The Opinion of the Indian Members of the Punjab Boundary Commission

The nominated members of the Boundary Commission were clearly sympathetic to the parties which had nominated them. Justice Din Muhammad and Justice Muhammad Munir supported the Muslim League stand and claim without reservations. Justice Teja Singh deviated slightly from the Sikh position, while although Justice Mehr Chand Mahajan took a stand sympathetic to the Congress-Sikh demands his was a relatively independent position. He not only rejected the Muslim League claim but also the Congress-Sikh one by proposing the international boundary to be demarcated near the Ravi. In his report however, Lahore and Nankana Sahib fell into eastern Punjab.

8) The Radcliffe Award

The great controversy surrounding the Radcliffe Award constitutes one of the major legacies of the partition of India. It is likely to remain a permanent feature of political debate and scholarly curiosity which has as its focus the continuing India-Pakistan relations or Hindu-Muslim-Sikh interaction or both. Largely the controversy originates in the equivocal terms of reference. The principle of contiguous Muslim and non-Muslim areas could not be applied neatly to Punjab where historically communal segregation was the exception while pluralism was the rule. Despite the constant waves of invasions from the north-western passes of the subcontinent the Bhakti, Sant and Sufi traditions embedded in the popular culture of Punjab for at least the past five hundred years had been quite successful in promoting communal peace. The partition of Punjab was thus destined to undo the common wisdom of Punjab. This could not have been achieved without profound injury — physical and spiritual — being meted out to its people.

However, in choosing the boundary at the Ravi rather than Chenab on the west (as the Congress-Sikh alliance wanted) or Sutlej on the east (as the Muslim League had argued), Radcliffe sought to balance the claims of the two contending groups, but also sought some sort of 'natural frontier' which could satisfy the need for security and stability. Consequently Lahore was awarded to Pakistan and Amritsar to India with necessary adjustments.

It can be argued that the awarding of the seven Muslim-majority *tehsils* to East Punjab was a way Radcliffe sought to meet in some substantial way the Sikh demand to be consolidated in East Punjab. Such an inference is plausible because in the various public statements of the British government a consideration of the special status of the Sikhs had been mentioned. Had Radcliffe openly admitted this perhaps the controversy which has surrounded his decision would not have given birth to so many conspiracy theories. That the awarding of the two Muslim majority *tehsils* of Gurdaspur and Batala to India was part of a conspiracy to provide it access over the land route to Kashmir enjoys wide support among most Pakistani and pro-Pakistani writers and scholars. The accusations are to the effect that Radcliffe was pressured by Mountbatten at the behest of Nehru to award Gurdaspur to India. However, unless one proceeds from the assumption that the Maharaja of Kashmir had joined this conspiracy already before the Radcliffe Award was announced such a position remains far from convincing. As Robert G. Wirsing has argued the benefit of such a division to India in the context of the Kashmir dispute has been fortuitious rather than deliberate.[125] It can be pointed out that there are conspiratorial theories in the other direction too, suggestion that the partition of British India and the creation of Pakistan was masterminded by imperialist British bureaucrats who wanted to create a ring of reactionary Muslim states as a buffer between the Soviet Union and secular India.[126]

As far as Punjab is concerned, after a careful perusal of the discussions of the Punjab Boundary Commission, another thesis can be put forth: the Radcliffe Award basically relied upon the principle of Muslim and non-Muslim majority contiguity and did not recognize claims to property as a valid basis for awarding territory. In particular the Congress-Sikh claim to Lyallpur and Montgomery, other canal colonies and to Lahore, which was based on the ownership of overwhelming property rights in these places, was not considered legitimate to override the population factor. Therefore these areas in which Sikhs in particular owned much of the land and Hindus and Sikhs together most of the urban property, went to Pakistan. In this sense, therefore, the Radcliffe Award was more sympathetic to the claims of the Muslim League than to that of the Congress and Sikhs.

9) The Losers and Winners in the Partition of Punjab

The greatest losers in the partition of Punjab were, of course, the common people who lost hearth and home through forced migration. More than half a million, men, women and children lost their lives. In cultural and religious terms, the Sikhs — who themselves demanded the partition of Punjab — were the main losers. Their most holy shrine at Nankana Sahib fell in the areas which were to constitute West Punjab. Also Lahore and Gujranwala where many of their Gurus and military heroes had lived became a part of Pakistan. The great efforts of the Sikh peasant-proprietors in turning waste land in the canal colonies into the granary of Punjab could not weigh heavier than the efforts of the smaller Muslim peasant-proprietors who also had worked hard to convert the canal colonies into rich agricultural land. Thus both Lyallpur and Montgomery were awarded to Pakistan because Muslims were in a majority in these areas.

An irony inherent in the partition of Punjab was that the Ahmadiya community (half a million in Punjab at that time according to its own estimate) which played a significant role in supporting the claims of the Muslim League to Gurdaspur district — because the founder of their movement was buried in Qadian — came under a cloud in Pakistan soon after independence and its members were finally declared non-Muslims in 1974 by the Pakistan National Assembly. That Qadian remained in India may have been an unintended blessing for them. Sir Muhammad Zafrullah Khan, himself a devout Ahmadi, had waxed eloquent about Islamic tolerance before the Boundary Commission against non-Muslims. All that proved nothing more than empty rhetoric in post-independence Pakistan.[127]

As to who were the main winners in the partition of Punjab, the answer is more difficult to give. The criminal elements —

Hindu, Muslim and Sikh — no doubt made the most of the opportunities which societal breakdown brought. The departure of the Hindus and Sikhs, however, did facilitate the advancement of the intelligentsia and sections of the depressed peasantry and poorer classes in western Punjab while the landlords could continue to enjoy their traditional privileges. In ideological terms the forces of reaction won the day on both sides. In the longer run the predominantly Punjabi army officers and bureaucrats came to dominate Pakistan. Under General Ziaul Haq this trend reached consummation.[128]

Partition of Punjab and Punjabis

The cultural and political impact of the partition of Punjab is difficult to grasp separately from the overall partition of India. The idea that people belonging to different religions cannot live together in the same state was given recognition when partition of India and its provinces of Bengal and Punjab was conceded. A question can be asked in the context of Punjab: Had Hindus and Sikhs stayed behind in Pakistan would that have helped avert its degeneration into a theocratic state? Any answer to this can at best be a reasonable guess, although the presence of a large number of non-Muslims in Pakistan would have confounded the creation of an Islamic state. This was admitted by the arch champion of a theocratic Islamic state in Pakistan, the late Abul Ala Maududi.[129]

It seems reasonable, however, to assume that the Calcutta killings of 16 August 1946 and the communal riots which followed in Noakhali, Bihar and the NWFP created considerable anxiety and fear among Sikhs and Hindus in western Punjab. From early 1947 Punjab had gradually been succumbing to communal violence which after 4 March become more brutal and widespread. In these circumstances the Sikhs demanded the partition of Punjab and were supported readily by Congress.

The long term ramifications of religious nationalism for politics in the subcontinent have definitely not been benign.

Pakistani history has been one of the gradual ascent of religious obscurantism in both constitutional and legal terms. Today not only non-Muslims but also deviant sects and women are denied many fundamental human rights in Pakistan.[130] As for India, religious nationalism became a permanent threat to the democratic secular model it had adopted at the time of independence. On the larger Indian political landscape, Hindu nationalism became a constant factor and the Jana Singh, the Bharatiya Janata Party (BJP) and other extremist organizations appeared as veritable threats to minority communities. In East Punjab, the Sikh claim to a Punjabi *Suba* became suspect and the Hindu nationalists and even Congres tried to stop its establishment. Its creation in 1966 did not mean the end of ethnonationalism and the Khalistan movement became the next stage in this ongoing drama.[131] In West Punjab, the Punjabi language was completely denied official patronage and literacy in Punjabi experienced extreme underdevelopment. It was first in the early 1990s that the speaker of the West Punjab Assembly, Muhammad Hanif Ramay, allowed an MLA to make a speech in Punjabi in the Assembly. The neglect of Punjabi continues to be the consistent policy of all governments in Pakistan.

The secular patriotic cultural identity of Punjab epitomized by Udham Singh — the assassin of the former Punjab Governor, Michael O'Dyer, during whose rule the Jallianwala Bagh massacre took place — who upon being questioned about his name by the British interrogators replied 'Ram Muhammad Singh' was mutilated forever as partition found its consummation in the murder of hapless human beings who suddenly could not find any protection in their Punjabi identity and were killed mercilessly by fanatical communal mobs who only saw them as Hindu, Muslim or Sikh enemies. Some 11 million Punjabi men, women and children fled their ancestral homes and the old Punjab was no more. Rajinder Puri laments this holocaust in the following words:

> After partition the Punjabis disappeared. In West Punjab they became Pakistanis. In East Punjab they became Hindus and Sikhs.

They also became Akalis and Congressmen. Arya Samajists and Jan
Sanghis. Never Punjabis.[132]

NOTES

1. M. A. K. Azad, *India Wins Freedom* (Bombay, Orient Longmans, 1959),
    p. 155.
2. G. D. Khosla, *Stern Reckoning* (Delhi, Oxford University Press, 1989).
3. Satya, M. Rai, *Legislative Politics and the Freedom Struggle in the
    Punjab 1897-1947* (New Delhi, India Council of Historical Research,
    1984), p. 326.
4. Chaudhri Muhammad Ali, *The Emergence of Pakistan* (Lahore, Research
    Society of Pakistan, 1973), pp. 210-21.
5. The Documentation Centre at Lahore first published, *The Partition of the
    Punjab 1947*, in 1983. Later it has been published by Sang-e-Meel
    Publications for Lahore in 1993 in four volumes.
6. *The Partition of the Punjab 1947*, Vol. I, (Lahore, Sang-e-Meel
    Publication, 1993), pp. 1-2.
7. Ibid., pp. 5-6.
8. Ibid, p. 13.
9. *The Partition of the Punjab 1947*, Vol. II., pp. 2-4.
10. Ibid., p. 6.
11. Ibid., p. 21.
12. Ibid.
13. Ibid., p. 24.
14. Ibid., pp. 38-9.
15. Ibid., pp. 46-7.
16. Ibid., p. 34.
17. Ibid., p. 37, 54.
18. Ibid., pp. 37-9.
19. Ibid., p. 38.
20. Ibid., p. 40.
21. Ibid.
22. Ibid., p. 41.
23. Ibid., pp. 41-2.
24. Ibid., p. 45.
25. Ibid., p. 48.
26. Ibid.
27. Ibid., pp. 54-5.
28. Ibid., pp. 49-51.
29. Ibid., p. 55.
30. Ibid., p. 59.

31. Ibid., pp. 51-2.
32. Ibid., pp. 69-72.
33. *The Partition of the Punjab 1947,* Vol. I, pp. 342-3.
34. Ibid., p. 322.
35. *The Partition of the Punjab 1947,* Vol. II, p. 106.
36. Ibid., p. 107.
37. Ibid., p. 108.
38. Ibid., p. 109.
39. Ibid., p. 123.
40. Ibid., p. 125.
41. Ibid., p. 126.
42. Ibid., pp. 132-3.
43. Ibid., p. 133.
44. Ibid., pp. 133-4.
45. Ibid., pp. 138.
46. Ibid., pp. 486-9.
47. *The Partition of the Punjab 1947,* Vol. I, p. 350.
48. *The Partition of the Punjab 1947,* Vol. II, p. 143.
49. Ibid., p. 144.
50. Ibid., p. 146.
51. Ibid.
52. Ibi.d, p. 165.
53. Ibid.
54. Ibid., p. 168-9.
55. Ibid., p. 131.
56. Ibid., p. 175.
57. Ibid.
58. Ibid., p. 180.
59. *The Partition of the Punjab 1947,* Vol. I, p. 396.
60. Ibid., pp. 37-9.
61. *The Partition of the Punjab 1947,* Vol. II, pp. 254-6.
62. Ibid., p. 253.
63. Ibid., p. 256.
64. Ibid., p. 259.
65. Ibid., p. 260-1.
66. Ibid., pp. 292-6.
67. Ibid., pp. 296-8.
68. Ibid., p. 322-3.
69. Ibid., p. 329.
70. Ibid., pp. 332-40, 413.
71. Ibid., pp. 334-7, 341, 344-6.
72. Ibid., pp. 352-5.
73. Ibid., p, 349.
74. Ibid., p. 350.

75. Ibid., pp. 350-1.
76. Ibid., pp. 351-8.
77. Ibid., p. 367.
78. Ibid., p. 379.
79. Ibid., p. 405.
80. Ibid., pp. 410.
81. Ibid., pp. 407-8.
82. Ibid., p. 409-10.
83. Ibid., pp. 415.
84. Ibid., p. 419.
85. *The Partition of the Punjab 1947,* Vol. I, p. 289.
86. Ibid., 289-90.
87. Ibid., 468-75.
88. *The Partition of the Punjab 1947,* Vol. I, p. 297.
89. *The Partition of the Punjab 1947,* Vol. II, pp. 191-202 (all three positions are covered).
90. Ibid., pp. 220-35.
91. Ibid., pp. 240-50.
92. Ibid., p. 245.
93. Ibid., p. 250.
94. Ibid., p. 252.
95. Ibid., p. 434.
96. Ibid.
97. *The Partition of the Punjab 1947,* Vol. III, p. 26.
98. Ibid., p. 10-53.
99. Ibid., p. 53.
100. Ibid., pp. 118-23, 144-7.
101. Ibid., pp. 127-9.
102. Ibid., pp. 133-7.
103. Ibid., pp. 144.
104. Ibid., p. 149.
105. Ibid., p. 223.
106. Ibid., p. 224.
107. Ibid., pp. 224-5.
108. Ibid., p. 225.
109. Ibid.
110. Ibid., p. 227.
111. Ibid., p. 231.
112. Ibid., p. 251.
113. Ibid., p. 163.
114. Ibid., pp. 206-7.
115. Ibid., pp. 207-9.
116. Ibid., pp. 205-6.
117. Ibid., p. 197.

118. Ibid., p. 211.
119. Ibid., p. 282.
120. Ibid., pp. 283-4.
121. Ibid., pp. 286-8.
122. Ibid., pp. 535-6.
123. Muhammad Munir, *From Jinnah to Zia* (Lahore, Vanguard Books Ltd), p. 17.
124. Paul R. Brass, *Language, Religion and Politics in Northern India* (Cambridge, Cambridge University Press, 1974), pp. 319-20.
125. For a detailed treatment about the Radcliffe Award and the controversies surrounding it see Robert G. Wirsing, *India, Punjab, and the Kashmir Dispute* (London, Macmillan, 1994).
126. This type of conspiratorial theories is best represented by Wali Khan, *Facts Are Facts: The Untold Story of India's Partition* (New Delhi, Vikas Publishing House Pvt Ltd).
127. Ishtiaq Ahmed, *The Concept of an Islamic State: An Analysis of the Ideological Controversy in Pakistan* (London, Frances Pinter, 1987).
128. Yunas Samad, 'Pakistan or Punjabistan: Crisis of National Identity' in *International Journal of Punjab Studies,* Vol. No. 1, January-February 1995, pp. 31-41.
129. Muhammad Munir, *From Jinnah to Zia,* pp. 33-4.
130. Ishtiaq Ahmed, *State, Nation and Ethnicity in Contemporary South Asia,* (London and New York: Pinter Publishers, 1996), pp. 176-82.
131. Ibid., pp. 120-36.
131. Rajinder Puri, 'What it's all About?' in Amrik Singh (ed.), *Punjab in Indian Politics: Issues and Trends* (Delhi, Ajanta Books International, 1985), p. 54.

Chapter Five

The Making of a Borderline:
The Radcliffe Award for Bengal

Joya Chatterji

The partition of India is customarily described using surgical
metaphors, as an operation, an amputation, a dismemberment or
a vivisection. By extension, the new borders created in 1947 are
often thought of as incision scars.[1]

At first sight, it seems unremarkable that this surgical imagery
has been so central to the way in which the process of partition
has been represented. It is consistent with the British portrayal of
their position in these events as one of clinical detachment. It
also complements the anthropomorphic conception of the nation-
as-mother that was evoked so often in the Indian nationalist
discourse. From the standpoint of the independent Indian state,
moreover, it is easy to see why it has been convenient to depict
Pakistan as a diseased limb that had to be sacrificed for the
health of the national body-politic.

The surgical analogy is, however, as misleading as it is vivid.
For the deployment of medical phraseology has lent weight to the
impression that partition was a necessary part of a process of
healing: that it was a surgical solution to the communal disease.
Fifty years on, however, it is clear that partition has not cured the
subcontinent of communalism and the idea that partition was a
remedy has been widely challenged. The surgical metaphor
suggests, furthermore, that partition was something that was done
to India: that she was the passive object of the surgeon's knife and
therefore not responsible for the act or its consequences. Recent
research has shown, however, that India's leaders were actively
involved in the partition and their agency and culpability in the
tragic event of 1947 is increasingly coming to be recognized.

But there are other implications of conceiving of partition in this way, some of which have not seriously been questioned. One consequence of the popularity of the surgical metaphor has been the tendency to regard the actual business of drawing the borderline as a technical affair informed by detailed specialist knowledge, just as the work of a surgeon is based upon specialist scientific knowledge. This could hardly contrast more sharply with the facts. Sir Cyril Radcliffe, author of the boundary awards of 17 August, 1947, was a rank outsider to India. He had no background in Indian administration, nor did he have any prior experience of adjudicating disputes of this sort.[2] If his appointment to the position of Chairman of the Boundary Commissions did not generate controversy it was because it was a well-established tradition in British Indian civil administration to confer the most responsible and prestigious jobs upon the 'confident amateur' rather than the 'narrow technician'.[3]

It does not follow from this, however, that the actual business of partition was merely the administrative implementation of a previously-concluded political agreement. The administrators of British India were accustomed to regard themselves as 'agents of justice and effective action, having the fairness and thoroughness to examine facts and the integrity to act upon [their] findings.'[4] Those who 'implemented' partition may have been, in their own eyes, disinterested professionals who simply carried out their orders to the best of their ability, who did their job in the best traditions of the administrative professionalism: rationally, carefully and deliberately, without fear or favour. Yet because they regarded themselves as non-partisan, it will not do to assume that the process by which they partitioned India was apolitical or neutral. Not only does this assumption greatly simplify the relationship between politics and administration, which have never been mutually exclusive domains; it also bolsters the prevailing impression that while politics informed the decision to partition India, politics and politicians had little bearing on the execution of partition. Chronologically speaking, 3 June 1947, the date of Mountbatten's partition plan, is assumed to be a dividing line. Before 3 June, politicians are known to have jockeyed to influence the terms of partition and the transfer of power. After 3 June, the bureaucrats are beleived to have taken over to sort out the administrative technicalities. As a result of this, historians of partition, all of whom have been interested in the political rather than the administrative issues involved, have tended to end their stories with the 3 June plan. Few have ventured beyond this date.

Yet the moment one crosses this Rubicon, the picture that emerges is much more complex. This chapter will set out briefly the stages of the partition process from 3 June until 17 August, 1947, when the Radcliffe Award was published. It will look specifically at the making of the Boundary Commission Award for Bengal, which defined the borderline between West Bengal and East Pakistan. By attempting to tease out the various shifting and competing priorities of those immediately involved, this chapter will reveal how political concerns continued to play as much of a part in the drawing of this borderline as they had ever done at any stage of the partition saga.

The 3 June Statement

Before we begin to look at this process, it is worth recalling that certain significant political choices on the form that partition would take had been written into the 3 June Plan itself. Though apparently leaving the entire question of partition open, the Plan delimited the parameters within which a division could take place. According to the Plan, the Bengal Legislative Assembly was to divide itself into two parts, one consisting of the representative Muslim-majority districts and the other of the Hindu-majority districts. Each assembly was to meet separately to ascertain whether the majority of its members favoured partition. In the event that they did, they were to indicate whether they wished to attach their half of the province to India or to Pakistan.[5] Accordingly, on 20 June, these two provisionally partitioned units met to vote on the question of partition. The majority of representatives of the Hindu majority districts voted in favour of the partition of Bengal, while those of the Muslim-majority districts voted against it.[6] On the basis of this vote, it was taken that the will to partition had been sufficiently established. It was only after this vote that the Boundary Commission was set up to determine the real or final border between the two Bengals.

This procedure, though seemingly uncontentious, had some remarkable features. These become apparent if we consider the process by which the people's will to partition was assumed to have been established. Even if we disregard the fact that members of the voting Assemblies had been elected by a very limited segment of the population, and ignore altogether the more fundamental questions regarding the representativeness of elected representatives, there were significant flaws in the process that was chosen to ascertain their will. The vote that was taken to establish their will to partition had been cast in an Assembly temporarily or notionally divided into two parts. Before the Boundary Commission had given its Award, there was no knowing to what extent these notional units would match the final shape of the two partitioned states. The partition vote was therefore necessarily an imperfect one. Many members of the notional West Bengal Assembly voted for partition without knowing for certain whether their constituencies would continue to be in West Bengal when the Award was finally made. For instance, members from Khulna, a Hindu-majority district that was included in the notional West Bengal, might conceivably have voted differently had they known that Khulna would eventually be awarded to Pakistan. Whether or not such fore-knowledge would have made a difference to the final outcome—the majority in the West Bengal assembly deciding in favour of partition—must remain a matter of conjecture. But it is significant that the procedure for establishing will on a question of such momentous importance was dealt with so summarily.

Yet if we think about it more closely, this is not as surprising as it seems. This entire proceeding was essentially tautological: the election was set up in such a way that its result could not possibly be any different. First the electorate (consisting of members of the assembly) was divided up into two parts in such a way that in one part partitionists were in the majority. Then it was decided on the basis of their majority vote in favour of partition that a majority will for partition had been adequately demonstrated. The procedure, though apparently careless, was in all likelihood deliberately designed to produce the specific result that it did: i.e., to prove the existence of a convincing majority in favour of the partition of Bengal. From Mountbatten's point of view, it was necessary to have such a result because the success of the entire partition plan hinged on the partition of Bengal (and Punjab). This was after all, the condition on which the Congress leadership had given its consent to the plan as a whole. In this sense, the whole exercise of voting was little more than window-dressing designed to create the impression that the representatives of the people of these two provinces had exercised their choice in favour of partition. It was certainly not designed to yield any surprises.[7]

One other notable feature of these arrangements was that the two voting blocs were divided on territorial lines. This is significant because everyone agrees that the basis of the partition was to satisfy a communal demand for autonomy: that its purpose was to ensure, for those who demanded it, a communal right to self-determination. But from the very start of the process of implementing the partition, this principle had to be tempered by a host of other considerations, amongst which territorial questions were paramount. The two voting groups into which the Bengal Assembly was divided were composed of the representatives of territorial rather than communal units: Hindu-majority and Muslim-majority districts respectively. Hindu and Muslim members were not invited to meet separately to determine their collective communal will on what was in its primary form, a communal question. There is little doubt that the result of the voting (Hindus voting aye and Muslims nay) would have been the same. But it is interesting that the option of a communal vote was not raised by any of the parties concerned.

By this stage, therefore, the parties appear to have accepted that communal autonomy was to be realized by the creation of separate territorial sovereignties. There are subtle but significant differences between the notions of communal autonomy and territorial sovereignty. The first emphasizes the rights of the people of a community to self-determination, rights which could in theory be achieved within a single state. The second stresses the bounded space within which a community is sovereign, and could be realized only by a territorial separation.[8] This difference was, we may recall, also the essence of the difference between the Cabinet Mission's Plan A (which provided for a single loose federation with a greater degree of autonomy for its constituent, communally determined units) and its Plan B, which provided for a separate, sovereign (albeit truncated) Pakistan. It is also interesting that no one objected that the package being offered to the members for their approval was in fact the Cabinet Mission's Plan B—which had not been officially accepted by either of the two parties involved. What had been accepted by both parties, albeit grudgingly, was the Cabinet Mission Plan A. Once again, it was crucial to the success of Mountbatten's Plan that this little detail should pass unnoticed. To succed in getting partition through by 15 August (or indeed to get it through at all), Mountbatten had to avoid running up against the requirement that his 3 June Plan be ratified by the All-India Committees of the Congress and the League. To side-step this eventuality, he went along with the Congress Party's effort to pass his 3 June Plan off as a modified version of Plan A. In other words he proceeded as if the support of the political parties for his Plan had already been constitutionally obtained and that the leaders who signed on the dotted line on behalf of their parties actually had the authority to do so.[9] This suggests that Mountbatten shared the fears of the Congress leaders who gave their assent to the Plan that their party was not behind them. Together they colluded to push through a partition that even their own committed followers might conceivably have rejected.[10]

Once it had been thus decided that Bengal was to be divided into two separate states, the focus of attention shifted with extraordinary speed from the question of how communal autonomy could be realized to the issue of how much territory was to be made available to each state. The tension underlying the two issues was not always apparent but nevertheless emerged quite sharply, as we shall see, when the actual process of division began.

The Constitution of the Bengal Boundary Commission

Once the will to partition had been established in this singular fashion, the next step was to set up a Boundary Commission that would draw up the final or 'real' border, on the basis of which power would be transferred to the two dominions.

The establishment of the Commission, though on the face of it uncontroversial, reveals some of the priorities of the key players at this stage of the negotiations for the transfer of power. Jinnah had been in favour of having a commission composed of three 'impartial' non-Indians, appointed on the recommendation of the United Nations.[11] But his proposal had not found favour with the Earl of Listowel, then Secretary of State for India. Listowel was not only worried that 'the Russian and other Slav states [might] create... difficulties'; he was also concerned that an appeal to the UN might 'suggest that we ourselves had proved incapable of transferring power without recourse to that body....'[12] The Congress also opposed Jinnah's proposal, though for different reasons: Nehru feared that going to the UN would cause an unacceptable delay. He suggested instead that 'each Commission should consist of an independent Chairman and four other persons of whom two would be nominated by the League and two by the Congress'; that they should all be 'of high judicial standing' and should elect their own Chairman.[13] Eventually, Mountbatten accepted this proposal, word for word.[14]

The significance of all this lies not only in its demonstration of the extent to which, by this stage, Mountbatten was happy to take his cue from Nehru and the Congress.[15] The fact that the members of the Boundary Commissions were to be nominated by political parties indicates the degree to which party considerations were expected to play a part in the Commission's findings. No one at the time appeared to have any doubt that the work of the commissions was not going to be simply technical. In the circumstances, the fact that the Commissioners were to be judges of the highest standing was neither here nor there.

If the impartiality and professionalism of the Commissioners had already been vitiated by the manner of their appointment, every effort was made to protect the credibility of Sir Cyril Radcliffe, whose name Mountbatten proposed as Chairman jointly of the Bengal and Punjab Boundary Commissions.[16] Perhaps one reason for this was that the Congress party had initially objected to Radcliffe, apparently under the impression that he was a conservative and therefore likely to favour the Muslim League.[17] (Here was another example of the part that party-political bias was expected to play in these events. It is significant that when Radcliffe's appointment was being considered by the Indian leaders, no one objected that he had no knowledge of the Indian problem and no experience of this kind of arbitration.) Mountbatten took pains to ensure that Radcliffe as Chairman 'should not only be, but appear to be, free from official influence'. He insisted, for instance, that Radcliffe should be housed neither in the Governor's residence while at Calcutta nor in the Viceroy's house in Delhi and refused to entertain any petitions on the boundary question before the Award was made.[18]

None of this, however, appears to have had any effect on what one observer described as 'the obstinate popular belief that Radcliffe [would] award as he [Mountbatten] dictates....'[19] And there are reasons to believe, despite all protestations to the contrary,[20] that this belief was not entirely unfounded. Mountbatten did not influence the fine print of the Award, but he undoubtedly inspired some of its broader features. For one thing, it was Mountbatten's idea that Radcliffe should chair both Commissions with the idea that a single chairman would keep the larger picture in mind.[21] No doubt with an eye to enhancing the palatability of the Awards, he went so far as to advise Radcliffe to compensate each party's gains on one border with losses on the other.[22] So although the two Commissions were intended to be

entirely independent, in fact they were not. This brought into play
the prospect of a *quid pro quo* between Bengal and Punjab.

Radcliffe has subsequently insisted that he paid no heed to
Mountbatten's advice and treated each Commission strictly
independently.[23] Nevertheless the parties framed their respective
cases before the Commissions under the impression that the two
Awards would be linked, and that some loose principle of
balance between them would be followed. This certainly
influenced the final contours of both borders.

It is also true that Mountbatten, by and large, left Radcliffe to
interpret his own terms of reference.[24] But the terms themselves
were set out by the Viceroy, who once again saw fit to accept
Nehru's advice on the subject. Nehru was clear that the work of
the Boundary Commission was to be done as quickly as possible,
believing (with characteristic naïveté) that 'when the two States
have been formed, those States will mutually consider
modifications and variations of their frontiers so that a
satisfactory arrangement is reached' and that 'this was likely to
be a fairly lengthy process involving the ascertainment of the
wishes of the people concerned in those areas'.[25] If, he argued,
this was left to the Boundary Commission, its work would be
'heavy and prolonged',[26] making it unlikely that the borders
would be defined by 15 August. In these circumstances, the
transfer of power would either have to be delayed or be carried
out on the basis of the existing notional boundaries. Nehru was
convinced that both these options were unacceptable and that, for
the purpose of transferring power, a makeshift border would do.
Mountbatten (at least on the face of it) argreed with him. So
when Nehru suggested that the Boundary Commission be
instructed only 'to demarcate the boundaries of the two parts of
Bengal on the basis of ascertaining contiguous majority areas of
Muslims and non-Muslims', taking 'into account other factors',[27]
Mountbatten accepted Nehru's proposal to the letter.[28] The fact
that the border was never intended to be anything other than a
rough-and-ready improvisation was impressed upon Radcliffe,[29]
and the result of his labours bore all the marks of the rush job
that it was.

This insistence on speed flew in the face of the administrators' advice. The clearest warning came from Evan Jenkins, Governor of Punjab, a man who was often described as being the best administrator in India. His assessment was that '...in the time available it [would] be quite impossible to make a clean job of partition, and even if... disorder [were checked] upto 15 August... there [would] be appalling confusion [afterwards]...' Making a pointed reference to Mountbatten's ignorance of civilian (as opposed to military) affairs, he stressed that '...in civil administration, certain things cannot be done in a matter of days or weeks, and 'standstill' orders (most of which will be accepted very grudgingly by the Parties) do not really solve the administrative problem....' [30] But his counsel was not heeded by the Viceroy, whose entire strategy for partition appears to have been to rush it through without giving anyone a moment to pause for thought. [31] And the Indian leaders, no doubt tempted by the short-term gains that a speedy settlement seemed to offer, went along with him. [32]

Radcliffe's Awards were ready on 12 August, well in time for the transfer of power in Pakistan on the fourteenth. But in a remarkable last-minute about-turn, Mountbatten suddenly developed cold feet about publishing it. He brought his influence to bear upon Radcliffe, who agreed reluctantly to post-date the Award for the thirteenth, by which time Mountbatten had already left for Karachi, and ultimately the Award was only published on 17 August.

We cannot be certain whether Mountbatten genuinely changed his mind upon realizing late in the day just how unpopular the Award would be, or whether delaying the announcement had been his intention all along. Once again, he ignored administrative advice, this time from the Supreme Commander of the Armed Forces. Auchinleck warned that because it was already widely known that the Award was ready, the delay in announcing it, by allowing 'the wildest rumours' to gain currency, was 'having the most disturbing and harmful effect.' [33] But Mountbatten's concern to protect his Government's image overrode all other factors. As he explained to the British

Government, although 'from the purely administrative point of view there were considerable advantages in immediate publication so that the new boundaries could take effect on 15 August...it had been obvious all along that, the more we postponed publication, the less would the inevitable odium react upon the British...' [34] More personal considerations also appear to have been involved in this decision. By all accounts, Lord Mountbatten was a man who enjoyed pomp and circumstance more than most. So he was particularly anxious that no unpleasantness should mar the transfer of power celebrations in which he would play Viceroy for the last time.

For reasons of this sort, power was transferred on the basis of the notional boundaries after all, and the hurry with which the Radcliffe line was drafted turned out to have been completely (and indeed tragically) unnecessary.

Claims and Counterclaims: Arguments Presented to the Bengal Boundary Commission

Political imperatives of the statesmen in Delhi and London thus profoundly shaped not only the character of the Boundary Commission but also the nature of its Awards and the timing of their announcement. In Calcutta too, the sittings of the Bengal Commission attracted the keenest political interest. The Commission was supposed to arrive at its decision by studying closely the claims and representations put to it by members of the public. But in fact, constraints of time meant that only the petitions presented by the key political parties could be examined with any degree of thoroughness. Also, as we have seen the four presiding judges were party-political appointees, it was only to be expected that their recommendations to the Chairman would be deeply partisan. [35] And because Radcliffe arrived at his Award essentially through evaluating their respective arguments, the claims and counter-claims of the political parties had a direct bearing on the final outcome.

The Bengal Boundary Commission's brief was to 'demarcate the boundaries of the two parts of [the province] on the basis of ascertaining contiguous majority areas of Muslims and non-Muslims' while also taking into account 'other factors.' [36] The cases put before the Boundary Commission by the Muslim League and the Hindu 'Co-ordination Committee' both used this last ambiguously-worded clause to press for the inclusion of territories that could not conceivably have been claimed on the grounds of contiguous majority areas. But there were significant differences of emphasis between the two representations made before the Commission. Within the Hindu Co-ordination Committee, inter-party disagreements broke out on the question of what constituted a reasonable claim. There are also tantalizing hints of schisms within the Congress party's ranks on the question of the shape and size of the new West Bengal. These dissensions throw light on the kind of concerns that were uppermost in the minds of the politicians when they lobbied before the Commission.

One striking feature of both cases was the language in which they were couched. Both cases were written in a highly legalistic, technical style that could not have been more different from the hyperbole of the communal propaganda generated for popular consumption. Both were persuasive and insisted on the reasonableness of their respective demands. Both were backed with reams of 'evidence' and called on 'experts' to validate their arguments. The style in which the arguments were presented (and also much of their substance) calls to mind a property dispute being fought in a court of law. Also the fact that all the commissioners were judges and the Chairman was a lawyer, has bolstered the prevailing impression that the Award and the cases on which it was based were the product of legal expertise, resting on judicial (rather than political) rationality; and by extension that the Commission's rulings met the technical requirements of legal justice. But the picture that emerges from a closer reading of the Commission's deliberations is not so clear-cut.

The 'Muslim' case was the simpler of the two. For one thing, there was just one party involved: only the Muslim League came forward to represent the Muslims before the Commission. The

Bengal Provincial Muslim League was deeply divided by this time and the two main factions, led by Huseyn Shaheed Suhrawardy and Khwaja Nazimuddin respectively, were on the bitterest of terms. But these differences did not affect the Muslim League case before the Commission, because only Nazimuddin's party took any interest in it. It will be recalled that Suhrawardy and Abul Hashim had co-authored a proposal for a united and sovereign Bengal, independent of both India and Pakistan. Having made public their opposition to the partition of Bengal, the two men were not disposed to sit down to work out the details of a division they had rejected.[37] And for obvious reasons, Congress-minded Muslims (such as Ashrafuddin Ahmed Chowdhury), who were staunchly opposed to partition in any form, took no part in the Boundary Commission's proceedings. Nazimuddin's group, on the other hand, supported the creation of single Pakistan: they had opposed the partition of Bengal only because they wanted the whole of the province for Pakistan. Moreover, enjoying the closest ties with Jinnah and the All-India Muslim League, Nazimuddin's group could confidently expect to take charge of East Pakistan after partition and they therefore had the greatest stake in the Commission's proceedings.[38] So at the end of the day, Nazimuddin's party took charge of the 'Muslim' case on its own.

But the 'Muslim' case was also simpler in another sense: it had the single objective of extracting for East Bengal as much territory as possible. In order to achieve this, it insisted on particular principles. The first was that the scope of the term 'contiguity' was to be limited to areas *within* Bengal; i.e., that if a Hindu-majority area was not contiguous to any other Hindu-majority area in Bengal it should go to East Bengal, even if it were contiguous to any other Hindu-majority outside Bengal in the Indian Union. On this basis, the League claimed for East Bengal three districts where Muslims were only a small minority of the population, namely the Chittagong Hill Tracts, Darjeeling and Jalpaiguri. [39]

The next point that the League insisted upon was that the unit of partition should be either the union or the sub-division. As the smallest units of administration, it was argued, they were cohesive and integrated in terms of politics and governance and could not easily be divided. Of the two, it favoured the sub-division, which would, it claimed, yield a straighter border-line. The League's spokesmen urged that the communal majority of each sub-division be worked out and that contiguous Muslim-majority sub-divisions be allotted to East Bengal. Of course there was merit in the argument that administrative and political units (such as unions) might have real advantages as units of partition over *thanas* (or police stations), which were merely criminal jurisdictions. But the point was more that a division based on contiguous majority sub-divisions or even unions would give East Bengal more territory.

In addition, the Muslim League claimed huge territories for East Bengal on the basis of a variety of 'other factors'. The scope of the 'other factors' clause was interpreted most liberally to make a bid for Calcutta. The League insisted that East Bengal must be given a share of the provincial revenue proportionate to its share of Bengal's population, and this could only be achieved if Calcutta went to the East. [40] On these grounds, not only did the League demand for East Bengal the whole of the Calcutta urban agglomeration, it also staked its claim to areas west of Calcutta where jute mills, military installations, ordnance factories, railway workshops and lines were located, on the grounds that these facilities were essential for East Bengal's economy, internal communications and defence. [41]

In effect, the Muslim League was asking for all the territory east of the Hooghly and Bhagirathi rivers. Its representatives knew that this scheme would place roughly two thirds [42] of Hindu population of Bengal in East Pakistan. But they insisted that '...the partition [was] not to be effected on the basis of putting the maximum percentage of any class of population on one side or the other or balancing the populations in the two provinces. The basis is the determination of contiguous majority area....' [43]

Hence in order to claim for East Bengal the greatest possible amount of territory, the Muslim members of the commission were driven to insist that the aim of partition was *not* to ensure self-determination for the largest possible number of each community, apparently reversing the Muslim League's proclaimed objectives. Their reasons for taking this position become clearer if it is borne in mind that the party had opposed the partition of Bengal. It had good reasons for this. Muslims constituted a majority of roughly 55 per cent in Bengal as a whole. If Bengal were not divided, a government elected by the Muslim majority would exercise sovereignty over the entire territory of Bengal. The 1946 elections had proved beyond doubt that this would be a Muslim League government.[44] A partition could only serve to reduce the extent of territory over which the League's sovereignty could extend. Once the partition of Bengal had been accepted in principle, the logical aim for Muslim spokesmen was to limit, as far as possible, the loss of territory and assets to West Bengal. By claiming almost four-fifths of the province, they had nothing to lose and everything to gain.

For the Hindu members of the Commission, however, the position was not so straightforward. The Hindu members of the provisional West Bengal Assembly had voted for partition so as to secure a 'homeland' for the Hindus of Bengal. They had wanted, in other words, to create a separate space within which Hindus, by virtue of their larger numbers, would determine their own future.[45] So it was crucially important to have a homeland with an outright and sizeable Hindu majority. Like their Muslim counterparts, on the other hand, they also wanted enough territory to accommodate the population and sustain a viable economy. The imperative for a communal majority had to be balanced against the requirements of space and economic rationality. How much territory was 'enough'? How far could the communal majority be safely watered down? These were questions with no obvious or determinate answers. Inevitably, there were differences amongst the spokesmen for Hindu interests on what constituted the best possible solution.

These disagreements were accentuated by the fact that four parties jointly presented the Hindu case before the Boundary Commission. In addition to the Congress, the Hindu Mahasabha, the Indian Association and the New Bengal Association[46] were represented on the Central Co-ordination Committee. The barrister Atul Chandra Gupta was appointed by the Congress president J. B. Kripalani as its chairman; he also led the Congress camp on the Committee.

Differences emerged when the four parties put their heads together to formulate the case to be argued before the Commission. The three smaller parties, whose representatives constituted a majority of ten of the twelve-member Co-ordination Committee, insisted that the maximum possible extent of territory must be claimed. In addition to the ten Hindu-majority districts (Burdwan, Midnapore, Birbhum, Bankura, Howrah, Hooghly, 24 Parganas, Khulna, Darjeeling and Jalpaiguri), they demanded that two entire Muslim-majority districts (Malda and Murshidabad), large parts of Nadia, Faridpur and Dinajpur, and selected *thanas* (police stations) in Rangpur and Rajshahi, be given to West Bengal. This would have given West Bengal roughly 57 per cent of the total area of Bengal (less the Chittagong Hill Tracts, which were claimed for the Indian Union but not for West Bengal).[47]

It made sense for the smaller parties such as the Mahasabha and the New Bengal Association, susceptible as they were to pressure from Hindu extremist fringe groups, to put forward this maximum demand. Indeed, even this maximum claim fell far short of what was being demanded by some of their wilder supporters. The Arya Rashtra Sangha, for instance, insisted that as much as four-fifths of the territory of Bengal be made over to West Bengal, on the grounds that four-fifths of all lands were owned by Hindus; that every single town in Bengal should go to the West because over 75 per cent of their population was Hindu, and so on.[48] The New Bengal Association itself was a right-wing pressure group which had come into existence in 1946 as a forum to lobby for the partition of Bengal. Run by a self-styled Major General, it was a front-runner in all subsequent campaigns to demand more Bihari areas for West Bengal.[49] Not much is known about the association or its leaders, but its pamphlets suggest that for 'Major General' A. C. Chatterjee and his cohorts, Hindu Bengalis were a distinct race of people, and that they were of the view that for this people to fulfil its destiny, it was crucial to have enough space.[50] Territory was clearly central to the Association's vision of 'New Bengal'.

The Bengal Provincial Hindu Mahasabha, as a branch of a larger all-India organization, could not advocate patently aggressive Bengali chauvinism of this sort, however much some of its members may have shared the New Bengal Association's world view. But there were other important party-political considerations that pushed the Bengal Mahasabha to make implausible demands for territory. Such inroads as the Bengal branch of the Mahasabha had been able to make in building an organization were chiefly limited to the eastern districts, to Barisal and Dhaka in particular.[51] The party had also worked hard to woo the Scheduled Castes into the Mahasabha fold through *shuddhi* and *sangathan* campaigns in the early forties.[52] The largest and most influential of these castes, the Namasudras, were clustered in the districts of Jessore and Faridpur: this was one persuasive reason for the Mahasabha to demand that these areas be included in West Bengal.[53] In the aftermath of the 1946 elections, in which the Mahasabha had been humbled by the Congress, it was understandably anxious to salvage as much of this base as possible. It also clearly hoped to recover some lost ground by winning the allegiance of Hindu refugees from East Bengal, who had begun to arrive in thousands after the Noakhali riots. So it justified its excessive territorial claims on the grounds that 'the new State of West Bengal should be in a position to provide for the inclusion and accommodation of immigrants from Pakistan'.[54] Though undoubtedly aware that it was very unlikely to succeed in persuading the Boundary Commission that its demands were fair or reasonable, its leaders probably calculated that it could do the party no harm to try. If they failed, as they almost certainly would, they could still claim to have fought for the Hindu cause until the bitter end. If, on the other hand, they succeeded in winning for West Bengal even the smallest piece of extra area (in excess of the Congress demand), they would come out as heroes who had stood up for Hindu rights, in contrast to the weak-kneed moderacy of the Congress.

Atul Chandra Gupta, the lawyer who represented the Congress party, took a very different view of the Hindu case. He was convinced that to put forward this maximum demand, which claimed over 57 per cent of the land for 46 per cent of the population, would be suicidal because 'no one seriously thinks that it will be accepted by the Commission.'[55] It was, he argued, bad legal strategy to argue a case that could so easily be shot down. He held that it was more crucial for the Hindu side to present a patently reasonable case, because it was the Hindu side that had called for partition in the first place. When the other Hindu parties refused to accept this argument, he offered to put two plans forward. The first, called the 'Congress Scheme', outlined the Congress party's maximum demand. Although it called upon 'other factors' to demand a good number of Muslim-majority *thanas,* it still fell considerably short of the Mahasabha's more fantastic claims.[56] The second plan (known as the 'Congress Plan') was a lesser, more plausible claim, drawn up strictly on the basis of contiguous majorities. As Gupta explained, the point of having two plans was tactical: he wanted to demonstrate the shortcomings of the plan to strengthen the larger claims put forward in the Congress Scheme.[57] But the other parties felt that this procedure was so complicated and devious that it was likely to fail, and they voted (by ten votes to two) to include only the maximum demand in the final memorandum. Gupta then threatened to resign from the Committee.[58] At this point, the Congress leadership intervened: Dr Prafulla Ghosh wrote to Kripalani in support of the Chairman's view,[59] Gupta retracted his resignation and the two cases were presented side by side.

Why did the Congress dig in its heels, even to the extent of overruling the majority in the Hindu Co-ordination Committee? At one level, the party was merely following its lawyer's advice on the best strategy (and that it was sound advice was proved subsequently when the Award was made). But would Atul Chandra Gupta's purely technical view of the case have prevailed had there not been good political reasons to support it? Dr Prafulla Ghosh, as Chief-Minister-in-waiting and as leader of the shadow cabinet, was obliged to take a more responsible position than the Hindu opposition.[60] He was also alive to the security implications of the border and was concerned that no demands be made that might jeopardize the safety of Calcutta.[61] But perhaps more importantly, the Congress leadership in Bengal was enjoying its first ever taste of power. Like the all-India Congress leadership, it could see the logic of cutting out potential trouble spots where its writ might be challenged.[62] It could also see clearly that it was inadvisable to include large Muslim-majority areas. From the point of view of those who would take over the reins of the West Bengal government, a compact state with a clear-cut Hindu majority would be the best guarantee for the future. In other words, for Prafullah Ghosh and the Congress establishment, a bird in hand was worth two in the bush.

But there were also different sorts of rumblings within the Congress party. Now that power was at last within reach, it was hard indeed to accept a lesser share in it. Once the decision to partition Bengal had been made, cracks began to surface in the alliance that had led the Jatiya Banga Andolan (or the 'Bengal National Movement' as the Congress described the movement for partition it had led). In May 1947, a pamphlet entitled *The Origin and Progress of the Partition Movement in Bengal* was published by the West Bengal Provincial Committee. The Provincial Committee was a Congress-sponsored body which had been set up in December 1946 at Calcutta with the object of mobilizing support for partition.[63] The pamphlet alleged that in January, 1947 dissensions had emerged within the Committee on the question of the boundaries of the proposed new West Bengal state. The dissidents within the Committee had formed the Jatiya Banga Sangathan Samiti, with Jadabendranath Panja of the Burdwan District Congress Committee as president and Atulya Ghosh, secretary of the Hooghly Congress, as its secretary. This Samiti lobbied for the exclusion of the entire Muslim-majority districts of Nadia, Jessore and Murshidabad, and also of the Hindu-majority districts of Jalpaiguri and Darjeeling in North Bengal. It also opposed plans to demand the inclusion of Bengali speaking areas of Bihar in the new West Bengal state.

This proposal points to the existence, within the Congress Party, of minimalist pressures for the creation of a small and territorially compact state that would include only the districts of south-west and central Bengal. This is significant in itself, particularly as a counterpoint to the wild claims of Mahasabha and other parties, and also to the expansionism of the West Bengal Congress in later years.[64] But it is also revealing to look at the particularities of the plan: at what areas it proposed to include and what it wanted to jettison.

The demand to exclude North Bengal was particularly significant. North Bengal was something of a frontier region, ethnically and culturally distinct from the Bengal heartland.[65] It had long been a political backwater, although in recent years it had been the locus of communist campaigns among share-croppers and plantation labour. But from the economic point of view, North Bengal was enormously important. Darjeeling and Jalpaiguri produced practically all of Bengal's fine teas and were destined to be key revenue earners for the new state. Indeed, so great was the economic potential of these two districts that neighbouring states coveted them for themselves. In September, 1947, there were reports that Assamese politicians were encouraging anti-Bengali movements in North Bengal. In Darjeeling, the Gurkha League demanded independence from West Bengal, allegedly with the backing of Assamese politicians and British tea planters (the latter no doubt could see the advantages of having their estates in the less volatile state of Assam, safe from the communist menace). At the same time the Raja of Cooch-Behar began a campaign against Bengali *bhatias* (outsiders), insisting that the autochthonous Rajbangshi tribals of Jalpaiguri and Cooch-Behar had more in common with their neighbours in Assam than with the Bengali babus.[66] If Cooch-Behar could not be allowed to exist as a separate state, he insisted that it must go to Assam rather than to Bengal. Not long afterwards, when the boundary disputes between West Bengal and Bihar began to gain gound, the police reported secret

meetings between Bihari and Gurkha leaders, at which they
discussed the possibility of Darjeeling's transfer to Bihar.[67] It was
plain to all, therefore, that North Bengal was a glittering prize.
Yet there were Congressmen in West Bengal who would gladly
have thrown it away.

Murshidabad also had a special significance as the site of the
headwaters of the Hooghly. It was generally agreed that the
survival of Hooghly as a port (and of Calcutta as an *entrepot* of
trade) depended on its link with the River Ganges (or the Padma,
as it is known in parts of Bengal), which flowed through the
northern edge of Murshidabad. The representatives of all four
Hindu parties had therefore insisted that Murshidabad be
included in West Bengal, although it was a Muslim-majority
district. There appears to have been an unspoken understanding
that if it came to a trade-off, they were prepared to exchange
Khulna, a large Hindu-majority district to the east of the twenty-
four Parganas, for Murshidabad.[68] So the Jatiya Banga Sangathan
Samiti's case went against the tide of opinion on the Hindu side.
If, moreover, these three districts were sacrificed, it would mean
that the claim to parts of Dinajpur and Malda (and eventually
Cooch Behar) on the ground of contiguity would also have to be
given up. All in all, six districts (Darjeeling, Jalpaiguri, Cooch
Behar, Dinajpur, Malda and Murshidabad) were being written off
in exchange for one: Khulna. Three of the six, Darjeeling,
Jalpaiguri and Cooch Behar) had outright, unequivocal, Hindu
majorities. What imperatives could have prompted this
exceptional demand?

One obvious probability is that Khulna Congressmen were
involved in this move. From their point of view, any economic
losses that the state might have to suffer in the future would be
preferable to the immediate loss of Khulna to Pakistan. But
neither of the office holders of the Samiti was from Khulna, nor
is there any evidence that Khulna men were particularly strongly
represented on the Samiti. So clearly this was not the only
consideration.

It seems very likely that the formation of the Samiti was the
first phase in the process by which territorial factionalism

emerged as a powerful force within the West Bengal Congress. The notorious fractiousness of the Bengal Congress had not been much in evidence during the forties. Once Subhas Bose and his supporters had been expelled from the party, the Congress leadership that took over, had displayed a rare cohesiveness and unity of purpose, particularly during the campaign for the partition of Bengal. But immediately after Independence, groupism re-emerged with a vengeance. For three or four years afterwards, Congressmen in West Bengal would engage in a rancorous contest for the control of the party organization, in which the battle lines were drawn on territorial lines. Partymen from the West Bengal heartland (chiefly Hooghly, Burdwan and Midnapore) would form themselves into an alliance in order to wrest control of the party from the refugee Congressmen from East Bengal who, by virtue of their larger numbers, continued to dominate the organization after partition, despite the fact that they had left their constituencies behind in Pakistan. Atulya Ghosh of Hooghly and Jadabedranath Panja of Burdwan were key players in this battle in which the stake was nothing less than the capture of political power.[69] The involvement of these two men in the Jatiya Banga Sangathan Samiti suggests that the nucleus of the new alliance had begun to crystallize well before 15 August 1947. The move to limit the boundaries of the new state to the West Bengal heartland may well have been a pre-emptive strike by Atulya Ghosh, a man whose foresight and ruthlessness would win him the secretaryship of the West Bengal Congress in 1950. By January 1947, when the Jatiya Banga Sangathan Samiti was formed, it must have been clear to him that while nothing could stop the Congress party from taking office in West Bengal after partition, it was still a matter of opinion which Congressmen would seize power in the divided party. If the state boundaries were drawn so as to include only the districts of the Burdwan and Presidency divisions in the new West Bengal, Congressmen from these districts would have the best chance of controlling the party and the government after partition and independence. Atulya Ghosh and the members of the Sangathan Samiti seem not to have been unduly concerned about the fact that such a partition would involve sacrificing to Pakistan the sizeable Hindu population of six northern districts.

If this is correct it would seem that canny politicians had realized very early on that the Radcliffe line would do much more than demarcating the boundaries between two nations. It would shape the very contours of control and influence in the divided successor states. It would help to define not only the political futures of political parties in the two successor states, but also of the individuals and factions within the parties that would rule them. The disputes between the Congress and the Mahasabha on the boundary question indicate that their leaders could see that the shape of the border would have implications for the future of their respective parties. Within the Congress, equally, at least some partymen seem to have been keenly conscious of the part which the borderline would play in determining who would capture the organization.

The Hindu and Muslim cases presented before the Boundary Commission thus reflected concerns and aspirations that had little to do with a communal vision of the welfare of the 'communities'. In the making of the Radcliffe Award, questions of economic rationality, geographical coherence and strategic necessity were not the only 'other factors' that tempered the fundamental principles of contiguity and communal majority on which partition was supposed to be based. Party-politics, factional goals and personal ambitions were also very much in evidence in the list of issues that influenced the final shape of the border.

To return to the metaphor of the surgical operation, this would suggest that by the time the surgeon began his task, the original problem he had been called in to solve was so overlaid with other secondary factors that it had been all but forgotten; or if not forgotten then certainly pushed far into the background.

Radcliffe's Award

These were some of the pressures and counter-pressures that Radcliffe had to try and balance off against each other while making his Award. He had to appear to be even handed to all sides, while keeping in mind the imperatives of British policy for the future of the subcontinent. Inevitably, his Award would please no one entirely, but there is little doubt that it displeased some people less than others.

The Award gave West Bengal an area of 28,000 square miles, containing a population of 21.19 million people of which nearly 53 lakhs (or 29 per cent) were Muslims. East Bengal got 49,000 square miles for a population of 39.11 millions, of which 29.1 per cent (11.4 millions) were Hindus.[70] West Bengal got 36.36 per cent of the land to accommodate some 35.14 per cent of the people, while East Bengal got 63.6 per cent of the land to accommodate 64.85 per cent of the population.

These figures make it immediately obvious that Radcliffe accepted the two 'cardinal principles' of the Congress case: firstly that the two parts respectively were to contain as large a proportion as possible of the total Muslim and non-Muslim population of Bengal, and secondly that 'the ratio of Muslims in one zone must be as nearly equal as possible to the ratio of non-Muslims to Muslims in the other'.[71] Radcliffe's Award created two states in which the ratio of the majority to the minority population was almost exactly the same.

Radcliffe also conceded the Congress argument that *thanas* as the smallest units for which census figures had been published, were the most acceptable units of partition.[72] He likewise accepted the Congress argument about the importance of the Murshidabad and Nadia river system for the survival of the Hooghly and gave the whole of Murshidabad to West Bengal. Khulna went to Pakistan except for those parts of it that fell to the east of the river Mathabhanga. It goes without saying that Calcutta went to West Bengal. The tea producing districts of Darjeeling and Jalpaiguri also went to West Bengal,[73] with the exception of the five Muslim-majority *thanas* of the Boda-Debiganj-Pachagarh area.[74] In awarding these areas to West Bengal, Radcliffe rejected the first principle of the Muslim League's case: namely that the scope of the term 'contiguity' was to be limited to areas within Bengal.

In its broad principles, therefore, the Radcliffe plan looked remarkably like the Congress scheme. The only major point the Congress did not win was its insistence that the boundary must be continuous.[75] Radcliffe would not allow this, so there were in effect *two* Radcliffe lines.[76] A continuous boundary would have given West Bengal a corridor connecting the two North Bengal districts with the rest of the province: as it was, the two halves were separated from each other by a substantial stretch of foreign, (and for the most part) hostile, territory.[77] This awkward arrangement was not put right until 1956, when the States Reorganization Committee awarded a narrow piece of Bihar to West Bengal.[78]

Nor would Radcliffe allow the principle of contiguity to be compromised too much: so the *thana* of Boalia in Rajshahi, the four *thanas* in Bakarganj and the areas of Faridpur claimed for West Bengal by the Congress, all went to East Bengal. Despite this, Radcliffe's package was very similar, on the whole, to the Congress proposal. The award placed 71 per cent of the Muslim population in East Bengal and 70.8 per cent of the Hindu population in West Bengal. Had the Congress scheme been followed in its entirety, the figures would have been 73 per cent and 70.67 percent respectively.[79]

Why did Radcliffe accept so much of the letter and spirit of the Congress scheme? Was he simply guided by his legal training to accept what was undoubtedly the soundest and best reasoned case? The Award itself, brief and baldly stated as it is, gives no indication of Radcliffe's mind. Moreover, since Radcliffe refused steadfastly to further elaborate upon, supplement or discuss his Awards once they had been made, perhaps we shall never know the reasons for certain.[80] But if it is recalled that Mountbatten had allowed the Congress leadership not only to determine the structure and composition of the Boundary Commission but also to draft their terms of reference, it is not entirely surprising to find that the Commission awarded, to such extent as it did, in the Congress party's favour.

Conclusion

From start to finish, the making of the borderline was shot through with politics. Far from being just a matter of sorting out the technical details, it was a process in which from the word go, legal niceties were ignored and purely administrative imperatives disregarded. Everyone involved at every level of this process, from the plenipotentiaries and statesmen down to district party bosses, is seen to have had political interests at stake in the Radcliffe line.

This is in itself quite unremarkable. More startling is the revelation that their calculations so often had little to do with 'communal' or even 'national' interest. This chapter has shown how quickly the communal and national solidarities that had been invoked so noisily in the run up to the 3 June declaration, dissolved and splintered in its immediate aftermath. The arguments and appeals presented before the Boundary Commission demonstrate, if anything, how rapidly communal cohesion could fall apart on lines of party, territory, faction and personal ambition when it ran into the harsh reality of partition. If the original purpose of partition was indeed (in the case of Bengal) to wrest a separate homeland for the Hindu 'community', it is striking how many Hindus were sacrificed in order to achieve it, and how willingly these sacrifices were made.

This chapter reveals how unwise it is to assume that the political concerns that shaped the partition demand were the same as those that shaped its fulfilment. If demands for communal self-determination were the 'cause' of the 3 June Plan, and the Radcliffe line was its 'effect', it is remarkable how little correspondence there was between the two. If there is a wider lesson to be drawn from this, perhaps it is to remind us that the link between historical causes and their effects are never simple or direct. As this chapter has shown, a few months (from June to August in this case) are indeed a long time in politics; and in practice, the conceptual separation between the formulation of policy (as the job of politicians) and their execution (the task of professional administrators) does not often hold water: policy is seldom implemented in an apolitical or neutral way. Or perhaps we can conclude that there was something about this particular demand—the demand for a separate communal homeland—that was inherently unrealizable: that it was a chimera that was bound to dissolve in the clear light of day when faced with the realities of execution.

NOTES

1. Medical and surgical analogies have been used to describe partition ever since 1947. In fact, Jinnah first spoke of it thus in a meeting with Mountbatten in April 1947: 'It would have to be a surgical operation.' (Mountbatten replied, 'An anaesthetic is required before the operation'.) Alan Campbell-Johnson, *Mission with Mountbatten,* (London, Robert Halea Company 1951), 1985, p. 57. In 1969, Hodson described partition as 'a period of dissection', another variation on the surgical theme. See H.V. Hodson, *The Great Divide: Britain-India-Pakistan,* (London, Hutchinson & Co. 1969) 1993, pp. 322-55. It was also very common to talk of communal violence as 'blood'-letting', another expression that harks back to an earlier era of medicine.

2. Sir (later Viscount) Cyril John Radcliffe (1899-1977) was, by 1938, 'the outstanding figure at the Chancery bar'. His 'meteorical [sic] legal career' was interrupted only by the Second World War, when he joined the Ministry of Information, becoming its director-general in 1941. This had been his only experience of administration when in 1947, he was called upon to chair the boundary commissions in India. Subsequently, however, he chaired so many public enquiries in Britain that one critic was led to comment on 'Government by Radcliffery'! Lord Blake and C.S. Nicholls (ed.), *The Dictionary of National Biography 1971-1980,* (Oxford and New York, OUP 1986), pp. 696-97.

3. In his discussion of the ICS tradition, Potter observes that 'the whole structure of the raj celebrated generalist control and continuity, not specialist expertise and innovation.' He argues that 'the amateur ideal was linked to the older idea of a man of leisure, with the time and ability to engage in a wide variety of pursuits that were unremunerative. The professional, by contrast, was a narrow specialist paid for his technical skills....' See David C. Potter, *India's Political Administrators. From ICS to IAS,* (Delhi, OUP 1996, pp. 34, 74-75.

4. Simon Raven, *The English Gentleman,* (London, 1961), pp. 58-9.

5. 'Statement by His Majesty's Government, dated the 3rd June 1947'. *Partition Proceedings*, I, Government of India Press, New Delhi, 1949, p. 2. (Hereafter *PP*, followed by volume and page numbers).

6. The provisional West Bengal Legislative Assembly voted by 58 votes to 21 that the province should be partitioned and that West Bengal should join the existing Constituent Assembly. At a separate meeting later on the same day, members of the East Bengal Assembly voted against partition by 106 votes to 35. Burrows to Mountbatten, telegram dated 20 June, 1947. Document No. 278, N. Mansergh and P. Moon (eds.), *Constitutional Relations between Britain and India: The Transfer of Power 1942-1947*, (London, HMSO 1970-82), Vol. XI. (Hereafter, *TP* XI, No. 278, and so on.)

7. The other obvious example for this sort of procedure was of course, the famous 'referendum' in the North-west Frontier Provinces, whose findings were accepted as proof of the popular will that the province should join Pakistan, despite the fact that it was boycotted by large sections of the population. Baren Ray has argued that 'British military interests were determined that the NWFP would go to Pakistan in the event of partition, no matter what the results of the elections....' Baren Ray, 'A unique leader of a unique movement: Abdul Ghaffar Khan and the Pakhtun national struggle', NMML Research-in-progress papers, second series, No. LXXIII, May 1993, p. 22.

8. Indeed, it has been argued that it was precisely this ambiguity that Jinnah exploited when he refused to define Pakistan in precise terms. Ayesha Jalal, *The Sole Spokesman. Jinnah, the Muslim League and the demand for Pakistan*, (Cambridge, Cambridge University Press 1985).

9. As Kripalani wrote to Mountbatten, 'any proposal... which might bring about the separation of a part of India.... would normally have to be considered by the All-India Congress Committee. The Working Committee would make its recommendations to that Committee, but the final decision would rest with the All-India Congress Committee, or the full session of the Congress itself. ...[However] in view of... the situation today, we are *willing to accept as a variation of [the Cabinet Mission Plan A] the proposal now being made....*' J. B. Kripalani to Mountbatten, 2 June 1947, *TP* XI, No. 35 (emphasis added). Nehru similarly insisted on describing Mountbatten's 3 June Plan as a *modified version* of Cabinet Mission Plan A. Nehru to Mountbatten, 10 June 1947, *ibid.,* No. 129. Jinnah refused to go along with this bit of casuistry, insisting that the Cabinet Mission Plan had been abandoned, and getting special authorization from his party to accept the 3 June Plan. His objections, however, were ignored. See Liaquat Ali Khan to Mountbatten, 10 June 1947, ibid., No. 127.

10. Indeed, when the plan was finally put before a full session of the Congress, it 'encountered heavy weather' and only went through at all

'because of the stand taken by the leaders'. Krishna Menon to Mountbatten, 14 June 1947, *TP* XI, No. 201.

11. Mountbatten to Listowel, telegram dated 9 June 1947, ibid., No. 120.
12. Listowel to Mountbatten, telegram dated 13 June 1947, ibid., No. 195.
13. Nehru to Mountbatten, 10 June 1947, *ibid.,* No. 128.
14. 'Minutes of the Viceroy's Eighteenth Miscellaneous Meeting', *ibid.,* No. 175.
15. Mountbatten had initially agreed with Jinnah, telling Listowel that personally, he 'could think of no better proposal'. Mountbatten to Listowel, telegram dated 9 June 1947, ibid., No. 120. But he did a volte-face as soon as Nehru made his objections known. No doubt the arrangement recommended by Nehru suited his strategy better: it would give an Indian gloss to the Commission while ensuring that the effective deciding voice would be that of an 'independent' (non-Indian) chairman in whose appointment the Viceroy could confidently expect to have a say.
16. Radcliffe had been recommended to Mountbatten for the job by the Secretary of State 'as a man of high integrity, legal reputation and wide experience: Apart from his great legal abilities, he has just the right personality and acquired during the War administrative experience which would be of great assistance to him....' Listowel to Mountbatten, 13 June 1947, ibid., No. 182.
17. Viceroy's Personal Report No. 10 dated 27 June 1947, ibid., No. 369.
18. Abbott to I. D. Scott, telegram dated 5 July 1947, ibid., No. 529.
19. Major Short to Stafford Cripps, 3 August 1947, ibid., No. 326.
20. See, for instance, Alan Campbell-Johnson's defence of Mountbatten's 'honour' in his *Mission with Mountbatten,* London (1951) 1985, p. 308; and also Hodson, *The Great Divide,* p. 352-5.
21. The suggestion that Radcliffe should chair both commissions first came from Jinnah. Record of meeting between Jinnah and Mountbatten, 23 June 1947, *TP* XI, No. 311. Mountbatten was quick to take it up, explaining that one chairman could usefully make adjustments of losses and gains between the two borders. Meeting of the Special Committee of the Indian Cabinet, 26 June 1947, ibid., No. 354.
22. Hodson, *The Great Divide,* p. 355.
23. Ibid., pp. 354-5.
24. With some notable exceptions: on the question of whether only those districts of Assam contiguous to Sylhet were to be considered for transfer, Mountbatten informally advised Radcliffe in favour of the former interpretation, though he refused to give a ruling on the matter. Abell to Radcliffe, 2 August 1947, *TP* XII, No. 318 (enclosure); No. 326. This drastically limited the scope for the transfer of territories from Assam to East Bengal. It has also been revealed by Christopher Beaumont, who acted as Private Secretary to Radcliffe, that Mountbatten (allegedly under pressure from Nehru) persuaded Radcliffe to change the Punjab borderline

in India's favour, so that Ferozepur *tehsil* was awarded to India instead of Pakistan. Statement by Christopher Beaumont, (1989), Appendix VI, in Ansar Hussain Khan, *The Rediscovery of India. A New Subcontinent,* (London, Sangam 1995).

25. Nehru to Mountbatten, 12 June 1947, *TP* XI, No. 158. This was, incidentally, as close as he or anyone else came to recognizing that the way in which the people's wishes had been ascertained under the terms of the Plan had been far from satisfactory. Nehru himself did not refer again to the need for any further investigations into the people's wishes once the Award had been made.

26. Nehru to Mountbatten, 12 June 1947, ibid, No. 148.

27. Enclosure to ibid.

28. See the 'Announcement by His Excellency the Governor General' dated 30 June 1947, in *PP* VI, pp. 8-9.

29. Hodson, *The Great Divide,* pp. 347-48; Minutes of the Viceroy's 54th Staff Meeting, 8 July 1947, *TP* XI, No. 12.

30. 'Meetings of the Partition Committee', he said, 'resemble a peace Conference with a new war in sight.... The Chairman of the Boundary Commission does not arrive until 14 July. His colleagues have given the Punjab Government an enormous questionnaire, the replies to which cannot be ready before about 20 July. Thereafter, if all the information is to be studied and transferred to special maps and if the parties are to be heard at any length it is difficult to see how the Commission can report by 15 August....' [Punjab] Governor's Appreciation, *TP* XII, enclosure to No. 81.

31. For a more sympathetic assessment of Mountbatten's gameplan, see H.V. Brasted and Carl Bridge, 'The Transfer of Power in South Asia: an historiographical review', *South Asia,* Vol. XVII, No. 1 (1994), pp. 93-114.

32. Commenting on the extreme haste with which the partition plan was settled and then executed, Azad writes, 'Why was there such a hurry in taking a decision which almost everybody regarded as wrong? If the right solution to the Indian problem could not be found by 15 August, why take a wrong decision and then sorrow over it? I had again and again said that it was better to wait until a correct solution was found. I had done my best but my friends and colleagues did not support me. The only explanation I can find for their strange blindness to facts is that anger or despair had clouded their vision. Perhaps also the fixation of a date–15 August acted like a charm and hypnotized them into accepting whatever Mountbatten said....' Maulana Abul Kalam Azad, *India Wins Freedom,* (New Delhi, Orient Longman 1959) 1988, p. 226.

33. Note by Auchinleck dated 15 August 1947 *TP* XII, No. 486.

34. Viceroy's Seventeenth Personal Report, 16 August 1947, ibid., No. 489.

35. See the 'Report of Non-Muslim Members' and the 'Report of Muslim Members', in *PP* VI, pp. 29-70; 71-115.
36. 'Statement by His Majesty's Government, dated the 3rd June 1947', *PP* I, p. 2.
37. Hamidul Huq Chowdhury, who framed the Muslim League's case, thus recalls, 'I did not receive any assistance from... Suhrawardy... [The] group represented by... Suhrawardy was not on talking terms with me or my group... As a result, during... the Boundary Commission I was left entirely to my own resource[s] without any assistance or help from the [Suhrawardy] party. Not for one single day did any member of the party of the Ministry take any interest in the Boundary [Commission] proceedings in Sylhet or Bengal....' Hamidul Huq Chowdhury, *Memoirs,* Dhaka, 1989, pp. 118-19.
38. For more details on the differences within the Bengal Muslim League on the partition issue, see Shila Sen, *Muslim Politics in Bengal, 1937-47,* (New Delhi, Impex India 1976), pp. 203-45.
39. This description of the Muslim League representation before the Bengal Boundary Commission is based on the 'Report of the Muslim Members' before the Bengal Boundary Commission, reproduced in *PP* VI, *Reports of the Members and Awards of the Chairman of the Boundary Commission,* West Bengal Government Press, Alipore, 1950, pp. 71-82.
40. It asserted that 'The total revenue of Bengal is about forty crores [rupees] of which thirteen crores are... contributed by Calcutta alone. If Calcutta goes to West Bengal, the result will be that West Bengal with about one third of the total population of the Province will appropriate 66.9 per cent of the revenue, while East Bengal with two thirds of the population will have at its disposal only 33 per cent of the revenue....' Ibid., p. 81.
41. This very loose reading of the 'other factors' clause contrasted sharply with the case presented by the Muslim League appointed judges in the Punjab, who insisted on the narrowest possible interpretation fo the same clause. See for instance, the report of Mr Justice Muhammad Munir, 6 August 1947, in Kirpal Singh (ed.), *Select Documents on Partition of Punjab 1947. India and Pakistan,* (Delhi, National Book Shop 1991, pp. 419-420.
42. The exact figure was 66.89%. *PP* VI, p. 78.
43. Ibid.
44. The League had won a spectacular victory in the Bengal Assembly elections, polling over two million Muslim votes and capturing 114 out of 121 Muslim Seats. 'Franchise, Elections in Bengal, 1946', File No. L/P&J/8/475, India Office Library and Records.
45. For more details on the Hindu communal campaign for the partition of Bengal in 1947, see Joya Chatterji, *Bengal Divided. Hindu Communalism and Partition, 1932-1947,* (Cambridge, Cambridge University Press 1994).

46. The New Bengal Association was formed towards the end of 1946 to agitate for the partition of Bengal. Government of [West] Bengal, Intelligence Branch (hereafter GB IB) File No. 1009-47.
47. *Memorandum for the Bengal Boundary Commission. Submitted by the Bengal Provincial Hindu Mahasabha and the New Bengal Association.* Dr. S. P. Mookerjee Papers, 1st Instalment, Printed Material, File No. 17 (Serial No. 8), (Nehru Memorial Museum and Library, hereafter NMML).
48. Krishna Kumar Chatterjee, *Arya Rashtra Sangha: Warning,* undated, in AICC Papers, First instalment, File No. CL-14 (D)/1948, NMML (hereafter AICC-I/CL-14(D)/1948, and so on).
49. From September, 1947, the New Bengal Association began a vocal campaign for the amalgamation of Bengali-speaking tracts of Bihar with West Bengal. It circulated several pamphlets which alleged that the Bihar government was systematically ill-treating Bengalis, in which it threatened to undertake 'direct action' if its demands were not fulfilled. 'A brief note on the New Bengal Association', dated 16 December 1948. GB IB File No. 1009/47.
50. There was a distinctly fascist tenor to some of the New Bengal Association's fulminations. See 'A brief note on the 'New Bengal Association', ibid.
51. Writing in August 1945, Asutosh Lahiry, the Secretary of the Bengal Provincial Hindu Mahasabha claimed that there were 1400 branches all over Bengal. Ashutosh Lahiry to Rai Bahadur Surendra Nath Gupta Bhaya, 14 August 1945. Dr S. P. Mookerjee papers, II-IV Instalment, File No. 90/1944-5. His claim cannot be substantiated, but the party's papers indicate that the most dynamic branch was in Barisal, while those in Narayanganj, Dhaka, Sirajganj, Noakhali, Brahmanbaria, Pabna and Chandpur were active.
52. For further details on the Mahasabha's campaign for the allegiance of the Scheduled Castes, see Chatterji, *Bengal Divided,* pp. 195-203.
53. The Mahasabha Memorandum insisted that '...all the Scheduled Caste members from West Bengal had voted for the partition of Bengal and had joined the Hindu campaign for a separate homeland. It is the universal desire of all sections of Scheduled Castes to remain as citizens of the Indian Union. The recognized leaders of the Scheduled Castes have in unequivocal terms demanded their inclusion in the West Bengal Province and declared their unwillingness to join the Pakistan State. For this reason we demand the inclusion of the Sub-Division of Gopalganj which is predominantly a Scheduled Caste area as well as the adjoining territory in the districts of Faridpur and Bakarganj....' *Memorandum for the Boundary Commission submitted by the Bengal Provincial Hindu Mahasabha and the New Bengal Association,* p. 4. Dr S. P. Mookerjee Papers, (NMML) First Instalment, Printed Matter, Serial No. 8, File No. 17/1947.

54. *Ibid.*, p. 2. Indeed, even after the Radcliffe Award was announced, Dr Shyama Prasad Mookerjee continued to insist in Parliament that more East Pakistani areas be seized so as to accommodate the refugees in West Bengal, and the issue remained one of the focal points of Mahasabha campaigns at least until the first general elections in 1952.

55. Atul Chandra Gupta to J. B. Kripalani, 12 July 1947, AICC-I/G-33/19478.

56. So, for instance, while the Mahasabha demanded the whole of Malda (a Muslim-majority district), the Congress scheme did not claim its five eastern *thanas*. Similarly, while the Mahasabha wanted all of Jessore, the Congress asked only for those parts of that district that lay to the west of the River Gorai. In Rajshahi, the Mahasabha asked for three *thanas*, the Congress scheme asked for only one: namely Boalia. See the *Memorandum on the Partition of Bengal Presented on Behalf of the Indian National Congress before the Bengal Boundary Commission* (filed on 17 July, 1947), AICC-I/CL-14(D)/1947-8.

57. As he explained to Kripalani, his purpose was 'to show the defects of the plan to strengthen our argument for adopting the Scheme of Partition... this cannot be done by keeping Plan I up the sleeve and bringing it out only after the attack on the Scheme of Partition by the Muslim League and Muslim commissioners....' Atul Chandra Gupta to J. B. Kripalani, 12 July 1947, AICC-I/G33/1947-8.

58. Ibid.

59. Prafulla Ghosh to J. B. Kripalani, 12 July 1947, AICC-I/G-33/1947-8.

60. He explained to Kripalani, 'I do feel that it would be wrong not to put [the Plan] [forward]. In my humble opinion the Scheme of Partition can never be accepted. So Plan No I should be submitted as a proposal. Unreasonableness of the Scheme of Partition will be apparent and if we do not put this plan before the judges we shall lose our case....' Prafulla Ghosh to Acharya Kripalani, 12 July, 1947, AICC-I/G-33/1947-48.

61. As he pointed out, 'According to Plan No. 1, the boundary of Pakistan will be 40 miles off from Calcutta. If we demand more than that, we shall have to concede that as far as the Pakistan capital is concerned....' Ibid.

62. For similar sorts of reasons, for instance, there were those in the Congress who were not averse to surrendering Kashmir to Pakistan. Sheikh Abdullah clearly believed that Sardar Patel was amongst them. See the Patel-Abdullah correspondence in Durga Das (ed.) *Sardar Patel's Correspondence 1945-1950*, I, Ahmedabad, 1971, pp. 228-45. Also see Prakash Chandra, 'The National Question in Kashmir', *Social Scientist,* 13, 6, (June 1985), p. 50.

63. Hemanta Kumar Sarkar was its General Secretary and Upendranath Banerjee its President. *The Origin and Progress of the Partition Movement in Bengal,* West Bengal Provisional Committee, Calcutta, 1 May 1947. AICC-I/CL-14(D) /1946.

64. For details on the West Bengal Congress party's role in the movement for a greater Bengal, see Marcus Franda, *West Bengal and the Federalizing Process in India,* (Princeton, Princeton University Press 1968).

65. For an excellent ethnography of the area, see Ranajit Das Gupta, *Economy, Soceity and Politics in Bengal: Jalpaiguri 1869-1947,* (Delhi, OUP 1992), pp. 5-26.

66. Secretary, Dacca District National Chamber of Commerce to Prafulla Chandra Ghosh, 5 September, 1947. AICC-I/G-30/1947-8.

67. Superintendent of Police (Intelligence Branch), Darjeeling, to Special Superintendent of Police (Intelligence Branch), West Bengal, 15 July, 1953. GB IB File No. 1034/48.

68. Murshidabad had a Muslim majority of 56.55 per cent. Atul Gupta, in his letter to Kripalani, insisted that this district had to be claimed for West Bengal 'in any event'. Atul Chandra Gupta to J. B. Kripalani, 12 July 1947, AICC-I/ G-33/1947-8.

69. Some details on this struggle within the West Bengal Congress are available in Prasanta Sengupta, *The Congress party in West Bengal. A Study of Factionalism 1947-86,* (Calcutta, 1986).

70. Saroj Chakrabarty, *With Dr. B. C. Roy,* pp. 59-0.

71. See *The Memorandum on the Partition of Bengal Presented on Behalf of the Indian National Congress Case before the Bengal Boundary Commission,* Calcutta, 1947, in AICC-I C.14 (D)/ 1946; and 'Report of the non-Muslim member', *PP* VI, p. 30.

72. *The Memorandum on the partition of Bengal Presented on Behalf of the Indian National Congress Case before the Bengal Boundary Commission,* p. 27.

73. 'The schedule', Sir Cyril Radcliffe's Award, 12 August 1947; in *PP* VI, p. 119.

74. See the telegram from Kaviraj Satish Chandra Lahiry to J. B. Kripalani dated 4 September 1947 in AICC-I/G-33/ 1947-8; and Ranajit Dasgupta, *Economy, Society and Politics in Bengal* pp. 237-9

75. See point number two of the 'Guiding Rules' set out in *The Memorandum on the Partition of Bengal Presented on Behalf of the Indian National Congress Case before the Bengal Boundary Commission.*

76. The first started at the point where the border between Darjeeling and Jalpaiguri districts met the border of Bihar near Tetulia. It worked its way eastwards along the northern borders of Tetulia, Pachagarh and Debiganj, until it met the Cooch Behar border in the northern corner of Debiganj. Darjeeling and the *thanas* of Jalpaiguri to the north of this line went to West Bengal, those to the south of it went to East Bengal. The second line began at the point where the Bihar border met the border between the Haripur and Rajganj *thanas* of Dinajpur. It worked its way south westwards, cutting through Dinajpur until it intersected and Malda until the point where the district boundary between Malda and Murshidabad

met the river Ganges. The line continued along the course of the Ganges along the border between Murshidabad and Nadia, until it met the confluence of the Ganges with the Mathabhanga in the north-eastern corner of Nadia. It followed the Mathabhanga southwards until it touched the *thana* border between Daulatpur and Karimpur, and worked its way through *thanas* of Nadia and Jessore until it met the district boundary between Khulna and the 24 Parganas. It then followed this district boundary unitl the point where it reached the Bay of Bengal. Sir Cyril Radcliffe's Award, 'The Schedule', (Annexure A); in *PP*, VI, pp. 119-20.

77. It would have been difficult to justify giving West Bengal a corridor after Nehru himself had denounced Jinnah's demand for a corridor to link West and East Pakistan as 'fantastic and absurd'. Campbell-Johnson, *Mission with Mountbatten,* p. 94-6.

78. *Report of the States Reorganization Committee,* New Delhi, (Manager of Publications), 1995, pp. 174-80.

79. See the *Memorandum on the Partition of Bengal Presented on Behalf of the Indian National Congress before the Bengal Boundary Commission,* p. 4.

80. Hodson, *The Great Divide,* p. 353.

Chapter Six

Partition, Migration and Assimilation: A Comparative Study of Pakistani Punjab

Mohammad Waseem

This chapter seeks to introduce a comparative analysis to the partition of Punjab which accompanied the emergence of Pakistan. It plans to focus initially on the controversy about the partition plan in Punjab, communal disturbances and the migration. The phenomenon of migration represents one of the most violent processes of ethnic cleansing in recent history. This was effected through a mass movement of Hindus, Sikhs and Muslims across the new international borders dividing the two successor states of British India in 1947. The magnitude and character of cross migration in Punjab differed from its counterpart in Bengal, with the result that the pattern of demographic changes through the process of refugee rehabilitation and ascendancy of migrants in the new state system also differed in the two provinces. In Pakistan, the partition of Punjab turned out to be politically far more significant than the partition of Bengal inasmuch as it determined political attitudes towards India, composition of the governing elite and commitment to the cause of Kashmir. Not only that, the partition of Punjab was far more controversial than that of Bengal. It also grossly differed in magnitude because, in the immediate aftermath of the partition, 73 per cent of migrants from India landed in Punjab while only 9 per cent of them came to East Bengal. The political fallout of the gruesome process of partiton and migration needs to be discussed in terms of the emergent political attitudes of West Punjab *vis-a-vis* India, Islamic solidarity, national security and foreign policy.

While the two partitions provide a basis for a comparative study in terms of their impact on the post-independence politics of Punjab and Bengal respectively as well as on the state of Pakistan in general, another comparative framework is provided by the way the migrant communities in the two provinces of Pakistan, Punjab and Sindh, interacted with their host societies. It is hereby argued that significant differences existed between the two waves of migration in terms of both the internal composition of the migrant community and patterns of its settlement. West Punjab provides a unique example of relative assimilation of more than five million migrants which constituted one-fourth of the population in the province after the process of migration came to an end. This contrasted with the situation in Sindh where it was the non-assimilation of migrants in the local society which represented the dominant pattern. Thus, we plan to focus on the way migrants from East Punjab were relatively integrated in West Punjab within a generation on the one hand and the way their counterparts from elsewhere in India remained generally unassimilated in Sindh.

Finally, we shall argue that West Punjab in Pakistan developed certain modes of political behaviour after 1947 which stood in direct contrast with political developments of East Punjab in India. The partition led to inherently different political processes in the two parts of the divided province. This brings in the question of the status of a province in the political, religious, demographic and economic landscape of a country. While the Pakistani Punjab acquired centre-stage in Pakistan in terms of military, bureaucratic and economic power, the Indian Punjab moved away from the centre and produced a militant Sikh nationalist movement after a generation. The purpose of our enquiry is to locate the origins of political development in West Punjab as it fundamentally differed from its counterpart in India within the larger framework of their respective political systems.

Partition of Punjab: A Legacy of Perceived Injustice

Muslims of India sought to escape their political dilemma as a permanent minority in the face of the expanding majoritarian democracy in British India through partition. Their cherished homeland was to be established on the territory of Muslim majority provinces. The Viceroy Mountbatten announced the partition plan on 3 June 1947 which included the scheme for partition of the two provinces of Punjab and Bengal. Muslims did not want partition of these provinces but Hindus and Sikhs vehemently demanded it. As Mountbatten aptly remarked, the Congress used the same argument for demanding the partition of provinces as the Muslim League used for demanding the partition of India. The idea was that neither Muslims nor Hindus or Sikhs wanted 'to live against their will under a Government in which another community has a majority and the only alternative to coercion is partition.'[1] Not suprisingly the West Punjab Assembly representing Muslim majority districts voted against partition 99 to 27 while the East Punjab assembly representing non-Muslim majority districts voted for it 50 to 22. Similarly, the members of the Bengal Assembly belonging to the Muslim majority districts rejected partition 106 to 35 while their counterparts from Hindu majority districts voted for it 58 to 21. This was followed by the formation of two boundary commissions for Punjab and Bengal.

The Radcliffe Award on the partition of Punjab, which was announced three days after partition, shocked public opinion in Pakistan. Earlier, a 'notional' award was contained within the Second Schedule of the India Independence Act which had actually allocated Muslim majority areas such as the Gurdaspur district to Pakistan. The Award was widely condemned in Pakistan as partisan and 'a deliberate perversity of justice'.[2] It led to a permanent sense of injury in Pakistan at the hands of Lord Mountbatten, Sir Radcliffe as well as the Indian authorities in general who were perceived to have manipulated the Award in their own favour. The Pakistani sense of injustice over the rendering of certain Muslim majority areas to India was compounded by the fact that these areas provided access to the State of Jammu and Kashmir and thus involved issues relating to larger factors operating outside Punjab. It has been suggested that Sir Radcliffe was offered a *fait accompli* by Lord

Mountbatten and his assistant V.P. Menon to announce an award which was more geopolitical than judicious in nature.[3] The fact that India and Pakistan entered into a bitter dispute over Kashmir immediately after partition and that the Radcliffe Award was considered by Pakistanis to be a part of the Indian conspiracy to secure a practicable access to Kashmir points to the extra-local nature of the controversy. Books written on Kashmir typically carry a discussion of the Radcliffe Award and the way it was widely understood in the strategic context of linking India with the Himalayan state.[4] Indeed Kashmir and the defence of Pakistan have been closely linked in the national consciousness of Pakistan.[5] In other words, it was not merely the Punjab question: there was a sense of loss throughout Pakistan attached to the way the partition of Punjab was brought about which was feared to have put the country at a disadvantage *vis-a-vis* its stand on Kashmir.

A major factor which complicated the Punjab scene was the Sikh question. The Sikhs did not constitute a majority in any district of Punjab. Their population did not exceed 14 per cent of the whole of the province. Obviously they stressed 'other factors' such as their substantial role in the agricultural life of the canal colonies and the relatively high ratio of land revenue paid by them, which was 46 per cent in Lahore division alone.[6] Justice Teja Singh, the Sikh representative on the Punjab Boundary Commission stressed 'the necessity of preserving the solidarity and integrity of the Sikh community and the situation of their shrines'.[7] He pointed to the 'special circumstances of Sikh community in the Punjab' which needed to be taken into account in addition to the factor of population as per terms of reference of the Commission.[8] The Sikhs had over the years projected a political profile distinct from the two communities of Hindus and Muslims. They had floated the idea of 'Azad Punjab' in 1942 and Sikhistan in 1944, and later demanded constitutional guarantees for Sikhs in case India was not divided but an independent Sikh state if India was partitioned.[9] It has been suggested that 'the Sikh problem' was always taken into account when Mountbatten communicated with Radcliffe, the Governor

Punjab, Jenkins, and other colleagues on such issues as inclusion of Ferozepur and Zira *tehsils* — which contained a large Sikh minority—in Pakistan, on the postponement of publication of the Radcliffe Award for fear of a hostile reaction from the Sikhs and, interestingly, on the need to show more generosity to Pakistan in Bengal (which had no Sikh problem) than in Punjab.[10] As a consequence, the Punjab Boundary Commission produced an Award which turned out to be extremely controversial as far as Muslims of Punjab and Pakistan were concerned.

The partition of Bengal was far less controversial. Of course, Muslims expressed their grievance over the fact that the Muslim majority district of Murshidabad was not included in Pakistan and that certain parts of other districts such as *Niadia* and Jessore had been transferred to India. On the other hand, the Chittagong Hill Tracts with its predominant Buddhist population was included in Pakistan because the area was completely isolated from West Bengal and depended for its economic survival on East Bengal.[11] Criticism of the Radcliffe Award on partition of Bengal was confined to the unsocial and ugly line of demarcation passing through historically established localities. It was nowhere near the national outcry over the partition of Punjab in terms of the intensity of feelings evoked or in terms of the political significance percieved, for the future.

Apart from the controversy about demarcation, the partition of Punjab involved a high level of organized violence which was unparalleled elsewhere in India, especially Bengal. Violence related to migration as a push factor involving arson, murder and rape. Accounts of vandalism, attacks on trains carrying refugees across the border and of uncivil behaviour of one community against the other reflect partisan views depending on whether the victims were Hindus, Sikhs or Muslims. There is no doubt that all communities were ready to perpetrate violence on their perceived enemies given the opportunity and resources. However what concerns us here is that the level of communal violence in Punjab was much higher than in other provinces of India. About half a million people died within a few months surrounding partition. The pattern of violence in Punjab especially in the

form of attacks on refugee trains was characterized by 'the use of
military tactics', 'the methodical and systematic manner', 'a high
degree of planning and organization' and 'military precision with
one half of the gang providing covering fire while the others
entered the train to kill.'[12] The fact that Punjab was the premier
recruitment area was responsible for a general militarization of
the society. At the beginning of the Second World War, 48 per
cent of the Indian army comprised men from Punjab, meaning
that one out of three able bodied men between the ages of
seventeen and thirty in Punjab and one out of two in Rawalpindi
district belonged to the army.[13] A relatively high level of group
solidarity in a situation of confrontation characterized the
communal strife in Punjab, especially on the side of Sikhs. The
1919 Montagu-Chelmsford Reforms ensured that the 'martial
castes' of Punjab constituted a majority of the electorate in the
recruitment area and, as a consequence, occupied patterns of
leadership in the locality.[14] At the end of the Second World War,
the large demobilized soldiery of Punjab mainly belonging to the
Sikh and Muslim communities perpetrated violence of all kinds
on each other. Many ex-servicemen carried weapons with them
which enhanced their powers to inflict damage on the rival
community because of their professional training in the use of
arms and the recent experience on the war front. Attacks on non-
Muslims in the Attock district were reportedly led by retired
Muslim army officers.[15] The Darbar Sahib Committee based in
Amritsar similarly employed ex-soldiers.[16] It was observed that
Sikhs were generally well-organized in their effort to inflict
maximum damage on the departing Muslims. *Akali jathas* were
organized in many districts. An *Akali Fauj* was also recruited
and organizations like *Shahidi Dal, SGPC Fauji Guard, Tarna
Dal, Buddha Dal, Deshmesh Dal* and *Naujwan Singh Sabha*
mushroomed in an effort to prepare for a civil war.[17] Similarly,
the Muslim National Guards were involved in organized acts of
communal violence.[18] As opposed to this pattern of organized
violence in Punjab, the scene in Bengal was characterized by
sporadic and relatively unplanned violence.

A closely related phenomenon in Punjab was the deep commitment with which religious minorities were harassed and pushed across borders by religious majorities, ostensibly to put an end to religious pluralism. It was this vision of a society based exclusively on one's own religion which led to extreme cases of violence in the province. Indeed, there were revivalist movements among all the three religious communities during the first half of the twentieth century, led by the *Arya Samaj* among Hindus, *Singh Sabha* among Sikhs and *Ahrar* among Muslims. These organizations caused rectification of identities through such movements as *Shuddhi* (purification), *Gurdawara* reform movement and *Tabligh* (proselytization) respectively. However, the Sikh revivalism displayed a quantum of political dynamism which was unrivalled by other communities, not the least because the relatively egalitarian structure of the Sikh community provided a greater scope for collective action.[19] This potential found a vehement expression during the partition when the acute minority situation of Sikhs in both parts of the divided province led them to devise a strategy for consolidating their position in East Punjab.

The ultimate goal of the Sikh community was conceived in terms of the establishment of a Sikh State in Punjab. Not surprisingly, the pattern of organized violence on the Sikh side drew upon a common source of inspiration in the form of what was understood as a project for a federation of Sikh states and districts of Punjab under the leadership of Patiala state.[20] The official view on the Pakistan side was that the August killings of Muslims at the hands of Sikhs were a part of the plan to liquidate the entire Muslim population of East Punjab and bring in Sikhs from West Punjab in order to lay claim for the formation of a Sikh state adjoining the Sikh states of Patiala, Faridkot and others.[21] The Governor of Punjab Sir Evan Jenkins claimed to have noticed a similar commitment among the Muslims of West Punjab, especially in the Rawalpindi division, to exterminate non-Muslims in their districts.[22] This tendency on both sides led to a pattern of total migration of religious minorities, Muslims from East Punjab and Hindus and Sikhs from West Punjab. This

mode of migration differed from the pattern in Bengal where
minority communities continued to live in the shadow of
majority communities even as communal hatred instigated target-
killings on both sides and pushed migrants across the border in
steady waves. The partition had left 42 per cent of the non-
Muslim population of Bengal, i.e., twelve million Hindus on the
Pakistan side.[23] The better-placed Hindus looked towards
Calcutta as a safe haven and continued to migrate to India for a
generation.

Table 1: The Two Partitions

Punjab	Bengal
Controversial	Non-controversial
National tragedy	Local problem
Organized violence	Sporadic violence
Total migration	Selective migration

The determinant potential of the partition of Punjab on the
emerging relations between India and Pakistan cannot be
overstated. The deep sense of injustice among Pakistanis *vis-a-
vis* the Radcliffe Award created a legacy of hatred against India,
especially as it was directly related to the Kashmir dispute. Also,
communal riots surrounding migration created an atmosphere
which made large sections of Muslims deeply suspicious of
Hindus and Sikhs with consequences for constitution-making in
future. It was reflected through the demand for an Islamic
character of the constitution and a provision for separate
electorates for minorities. The difference between the political
attitudes of the Punjabis and Bengalis *vis-a-vis* non-Muslims can
be traced down to the fact that migration in Punjab was total in
character leaving no trace of Hindus or Sikhs, while migration in
Bengal was selective in nature leaving a large Hindu minority in
place.

Punjab: From Migration to Assimilation

West Punjab presents a unique example of the general assimilation of a huge migrant community in the host society within a relatively short period of time. The partition of India was geographically achieved through the two partitions of Punjab and Bengal where a large number of people fled across borders due to communal disturbances. However, the partition of India also had a distinct character of its own whereby whole provinces were included in one country or the other in addition to the two provincial partitions. It was characterized by a slow-moving, selective and voluntary process of migration from various areas other than Punjab and Bengal in India to the province of Sindh in Pakistan. While West Punjab presented a scene of immediate and *en masse* migration as a direct result of breakdown of communal relations, Sindh presented a scenario where migrants continued to come for a generation. Migration in Punjab was directly related to the issue of physical security of Muslims in East Punjab when they found themselves on the wrong side of the border after the announcement of the Radcliffe Award in the midst of communal riots. As opposed to this, migration in Sindh came about essentially due to ideological and political reasons as well as due to the pull of new job opportunities. Not surprisingly the latter developed a perspective on social and political issues which was different from the view of their compatriots in Punjab.

The two cases of Punjab and Sindh represent the two models of assimilation and non-assimilation respectively. The Punjab accommodated 5.3 million refugees, which accounted for 25.6 per cent of its population.[24] Thus every fourth person in West Punjab was a refugee from across the border. Refugees were dispersed in a large number of villages, towns and cities. They profoundly influenced the local population in terms of a heightened sense of insecurity *vis-a-vis* India and the relatively enhanced consciousness about Islam. This process was facilitated by the fact that both migrants and locals shared linguistic and cultural traditions. Almost all refugees in Punjab were Punjabi-speaking while no refugees in Sindh were Sindhi-speaking. Similarly, refugees in Punjab typically belonged to one Punjabi-speaking community, but refugees in Sindh spoke a variety of languages including Urdu, Punjabi, Gujarati and Kutchhi. The place of origin of refugees in India was a significant factor in their prospects of assimilation in the host society. In Punjab, 97.5 per cent refugees came from the north-west zone, comprising essentially East Punjab—which was geographically contiguous with and culturally similar to West Punjab—in addition to Ajmer, Delhi, Rajputana states and Jammu and Kashmir.[25] But, the migrant community of Sindh was totally non-Sindhi in ethnic, linguistic and geographical terms. This represented a radical break with the situation in Punjab. In Sindh (excluding Karachi), out of 5,40,278 refugees, 30 per cent came from East Punjab, 21.7 per cent from UP and 25.6 per cent from Rajputana states along with small pockets from Ajmer, Bombay, Delhi, CP and Bihar.[26] Similarly, out of 6,16,900 refugees in Karachi, 35 per cent came from East Punjab and adjacent areas, 32 per cent from UP and 19 per cent from Bombay and West India, in addition to 8 per cent from the central zone (CP, Central Indian states and Hyderabad state).[27]

It is clear that the largest single ethnic community among refugees in Sindh belonged to East Punjab. Indeed, Punjabis had been coming to Sindh from the 1890s onwards when canal irrigation started in large areas and commercial agriculture flourished in the form of cultivation of cash crops. The completion of the Sukkur Barrage in 1932 led to a new influx of Punjabi peasant proprietors which elicited a hostile reaction from Sindhis.[28] After independence, especially after the One-Unit was formed in 1955, the perceived 'Punjabization' of Sindh was reflected in the allotment of land to civil and military officers, a majority of whom were Punjabis, and through recruitment to jobs along with the establishment of industries.[29] In this way, the Urdu-speaking bureaucracy, the Gujarati-speaking businessmen and the Punjabi-speaking elite farmers, peasants and civil servants together occupied large parts of the social and economic space available in the province. It was not surprising that, while refugees in Punjab had a good chance of assimilation, refugees in Sindh defied integration because of a certain dominant otherness that their linguistic, cultural and historical background encouraged from the local population. In addition, these ethnolinguistic differences were patterned along sectoral lines. *Mohajirs* generally settled in cities while Sindhis over-whelmingly belonged to the rural sector. 63.9 per cent of refugees in Sindh lived in urban areas, 86.16 per cent in Hyderabad district and 71 per cent in Sukkur.[30] In Karachi, there were only 14.28 per cent speakers of Sindhi as opposed to the 58.7 per cent who had Urdu as their mother tongue.[31] Migrants in Punjab settled in both rural and urban areas, but migrants in Sindh emerged as an urban community pitted against rural Sindhis who were overnight relegated to the position of a rural community. The fact that the sources of identity for migrants in Sindh in cultural, linguistic and even sectoral terms were different from those for Sindhis was an obvious deterrent to integration between the two communities.

A crucial factor in the successful integration of migrants with locals in West Punjab was the relative balance of power between the two segments of the society. Migrants from East Punjab had an edge in education and jobs in selective fields over the 'locals' who dominated electoral politics, commercial agriculture in the canal colonies as well as the army. This situation indirectly paved the way for assimilation because no real clash of interests developed along sectoral, class, professional or institutional lines involving a vast number of people in the society. While the host society in West Punjab had a somewhat credible power base of its own which enabled it to compete with refugees, its counter-part in Sindh was no match for the *mohajirs*. The 'ruling' dispensation in Punjab led by the Unionist Party for two decades prior to independence comprised the Muslim Rajput landlords and *sufi pirs* from West Punjab who were also politically ascendant in the Muslim League at the time of partition while East Punjab was typically represented by the *biradris* (small communities) of peasant proprietors.[32] The outgoing Hindu officers and professionals from West Punjab were replaced in many cases by their Muslim counterparts from East Punjab. As opposed to this pattern, the pre-partition exercise in political coalition-building in Sindh presented an extreme case of faction-ridden politics.[33] Here, the migrant elite represented the new state almost to the total exclusion of the Sindhi leadership. It pushed the latter out of Karachi to Hyderabad and turned it into a pawn in the hands of the Centre. Similarly, the most prosperous region of Punjab in terms of commercial agriculture lay in the canal colonies and central districts on the Pakistan side. In contrast, Sindh lacked a progressive peasantry. Because the Urdu- (and Gujarati-) speaking migrants, the *mohajirs,* had overnight begun to dominate the political, administrative and cultural life of Sindh, especially in the capital cities of Karachi and Hyderbad, Sindhis looked at them as land grabbers and imperialists. As opposed to this, refugees in Punjab were too integrated with the host community to project themselves as a distinct social, cultural or sectoral entity.

The migrants in Punjab were settled on agricultural land or urban property in the form of large communities. The official policy focused on preservation of group identity and familial bonds amidst the anarchic situation prevailing at that time. Refugees who came from East Punjab, Delhi and Jammu and Kashmir were largely accommodated in West Punjab districts. Almost half of the refugees from East Punjab, i.e., 26 million, were agriculturists out of whom 22.5 million had already been rehabilitated by July 1948.[34] The government tried to keep whole communities belonging to the same area of origin together in the process of rehabilitation.[35] It is interesting to look at the pattern of refugee rehabilitation across the border. The Government of India also believed that refugees from West Punjab should ultimately settle in East Punjab and their migration to Delhi, UP, and other areas should be discouraged. Only refugees from non-Punjab areas such as Sindh, NWFP and Balochistan were likely to settle in areas to the east of Punjab.[36] Following the policy of settlement of whole communities in specific places, refugees from the canal colony districts of West Punjab were settled in the areas from where they had initially migrated. Similarly, refugees from Lahore *tehsil* settled in Ajnala *tehsil,* those from Sialkot in Gurdaspur, those from Rawalpindi division in parts of Ambala division, and Sikhs were settled in the riverrain area of Ferozepur, Fazilka and so on. On both sides of the border, the governments thought that rehabilitation should be on a communal basis. The idea was that individuals should be safeguarded from the devastating effects of breakdown of support structures such as family, tribe and community.

The scene in Sindh presented a different model. First, unlike West Punjab where the bulk of refugees came from East Punjab, in Sindh refugees came from all over India speaking different languages and representing different cultures. Second, they did not come *en masse.* Instead, their arrival was spread over a quarter of a century. Third, the political and administrative machinery handling the refugees in Punjab was itself dominated by migrants from East Punjab and elsewhere in India. This tremendously facilitated the process of rehabilitation. As opposed to this, the Sindh government which was Sindhi in character had to deal with refugees who were non-Sindhi. Not surprisingly, the two sides were full of mistrust for each other. When the process of refugee rehabilitation started in Sindh, relations between refugees and Sindhis steadily grew tense. The process of their rehabilitation was very complex and traumatic because it involved settlement of migrants in an alien geographic, cultural and social milieu. Indeed, it forced many to go back to India. Karachi blamed the Sindh government for not doing enough for refugees and thus forcing them to return to their places of origin.[37]

A significant part of the rehabilitation process was the provision of jobs and shelter to refugees. In Punjab, claims to evacuee property were filed and disposed of in a relatively smooth way, especially as the governments of India and Pakistan cooperated with each other in the matter of exchange of information about property, leading to allotment of 350,000 acres of evacuee land to the incoming Muslim refugees within a short time.[38] The performance of the two provinces of Punjab and Sindh differed in the matter of the disposal of property claims especially as the distinction of 'agreed' and 'non-agreed' area cropped up for determining the legal status of evacuee property. The areas 'agreed' for disposal of evacuee property belonged basically to West and East Punjab on the two sides of the border. Following the agreement, revenue records of agricultural land were exchanged between the two governments, followed by verification of claims by a Central Record Office. Out of a total of 11,43,102 claims dealt with 95 per cent belonged to Punjab.[39] Refugees from 'agreed areas' were therefore allotted land on permanent basis. This pattern of handling the claims to evacuee property led to the emergence of refugees as a more or less propertied class, especially in cities where they assumed a relatively middle class status. Having passed through the bloodbath of migration which enhanced their sense of insecurity, Islamic identity and dependence on armed forces, these migrants generally behaved as a constituency for martial law governments, or as a lobby for right-wing parties in pursuit of anti-India and Pan-Islamic policies.[40] On the other hand, refugees in Sindh who hailed from 'non-agreed areas' were allotted land only on a temporary basis and on a smaller scale. This led to gross misgivings among *mohajirs* of Sindh. This issue resurfaced thirty years later from the platform of the *mohajir* ethnic party MQM, (Mohajir Qaumi Movement) which projected it as one of the gross injustices done to *mohajirs* in Sindh.[41] The process of refugee rehabilitation in Karachi and Sindh generally remained far from satisfactory. Even in 1954, seven years after partition, no less than 2,40,000 out of a total of 7,50,000 refugees in Karachi were still to be rehabilitated.[42] While in Punjab, immigration had virtually stopped in 1948, in Sindh it continued even after the passport and visa system was introduced for travel between India and Pakistan.

Table 2: Patterns of Refugee Rehabilitation

Punjab situation	Sindh situation
Settlement: smooth; quick (90% by July 1948)	Settlement: Problematic; delayed (30% unsettled by 1954);
No returnees	Refugees returning to India
Refugees spread over Punjab	Refugees concentrated in Karachi
Permanent allotment	Temporary allotment

The trauma of migration in Punjab had involved sacrifices of life and property and therefore a relatively enhanced consciousness about national security. It meant that the settlers generally deified the state and depended on religious sources of identity and inspiration, especially against the perceived bellicosity of India. In political terms, they tended to dislike what they considered selfish, corrupt and parochial politicians and acted as a support base for military intervention in politics. Alternatively, they preferred a presidential system over the parliamentary system as it symbolized the unity of authority. Migrants' political attitudes carried extra weight because of their presence in cities in large numbers. For example, Lahore city was 43 per cent migrant, Multan 49 per cent, Gujranwala 50 per cent, Jhang 65 per cent and both Faisalabad and Sargodha 69 per cent.[43] The fact that migrants in Punjab were increasingly assimilated in the wider society made their influence indistinct and relatively diffuse. Their attitudes were gradually identified with the whole of Punjab, not the least because of the locals' own recent experience of the bloody Hindu-Muslim riots. Also, northern Punjab was the traditional recruitment area for the army which had been recently deployed along the border area in Punjab for evacuation of Muslim refugees from India as well as along the cease-fire line in Kashmir where it fought with Indian forces alongside the mujahideen. All this meant that there was no major difference in political attitudes of locals and migrants in Punjab. The pattern in Sindh was different. Here, the *mohajir* attitudes which were characterized by a rampant anti-Indianism and commitment to centralization of authority, were resented by Sindhis who took an opposite stand on such issues as provincial autonomy, political role of the army, Islamization and foreign policy orientations especially towards India. In other words, assimilation in Punjab did not mean only that the potential sources of conflict between locals and migrants were rendered ineffective. It actually led to consolidation of certain political attitudes which spread all around because of the absence of conflict between the two segments of the population.

Punjab: Pattern of Domination

We have observed that the partition of Punjab led to the emergence of a wholly Muslim society in the western part. The bulk of East Punjabi refugees had been settled on land and in cities within a year. Their claims to property had been settled with the help of exchange of revenue records with India, although many were able to amass wealth on the basis of fake claims supported by the refugee elements in the bureaucracy. It has been observed that 75 per cent of the urban immovable property in the Pakistan areas belonged to Hindus in pre-partition days.[44] A large beneficiary of this pattern of allotment was the relatively enterprising section of migrants from Jullundar, Amritsar, Ludhiana, Ambala, Hoshiarpur, Gurdaspur and other cities of East Punjab where the relatively prosperous Hindu professional and commercial classes had evacuated their own property. In operational terms, they were able to start new businesses, expand the transactional network of commercial activity and install industry with the help of the development-oriented ruling elite of Pakistan.

Punjab emerged as the largest province of West Pakistan with a population more than that of all other provinces of that wing combined. As long as East Bengal was part of Pakistan, its overwhelming demographic weight at 55 per cent shaped the political attitudes of Punjab which accounted for a mere 38 per cent. These attitudes were characterized by the commitment to One-Unit comprising the whole of West Pakistan — the inter-wing party thus denying the numerical advantage to East Pakistan; reliance on Punjabi-dominated army for overt or covert operations in the civilian field; and, a focus on Islamic ideology as the principle of national integration largely at the expense of the principle of equitable distribution of wealth between provinces. After the emergence of Bangladesh, the logic of numbers favoured Punjab, and electoral democracy no more threatened its preponderant representation in the elite structure. During the 1970s, a 'leftist' party PPP (Pakistan People's Party) came to power which soon became an irritant for the elite and was dismissed from office after the controversial 1977 elections. Later Zia's martial law government indirectly caused de-radicalization of that party because now it had to adjust to the 'rightist' thinking of the military-bureaucratic establishment in order to continue to be in the field as a legitimate contender for power. The subsequent political developments in Pakistan led to the emergence of the *de facto* two-party model because the Zia government had also put together most of the anti-Bhutto elements, especially from Punjab, in the form of a revived and refurbished Muslim League. Not surprisingly, Pakistan has experienced five general elections during the last eleven years, and the process of democratization is well on its way despite acute problems of governance. Some writers explain the 'predicaments' of democracy in Pakistan as the upshot of Bhutto's 'open violation of Muslim religious sensibilities', coupled with the resurgence of Islam from the platform of the League-dominated IJI.[45] This, however, does not seem to be the actual case. The problems of governance in Pakistan relate essentially to the way the restoration to democracy in 1985 was effected through an institutionalized form of patronage extended to local influence-holders who got elected in the non-party elections. This bypassed the need for policy and accountability. The relative political instability in the form of successive dismissals of elected governments in 1988, 1990, 1993 and 1996 can be explained with reference to the extreme polarization between the pro-Bhutto and pro-Zia elements with its epicentre in Punjab. The simple political dichotomy has been convoluted by the diarchal split of constitutional powers between the president and the prime minister as per the Eighth Amendment.[46]

West Punjab enjoys a pivotal position in post-independence Pakistan. Some wonder if the country should be called Punjabistan.[47] As a self-conscious heartland of the country, it functions as the power base of Pakistan. Initially, the patterns of migration and settlement of refugees in various Punjab districts had led to emergence of various lines of conflict. For example, when the Hindus and Sikhs emigrated, their urban and rural property was selectively occupied by the more 'enterprising' sections among neighbours. However, soon the government allotted evacuee property to the incoming refugees from India. The local occupants of the evacuee property who were thus forced to vacate it for the latter in many cases developed antipathy towards them.[48] It was not uncommon to see the local-*mohajir* conflict in various localities. The large settler-communities in Sargodha, Lyallpur (now Faisalabad), Multan, Jhang and Sialkot districts as well as the Bahawalpur state evoked resentment among the local population once the sympathetic excitement of helping the calamity-ridden refugees was over. However, the two sides were internally too differentiated in tribal, caste and sectarian terms and externally too open-ended to operate as distinct communities, especially in the absence of separate sources of identity such as language, history and culture. The only area where linguistic differences could have triggered such a reaction was south-western Punjab. Here, an incipient Siraiki movement emerged first as a move to make the erstwhile Bahawalpur state a province and then as a campaign to create a Siraiki province with its epicentre at Multan. The Siraiki activists took umbrage at the allotment of 6,00,000 acres of local land to non-Siraikis, at the neglect of Siraiki-speaking people in the quota system and at the hurdles put in the growth of a Siraiki culture through the print and electronic media.[49] However, the movement has not taken off despite the presence of half a dozen political parties and groups pursuing this agenda. Indeed, the local elite seeks to operate at the full provincial level and does not want to limit itself to the 'poorer' regions of Punjab. Also, the status of Siraiki as a language separate from Punjabi as claimed by its protagonists remains controversial and both scholarly and political opinion consider it a Punjabi dialect.[50] Therefore, it can be safely maintained that there have been no internal challenges threatening to divide the present make-up of the province.

The Punjabis in Pakistan have generally developed a strong outward-orientation in terms of identifying themselves with larger entities both present and past. For example, they have all along felt nostalgic about the Delhi-based Moghul imperium of the past, upheld the cause of Urdu and operated along concentric identities of Punjab, Pakistan and the Muslim world. Other communities of Pakistan, including the Sindhis, Balochis and ironically, *mohajirs*—who largely shared political attitudes of the Punjabis till the emergence of the MQM in 1984—have often challenged the pre-eminent position of Punjab and sought to carve out a political space for themselves through pressure, bargaining and occasionally through armed struggle. Out of the lands in Sindh brought under irrigation by the Ghulam Mohammad Barrage, 0.87 million out of 1.48 million acres were allotted to the serving and retired civil and military officers, a vast majority of whom belonged to Punjab.[51] Not surprisingly, the Sindhi nationalists consider the Punjabis as grabbers of vast agricultural lands along river Indus and accuse them of expansionist designs. The MQM leadership also accused Punjab of pursuing plans to turn Karachi into its satellite.[52]

The language situation in Punjab has directly contributed to disaffection between the Punjabis and other ethnic communities of Pakistan. When the British annexed Punjab in 1849, Urdu, not Punjabi, was declared the language of administration and education in the province. Thus, Urdu emerged as a language of literacy in Punjab, whereas Punjabi was never taught even at the primary level. Later, as the language of Muslim nationalism in

British India in the twentieth century, Urdu served as a potent symbol of Indo-Muslim civilization second only to Islam in political importance. At the same time, the proximity between Punjabi and the Sikh revivalist movement pushed Muslims away from their ethnic and regional identity as Punjabis. The 'soft' boundaries between Urdu and Punjabi further helped blur the Punjabi identity.[53] Various Punjabi revivalist groups such as *Dulla Bhatti* Academy, Punjabi *Majlis* and *Khaddar posh* Trust continue to exert pressure in favour of restoring Punjabi to its rightful place.[54] However, with Urdu as the language of literacy in Punjab, an absolute majority of the literate people in that province are cut off from the written shape of their language. This has converted Punjabis into linguistic agnostics. They are generally impervious to the language-based demands of other communities and consider linguistic identities as inherently centrifugal. The articulate sections of the Punjabis tend to identify themselves with Urdu rather than Punjabi. They define the Urdu-based Pakistani nationalism as the real legacy of the Two-Nation Theory and the source of their political identity. However, it is true that commitment to Urdu is more symbolic than real, since an absolute majority of Punjabis continues to express itself in its mother tongue. In fact, the lack of perceived linguistic boundaries in the absence of written Punjabi has indirectly helped expand the Punjabi vision and ambitions beyond ethnic realities. The expanding world of the Punjabis can be contrasted with the contracting world of Urdu-speaking *mohajirs*. The latter previously operated in the circuit of jobs and socio-cultural activity encompassing large areas of the non-Urdu speaking population in Pakistan. However, they have been obliged to fall back on their linguistic identity as a security mechanism against the perceived dominance of the Punjabis in economic, political and cultural fields.

East Punjab represents the antithesis of all that West Punjab symbolizes. It is marginal, not central, to the state of India, with a population not exceeding two per cent and a territory reduced to one-fifth of what was once the mighty province of Punjab in British India, after separation of Haryana and Himachal Pradesh.

The obvious gain of the migration for the Akali Movement was the concentration of the Sikh community in the north-western districts of East Punjab which could provide it with a demographic support base. However, the more the Akali Dal focused on the demand for a separate Punjabi province, the more the Hindu communal organizations such as the Jana Singh and Hindu Mahasabha grew hostile and the greater became the inter-communal divide.[55] Thus, unlike the West Punjab scenario where communal divisions had disappeared after the migration, East Punjab was given to bipolarity immersed in communal hostility. The two traditions of the pro-Centre Congressite politics and the Sikh revivalist Akali Dal politics competed for influence. In the face of the former's domination over the state politics for a quarter of a century the latter resorted to upholding the cause of state autonomy culminating in the form of the Anandpur Sahib Resolution in 1974. What followed was a further sharpening of the divide between the two communities.[56] It has been suggested that the green revolution led to economic competition between the two communities and alienated the educated unemployed among the Sikh youth who formed the All-India Sikh Students Federation (AISSF).[57] One is reminded of the All Pakistan Mohajir Students Organization (APMSO) which drew upon the alienated *mohajir* youth of Karachi for its support and which similarly embraced political violence as a strategy in pursuit of nationalist goals. The East Punjab situation deteriorated from the early 1980s, punctuated by the June 1984 Operation Bluestar. The assasination of Indira Gandhi was followed by the anti-Sikh riots and a series of repressive counterinsurgency measures. There is more to the nationalist movement of Sikhs in the 1980s and 1990s than what is described as the failure of democratic governance, which is supposed to have channelled the potential volatility of the participant group into constructive behaviour.[58] The Sikh movement failed to de-legitimize the federal government in Delhi which crushed it in a low intensity war, although at the cost of the militarization of Punjab.[59] From East Punjab's perspective, India represents an ethnic democracy because it upholds 'a form of pan-Indian ethnicity' represented by Hindusim.[60] Nostalgia for Lahore-based Sikh rule in the late eighteenth and early nineteenth centuries generally characterizes East Punjab's assertion of identity which is incommensurate with the prevalent political and ideological realities of India as well as demographic and sectoral realities of East Punjab. As opposed to the linguistic agnosticism of West Punjab, it is the Punjabi-based linguistic nationalism which represents the Sikhs' vision and their political aspirations. The Sikhs of East Punjab tend to operate in multiple identities — Sikh, Punjabi, Indian, which are often conflicting and even at the best of times hardly as harmoniously integrated as in West Punjab. Some Sikh leaders are essentially committed to the abolition or at least, reduction of central government control as opposed to the unitarian tendency of the strident West Punjabi political opinion.

Table 3: Punjab: East and West

West Punjab	East Punjab
Heartland	Rimland
Unity of community	Bipolarity
Linguistic agnosticism	Linguistic nationalism
Concentric identities	Conflicting identities
Centralist/Unitarian	Provincialist/separatist

It is interesting to see how certain communities in India and Pakistan reversed their ethnic profile after cross-migration at the time of the partition. West Punjab continues to be the least ethnically conscious province of Pakistan, whereas East Punjab witnessed a fierce Sikh Ethno-Nationalist movement in India during the 1980s and 1990s. Similarly, ethnic consciousness is least developed in the UP in India, whereas *mohajirs*, a majority of whom belong to the UP, have developed a militant ethnic movement in Pakistan. We can argue that a community defines its ethnic profile in terms of its position *vis-a-vis* the state as well as such vital sources of identity and legitimacy as language, geography and demography. Identification with a perceived All-Pakistan lingua franca, Urdu, has cut across ethnic boundaries in West Punjab. Similarly, Hindi in India does not serve the nationalist purposes of its home state UP and has a constituency effectively spread over the Hindi belt and somewhat thinly spread over the rest of India. In geographical terms, the UP in India and Punjab in Pakistan have a self-image of being the heartland of India and Pakistan respectively, while Sikhs in East Punjab and *mohajirs* in Sindh feel that they have been pushed to the periphery.

We have observed that the primordialist logic about the relatively permanent sources of ethnic movements does not hold ground in the face of the rapidly changing political attitudes of communities. On the other hand, the circumstantialist or instrumentalist logic tends to concentrate on voluntarist aspects, especially in terms of the policies of the ruling elite. It is argued that large-scale phenomena such as the Hindu-Muslim dichotomy impinge on more specific and local conflicts where they bring about changes along the potential lines of division within and between communities. The shape of politics in a community is finally determined by its location in the changing matrix of power in social, economic, cultural and administrative fields of public activity.

NOTES

1. Viscount Mountbatten's broadcast on the All-India Radio, 3 June 1947, National Documentation Centre (NDC), *The Partition of the Punjab 1947: A Compilation of Official Documents,* Vol. I, (Sang-e-Meel Publications, Lahore, 1993), 1-2.
2. *The Pakistan Times,* 19 August 1947.
3. For a discussion of the controversial nature of the Radcliffe Award, see Alastair Lamb, *Birth of a Tragedy.,* (Oxford University Press, Karachi, 1994), 37-40.
4. See for example, Victoria Schofield, *Kashmir in the Crossfire,* (I.B. Tauris, London, 1996), 125-30; and Mushtaqur Rehman, *Divided Kashmir,* (Lynne Rienner, Boulder, London, 1996), 57-60.

5. Hasan Askari Rizvi, *Military and Politics in Pakistan,* (Progressive Publishers, Lahore 1986), 39.
6. Mushtaqur Rehman, *Divided Kashmir,* 56.
7. NDC, *The partition of the Punjab,* Vol. III, 230.
8. Ibid., 231.
9. Gurharpal Singh, *Communism in Punjab,* (Ajanta, Delhi, 1994), 90-1.
10. Mosarrat Sohail, *Partition and Anglo-Pakistan Relations 1947-51,* (Vanguard, Lahore 1991), 72-4.
11. Ibid.
12. Swarna Aiyer, 'August Anarchy: The Partition Massacres in Punjab 1947', *South Asia,* Special issue, xviii, 1995, 23-4.
13 Ibid., 28.
14 Clive Dewey, 'The Rural Roots of Pakistani Militarism' in D. A. Low (ed.), *The Political Inheritance of Pakistan,* (Macmillan, London, 1991), 265.
15 Sir E. Jenkins to Lord Wavell, 17 March 1947, OIOC Cat No R/3/1/176, NDC, *Disturbances in the Punjab 1947,* henceforth DIP, (Islamabad, 1995), 100.
16. Punjab Police Abstract of Intelligence for the week ending 22 March, 1947, NDC Accession No S 415, DIP, 107.
17. Punjab Police Abstract of Intelligence for the week ending 29 March 1947, NDC Accession No S. 415, DIP, 113.
18. S. Gurbachan Singh Talib, *Muslim League Attack on Sikhs and Hindus in the Punjab 1947,* (*Voice of India*, New Delhi, 1991) Reprint, 20
19. Ian Talbot and D. S. Tatla, (eds) *Punjab* (World Bibliographical series, Clio Press, Oxford, 1992, xxi.
20. Note by E. Jenkins, 9 April 1947, OIOC Cat. No. R/3/1/19, NDC MFU Accession No. 34, DIP, 136.
21. Message from Prime Minister of Pakistan to Prime Minister of United Kingdom dated 10 September 1947; FO 371/65574.
22. Sir Jenkins to Lord Wavell, NDC, DIP, 101.
23 Gyanesh Kudaisya, 'Demographic Upheaval of Partition: Refugees and Agricultural Resettlement in India 1947-67', *South Asia,* Special issue, 86.
24. *Census of Pakistan 1951,* Karachi Vol 1, Table 19-A; Vol. 6, 65.
25. Ibid. Vol. I, 30, 5-1.
26. Ibid. Vol. 6, Statement 6-B, 65.
27. Ibid. Vol. 1, Sttement 2-E, 31.
28. Sarah Ansari, 'Punjabis in Sind: Identity and Powers, in Gurharpal Singh and Ian Talbot (eds), *Punjabi Identity: Continuity and Change,* (Manohar, Delhi, 1996), 93-7.
29. Ibid. 100-102.
30. Ibid. Vol. 6, Statement 3-R, 36.
31. Ibid. Vol. I, Statement 5-C, 87.

32. Ian Talbot, 'The Unionst Party and Punjab Politics 1937-1947', in D.A. Low ed., *The Political Inheritance of Pakistan*, 88.
33. Ayesha Jalal, *The Sole Spokesman*, Cambridge, 1985, 110-13.
34. R.F. Mudie Governor West Punjab, 'A Note on Rehabilitation of Refugees', NDC, *The Journey to Pakistan*, (Islamabad, 1993), 78-9.
35. Ibid.
36. *Statesman*, 18 September 1947.
37. *Constituent Assembly of Pakistan Debates*, 20 May 1948, 713.
38. Ayesha Jalal, *The State of Martial Rule*, (Vanguard, Lahore, 1991), 79.
39. *Constituent Assembly of Pakistan Debates*, 12 March 1953, 48.
40. Mohammad Waseem, *Politics and the State in Pakistan*, (Islamabad, National Institute of Historical and Cultural Rsearch 1994), 110-11.
41. For a profile on the MQM, see Feroz Ahmed, 'The Rise of Mohajir Separatism in Pakistan', *Pakistan Progressive*, 10, 2/3, Summer/Fall 1989
42. *Constituent Assembly of Pakistan Debates*, 23 March 1954, 405
43. *Census of Pakistan 1951*, vol. I, 44.
44. C. N. Vakil, *Economic Consequences of Divided India*, (Bombay, 1950), 13.
45. Seyyed Vali Reza Nasr, 'Democracy and the Crisis of Governability in Pakistan', *Asian Survey*, xxxii, 6, 1992, 524.
46. Mohammad Waseem, 'Pakistan's Lingering Crisis of Dyarchy', *Asian Survey*, July 1992, 622-30.
47. Yunas Samad, 'Pakistan or Punjabistan: Crisis of National Identity', in Gurharpal Singh and Ian Talbot (eds), *Punjabi Identity*, 61-87.
48. For a discussion of such conflicts, see Ayesha Jalal, *State of Martial Rule*, 79.
49. Tariq Rahman, 'The Siraiki Movement in Pakistan', *Language Problems and Language Planning*, Vol. 19, 1, 1995, 19.
50. Ibid. 16-17.
51. Abbas Rashid and Farida Shaheed, *Pakistan: Ethno-Politics and Contending Elites*, UNESCO Discussion Paper 45, 1993, 16.
52. *Dawn*, 12 March 1995.
53. Sabiha Mansoor, *Punjabi, Urdu, English in Pakistan*, (Vanguard, Lahore, 1993), 16.
54. Ibid. 27.
55. Ian Talbot and D. S. Tatla, (eds), *Punjab*, xxx.
56. Ibid. xxxi.
57. Ibid.
58. Ajay K. Mehra, 'Ethnicity, Democratization and Governance: The Case of India', *Ethnic Studies Report*, Colombo, July 1993, 230.
59. Shinder Singh Thandi, 'Fighting Sikh Militancy: Counter-insurgency Operation in Punjab', in Iain Hampsher-Monk and Jeffrey Stanyer (eds), *Contemporary Political Studies 1996*, (Belfast, 1996), 550-4.
60. Gurharpal Singh, 'The Punjab Crisis Since 1984: A Reassessment', *Ethnic and Racial Studies*, July 1995, 481.

Chapter Seven

Literature and the Human Drama
of the 1947 Partition

Ian Talbot

Independence brought forth a bitter harvest in the North Indian region of Punjab. The grim reaper claimed hundreds of thousands of lives, while a further ten million people were uprooted from their ancestral homes. The partition related massacres and migrations represented an unfolding human tragedy of enormous proportions. Nevertheless, historical studies have tended to focus on the causes of partition rather than its impact.[1] Sustained treatment of its consequences has largely been limited to accounts whose main purpose is to apportion blame for the related massacres.[2] In this great human event, human voices are strangely silent.[3]

Yet the sheer scale of the turmoil justifies its examination, if a serious distortion is not to enter into the historical discourse. Moreover, valuable clues to the future circumstances of North India may be lost by the failure to address the human dimension of partition. It should not be forgotten that in this, the century of the displaced person, India's partition still remains one of the greatest social upheavals.

This chapter explores the human dimension of partition through the physical and psychological impact of the four experiences of violence, abduction, migration and resettlement. It deploys a fresh range of source materials including autobiographical accounts. The most sustained use however is made of literary 'representation'. Before turning to insights which can be derived from works of fiction, it is necessary to consider the range of such sources and the problems associated with their utilization.

Novelists, unlike historians have fully addressed the human agonies which accompanied partition. Hundreds of novels, short stories and plays have taken these as their theme. Much of this outpouring has been catharthic as the writers relate their own experiences. Whilst many of the works lack artistry, some of the greatest pieces of literature from the subcontinent have also been produced. The contributions in English of Khushwant Singh[4] and Chaman Nahal[5], of Kartar Singh Duggal[6] in Punjabi, of Bhisham Sahni[7] in Hindi and Saadat Hasan Manto[8], Rajinder Singh Bedi[9] and Intizar Hussain[10] in Urdu spring readily to mind. Historians of Indian independence have been much more reluctant than their colleagues in other fields to utilize such creative out-pourings as source material. There are of course methodological problems in the use of literature[11], but it is curious that standard historical accounts of partition have not seized on this rich vein of material to begin to uncover the human dimension of the experience.

The most immediate physical and psychological impact of partition was the brutal violence which it brought. Before examining autobiographical and literary accounts of its impact, it is necessary to understand, firstly how creative writers have responded to this phenomenon and secondly to differentiate between the partition related massacres and earlier episodes of 'communal' conflict.

Such novelists as Manto[12] have derived much black humour from the partition violence. Others such as the progressive[13] author Krishan Chander[14] have attempted to underline the moral that all communities were equally guilty. Another common theme is the role of politicians in inciting hatred to serve their own purposes. This is addressed with considerable subtlety and power by Bhisham Sahni[15] in his award winning work, *Tamas*[16] which is based on his experiences during the time of partition. Novelists have also commented on the brutalizing effects of violence on its perpetrators and on its elemental ferocity. Especially with regard to this latter point, art closely mirrors reality.

Kirpal Singh in his recently published compilation, *Partition of the Punjab, 1947*[17] provides a graphic account of the impact of violence on non-Muslims by reproducing the evacuation reports of the District Liaison Officers. Similar material can be drawn from the private papers of the West Punjab Governor, Sir Francis Mudie to build up a Muslim perspective. What emerges from such accounts is the ferocity and cold bloodedness of the violence. This had a severe traumatic effect on survivors which has not been adequately researched and can only be glimpsed in autobiographical and literary accounts. The violence in Punjab in 1947 was in fact of a different character to earlier 'communal riots' and should be treated in a distinct category.

Attacks on refugee trains, and minority villages for example were often carried out with a military precision which was not surprising given the role played by ex-servicemen from both the Indian Army and the INA.[18] Light tanks were even deployed in the attack against the heavily fortified Harnoli *mandi*. in the Mianwali district in which three thousand inhabitants were massacred.[19] Moreover, while revenge and bloodlust were motives, Punjabi Muslims and Sikhs alike turned to violence to ensure 'ethnic cleansing'.[20] Force was also of course used in boundary demarcation in the Frontier and Bengal. During the Noakhali riots, one British observer spoke of a 'determined and organized' Muslim effort to drive out all the Hindus.[21] But the partition related violence should not be treated as merely an extreme variant of earlier 'communal' outbreaks, although it shared similar features; such as attacks on mosques, temples etc, attempts at forced conversion and endeavours to 'dishonour' the 'other' community by molestation of females.[22]

This section will examine the impact of violence on both its victims and perpetrators through the insights of autobiographical sources and fictional 'representation'. The authors will be allowed to speak for themselves once the background to the text has been explained. We shall turn first to the horrific picture of violence painted by the novelist Bapsi Sidhwa[23] in her compulsive work, *Ice-Candy Man*. The book's heroine, Lenny, a young Parsee girl growing up in Lahore is drawn from the author's own experience. Similarly, the sub-plot Ranna's Story given in extract below is based on the childhood recollections of one of her friends.

The attack came at dawn. The watch from the mosque's single minaret hurtled down the winding steps to spread the alarm. The panicked women ran to and fro snatching up their babies, and the men barely had time to get to their posts. In fifteen minutes the village was swamped by Sikhs – tall men with streaming hair and thick biceps and thighs, waving full-sized swords and sten-guns roaring, 'Bolay so Nihal! Sat Sri Akal!'

They mowed down the villagers in the mosque with the sten-guns. Shouting 'Allah-o-Akbar' the peasants died of sword and spear wounds in the slushy lanes and courtyards... Ranna awoke with a start. Why was he on the floor? Why were there so many people about in the dark? He felt the stir of men getting to their feet. The air in the room was oppressive: hot and humid and stinking of sweat. Suddenly Ranna remembered where he was and the darkness became charged with terror... Suddenly the noon light smote their eyes... Ranna saw his uncles beheaded, his older brothers, his cousins. The Sikhs were among them like hairy vengeful demons, wielding bloodied swords, dragging them out as a sprinkling of Hindus, darting about at the fringes, their faces vaguely familiar, pointed out and identified the mussulmans by name. He felt a blow cleave the back of his head and the warm flow of blood... Later in the evening he awoke to silence. At once he became fully conscious. He wriggled backwards over the bodies and slipping free of the weight on top of him felt himself sink knee-deep into a viscous fluid. The bodies blocking the entrance had turned the room into a pool of blood.[24]

This account brings out clearly the ferocity and suddeness of the violence in the rural Punjab in August 1947. Standard historical accounts tend to overlook this altogether. Its counterpart written from the non-Muslim perspective is the equally harrowing account of the attack on the Sikh minority of Sayyedpur contained in *Tamas*.[25] This reaches a climax with the mass suicide of the Sikh women in the village well. Common to both accounts is the elemental violence let loose by communal animosity and the coming together of past and present hatreds. Interestingly, Sahni has the Sikhs of Sayyedpur call their attackers 'Turks' although they were near neighbours.

Such fictional 'representations' of the bloodshed in rural Punjab minimize rather than exaggerate it. The real life equivalent of Sayyedpur was the episode at Harnoli in the Mianwali district where hundreds of women jumped into wells or threw themselves into burning houses to escape molestation.[26] An equally chilling actual episode this time in East Punjab is contained in Mashkur Hassan's autobiography, *Azadi ke Charagh*.[27] The writer recalls that his Hissar home was attacked on 29 August. When the police were called, they joined in the assaults. Like the 'fictional' character Ranna, Hassan was an injured witness to the death of his family and friends. Parched by the heat of a fire elsewhere in the building he licked the blood which was flowing from the victims. Twelve hours elapsed before he was able to stagger from the building's shattered remains.

The following extract from Bhisham Sahni's *Tamas* focuses on the cold blooded stray stabbings which were a marked feature of urban violence in North India during the partition period. This aspect has been similarly overlooked by historians. The passage must be read in the context of Sahni's general belief that violence resulted from the manipulation of simple people by the power-hungry to serve their selfish ends. A Hindu communalist, Master Devbrat has trained a group of young school boys to kill their Muslim 'foe'.

The four warriors in the squad were spoiling for action. Stationed on the roof they felt like gallant Rajputs waiting for the Muslim foe down in the Haldi Ghati.

Being rather short Ranvir liked to believe he was like that other great short-statured hero Shivaji... Sometimes he wished he were wearing a long Rajput coat, a Saffron turban on his head and a long sword hanging from a cummerbund round his waist. To take part in a fierce fight in loose pyjamas, an ill-fitting shirt and worn out *chappals* didn't seem right; it was not the dress of a fighting man... There was not a moment to be lost. He must decide and decide quickly. This man was a Muslim and a stranger to the place, carrying a heavy load of bags. He could neither flee nor protect himself. And he looked so tired. Everything was in favour of attacking. Ranvir's eyes met Inder and he signalled his decision..

Inder was very composed. He kept walking steadily, his hand firmly gripping the knife in his pocket, his eyes fixed on the perfume seller's waist. Even Arjuna who had killed a bird by looking at its reflection in a receptacle of oil would have envied Inder his concentration. As they walked past the tap Inder's energy suddenly concentrated in his right hand, his mind measuring each step as they walked on together.

'In the bazaar there is greater demand for cotton swabs while in the lanes I sell more bottles of oil and perfume,' the old man said.

Suddenly Inder lunged. The old man saw the boy's left hand move swiftly. Something bright flashed in the air. Before he could stop and feel his bag to see if anything had been taken, he felt a sharp agonising pain in his stomach. Inder twisted the knife he had plunged into the man's belly as he had been taught. Then leaving it where it was he ran.[28]

The artistic power of the extract lies of course in the contrast it presents between the romanticized view of violence which Master Devbrat has inculcated in his acolytes and Inder's futile murder of the helpless old man. The reader is left to ponder whether the boys themselves should not be viewed as victims.

The effect of violence on its perpetrators is a constant theme of partition literature. Chaman Nahal in *Azadi* for example excels in his depiction of the moral disintegration of Abdul Ghani, the *hookah* maker and neighbour of the novel's main protaganist, Lala Kanshi Ram. Saadat Hassan Manto's short story, *Thanda Gosht* remains, however the most notable work on this theme. Iswar Singh's impotence following his rape of a dead Muslim girl provides a compelling symbol of the loss of human sensibilities during the miasma terror and violence in August 1947.

Some may argue that little is to be served by cataloguing the horrors brought by the massacres of 1947. All that will be achieved is the reopening of old wounds. Indeed this argument was used to try to prevent the broadcasting of *Tamas* by Doordarshan. Yet to bury away these agonies is to deny the experience of countless people. In the name of both justice and truth, victims should be given their voice. Furthermore, it could be argued that a nation's maturity can be gauged by its ability to confront unpleasant aspects of its historical past. The more it does this the less likely they are to be repeated. By denying the horrors of the 1947 massacres, the courage and humanity which was displayed during them is also neglected. There were many who like the fictional character Jugga Singh in *Train to Pakistan* risked their own lives to save others. We shall conclude this section with three brief quotations from interviews conducted by Miriam Sharma and Urmila Vanjami amongst Hindu Jat refugees from the Multan district. The story they tell is however not confined to their community.

> The Muslims of our area were the ones who warned us to leave or we would be slaughtered. They were Rajputs before who had become Muslims in the old times and they had a certain amount of sympathy for us.
>
> A lot of people came to our village and I saw this happen – killings and murders with my own eyes. Actually many of the big land-holding Muslims were very helpful. They gave us shelter and tried to protect us from the others, from the small Muslim have-nots who wanted to push us out, kill us off and take our land.
>
> The five fingers are not the same. Some people want to trouble you and others want to help you. The Muslims were like that too... There was a Muslim man. He said, no matter what happens I will let nothing happen to these people. He was an officer on the Pakistan side. He made sure that we left safely. There were others who helped us. Like in our own village, there were people who extended hands of help to us and wouldn't let any harm come to us.[29]

2

The break-up of families through abduction and abandonment is a second largely untold aspect of the partition experience. The increasing incidence of abductions and attacks on women in 1946-7 undoubtedly reflected attempts to expose the most protected aspect of the 'other's' honour and self-identity.[30] Like other gender aspects of partition, the experience of women as both victims and survivors of violence is absent from the standard historical account. All we are given are the bald statistics that by October 1952 just over eight thousand women and children had been rehabiliated from Pakistan, whilst twice this number had been recovered from India.[31] These tell us nothing of the physical and psychological scars left by the experience of abduction. Did women as of other victims circumstances blame themselves for their sufferings rather than the male perpetrators of the violence against them? The comparative oral history project on women's experience of partition is beginning to address this question. Ritu Menon and Kamla Bhasin began the publication of the project's findings in an article in the *Economic and Political Weekly* in April 1993.[32]

Creative writers also provide some clues for the historian in the recovering of this neglected aspect of the reality of partition. Amrita Pritam in her novel, *Pinjer* through the character Pooro-Hamida explores the theme of abduction.[33] Bapsi Sidhwa in the following extracts from *Ice-Candy Man* approaches this through the sufferings of Lenny's Hindu *ayah*. The first gives a vivid account of her forcible abduction, next there is a description of the home for rehabiliatated women nearby to Lenny's house and finally there is the picture of the devastated *ayah* who has been married to one of her Muslim captors.

They move forward from all points. They swarm into bedrooms, search the servants' quarters, climb to the roofs, break locks and enter our *godowns* and the small store-rooms near the bathrooms. They drag *ayah* out. They drag her by her arms stretched taut, and her bare feet – that want to move backwards – are forced forward instead... Her violet sari slips off her shoulder, and her breasts strain at her sari-blouse stretching the cloth so that the white stitching at the seams shows. A sleeve tears under her arm.

The men drag her in grotesque strides to the cart and their harsh hands, supporting her with careless intimacy, lift her into it. Four men stand pressed against her, propping her body upright, their lips stretched in triumphant grimaces.

The mystery of the women in the courtyard deepens. At night we hear them wailing, their cries verging on the inhuman... One cold

night I am awakened by a hideous wail. My teeth chattering, I sit up.
I must have dozed off, because Hamida is still sitting by my bed..

'Why do they wail and scream at night?' I ask. It is not a subject I
have broached till now, mindful of Hamida's sensibilities.

'Poor fate-smitten woman,' says Hamida, sighing. 'What can a
sorrowing woman do but wail?'... My heart is wrung with pity and
horror. I want to leap out of my bed and soothe the wailing woman
and slay her tormentors. I've seen Ayah carried away – and it had
less to do with fate than with the will of men... I tell (Godmother) of
my conversation with Hamida.

'Hamida was kidnapped by the Sikhs,' says Godmother
seriously... 'She was taken away to Amritsar. Once that happens,
sometimes, the husband – or his family – won't take her back.'

'Why? It isn't her fault she was kidnapped!' 'Some folk feel that
way – they can't stand their women being touched by other men.'

It's monstrously unfair: but Godmother's tone is accepting.

'So!' whispers Godmother, blinking and nodding impishly. 'He
has christened our *ayah* Mumtaz!' 'Lenny baby, aren't you going to
embrace my bride?' Ice-candy-man asks.

And Ayah raises her eyes to me.

Where have the radiance and the animation gone? Can the soul
be extracted from its living body? Her vacant eyes are bigger than
ever: wide-opened with what they've seen and felt... 'I want to go to
my family.' Her voice is harsh, gruff: as if someone has mutilated
her vocal cords...

'Isn't he looking after you?

Mumtaz nods her head slightly.

'What's happened has happened,' says Godmother. 'But you are
married to him now. You must make the best of things.' . .

'I will not live with him'. Again that coarse, rasping whisper... 'I
cannot forget what has happened.'

'That was fated daughter. It can't be undone. But it can be
forgiven... Worse things are forgiven. Life goes on and the business
of living buries the debris of our pasts... That's the way of life.'

'I am past that,' says Mumtaz. 'I'm not alive'. 'What if your
family won't take you back?' (Godmother) asks.

'Whether they want me or not, I will go.'[34]

I wish to conclude this brief examination by citing two male writers who have provided the historian with sensitive insights into the impact of abduction on ordinary people. We shall turn respectively to the work of Rajinder Singh Bedi[35] and Saadat Hassan Manto.

Bedi's short story *Lajwanti*[36] which is set in the partition period is rightly regarded as an Urdu classic. The plot revolves around Sunder Lal and his wife Lajwanti who has been abducted. 'Sunder Lal had abdandoned all hope of finding Lajwanti', Bedi tells his readers. 'He had made his loss a part of the general loss. He had drowned his personal sorrow by plunging into social service.'[37] He daily led processions and remonstrated with those who refused to take back their abducted women. This existence was turned upside down by Lajwanti's unexpected return. Her Muslim style of dress disgusted him when he first saw her at the police station, but unlike the other men there he takes her in.

The story concludes, however on a poignant, rather than joyful note. For Sunder Lal refuses to allow Lajwanti to unburden her experiences. He treats her instead with an over-exaggerated respect calling her his *devi*. She had been rehabilitated but not accepted. Lajwanti is as much a victim in her own home as she was at the time of her abduction. But Sunder Lal has also been diminished.

Manto's short story, *Khuda ki Qasim*[38] also reflects on the emotional trauma of abduction. It too provides valuable insights which have surprisingly been ignored by historians. The narrator is a Liaison Officer involved in the recovery of abducted women. During his work he encounters an old Muslim woman who is searching for her daughter with increasing desperation. She refuses to return to Pakistan with him, as she is convinced that her daughter is still alive.

'Why?' I asked her.
'Because she is so beautiful – so beautiful that no one would dare kill her – no one will slap her even.' she replied to me.

The old woman is so distressed at the time of their final
meeting in Freed Chowk Amritsar that the Liaison Officer
decides to get her admitted to a lunatic asylum. Just at that
moment a 'sharp-faced' young Sikh walks by accompanied by a
veiled woman. The Sikh whispered to that 'goddess of beauty',
'Look – your mother.' The young woman looks for a moment
then averts her eyes and walks away. The old Muslim woman in
that moment recognizes her daughter and shouts after the Liaison
Officer, 'I have just seen her, just seen her.' He firmly replies,
fully aware of what is happening, 'By God, I do not lie. By God
she is dead.'[39] At that instant the old woman collapses to the
ground.

Manto's ending to the story is not only artistically powerful,
but reveals perhaps better than anything else that partition
involved the death of family ties as well as of individuals. The
character of the old woman, moreover, articulates the
uncertainties and anxieties of many relatives waiting to hear of
loved ones. Such fears overcame any personal relief at safely
crossing the great divide of 1947.

3

Migration was the single most important human agony which
attended the transfer of power. It brought in its wake a sense of
hopelessness and uprootedness. Around ten million people in all
were forced to flee from their homes. Delhi and Karachi took on
the character of refugee cities which they have never lost. The
subsequent historical development of large areas of the Indo-
Pakistan subcontinent has been profoundly shaped by the
migration experience. *Mohajirs* have played a crucial role, some
might add a divisive one, in Pakistan's post-independence
history.[40] Whilst much of post-1947 Sikh history and that of the
Indian Punjab has been shaped by the need to recover the
physical and psychological losses brought by the partition.

Yet despite the magnitude of the migration and its long term
consequences, comparatively little has been written about this

human aspect of partition. The aim of this section is to illustrate how historians could obtain fresh insights into the experience of migration by the use of both literary and autobiographical material. There will be an attempt to examine its psychological effects as well as its more immediate physical dangers and hardships.

Kartar Singh Duggal's[41] novel, *Twice-Born Twice-Dead*[42] centres around the physical hardships of those who were forced to flee their homes by communal violence. The main character Sohne Shah and his adopted Muslim daughter Satbharai wander from the Rawalpindi district to Lahore and thence to Lyallpur from where they are once again driven out. Duggal draws on first hand material to depict the refugees' plight. Towards the close of the novel he provides the following poignant picture of a refugee column which is unmatched in Punjabi literature and is of inestimable value to the historian concerned with understanding the partition experience 'from beneath'.

A caravan of Muslim evacuees was on the move. Whenever such a caravan was to pass, the police usually clamped down a curfew... Policemen lined both sides of the road to prevent incidents. Still the Hindu shopkeepers and their children poked fun at the cowed, miserable, hungry and emaciated evacuees.

The caravan was moving. Bullock carts were loaded with boxes, trunks and spinning wheels. On the top were *charpoys,* bedding and sacks. On the sacks were old men and women, carrying fowls, cats and lambs. From the bullock carts hung hubble-bubbles, baskets, prayer mats, odds, and ends. Holding on to the bullock carts for imaginary support walked women with babies at their breasts. Muslim women nurtured behind seven veils ran the gauntlet of hostile glances. The men were wounded; they had seen their relatives hacked to pieces with *kirpans.* There was not a single young man in the column... There were small boys, bare-footed, bare-headed, walking fast or slowing down to cast a longing glance at the hot *jalebies* in the sweet shops. The most yearning look however was cast at the running tap... No Muslim dared to take a drop of water from the Hindu tap. Men, women and children looked beseechingly at the water flowing from the tap and moved on.[43]

Those who migrated by train were spared such physical deprivations. But they faced a terrifying ordeal in that refugee trains were frequently attacked and their passengers murdered or abducted. The tense atmosphere which accompanied such journeys is powerfully recalled in the extract below. This is taken from an autobiographical account of the train ride from Delhi to Pakistan given by an educated Muslim woman, Dr Zahida Amjad Ali.

All passengers were forced into compartments like sheep and goats. Because of which the heat and suffocating atmosphere was intensified and it was very hard to breathe. In the ladies compartment women and children were in a terrible condition... Women tried in vain to calm down and comfort their children... If you looked out of the window you could see dead bodies lying in the distance... At many places you could see corpses piled on top of each other and no one seemed to have any concern. At one place we saw the dead bodies of innocent children, and in such condition that even the most stone-hearted person would draw breath for a moment if he saw them... These were the scenes that made your heart bleed and everybody loudly repented their sins and recited verses asking God's forgiveness... Every moment seemed to be the most terrifying and agonizing.[44]

Migration brought not only constant danger, but the emotional trauma of displacement and broken identities. Historians have totally neglected this aspect of partition, yet it lay at its very heart and still continues to exert a profound psychological effect. Saadat Hassan Manto explores this theme in his classic short story, *Toba Tek Singh*.[45] He approaches the subject through an allegory. This concerns the exchange of lunatics after independence.The plot increasingly centres around an aged Sikh inmate by the name of Bishan Singh. He is known to everyone as Toba Tek Singh because of his large landholdings there. Bishan Singh becomes obsessed with the question of whether Toba Tek Singh is in India or Pakistan. His insistence flusters a neighbour Fazal Din who visits him with the result that his reply is ambiguous. Bisham Singh only discovers the truth that Toba Tek

Singh is in fact in Pakistan when he is awaiting evacuation at the border. He then refuses to cross to India and is left standing on a spot midway between the boundary lines.

> Just before dawn, an ear-splitting cry issued from Toba Tek Singh's silent throat. Officials ran from both sides and discovered that the man who had remained upright on his legs for fifteen years was now lying on his face. On one side behind the barbed wire was India; Pakistan was behind the barbed wire on the other side. Between them, stretched on the ground of no-man's land, lay Toba Tek Singh.[46]

Manto makes the character Bishan Singh reflect the sense of confusion and displacement which many refugees faced. They were attached to their ancestral villages not out of mere sentimentality, but as the allegory reveals because it was there that the core of their identity resided. Chaman Nahal in *Azadi* makes a similar point through the chief protaganist Lala Kanshi Ram, a grain merchant who is forced to flee his native Sialkot. He arrives safely in Delhi with his family, but has suffered serious emotional loss, in addition to the loss of his extensive property which will never be restored.

> Lal Kanshi Ram would forgive the English and the Muslims all their sins, if only he could return. Return and die here and be cremated by the side of the river Aik! To be carried shoulder high on a bier through the streets of Sialkot, through all the streets in each of which somewhere sat a friend. Then at the last moment, for his Spirit to look at the Aik and the land of Sialkot from above, from the sky, or to come down and roll in the dust of the fields – that would be the very pinnacle of his delight.[47]

The sense of alienation brought by partition is explored with great subtlety by the Urdu writer Intizar Husain.[48] In the story *Sirhiyan*[49] he focuses on the loss of meaning and identity through the character Saiyid who has been robbed of his memory. He has also become unable to dream and subconsciously retrieve it in this way. One summer evening he is depicted lying on his *charpoy* along with three friends, Akhtar, Basher Bhai and Razi. Basher Bhai is interpreting a dream that Razi has related. It is suffused with past memories of a small town somewhere in east UP. When Razi mentions the *imambara,* a series of past memories and events are triggered in Saiyid's mind. He regains his power to dream and with it his wholeness and sense of identity and his past becomes again part of his present.

This strong feeling for the flow of Indian Muslim history and the sense that partition has sundered the past is further explored in Intizar Husain's short story, *Akhri Mom Bati.*[50] The Pakistani narrator returns to visit his aunt in the UP. He notices that everything in the village has changed and that his widowed aunt has suddenly grown old. On the eve of *muharrum,* he remembers how his aunt and his cousin Shamina who is now living in Karachi used to decorate the *imambara* and receive visitors. When he returns from a stroll to the railway station, the *imambara* is illuminated and Shamina is there to his amazement. His aunt, however laments that this will be the last such occasion. The narrator lies awake listening to the worship. When he falls asleep he dreams that all the candles except one have been extinguished and through it he can hear the sound of religious songs.

The mournful feeling of the work is impossible to capture in translation, but Intizar Husain's message is clear. He returns to the past, not to worship it, but to help understand the present. Only when this has happened, as for the character Saiyid, can the present be comprehended. Intizar Husain provides an illuminating insight into *mohajir* emotions. He articulates not only their sense of loss, but maintains that this is not self-indulgence. For in effect what he is saying is that a truly Pakistani ethos and sensibility can only emerge after a reassessment has taken place of past Indian Muslim cultural identity.

Intizar Husain's elegies harmonize with much autobiographical writing. The sense of loss and displacement is especially striking in the following two quotations from Shahid Ahmad and A. Hameed. Both men are renowned writers[51] in

Pakistan. They reflect the feelings of the North Indian Muslim professional class which migrated in 1947. Shahid Ahmad briefly returned to Delhi just six months after partition. He was at first struck by the physical changes which had resulted from the refugee influx; the congested streets and markets, the pavements crammed with migrants selling their wares on trays. In the midst of all this bustle, he became acutely aware of a deeper feeling of loss, of sundering links with the past. He poetically describes this as follows in his autobiography.

I came to my mother's lap with a broken heart and came back with a dead heart. I saw mother's widowhood, her widow's tears. I saw the Shah Jehan mosque in beautiful moonlight, and thought that mother had lifted her hands to the heavens in prayer. And like Mary her heart is full of flames. This vision has been engraved in such a way that I cannot forget. And repeatedly these questions come to my mind, 'Mother have you lost the happiness of your marriage for good?'[52]

For Shahid Ahmad, Delhi has been lost and widowed as were earlier Muslim cities of Cordoba and Granada. Like them it will continue to haunt Muslims as a memorial to their vanished glory. A. Hameed has expressed similar feelings when he recalls his former Amritsar home.

In fact Amritsar for me is Jerusalem, separated from me and I am her 'wailing wall.' Amritsar is circulating in my body, within my blood. I see Amritsar, before I go to sleep, and the first thing I see when I get up in the morning is Amritsar. When I walk Company Garden accompanies me. When I sit, the trees of Saktari Garden shadow me. When I speak, I hear the call for prayer from the mosques and when I am silent, I hear the hissing sound of flowing water in the canals of Amritsar, as if very close to my ears. When I look at one of my hands, I see the sleeping lanes and paths of the place (where I lived).[53]

Hameed visits in his imagination such places as Hal Bazaar, Chowk Farid, Katra Safaid and Company Garden, but finds them sad and desolate.

Even the ruins of Muslim culture were not visible. Mosques seemed to be reciting an elegy. Hindu women were plastering the walls which once formed the rendezvous for Kashmiris... In the dust of Amritsar's mosques are hidden the prints of the prostrations of my ancestors and its lanes are red with the blood of martyrs... O Spain! You are the trustee of the blood of Muslims. You are very sacred in my eyes. In your dust are hidden the prints of the prostrations and silent calls for prayer can be heard in your morning breeze.[54]

Spain is of course a popular symbol for Muslim writers concerned with past Islamic glories. But what we have here is something more than literary convention. It is an expression of deep pain and sense of loss and longing. This lies at the heart of the partition experience for many South Asian Muslims. It is of course part of a wider emotional current in Muslim society which Akbar Ahmed has termed the Andulas syndrome. He sees it existing wherever a great Muslim civilization has been lost and its descendants face an uncertain future. Akbar Ahmed's view is that it constitutes an unhealthy neurosis in which there is permanent perplexity and trauma.[55]

4

At the end of difficult and frequently terrifying journeys, migrants had to re-establish their lives in a strange environment. This brief examination of the human impact of partition will conclude by focusing on the experience of resettlement. Refugee experiences on arrival in their new homeland varied enormously. Some had relatives to smooth their paths and were soon able to pick up their old occupations. The less fortunate had to make their own way and faced both short term exploitation and months of demoralizing inactivity in refugee camps. Amir Abdullah Khan Rokri, for example, provides evidence in his autobiography, of bureaucrats and landlords feathering their nests at the refugees' expense. Pakistan government officials in connivance with local Muslim and Hindu businessmen sold goods on the black market which had been donated to refugees in the transit camp at Pathankot.[56] Shahid Ahmad recalls how he was fleeced by coolies and tonga drivers on his arrival in Lahore, when they heard him speaking Urdu.[57]

Kartar Singh Duggal whose Muslim wife Ayesha worked among the refugees in Jullundur has painted an especially vivid picture of refugee life in his novel *Twice Born, Twice Dead*. The first extract brings home the extent of the larger camps, whilst the second evokes the often desperate struggle for survival in the transit camps.

> The camp was like a small township. As far as the eye could see there were...tents. Living quarters, bathrooms, offices, hospitals, schools, *gurdwaras*, temples, the post office and shops were all housed in tents. Roads, lanes and by lanes criss-crossed the camp...Children were crying, men and women were shouting, there was uproar all around. Sohne Shah remembered the peace and quite of his village. He could walk miles there without meeting anyone.[58]

> Every instant flocks of refugees on bullock carts and trucks came to the camp under the protection of the army. Day and night the process continued... No one dared set foot outside the gates. Those who had gone outside without protection never returned. A few used to go out of the camp with the police. It transpired that a black market was flourishing: flour at ten rupees a seer and salt at a rupee. People were exchanging gold ornaments for bicycles, tongas and even camel coaches.[59]

Qudrat Allah Shahab's short story, *Ya Khuda*[60] is less well known than Kartar Singh Duggal's work, but provides similar insights into the hardships of refugee life, this time from the Muslim perspective. Dilshad, a *maulvi's* daughter arrives dishonoured and penniless in Lahore where she encounters indifference and contempt. Life is equally tough for her friend Zubeida who has to disregard her modesty to keep alive her son Mahmood during the bitter Lahore winter. The local shopkeeper meanwhile stockpiles blankets and sanctimoniously recites Iqbal's poetry.

Dilshad is tricked into going to the house of Mustafa Khan who claims to know the whereabouts of her beloved Rahim Khan who has disappeared during the journey from the East Punjab. Mustafa Khan makes sexual advances towards Dilshad as soon as they are alone, prompting the narrator to comment with bitter irony on the relationship between the *mohajirs* and their *ansar* helpers.

> Lahore was not Lahore, it was Medina; the people of Lahore were not of Lahore, they were the *ansars* of Medina offering help to the Holy Prophet. Here for Dilshad a new Rahim Khan was being born, for Zubeida a new grandfather was born daily, for daughters new fathers, for sisters new brothers, the relationship of flesh was meeting flesh and blood with blood.[61]

Not all Muslim refugee experiences were as painful as that. In Hyderabad even tonga drivers were found residing in the luxurious homes once occupied by Hindu businessmen. The first Muslim arrivals in the West Punjab canal colony areas vacated by Sikhs found the fields almost ready for harvesting, millet and rice crops provided the migrants with food, whilst cotton could be sold for cash. Shahid Ahmad encountered generosity as well as exploitation. When his refugee train reached the first station in Pakistan, hundreds of people were waiting, they descended on the carriages with gifts of bread, lentils and pickles.[62] There were many on both sides of the Punjab border like Amir Abdullah Khan Rokri who moved out of their houses to provide temporary accommodation for refugees. Moreover, for some Muslims the migration experience was viewed in terms of *hijrat* which transcended human sufferings. Looking back four decades later on her flight from Nikodar in East Punjab, Hurmat Bibi expresses this understanding on behalf of many other migrants.

> I had lost everything, forty people of our family were martyred, but the happiness I found when I saw the Pakistan flag flying at the Pakistan border, is still living in every cell of my body.[63]

Non-Muslim refugees could not of course seek a similar religious solace for their material losses. These were frequently greater than those of their Muslim counterparts as the Hindu and Sikh population of the West Punjab was far wealthier than the Muslims of the East. It owned the bulk of the businesses and factories and urban property in the 'Pakistan' areas. Non-Muslim farmers also cultivated around 6.7 million acres of land. This not only exceeded the land left by Muslims, but contained superior soil and irrigation facilities.[64] The fictional character, Lala Kanshi Ram's futile endeavours to secure compensation for his lost property, during his prolonged sojourn in a Delhi refugee camp is representative of the resettlement experience of many Punjabi non-Muslims.

Chaman Nahal, however, also makes his character express a sense of pride in the independent India which he has struggled so hard to safely reach. The novel closes with this short description following Gandhi's assassination.

> What impressed Lala Kanshi Ram was the pride with which the men stood... he thought of pre-independence days... An Indian leader dying and the crowd feeling openly for him? Today the men stood in pride... Lala Kanshi Ram raised his head with pride and stretched back his shoulders. He was unrestricted now, he was untramelled.[65]

5

Three themes emerge strongly from this brief exploration of literary representations of the human dimension of partition in North India. The first is that of the searing reality of the agony of the partition massacres and migrations. The emotional and physical pain of innumerable ordinary men and women is represented by such fictional characters as Lala Kanshi Ram. It is frequently forgotten that significant sections of the subcontinent's population entered the new era of independence severely traumatized. The social and political implications of this reality have been largely neglected.

The second theme is that of the conflicting human emotions evoked by partition. National pride and religious fulfilment mingled with a sense of loss and bewilderment. The primary concern was for immediate family and kin. The loss of her daughter meant far more to the old woman in Manto's story *Khuda ki Qasim* than the establishment of Pakistan or for that matter even her own life. Novelists repeatedly point to the reality of how violence from outside intruded into harmonious family and community relationships destroying that which it claimed to uphold.[66]

Third, there emerges a strong sense of the displacement brought by migration. The demented character Toba Tek Singh merely caricatures the fact that separation from the ancestral home threatened the core of many migrants' identity. Such varied authors as Duggal, Nahal, Intizar Husain and Manto reflect on an emotion which affected all communities. Shahid Ahmad in his autobiographical account articulates the same feeling on behalf of many Muslim *mohajirs* in a classic Urdu poetic convention. The Lahore educationist Dr Prem Kirpal in his autobiographical poem, *Spirit's Musings* expresses similar emotions for the non-Muslims whose familiar home had suddenly become a foreign land.

> My beloved city of Lahore
> Still standing not far from Delhi,
> Within quicker reach by air or train,
> Suddenly became a forbidden land
> Guarded by a sovereign state
> Of new ideologies, loves and hates.
> Homes were lost and hearts were bruised
> In both unhappy parts of Punjab.[67]

Historians have neglected the sense of loss and displacement brought by partition. Such emotions cut across community identity. They lie at the very heart of the human impact of partition. To omit this dimension is not only to distort the historical discourse, but to lose an important key to understanding social and political developments in the decades which have followed North Indian independence.

NOTES

1. A notable exception is Chapter Thirteen of C.M. Ali, *The Emergence of Pakistan* (New York, Columbia University Press 1967). See also, the recollections of the East Punjab Refugee Rehabilitation Commissioner, M.S. Randhwa, *Out of the Ashes* (Jullundur, Public Relations Department, Punjab 1954) and J. Nanda, *Punjab Uprooted* (Bombay, Hind Kitab Government Press 1948).

2. See for example, Pakistan Government, *Note on the Sikh Plan* (Lahore 1948).

3. In an attempt to remedy this situation, a recent study of the demographic consequences of the partition in Punjab concludes with sixty-two personal accounts of people caught up in the disturbances.
R.S. Corruccini and S.S. Kaul, *Halla: Demographic Consequences of the Partition in the Punjab, 1947* (Lanham, University Press of America 1990) pp. 60-93.

4. K. Singh, *Train to Pakistan* (London, Chatto & Windus 1956).

5. C. Nahal, *Azadi* (London, Orient 1976).

6. K.S. Duggal, (J. Ara trans.) *Twice Born, Twice Dead* (New Delhi 1979).

7. B. Sahni, (J. Ratan trans.) *Tamas* (New Delhi, Penguin 1990) also (J. Ratan trans) *We have Arrived in Amritsar and Other Stories* (London, Sangam Books 1990).

8. S. H. Manto, (C.M. Naim and R.L. Schmidt trans.) 'Thanda Gosht', *Journal of Asian Literature* 1, (1965) pp 14-19. also (R.B. Haldane trans) 'Toba Tek Singh' *Journal of South Asian Literature* 6, (1970) pp. 19-23 (M. Ali trans) 'Khuda ki Qasim' *Pakistan Review* (13 April 1965) pp. 33-4.

9. R. S. Bedi (M. Hasan (ed.) India Partitioned Lotus (New Dehi 1995) *Lajwanti* in R. Mathur and M. Kulasrestha (eds) New Delhi, 1995 (Lotus Collection) pp. 177-90.

10. I. Hussain, 'Akhri Mom Bati' in *Kankary* (Lahore, Maktaba-e-Jadid, 1995) pp. 90-104. See also, 'Ek bin likhi Razmiyah' in *Gali Kuche* (Lahore, Shahin Publisher 1952) pp. 193-221.

11. The novelist's art is subjective by its very nature. All literary sources must therefore be treated circumspectly by historians. It must be remembered that they have been produced by tiny elites in 'traditional' societies. The great writers can of course transcend their own experiences and echo the feelings of other classes and communities. But lesser novelists lack this

empathy and produce merely stereotypes and stylized emotional responses.

12. The collection *Siyah Hashiye* is particularly noted for its irony and black humour. The short story entitled 'Karamat' is typical. The miracle of the sweet water in a village well is really to be explained by the fact that a man drowned in it, whilst trying to hide a looted bag of sugar.

13. The Progressive Writers' Movement was launched in London in 1934 before being established at Lucknow in April 1936. Krishan Chander was its General Secretary for a number of years. For further details see, H. Malik, 'The Marxist Literary Movement in India and Pakistan' *Journal of Asian Studies* xxvl, 4 (August 1967) pp. 649-64;
K.H. Ansari, 'The Emergence of Muslim Socialists in India 1917-1947' London, Unpublished Ph. D. Thesis 1985.

14. See especially his noted short story 'Peshawar Express' translated in Mathur and Kulasreshtha, op. cit. p. 69 and ff.

15. Bhishan Sahni was born in 1915 in Rawalpindi. He was brought up in a devout middle class Arya Samajist family. He taught for a number of years at Delhi University College following partition before spending time working as a translator in the Soviet Union. He has written widely in Hindi.

16. *Tamas* was first published in 1974, the following year it received the prestigious Sahitya Akademi award. In 1988 it was dramatized for Indian television.

17. K. Singh (ed), *Partition of Punjab 1947* (Delhi, National Book Store 1991).

18. For the role of ex-INA men in organizing Sikh *Shahidi Jathas* see *The Sikh Plan,* op. cit., pp. 17-29.

19. *Ibid.,* (18) Report of Work in Mianwali District L.A.R file No Lic/7 p. 677.

20. The Akali leader Master Tara Singh emphasized that territory which contained Sikh religious places and property should not be included in Pakistan at any cost. *The Sikh Plan* op. cit., pp. 26-7.

21. S. Das, *Communal Riots in Bengal 1905-1947* (Delhi, Oxford University Press 1991) p. 199.

22. For a general discussion of patterns of communal violence see, I. Talbot, 'The Role of the Crowd in the Muslim League Struggle for Pakistan' *The Journal of Imperial and Commonwealth History* 21, 2 (May 1993) pp. 307-34.

23. Bapsi Sidhwa was born in Karachi, but brought up by her Parsee parents in Lahore. She has published a number of novels and has lectured in America. In 1975 she represented Pakistan at the Asian Women's Congress.

24. B. Sidhwa, *Ice-Candy Man* (London, Penguin 1989) p. 199 and ff.

25. B. Sahni, *Tamas* (New Delhi, Penguin 1990) p. 193 and ff.

26. Ibid. (18) p. 677.

27. M. Hassan, *Azadike Caragh* (3rd ed. Lahore 1986).

28. Sahni, *Tamas*, op. cit. p. 137 & ff.

29. M. Sharma and U. Vanjani, 'Remembrances of Things Past. Partition Experiences of Punjabi Villagers in Rajasthan.' *Economic and Political Weekly* 4 August 1990, p. 1731.

30. See, S. Das, *Communal Riots in Bengal 1905-1947* (Delhi, Oxford University Press 1991) p. 198.

31. C.M. Ali, *The Emergence of Pakistan* (New York, Columbia University Press 1973) p. 274.

32. R. Menon and K. Bhasin, 'Recovery, Rupture, Resistance. The Indian State and Abduction of Women during Partition', *Economic and Political Weekly* (24 April 1993) WS2-WS17.

33. The novel centres around the abduction of Pooro by a young Muslim farmer who is avenging his own 'dishonour'. The novel was published in Punjabi in 1950. It has been translated by Khushwant Singh. K. Singh, *The Skeleton* (Delhi 1984).

34. Sidhwa, op.cit., pp. 183, 212-15, 260-2.

35. Bedi was born into a lower middle class Punjabi family. He began his literary career in the 1930s and was associated with the Progressive Writers' Movement, although he never fully conformed to its ideology.

36. See (10) above.

37. Ibid. p. 127.

38. Muhammad Ali has rendered this into English in *Pakistan Review*, 13 (April 1965) pp. 33-4.

39. Ibid., p. 34.

40. The *mohajirs* dominated politics during the early years of Pakistan, more recently they have institutionalized claims to be Pakistan's fifth nationality through the MQM.
See, T.P. Wright, 'Indian Muslim Refugees in the Politics of Pakistan', *Journal of Commonwealth and Comparative Politics,* xii, (1975).

41. Duggal is a leading author in Punjabi. He moved to Delhi from the Rawalpindi district at the time of partition and is married to a Muslim.

42. K. S. Duggal (J. Ara trans.) *Twice-Born. Twice-Dead* (New Delhi, Vikas 1979).

43. Ibid., pp. 136-7.

44. K. Iftikhar, *Jab Amritsar jal raha tha* (9th ed.) (Lahore, Khwaja Ghafoor Ahmad 1991) pp. 259-61.

45. This has been translated into English by R.B. Haldane in the *Journal of South Asian Literature* 6 (1970) pp. 19-23.

46. Ibid., p. 23.

47. Nahal, op.cit., pp. 148-9.

48. Intizar Husain was born in the Bulandshehr district of UP and migrated to Pakistan in August 1947 cutting short his college career in Meerut.

49. This is summarized in M.U. Memon, 'Partition Literature: A Study of Intizar Husain' *Modern Asian Studies*, 14, 3 (1980) pp. 377-410.

50. This is included in Husain's collection entitled, *Kankary* (Lahore, Sangmail Publisher 1987) pp. 90-104.

51. Shahid Ahmad was a member of the Progressive Writers' Movement who migrated to Pakistan in 1947. He has left behind a valuable autobiographical account of this period entitled, *Dilhi ki Bipta.*

52. S. Ahmad, 'Dilhi Ki Bipta' in M. Shirin (ed) *Zulmat-i-Neem Roze* (Karachi, Nafees Academy 1990) p. 169.

53. A. Hameed, Foreward in Iftikhar op. cit., p. 35.

54. Ibid., pp. 42-43.

55. A.S. Ahmed, *Discovering Islam: Making Sense of Muslim History and Society* (London, Routledge 1988) pp. 159-60.

56. A. Abdullah Khan Rokri, *May awr Mera Pakistan* 2nd ed (Lahore 1985) p. 76.

57. Shirin, op.cit., p. 157.

58. Duggal, op.cit., pp. 143 and 136.

59. Duggal, op.cit., p. 130.

60. This is found in the collection edited by Mumtaz Shirin *op.cit.,* pp. 315-352.

61. Shirin, op. cit., p. 339.

62. Shirin, op. cit., p. 339.

63. These sentiments were expressed during the course of an interview with the researcher Tahima Farhi Manazar. This was published in M.M. Mirza and S. Bakht (eds) *Azadi ke Mujahyd* (Lahore 1989) p. 16.

64. For further details see, K. Singh, *The Partition of Punjab* (Patiala, Punjab University 1972) p. 151 and ff.

65. Nahal op. cit., p. 368.

66. See, for example, K.S. Duggal (J. Ara, Trans.) *Twice Born, Twice Dead* (New Delhi, Vikas 1979) p. 11 and ff.

67. Prem Kirpal, *Spirit's Musings* quoted in P. Nevile, *Lahore. A Sentimental Journey* (New Delhi, Allied Publishers 1993) p. 18.

Chapter Eight

The Partition of Punjab: Its Impact upon Sikh Sacred and Cultural Space

Gurdit Singh and Carol C. Fair

Introduction

The partition of Punjab in 1947 changed the religious and cultural landscape of Punjab for all time to come. For a plethora of reasons, structures inscribed by Sikh sacred and cultural space — historical gurdwaras, Sikh homes, *havelis*, shops, and so forth — that existed in Punjab assumed new, renewed, and greater significance after the partition. It is not that these areas of Sikh cultural and sacred space were insignificant or without importance prior to the partition; however, the partition added to and varied their significance in numerous ways. The purpose of this chapter is three-fold. First, we will highlight how pertinent examples of sacred and cultural space in West Punjab have been and currently are intrinsic to the multivalent Sikh traditions of history, society, culture, and religion. Secondly, we will describe the process by which the partition led to the inclusion and permanent enshrinement of these buildings in Sikh canonical literature such as the *Ardas*. Finally, we will examine how the partition has given rise to a cycle of annual pilgrimages in which specific sites of Sikh sacred and cultural space have been naturalized within the domains of sacred Sikh cartography.

Sikh Sacred and Cultural Space in History: Pre-partition

Gurdwaras have probably been the most important elements of Sikh sacred and cultural space ever since their inception during the time of the Sikh Gurus.[1] Literally, a gurdwara is 'the house of the *guru*,' a place meant for propagating the ideals of the religious tradition and in which the *Guru Granth Sahib* is installed. Gurdwaras have been and continue to be centres of numerous activities. Bhai Khan Singh Nabha, an influential scholar and historian of Sikhs and Sikhism, attributes the following characteristics to a gurdwara: a school for students, a knowledgeable guide for those seeking knowledge of the soul, a clinic for patients, a place where the hungry can be fed, a place where women can maintain dignity, and a rest house for travellers.[2] All these characteristics and many more are applicable to the different historical gurdwaras that exist in West Punjab.

Certain gurdwaras in West Punjab figure prominently in the evolving history of Sikhism in the subcontinent. Nankana Sahib, a complex of buildings encompassing about seven historical[3] gurdwaras in Sheikhupura including the birth place of Guru Nanak *(Janamasthan),* is an excellent case in point. In the late nineteenth century and the early twentieth century, a group of people called *mahants*[4] assumed responsiblity for maintaining and looking after gurdwaras in exchange for the offerings that Sikh devotees and other worshippers and visitors offered. Initially, the *mahants* were able to perform their duties without facing any opposition or hostility. However, after some time, there emerged groups of Sikhs who wanted to get rid of the *mahants* by removing them from the positions of authority that they had acquired over a period of time. These Sikhs resented the fact that the *mahants* had personally taken control of the farms, fields, estates, and other properties (affiliated to gurdwaras), that in their view, belonged collectively to the congregation.[5]

These groups of Sikhs started reform movements such as the *Gurdwara Sudhar Lahir* (lit., 'Gurdwara Reform Movement).[6] These reform movements were specifically important for three reasons. First, there was an exhortation to resume in its full vigour, the Khalsa code of discipline. Secondly, there was an insistence upon the paramount authority of the *Shabd* Guru. Thirdly (and this is the most important point), there developed a sustained campaign to secure control of the gurdwaras. It is here that Nankana Sahib and the *saka* or massacre that occurred there become very important in chronicles of Sikh history and religion.

After every direct effort by reformist Sikhs to reclaim control of the gurdwaras failed, they decided not to put up with the *mahants'* 'high-handedness' any longer. At a meeting in Amritsar, they decided that they would oust the *mahants* and their representatives would take complete charge of the management of the gurdwaras of Nankana Sahib. The entire process was supposed to be peaceful and the reformist Sikhs admonished their followers to abstain from violence, even in self-defence. On 20 February 1921, a group of one hundred and thirty people led by Bhai Lachman Singh went to Gurdwara Janamasthan to reassert their control over the shrine. The *mahant* of the gurdwara, Narain Dass, had his gunmen fire upon this crowd resulting in the death of many people and wounding many more. The news of this massacre and bloodshed spread very fast throughout Punjab and encouraged a group of more than 2,000 Sikhs to march to Nankana Sahib to avenge the killings of their brothers and sisters. Finally, government officials intervened, arrested the *mahant* and some of his accomplices, and turned Gurdwara Janamasthan over to a committee of seven Sikhs.[7]

The aforementioned incident at Nankana Sahib was the epitome of the entire Gurdwara Reform Movement which involved other important gurdwaras in West Punjab as well. The memories of the Sikhs, who were martyred while defending the gurdwaras in Nankana and other places against the *mahants,* are considered so important that they have been permanently enshrined in the Sikh liturgical prayer, the *Ardas:* 'Remember those Singhs and Singhnis... who served the gurdwaras by sacrificing their lives.'[8]

Sikh Sacred and Cultural Space in History: Post-partition

The significance of gurdwaras and other constituents of Sikh sacred and cultural space did not diminish with the partition of Punjab in 1947. On the other hand, the importance of these places evolved and increased with renewed vigour in remarkable ways. Gurdwaras, houses, *havelis,* shops, and schools that were once the *axis mundi,* to use Eliades' term, around which the lives of thousands of Sikhs revolved were now so close yet so far away.[9] As a result of being separated from space that was so integral to the lives of so many Sikhs, the attraction and longing for being close to this space increased with time. After the partition, Sikhs all over the world campaigned to win the Pakistan Government's official sanction to once again allow the Sikhs reasonable access to their sacred places. Between 1948 and 1975, only a few Sikhs in India were able to get special permission from Pakistan to visit their holy places under a highly restrictive arrangement.[10] Eventually, in 1975 a determined and successful endeavour was made to pursuade the Government of Pakistan to allow a large group of pilgrims to visit their holy places in Pakistan.

Continued Scriptural Canonization of Sikh Space after the Partition

As stated earlier, the *saka* or massacre of Nankana Sahib was enshrined in the Sikh *Ardas* as a continual and everlasting way to commemorate the Sikhs who died defending the gurdwara against the *mahants.* This process by which Sikh sacred space was canonized prior to the partition did not stop with the partition. Conversely, the way in which sacred space was canonized in the post-partition era became more explicit and detailed. For example, after the partition, a specific stanza pertaining to [the renewed significance of] Nankana Sahib and other gurdwaras in West Punjab was included in the *Ardas*:

> O Immortal One, always a helper of the Panth! Give your Panth the gift of free *darshan* and an opportunity to serve Sri Nankana Sahib and other gurdwaras and places of the guru from which the Panth has been separated.[11]

'Gurdwaras... from which the Panth has been separated' specifically refers to those gurdwaras that are currently in Pakistan and from which Sikh communities were separated as a result of the partition. The inclusion of this stanza in the standardized Sikh liturgical prayer that is recited in gurdwaras and by individual Sikhs all over the world makes the reinforced significance of Sikh sacred space quite evident. It is interesting to note that this passage in the Sikh liturgical prayer is, ironically, also read by Sikhs living in Pakistan, for example those living at Gurdwara Patti Sahib (Nankana Sahib), who are separated not from gurdwaras in Pakistan but from those in India.

Annual Pilgrimage of Sacred Sites: A Post-partition Phenomenon

A very interesting aspect of sacred Sikh space in West Punjab is that starting in the 1970s, specific sites became naturalized within the domains of sacred Sikh cartography as destinations of annual pilgrimage. These specific sites are Gurdwara Dera Sahib in Lahore, Gurdwara Panja Sahib in Hasan Abdal, and the seven historical gurdwaras in Nankana Sahib. Every year, large groups of Sikh pilgrims from India visit the aforementioned sites at the three different occasions: Guru Nanak's birthday celebrations (gurpurab) at Nankana Sahib in November, Vaisakhi[12] celebrations at Gurdwara Panja Sahib in Hasan Abdal in the month of April, and Guru Arjan's martyrdom day celebrations at Dera Sahib in May. Pilgrims receive a warm welcome by Pakistani governmental authorities and usually receive considerable media coverage in the form of television and radio news headlines and newspaper articles such as the one excerpted below:

> Earlier on arrival at the local Railway Station the yatris [pilgrims] were received by Khalid Majid Pirzada, Assistant Commissioner, Tariq Ahmad Rao, Resident Magistrate, officials of Evacuee Trust Property Board and elite of the town.[13]

Pilgrims, numbering in the thousands, not only visit this triad of holy Sikh sites but also stay at these gurdwaras for boarding and lodging purposes. For those who have never visited these gurdwaras before, pilgrimage to these sacred sites, their *darshan*, and the opportunity to perform *seva* (service) at these sites constitute fulfillment of long held dreams and prayers. For others, it is another rare opportunity to be at-one-ment with sacred and cultural space close to their hearts.

The Cultural Dimensions of Pilgrimage

Sikh doctrine describes liberation as a process that takes place concurrently with acts such as laughing, playing, changing clothes, and eating.[14] Perhaps, this explains why gurdwaras, in both pre-and post-partition eras, have been intrinsically linked to the mundane, down-to-earth world around them. At the time of the partition, Sikhs were separated not only from their places of worship but also from their ancestral home, shops, towns, and villages, many of which were situated in the vicinity of gurdwaras. The yearning to see latter elements of space is as strong, if not stronger, than the former, in the minds of Sikh pilgrims. This makes pilgrimage to gurdwaras a very 'wholesome' process and, consequently, highlights many cultural dimensions of pilgrimage. That is to say, international pilgrims not only come to Pakistan to visit sites of spiritual interests, but also their ancestral homes, markets, towns, and villages, Pakistani landmarks such as the Badshahi Masjid, Shalimar Gardens (including cultural ones such as popular Punjabi films), and so forth.

Some of the cultural activities, of Sikh pilgrims who came to Pakistan for *Vaisakhi* celebrations in April 1996, have been aptly and insightfully described in an article in an Urdu daily from Lahore:

Sikh pilgrims who had come from India a week ago departed for India yesterday amidst slogans of 'Pakistan Zindabad.' They included women who went around Lahore and saw Pakistani films on Friday and Saturday. They liked Sultan Rahi's films very much and expressed sorrow over his murder. Young Sikh pilgrims also bought video tapes of Sultan Rahi's films.... Seventy year old Amrit Singh, who is a resident of Amritsar, spent Friday searching for his house on Nisbet Road. Sardar Amrit Singh migrated from Lahore to Amritsar during the establishment of Pakistan.[16]

What is interesting about this particular article is that it presents the Sikh pilgrims' participation in Pakistani Punjabi culture (watching Sultan Rahi films and shopping) and their attempts to locate pieces of family history (homes etc.) fragmented as a consequence of partition.

The commercial aspects of the annual *melas* are non-trivial as they have a profound impact on local economies. Many Sikhs see the pilgrimage events as excellent shopping opportunities, stocking up on goods that are less expensive in Pakistan than they are in India. Shopkeepers and hotel owners of Nankana Sahib, Hasan Abdal, and Lahore also reach out to attract Sikh customers through advertisement banners specifically directed at Sikh pilgrims. For instance, during the Guru Nanak birthday celebrations in Nankana in 1995, we saw banners in Gurmukhi advertising hotels, video markers (selling video recordings of the procession that takes place as a climax to the celebrations), and pure almond extract. Furthermore, within the gurdwara complexes, there are rows of sidewalk vendors (many of them Afghani Sikhs) selling everything from artificial jewellery to candy and french fries. Curiously, some advertisement notices have a perplexing sense of purpose. For instance, a large poster, printed predominantly in Urdu, advertises the 'All Pakistan Baba Guru Nanak Memorial Football Tournament', to be held in the beginning of November. Most prominently featured is the picture of Guru Nanak in the centre of Pepsi endorsements in English. Many smaller endorsements are found at the bottom of the poster, mostly in Urdu but some in English. One must ask why this particular function is held exactly during the dates of the Gurpurab celebration and for whom these advertisements are intended.

The cultural dimension of the Gurpurab celebrations is also evident by the most prominent word used to describe them—, *mela* or 'fair.'[17] Before the celebrations, I was frequently asked on the streets of Lahore, 'Sardar ji, when is the mela?' The various ethnic dances performed each night in the main lawns and in the final procession at Nankana by Sikh men from Peshawar, Swat, and Sindh add to the mela-like image of the celebrations. These dances not only last late into the night but also attract sizeable crowds and audiences mostly comprising men. In additon, Bhangra, whether performed by Sikh men from East Punjab or by others, is a popular cultural item at these celebrations.

Apart from cultural entertainment and spiritual pursuits, many Sikhs from East Punjab specifically join the pilgrimage expeditions to meet with Muslim friends who live in West Punjab. Some of these individuals are writers, poets, and literary critics of Punjabi, a shared and common language which brings litterateurs on both sides of the border together. Since Punjabi writers in West and East Punjab use the Persian and Gurmukhi scripts for their writings respectively, the mela provides rare opportunities for them to keep up with literary ventures of the other side and to exchange literature for the purpose of reading and for transcribing into their respective scripts.

Preservation of Sacred and Cultural Space: The Triad v. Other Historical Monuments

In addition to the triad—Gurdwaras Dera Sahib (Lahore), Panja Sahib (Hasan Abdal), and the seven gurdwaras at Nankana Sahib—which has become normalized as the pilgrimage map or route of Sikh pilgrims, the entire country of Pakistan, especially Punjab, abounds in numerous other historical Sikh sacred and cultural monuments. Unlike the aforementioned three sites that are visited by Sikh pilgrims thrice every year,[18] other places are rarely visited by any Sikhs even by those who live in Pakistan. The three sites that have been naturalized within sacred Sikh cartography are different from the rest in a number of ways. First, since Sikhs keep visiting the buildings of the triad, they are physically much better preserved than most others. Second, unlike other Sikh sacred and cultural sites in Punjab resident Sikhs are employed as caretakers of the buildings at all three sites of the triad by the Archaeological Department of Pakistan. Furthermore, in the case of Gurdwara Patti Sahib in Nankana, the building is actually used as a place of residence and occupation by Sikhs who have migrated to Punjab from Afghanistan and Peshawar.[19] Third, as a result of individuals or communities of Sikhs who reside in or near the triad, these gurdwaras are actually operative, i.e., copies of the Guru Granth Sahib are installed and, small or large, services take place daily.

In stark contrast, most other gurdwara buildings in the rest of western Punjab are merely buildings that serve as historical treasures and hence, are inoperative as gurdwaras. They neither have copies of scripture installed within them nor individuals or communities living in their vicinity who worship there. In fact, the state of this very important religious and cultural Sikh heritage is quite precarious to say the least. Other gurdwara buildings are no better. Some have even lost their original status. For instance, there are gurdwara buildings that are currently used for civic and governmental purposes such as schools and police stations. Good examples of these include the Binat-ul-Islam High School located on Bairoon Sori Gali in Sahiwal, Gurdwara Nanaksar in Harappa which is now the only high school in town, and the police station in Mansehra which used to be a gurdwara. Other gurdwara buildings like the one in Gurdwara Bazaar, Abbotabad, are used by the Department of Archaeology as an office.[20]

Moreover, other Gurdwara buildings like Gurdwara Sri Guru Singh Sabha, Grain Market, Sahiwal, the Gurdwara at Dipalpur, and Gurdwara Guru ka Koth at Wazirabad are all used by people illegally[21] as places of residence. The structures of some of these edifices have been completely transformed. The place or platform where the Guru Granth Sahib used to be installed is often found removed or torn down for the convenience of the people who reside in the gurdwara building. Similarly, the poor state of preservation of historical Sikh space can also be seen in what is left of Gurdwara Tibba Nanaksar in Pakpattan. This historical gurdwara is significant because it marks the place where Guru Nanak met with Sheikh Ibrahim, a descendant of Baba Farid Ganj-i-Shakar, the famous Punjabi Sufi saint of the Chishtiya order. It is here that Guru Nanak is said to have collected the verses of Baba Farid that are included and preserved in the Guru Granth Sahib. This noteworthy Sikh treasure includes fascinating selections of rare[22] Gurmukhi scriptural verse etched on the inner and outer walls. Unfortunately, at the present time, the gurdwara building has been turned into a working barn where buffaloes and goats are being raised. Half the ceiling of the main hall has fallen and the rare Gurmukhi inscriptions seem to be slowly chipping off the walls.[23]

Gurdwara buildings are not the only entities that have been transformed due to inadequate preservation. Maharaja Ranjit Singh's birthplace in Gujranwala is in a similar state of neglect. The building has been variantly used as a fish shop, a place to cook samosas, and most recently, as a ground for playing cricket. Illias Ghumman, a well known Pakistani Punjabi writer and editor of the Punjabi magazine *Ravael*, wrote a very informative, insightful, and at the same time, a very melancholic article about his personal and reflective visits to Ranjit Singh's birthplace in *Ajit Magazine*, published from Jalandhar. His article, excerpts of which are translated below, talks about the tragic state of the building that has resulted from the absolute lack of its preservation despite the fact that it is the birthplace of one of the most renowned personalities that Punjab has ever produced:

These blue doors often remain shut. There is no need to lock them as the room which they belong to has nothing except darkness anymore. This room is part of a large *haveli* which is constructed from *Nanakshahi* bricks. The yellow paint that had long been covering its exterior has, to a good extent, come off now. Although I had intended to go to a different city, when passing through the city in which this *haveli* is located, I don't know why I got off the bus right here, and then, moving through the crowded bazaars covering a distance of about a kilometre and a half, ended up standing in front of this *haveli*.

What building is this? On this inquiry of mine, a young street vendor tells me very carelessly, 'Don't you know, this is the old police station. The police station moved from here a long time ago. Now only the name remains.'

'What will this kid of yesterday tell you, ask me,' an old shopkeeper gets up from behind the street vendor, comes close to me, and then, without my even asking him, starts telling me. 'This building was indeed a police station for a long time but in actuality it is not a police station. Wasn't there a Sikh king, dude, the one who conquered Lahore and Peshawar, he was born here... he had a beautiful name but what can I do, memory doesn't last with old age. Yeah, yeah, I remember, Ran....'

He couldn't even remember the full name when all of a sudden, a tall man comes from somewhere, drags him away from me, and murmurs something in his [the old man's] ear. I know this man too. He has collaborated with employees of the archaeology board and has taken control of the rooms on the lower floor of the *haveli*. He has a fish shop and the stench from the fishes kept in these rooms has destroyed the condition of the entire *haveli*. He knows me a little too. He thinks that I am either a government employee or a reporter. Whatever I may be, I am a danger to him and to his illegal business... he understands this completely.[24]

Later in the same article, Ghumman narrates a conversation that he has with one of the *Auqaf* (Archaeological Department) officers on duty. In this conversation, the Auqaf officer tells Ghumman that they have done their absolute best to protect the building. Responding to this self-praise, Ghumman remarks:

The hell you've done good work. Can't you see that the fish seller has now started keeping dirty baskets in the upper rooms as well.... The ceilings of the *haveli* are worse off than they were before. At many places, the ceiling has fallen down and the walls are further coming apart.[25]

Ghumman's article paints a very accurate and depressing picture of the calamitous state of Ranjit Singh's birthplace. What

Ghumman's article describes is not an exception but, more often than not, the norm. In other words, there are many more historical treasures of sacred and cultural Sikh space that are similarly being ravaged. Moreover, the number of historical buildings that are falling into oblivion unidentified and unrecognized is also on the rise every year. And finally, the rising wave of communalism and sectarian violence in the sub-continent is also having a serious impact on the vestiges of Sikh space in Western Punjab. This is specifically the case when buildings encompasing Sikh space resemble Hindu *mandirs* or are situated right next to them. Although the Pakistan Government attempts to protect such places, the vigorous response to incidents such as the demolition of the Babri Masjid in Ayodhya, India, cannot be fully contained.

The current state of Sikh buildings in West Punjab provokes many questions regarding the sacredness of Sikh space. For instance, what does it mean to call a place sacred when its sacredness is being or has already been radically transformed? If the integral elements of a gurdwara—a copy of the Guru Granth Sahib, an active congregation, and *kirtan* performers—are all absent from a gurdwara building, can it be considered sacred to the same extent as gurdwara buildings, for example those of the triad, that have all of the elements mentioned above? When the platform on which the Guru Granth Sahib was once installed has been removed for the convenience of the unauthorized residents of a gurdwara building, is not some degree of sacredness of the place lost?

Sikh doctrine and beliefs allow everyone, regardless of race, sex, religious, or national background, admission to gurdwaras. Non-Sikhs can not only eat the *langar* (food) provided by gurdwaras but can also stay at the rest-houses built within most gurdwara complexes. However, these principles of non-discrimination are easily transformed in West Punjab where Sikhs like myself have to obtain permission, either from Auquaf authorities or from the illegal residents of many gurdwara buildings,[26] to enter the sacred and cultural Sikh space. When the historic meeting point–Gurdwara Tibba Nanaksar, Pakpattan–of two very famous religious traditions of the subcontinent, Sikhism and Chishtiya Sufism, is turned into a barn for water buffaloes, goats, and a place for storing dried cow dung, what does it mean? How does an important centre like the birthplace of Maharaja Ranjit Singh, one of the most famous rulers of the Punjab, retain its significance when everything from selling fish to playing cricket is carried out there? Although the sacred, cultural, and symbolic significance of the aforementioned places will remain intact in the minds and hearts of those people who care about these places, their physical existence is certainly endangered by the kind of treatment that is meted out by different people.

Notes Towards Conclusion

Sacred and cultural Sikh space in West Punjab has undergone numerous changes as a result of the religious, social, and demographic shifts that were inflicted on Punjab in consequence of the partition. As we have seen in this chapter the changes, that Sikh sacred and cultural space experienced (as an outcome of the partition) are not only many in number but are also linked to different aspects of Sikh life. The partition and the resultant changes that accompanied it have definitely heightened the importance and symbolic significance of different gurdwaras, especially the triad which has been integral to and has figured prominently in Sikh history and religion for a long time. Furthermore the partition, as we have documented in this paper, has lead to the permanent scriptural canonization of Sikh sacred and cultural centres in West Punjab. We have also looked at annual pilgrimage processes, including the various cultural dimensions of such processes, all of which commenced and evolved only after the partition.

The changes that we have described and analyzed in this paper are only a small fragment of the many more that these buildings experience during their life cycles. More importantly, sacred and cultural Sikh space in Western Punjab continues to evolve rapidly. What will become of the hundreds of unattended gurdwaras that are scattered throughout West Punjab in the years to come? Will they achieve a fate similar to Ranjit Singh's birthplace in Gujranwala or Gurdwara Tibba Nanaksar in Pakpattan that has become a barn? Or will they survive like the buildings of the triad? What role will future governments and their appointees in the Department of Archaeology play in the preservation of this very important cultural heritage? Will the increasing number of Sikh pilgrims from India and other parts of the Sikh diaspora help in preserving and restoring Sikh sacred and cultural space in West Punjab? Only time will provide the answers to these aforementioned questions. While our research here is not definitive, it is our hope that our small inquisitive venture in documenting important Sikh religious and cultural heritage will generate greater interest and more extensive research of sacred and cultural Sikh space in West Punjab.

NOTES

1. The time period of the Sikh Gurus dates from the life of the founding Guru, Nanak (1469-1539) to the life of the last human Guru, Gobind Singh (1666-1708). Guru Nanak began establishing *dharamshallas,* which are distinct from the later structures, gurdwaras. The important question persists, though beyond the scope of this paper, as to when and how *dharamshallas* became gurdwaras. As they are both representative of Sikh cultural and sacred space, we are not drawing a functional distinction between the two.

2. Translated from the Punjabi, Bhai K. S. Nabha, *Gurshabad Ratankar Mahan Kosh* (Patiala, Languages Department, 5th ed. 1990), 416-17.

3. Although all gurdwaras are historical in one sense or another, for the purpose of this paper, 'historical gurdwaras' refers to those gurdwaras that are connected to any one of the the ten Sikh human gurus.

4. Literally, 'an elder'.

5. For a list of the estates adjoining different gurdwaras and their occupants, see Narain Singh, *Nankana Sahib* (Patiala, Languages Department, 1969). Text in Punjabi.

6. For more information on these movements, see Ganda Singh, ed. *The Singh Sabha and other Socio-Religious Movements in the Punjab 1850-1925,* vol. VII, part I (April 1973) of the *The Punjab Past and Present*

(Patiala, Punjabi University, 1984); Ruchi Ram Sahni, *Struggle for Reform in Sikh Shrines* (Amritsar, Sikh Itihas Research Board, 1964).

7. G.S. Dhillon, *Janamasthan: Yesterday, Today and Tomorrow* (Washington DC, Sri Nankana Sahib Foundation Inc., 1979) 35; for information on similar campaigns pertaining to other gurdwaras, see Narain Singh, *Nankana Sahib*.

8. ਸਿਨ੍ਹਾਂ ਸਿੰਘਾਂ ਸਿੰਘਣੀਆਂ ਨੇ . . . ਗੁਰਦੁਆਰਿਆਂ ਲਈ ਕੁਰਬਾਨੀਆਂ ਕੀਤੀਆਂ *'Ardas'* in *Nitnem te hor baNia(n)* Amritsar, Shirmonai Gurdwara Prabhandak Committee, 1986) 14.

9. Although important cities in East Punjab like Amritsar are so close to important centres of West Punjab like Lahore, it is extremely difficult for residents of either Punjab to visit the home towns that they had to leave because of the partition.

10. Dhillon, *Janamasthan*, 47.

11. ਹੇ ਅਕਾਲ ਪੁਰਖ ਆਪਣੇ ਪੰਥ ਦੇ ਸਦਾ ਸਹਾਈ ਦਾਤਾਰ ਜੀਓ! ਸ੍ਰੀ ਨਨਕਾਣਾ ਸਾਹਿਬ ਤੇ ਹੋਰ ਗੁਰਦੁਆਰਿਆਂ ਗੁਰਧਾਮਾਂ ਦੇ, ਜਿਨ੍ਹਾਂ ਤੋਂ ਪੰਥ ਨੂੰ ਵਿਛੋੜਿਆ ਗਿਆ ਹੈ, ਖੁਲ੍ਹੇ ਦਰਸ਼ਨ ਦੀਦਾਰ ਤੇ ਸੇਵਾ ਸੰਭਾਲ ਦਾ ਦਾਨ ਖਾਲਸਾ ਜੀ ਨੂੰ ਬਖਸ਼ੋ *'Ardas'* in *Nitnem*, 156.

12. *Vaisakhi* is an important Sikh festival celebrating the formation of the Khalsa in the month of Vaisakh, the first month of the Indian year, in 1699.

13. '526th birth celebrations of Baba Guru Nanak start', *The News* (Lahore), 6 November 1995.

14. ਹਸੰਦਿਆ ਖੇਲੰਦਿਆ ਪੈਨੰਦਿਆ ਖਾਵੰਦਿਆ ਵਿਚੇ ਹੋਵੈ ਮੁਕਤਿ *Guru Granth Sahib* (standard edition), 522.

15. Sultan Rahi is probably the most popular contemporary Pakistani Punjabi film star who died in 1996.

16. *The Daily Jang* (Lahore), 21 April 1996. Text in Urdu.

17. Unlike Gurpurab celebrations in Pakistan, the word mela is rarely used to describe important Sikh festivals in India.

18. This is not exactly true. For one thing, many Sikhs opt to visit a fourth Gurdwara, Sachaa Sauda, Sheikhupura.

19. For information on how the Afghani Sikhs have transformed the use of some of these buildings that were once historical treasures, see C. Fair and G. Singh, 'Afghani Sikhs: Interrogating Notions of the Sikh Diaspora,' unpublished paper.

20. Many such gurdwaras are listed in Khan, *Sikh Shrine in West Pakistan*, 1962.

21. All gurdwara buildings in Pakistan are supposed to be under the control and management of the Department of Archaeology.

22. The selections of verse present in this gurdwara building are inscribed in Gurmukhi words joined together. This is a rare phenomena as it is found in very old Gurmukhi books or manuscripts.

23. These observations are based on two extensive field visits to Gurdwara Tibba Nanaksar in Dec. 1995 and March 1996.

24. *Ajit Magazine* (Jullundur), 6 March 1994. Text in Punjabi.
25. Ibid.
26. In addition to many such gurdwaras in Rawalpindi and Sahiwal, gurdwaras in Dipalpur, Guru ka Koth (Wazirabad) are two prominent examples.

Chapter Nine

Partition and Kashmir:
Implications for the Region and the Diaspora

Patricia Ellis and Zafar Khan

As the processes associated with the act of partition unfolded in South Asia, the events in the princely state of Kashmir set the basis for a continuing dispute which fifty years later affects the relationship between India and Pakistan and reverberates throughout the Kashmiri diaspora. This is the longest running dispute on the books of the United Nations and is the reason given for the high level of current spending on military personnel and hardware in both Pakistan and India. It is also now recognized internationally as a potential nuclear flash point on the subcontinent. This lack of resolution not only affects the internal politics of India and Pakistan but also their positions within the world of international politics. For India it potentially threatens its political ambitions to be recognized as a 'superpower' through membership of the UN Security Council. For Pakistan it contributed to consideration by the USA of their inclusion on the list of 'Terrorist States'. It has been the basis of three military confrontations between India and Pakistan. When India became a republic in 1949, the Commonwealth Conference of that year not only adapted aspects of its constitution to allow for membership of a republic but also in its declaration made no mention of military security or political cooperation. This was without doubt partially in recognition of the aggression between India and Pakistan over Kashmir.[1] Jalal in her recent examination of political developments in South Asia concluded that

> By far the most serious problem in the region is the popularly backed armed uprising in Kashmir which raises the spectre of nuclear war between India and Pakistan. An acute manifestation of

India's federal dilemma, Kashmir also exemplifies the inter-connectedness of domestic, regional and international problems. It is a supreme irony of the times that a region with a long history of working out creative political arrangements based on layers of sovereignty appears today to have declared sovereignty a non-negotiable issue.[2]

When British Paramountcy lapsed, Kashmir was the only one of the 565 princely states to experience partition of its territory and the split of its control between India and Pakistan. This division of the state was not accepted by many of its population and still is the subject of dispute. Fifty years after partition, Kashmir is the only territory in the subcontinent whose situation has remained unresolved with the majority of its population not accepting the *status quo* thus placing it in a unique position within the region. These events have fuelled the development of Kashmiri nationalism which has erupted again strongly in the 1990s.

The history of Kashmir over the past fifty years is the history of two territories with different patterns of development but with the populations of both areas continuing to dispute the division. In spite of the incorporation of one part into the Indian state and the other into the jurisdiction of Pakistan, the expression of political militancy is 'state-wide' including the organization of specific political movements of which the prime ones are Jammu Kashmir Liberation Front (JKLF) and Hizb-ul-Mujahideen. Whilst the situation in the Indian controlled part of Kashmir has been the subject of analysis within the academic world[3] little has been written on the development of the situation over this period in Azad Kashmir which is under the control of Pakistan. For Indian politicians Azad Kashmir is seen as the training ground for terrorist incursions into the Valley and proof in their eyes of Pakistani support for destabilization of Indian territory.[4] Meanwhile for many British academics, Azad Kashmir or rather the district of Mirpur, is viewed only as the place of origin of the sizeable immigrant community now settled in the United Kingdom who most writers label as Pakistanis, Punjabis or Mirpuris without acknowledgement of their particular origin as Kashmiris and its significance.[5] This relative invisibility of Azad

Kashmir in literature hampers clear understanding, which is important for analysis of events in the subcontinent as well as for the development of the settled community of Kashmiris in the United Kingdom. The continuing consciousness of Kashmiri identity fifty years after partition and its expression in current organized political activity cannot be meaningfully analysed without acknowledgement of the pivotal links between the experiences of the population of Azad Kashmir, developments in the Kashmiri diaspora and the events in Indian-controlled Kashmir.

In the context of the events of partition and the division of the state of Kashmir, this chapter first examines the evolution of Azad Kashmir and its relationship with Pakistan over the fifty year period to date and includes a brief analysis of the impact of some of the developments in Punjab during this period. The chapter then explores the current situation in Azad Kashmir and the attitudes and actions of Azad Kashmiris both in the subcontinent and the United Kingdom in relation to the Kashmir dispute. Data on current attitudes amongst Azad Kashmiris and the situation in Azad Kashmir is drawn from fieldwork in the United Kingdom and Azad Kashmir.[6] Interviews were held across the social structure of Azad Kashmir and they include the views of articulate villagers and local professionals as well as those of government officials and senior politicians. In the United Kingdom, interviews and observational studies have involved a wide spectrum of members of the Kashmiri community including those with a high level of involvement in Kashmiri political activity. The views of those who are not themselves part of the political elite but who give time or money to support political activities, or of those whose lives have been touched by the situation in Kashmir and who care about the outcomes, make a valuable contribution to an understanding of the forces at work alongside the views of politicians and policy makers. As Talbot says, 'there is growing realization that the discourse centred solely on the 'high' politics of independence and partition is self-limiting.'[7]

Events at Partiton: Context for Kashmiri Nationalism

The final partition plan for the subcontinent excluded the 565 princely states. Congress maintained that once the Paramountcy of the British Crown lapsed the successor states (and Congress considered India as the successor to the British Rule in India) would assume rights over these states. Whilst as Saraf states 'Quaid-e-Azam was clearly of the view that Indian states were constitutionally entitled to resume their independence after the lapse of Paramountcy.'[8] Within this context, the reluctance and dithering of Maharajah Hari Singh to act in a decisive way before both India and Pakistan came into being as the successor states brought Kashmir into contention between the two future powers. Their involvement over Kashmir and the clash of arms further heightened their mutual distrust and fear. This confrontation has been called by Taylor a 'civil war out of time'[9] which brought into sharp focus to the outside world the existence of two hostile powers on the subcontinent.

For the overwhelming majority of the population of the Dogra Kingdom, the central issue since the 1930s and even earlier had been the establishment of political, economic and civil rights. They had been subjected to draconian laws and therefore a deep and abiding resentment and alienation existed against the autocracy of the last ruler of the Dogra dynasty. Fuelled by suspicions about the intentions of the various political actors involved with partition, a full scale uprising against the Maharajah took place in Poonch and other nearby areas which his government found increasingly difficult to control. This was the area which was subsequently to become Azad Kashmir. Recent writings on Kashmir suggest that the population was right in its suspicion. Wirsing and Malik agree that key leaders in both India and Pakistan without question harboured unambiguous territorial ambitions about Kashmir and this is perhaps epitomized in a much quoted report:

> VP Menon... raised his glass to Symon [British Deputy High Commissioner].' 'Here it is', he said, 'We have Kashmir. The

bastard [the Maharajah] signed the Act of Accession. And now we've got it, we'll never let it go.'[9]

Saraf considers the treatment meted out to the 90 million inhabitants of Indian princely states as the most tragic part of the partition. He particularly laments the fact that while in British India—even afterwards—Muslim members of the majority provinces were given the right to choose between the two dominions, similarly the non-Muslim minority was vested with the power of veto which brought about the partition of Punjab and Bengal, unlike them the inhabitants of the princely states were 'treated like a herd of dumb driven cattle who had no voice in deciding the question of accession to either of the two dominions.'[11] His reference here is particularly apt for Jammu Kashmir.[12] He also brings out the fact that the reason why the Congress and the Muslim League agreed the rulers could decide about the future of those states was that both parties expected the policy would benefit them.

The partition of Punjab is also considered central to Indian plans for future involvement in Jammu and Kashmir. Traditionally routes into the State of Jammu and Kashmir from India were either from Rawalpindi to Srinagar or from the Pathankot railhead. The Punjab Boundary Commission was therefore of decisive importance. Lamb advances a number of, what he calls, 'hypotheses' based on fragmentary but weighty evidence. He believes that research indicates that the government of India had worked out the kind of Punjab boundary they wanted well before Radcliffe and his judges set it down.[13] He also puts forward the thesis that the League and Congress leaders challenged initial ideas for the boundary line as both sides became increasingly aware that

> beyond the partition of the Punjab lay the prospect of yet another partition or redistribution of territory of enormous significance for the future. Jinnah and Liaquat Ali Khan who had hitherto assumed that Kashmir would become part of Pakistan now saw that it might very well not and that denial to India of trans Ravi *tehsils* of Gurdaspur began to assume a special significance.[14]

Wirsing points out that Lamb's views about Nehru's deliberate plans for acquiring Kashmir, find support in the recent writings of Congress members.[15] The suspicion of direct political interference in the making of the Punjab boundary has always been held by Pakistanis and Kashmiris. Increasingly scholars have lent credibility to the suspicion:

> it remains circumstantial; but over the years the circumstantial evidence has been accumulating at a rate and of a quality far in excess of anyone's ability to explain it away.[16]

While the extent of political manipulation surrounding the division and the transition from princely state to independence may never be fully revealed, perhaps the most critical aspect of these events is the continuing impact that the perceptions of injustice and illegality in relation to the Indian control of Kashmir still make, fifty years later, to the aspirations of Kashmiris in the subcontinent and in the diaspora.

The Formation and Political Development of Azad Jammu Kashmir

During the time the accession drama and boundary decisions on Punjab unfolded, the rebellion against the Jammu and Kashmir ruler became intense. In many areas particularly those which were later to comprise Azad (Free) Kashmir the state forces were not able to hold ground. The Maharajah asked India for help in quelling the rebellion while India presented him with a *fait accompli* 'accede to India or lose your power' at the hands of the rebels. Many areas of the state were liberated and in those areas a provisional government of the Republic of Kashmir was set up on 4 October 1947 under a man simply called Anwar. Many agree that he was Ghulam Nabi Gilkar, a prominent activist belonging to the Muslim Conference. The decision to set up a provisional government was no doubt right and timely according to Saraf, however it was taken at what he calls 'such a municipal level even without the knowledge of the party's top brass' (party being the All Jammu Kashmir Muslim Conference).[17] However this government was reconstituted under Sardar Muhammad Ibrahim Khan on 23 October 1947. This reconstituted government was answerable to the Working Committee of the Muslim Conference. Thus responsibility for governing became vested in the Muslim Conference.

However, the Government of Azad Kashmir was not fully in control of its affairs. As Saraf points out it was deprived of important powers through an agreement between the Government of Pakistan and the Azad Kashmir Government/ Muslim Conference. This agreement outlined the division of functions—defence, foreign affairs, negotiations with UNCIP, publicity in foreign countries and in Pakistan, responsibilities for relief and rehabilitation of refugees, the plebiscite, activities related to procurement of food, civil supplies, transport, refugee camps, and medical aid would be dealt with by Pakistan. Also the affairs of Gilgit, and Ladakh (Baltistan) previously under a political agent, became the responsibility of the Pakistan government. (These Northern Areas were not part of Pakistan constitutionally although this was the *de facto* position as they were managed by a Pakistani Political Agent.) All the other matters were essentially of a local nature and remained within the purview of the Azad Kashmir administration.[18] This agreement basically existed between the Government of Pakistan and the Muslim Conference until 1970. There were no direct elections for the Assembly and the practice had been to appoint a head of administration (government) after his approval by the Working Committee of the Muslim Conference. In 1961 an electoral College of Basic Democrats (under the BD system introduced into Pakistan by Ayub Khan) was also introduced into Azad Kashmir and these were elected through an adult suffrage. These basic democrats numbered 2400 and through this system they elected the charismatic K.H. Khurshid for the first time by a popular but indirect vote. The first State Council was set up in 1961 with two state councillors elected from each of the three districts of Azad Kashmir. This was increased to a total of twelve

in 1968 with the new Government Act and included
representation from the refugees from 1947 with two seats for
those from Jammu and two for those from the Valley. These four
refugee State Councillors were to be nominated by the President
on the recommendation of the Chief Adviser.

Such a set-up made Azad Kashmir no better than a municipal
committee and great resentment against this act developed in
Azad Kashmir. In 1968 Amanullah Khan and others took out a
procession of the All Parties Kashmir Committee in Karachi
representing various parties including the Plebiscite Front and
the Liberation League. The Plebiscite Front of Azad Kashmir
was the forerunner of JKLF of which Amanullah Khan is the
present head. It is at this point in the development of Azad
Kashmir that leaders such as Sardar Qayyum, Sardar Ibrahim
and K.H. Khurshid joined forces and demanded that Azad
Kashmir should be recognized as the sovereign government
successor of Maharajah Hari Singh for the whole of the state.

In 1970 the Legislative Assembly was set up and a
constitution drawn up for Azad Kashmir. It is said that under the
first election based on adult franchise, the elected president
Sardar Abdul Qayum Khan lifted the status of Azad Kashmir
from a hitherto municipal level to a provincial level and brought
home to Pakistan that

> …we are not a bunch of mountain dwelling simple folk who live on
> Pakistan's bounty but a dynamic people even capable of giving a
> lead to Pakistan despite having clipped our wings in the 1949
> Karachi agreement.'[19]

With the expression of such sentiments, Saraf also reflects a
growing restlessness among political parties and their leaders
about the lack of substance, political authority, credibility and
responsibility which could come with an enhancement of Azad
Kashmir's status.

Despite the emergence of institutions and indeed the
Legislative Assembly in Azad Kashmir, the power of Azad
Kashmir functionaries are always subject to the likes and dislikes
of the government in Islamabad. Direct influence and at times

control are exercised through the Ministry of Kashmir Affairs which is also responsible for the 'Northern Areas' (Gilgit and Baltistan). The Minister of Kashmir Affairs can exert enormous power and influence on the outcome of events that occur in Azad Kashmir politics. Furthermore the Chief Secretary of Azad Kashmir and the Director General (DIG) of Police are appointed directly by Pakistani authorities. Other similar 'lent officers' holding top posts in the civil administration have invariably come from Pakistan and still do. This practice continues and mirrors that of the Dogra rulers of Kashmir who would borrow civil servants from the Political Department of the British Indian government. Saraf's assessments of that practice is that 'lent officers' were 'petty minded and lived as high-caste Brahmins in what they considered a society of untouchables.'[20] While these attitudes may have changed somewhat since the era of the princely state, these 'lent' officers do however exert inordinate influence at times contrary to the wishes of the Azad Kashmir rulers.

In 1974 the constitution was amended and it was affected by the 1973 constitution of Pakistan in that the political parties of Azad Kashmir found it easier to demand from Pakistan greater and more meaningful representation. Under the 1974 constitution the President would be elected by the Legislative Assembly. The Kashmir Council was established as the Upper House. This comprises twelve members of whom six are elected by the Azad Kashmir Assembly and the President is the seventh member by virtue of his office and acts as the vice-chairman. The Prime Minister of Pakistan is the chair of the Kashmir Council and the Minister of Kashmir Affairs is its secretary. The other three members are appointed by the Prime Minister of Pakistan.

The political system has always been closely tied into that of Pakistan. Under Article 56 of the Pakistan Constitution, the Pakistan Government has the authority to remove any Azad Kashmir Government despite the fact that under the Pakistan Constitution Azad Kashmir is not part of Pakistan. Martial law was never imposed in Azad Kashmir although the Legislative Assembly was suspended by Zia from 1977 to 1985 and there was direct rule by the President who was appointed by Zia. When the Legislative Assembly was reconvened in the mid 1980s, an additional seat was created for a Representative of the Overseas Kashmiris in recognition of the significant size of the diaspora. This seat is an appointment by the Azad Kashmir Prime Minister. The British Kashmiri community is the largest in the diaspora and has been the scene of the greatest political activity in relation to both parts of Kashmir, so it is not surprising that the seat until now has always been held by someone from the British Kashmiri community. This appointment has always generated a fair amount of competition between potential candidates with a lot of energy and resources being utilized in both the United Kingdom and in Azad Kashmir to influence the decision. From 1993 this position is held by a German-based Kashmiri member of the AKPP who is close to Benazir Bhutto.

An Azad Kashmir branch of the People's Party was established in late 1969 and this heralded the start of party politics in Azad Kashmir. Jama'ati-Islami is also now established within Azad Kashmir politics. Although parties are nominally independent of their counterparts in Pakistan, the reality is that the Pakistanis are extremely influential and unofficially exercise a 'chief whip' role on the members of the Azad Kashmir government and this is particularly the case where the party in power in Azad Kashmir is the same as that in power in Pakistan. The political fraternity is pro-Pakistan and is like a political family although some seek their identity through local political symbols and some through Pakistani political symbols.

A constitutional crisis occurred in May 1996 which underlined how closely Azad Kashmir governance is tied into that of Pakistan politics. The maximum term of office was about to finish for the Muslim Conference government of Sardar Qayum at about the same time as the office of the President was coming up for re-election. The Prime Minister of Pakistan indicated a time for the presidential election which would potentially favour her party. In order to highlight the issue the President who had Muslim Conference affiliations resigned ahead of time so that the Muslim Conference government saw through the presidential election. Then, he immediately offered himself for re-election and was successful. Three weeks later however the Legislative Assembly elections returned a People's Party government which immediately deposed the President through a no-confidence vote challenging the legitimacy of the recent presidential election. It could be perceived that the Assembly was now exercising its democratic right to dissent through as, for example this vote of no confidence.

Sardar Ibrahim who headed the first official government of Azad Kashmir in 1947 and who is an AKPP member has now been appointed President for the period 1996-2001. This means that the fifty year period of the existence of Azad Kashmir starts and ends with the same person at the helm and a person who has clear memories of the traumas associated with partition and the division of Kashmir.

The constitution of 1974 excludes anyone who does not support the idea of accession to Pakistan for Kashmir from standing for the Legislative Assembly. It therefore excludes those who support ideas of Kashmiri self-determination and independence for Kashmir. Thirty candidates were barred from participating in the 1996 elections by this means. At the time of the fieldwork in Azad Kashmir some were in the process of appealing from within the legal system challenging the legality of such an obstacle and its consistency with the operation of natural justice. This means that the liberation movement and its different groups by definition must operate outside of the official political representation system in Azad Kashmir. A growing number of Azad Kashmiris question this constraint on standing for the Assembly and make comparisons with the political situation in the Indian controlled part of Kashmir which Azad Kashmiri politicians constantly denounce. The main party of the liberation movement, JKLF, whilst opposing this political constraint along with other parties does not see local electoral activities as significantly beneficial to the aim of self-determination for Kashmiris. During the election campaign in June 1996, JKLF held well-attended meetings across Azad Kashmir — even better attended than those of the main political parties, in which they advised their members to refrain from participating in the election as voting achieved little. During elections the flying of the party flag is a major way of denoting political allegiances. In the districts around Mirpur, Kotli, Rawalakot and Muzaffarabad there appeared to be more JKLF flags attached to houses and public buildings than those of any other political group. It is clear that political loyalties within Azad Kashmir are divided between support for the domestic parties of the country and for the liberation movement and that this split stretches across all the strata of the society.

The Development of Azad Kashmir Society

It is not only in its political development that Azad Kashmir is tied closely to Pakistan. The major economic and allied social policies that have shaped much of present day Azad Kashmir also come from Pakistan, leaving the country's administrative and legislative machinery a role in the less significant areas of decision-making. Pakistan is powerful in its control and influence in three ways: national economic and social decisions aimed at the development of Pakistan, or Punjab in particular, are either explicitly designed to relate also to Azad Kashmir or have a knock-on effect on Azad Kashmir; Pakistan controls defence and foreign relations policy in Azad Kashmir, the former of which has a significant impact not only on the economy but also on the social structures of Pakistani society and has an especially powerful and openly observable impact within Azad Kashmir because of the security issues arising from the Kashmir situation; finally, Pakistan is responsible for providing part of the budget of Azad Kashmir which places it in a strong controlling position when it chooses to exercise that power.

One crucial way in which Azad Kashmir has been tied up with Pakistan is in education. Schools and universities are not only the means by which a society educates and trains its workforce but they also operate for developing a national identity. The school curriculum in Azad Kashmir is that of Pakistan and is controlled from Pakistan. Azad Kashmiris are proud of their educational achievements particularly in the area of literacy, and female education in comparison to Pakistan. However a consistent criticism heard during the fieldwork from young people in particular is that a key thread to the curriculum is that of building a Pakistani identity even for Azad Kashmiris. School textbooks are written and published in Pakistan and until very recently none were available which included anything systematic for Azad Kashmiris about Kashmir, its geography, history, social and cultural development. The new texts that are just coming in at pre-primary and junior school level in Azad Kashmir are of a UNESCO funded development project rather than a Pakistani government intitiative. These texts will only be issued within Azad Kashmir which means that Pakistani school children will have little formal opportunity to understand the roots of current Kashmiri identity and its importance in the development of Azad Kashmir. Azad Kashmiris who had received university education in Pakistan, related that they had met a lot of negative stereotyping of Azad Kashmiris from Pakistani students who had little idea of, or sympathy for, the aspirations of the residents of Azad Kashmir. The postgraduate Kashmiri studies courses available at the Universities of Azad Kashmir and Punjab at Lahore were not seen to necessarily redress this imbalance. The criticism made was that the number of students doing these was very small, but much more importantly the curriculum was seen to be deliberately apolitical with the emphasis on art, literature, Kashmiri language (which is basically only spoken in the Kashmir valley part of the Indian controlled state) and history which focused on past centuries. The little discussion of the present day political situation and ideas on these courses was seen to conform compleletly with the Pakistani position on the Kashmir situation which condemned Indian actions and refused to accept the validity of debates amongst Kashmiris on both sides of the border about the type of political future for a re-united State of Kashmir and issues around its sovereignty. So Pakistani educational policy at all age levels was seen to actively promote the building of a Pakistani identity at the expense (for

Azad Kashmiris) of a Kashmiri identity and therefore to be further reinforcing the idea that Azad Kashmir is *de facto* a part of Pakistan.

Perhaps the most significant Pakistani policy decision that touched the lives of many Azad Kashmiris and significantly changed demographic and economic aspects of Azad Kashmiri society was the construction of the Mangla Dam by Pakistan in the early 1960s. The Mangla Dam was built in Azad Kashmir to generate electricity to meet the energy needs of Punjabi industry and the large cities of Punjab. This massive project brought upheaval into the lives of thousands of inhabitants of Mirpur District as the lake that was created removed over a hundred square miles of good agricultural land from the local economy and flooded 250 villages. This meant the move of whole villages, the recreation of village life in a new location and the disruption of local communication networks. Fifteen years ago Ballard found that agricultural productivity had not recovered from the impact of the dam's construction and that Mirpur District was 'no longer self-sufficient even in food grains: large quantities of wheat are imported from elsewhere in Pakistan.'[21] This is still the case fifteen years later and demonstrates how the long term knock-on effect of a Pakistani national development policy has been to bind Azad Kashmir more closely into the economy of Pakistan.

However, perhaps a more important consequence for Azad Kashmir was the enormous expansion of the diaspora. A significant proportion of those affected by the building of the dam used their compensation as an opportunity to fund a move to a new life either in Punjab or in the United Kingdom. The migration impact of this upheaval spread beyond the immediate environs of the reservoir and particularly to what was then the *tehsil* (and is now the district) of Kotli. This creation of a sizeable diaspora particularly in the United Kingdom has had two major consequences for Azad Kashmir: the first is the establishment of a remittance sub-economy in Azad Kashmir; the second is the strengthening active support for Kashmiri liberation political activity linking the diaspora with both parts of

Kashmir but particularly with Azad Kashmir. As Ballard commented fifteen years ago analyzing the consequences of the migration from Mirpur and Jullundur, 'migration is altogether more complex in both its context and its consequences than many commentators have yet recognized.'[22] However in his analysis he did not recognize the then emerging consequences for Kashmiri politics of the creation of such a large but geographically concentrated diaspora. Nor could he have anticipated the ways in which the technological advances and the globalization of telecommunication networks would work to support this development.

Ballard found that migrant remittances played a significant part in Mirpuri life and that those families with members abroad had become increasingly dependent on regular remittances to maintain their living standards and that the exodus of the males had in some ways exacerbated the situation by removing the labour power for cultivating the land productively.[23] He also observed that much of the women's time in the villages was spent in fetching water from the streams etc. Many of his observations are still true in the late 1990s but since that period there has been considerable investment in the water systems by local government and individual households. The building boom has continued with major expansion of towns. Also, some villages have been funded in great part by remittance income. When Ballard was researching in Mirpur he found

> no lack of money in Mirpur District itself: there can be few other places in the third world which are so capital rich. Yet development stubbornly refuses to take place. The reasons for this must be sought... in the structural context in which they find themselves.[24]

In the late 1990s, Mirpur is a major banking centre because of the remittance-based economy and this has resulted in the opening of so many banks in Mirpur that there are more bank-branches per capita than in Karachi, the commercial capital of Pakistan. However there are no Azad Kashmiri banks because, as senior bankers in Mirpur explained, Pakistan controls the banking sector and will not grant a licence to an Azad Kashmiri enterprise. Azad Kashmiris form the bulk of the 'Pakistani' migration to the United Kingdom and so it is likely that the majority of British remittances are coming back into Azad Kashmir rather than Pakistan. However thanks to the the control on the banking system, as various interviewees asserted, Pakistan gains foreign exchange benefit from the remittances and the use of investment opportunities through savings accounts within Pakistan. It was pointed out with some irony that in many cases the banks will be supporting new businesses in Punjab, adjacent to Azad Kashmir. This may go some way to explaining some part of the structural context that Ballard alluded to. However there are other factors at work affecting the economic development of Azad Kashmir in relation to the use of remittances.

In the interview with Sardar Qayum, the Prime Minister of Azad Kashmir at the time of the fieldwork, it was stated that the government considered the diaspora important in the development of the economy; although it was mostly through sharing of earning with their families in Azad Kashmir that resulted in improved housing and a rise in the standard of living. There was evidence of some remittances being used as investment in Azad Kashmir but also it was noted that some were being used in Pakistan. Raja Zulqarnain Khan, the Finance Minister,[25] felt the economy was progressing well but remittances were falling as British-based Kashmiris were no longer in a position to send money as plentifully as earlier. The Government did not have any policies aimed specifically at the diaspora in relation to the investment of remittances. Instead they had general investment policies targeted at funds from abroad, and Mirpur and Bhimber were held up as examples of these in operation. These policies included exemption from various types of taxes and provision of services at 'reasonable rates'. It was pointed out that Azad Kashmir was a very secure area in terms of law and order especially compared to Pakistan. But while there were instances of major foreign investment such as a European hydroelectricity project in the Neelum Valley and some World Bank money, there had been no investment from the British or

Japanese and this was attributed to the Kashmir situation. The unresolved nature of the Kashmir issue was recognized as having a very negative impact on investment. Not surprisingly senior members of other political groupings such as Abdul Rashid Turabi, the President of the Jama'at-i-Islami in Azad Kashmir[26] and Amanullah Khan, the Chairman of the JKLF, did not share the view that the government was doing all it could in terms of harnessing the potential of the remittance income and the contribution that members of the diaspora could make to the development of Azad Kashmir. From discussions with some 'returned' Kashmiris who were potential investors, it was evident that they shared this critical assessment of government strategy. But they also raised the issue of the unresolved political situation as a real disincentive to investment. So the policies of the Azad Kashmir government can be seen as a potential contributor to Ballard's structural context but it is probably far less important than the continuing impact of the Kashmir situation.

Political activists as well as government ministers in interviews deplored the check on Kashmiri resources by Pakistan. The low government budget resulting from the lack of revenue from the Mangla Dam was cited as contributing to the poor development and upkeep of the internal road network which in turn affected the development of the economy. It was also pointed out that ironically the residents of Azad Kashmir are victims of 'load shedding' because of the growing energy consumption of Punjabi industry. Kashmiri politicians raise these issues in their dialogues with the Pakistan Financial Ministry over budget allocation. They also point out the need for a State Bank of Azad Kashmir and question the payment of royalties on Kashmiri properties to the Pakistan government. However such issues can only be used with any continuing success if they are seen to have a substantive base in the feelings of the general population and if they can be channelized towards the mobilization of the nationalist sentiment.

The Diaspora and Azad Kashmiri Politics

The Kashmiri diaspora comprises two main groups: those who migrated mainly in the 1960s and 1970s and have 'settled' either in the United Kingdom, other Western European countries or the United States of America; and, those who are working as migrant workers for extended periods of time primarily in the Middle East and South-east Asia. This latter group though increasingly important for the remittance income within Azad Kashmir has a small profile in Kashmiri political militancy compared to that of the Western diaspora. The British Kashmiri diaspora have played the most important role in Azad Kashmiri politics both at home and abroad. The diaspora settled in the West primarily comes from two districts of Azad Kashmir, Mirpur and Kotli, whilst those working in the Middle East historically come from the other districts but this has changed as Western immigration legislation has made it increasingly difficult to enter let alone settle in the West.

In the past decades political activism of a nationalist nature found itself stifled in Azad Kashmir for some of the reasons explored in the previous sections. Ballard recognized the potential importance of diaspora politics in affecting radical change in his article in 1983, he asked 'Who knows what political movements may emerge from the contemporary Mirpuri...diaspora?'[27] He seemed unaware that diaspora political organization had already started. The Jammu and Kashmir Liberation Front (JKLF) was founded in Birmingham in 1977 with Amanullah Khan as its chairman. It is the most important manifestation of diasporic mobilization around the Kashmir situation. In August 1985 after ten years in the United Kingdom Amanullah Khan was arrested by the British police and held for fifteen months before his trial on charges of bomb making and other allied activities. At this point he was a resident of Luton living in a residence aptly named Kashmir House.[28] He was acquitted of all charges but in spite of this was deported in December 1986. Kashmiris in the United Kingdom and in the subcontinent believe that the trial and subsequent deportation were carried out under pressure from the Indian government. However, in spite of this JKLF developed and grew in political terms so that it spread into Azad Kashmir and then over the ceasefire line into the Indian-controlled part of Kashmir. It was a leading founder member of the All Party Hurriyet Conference and is regularly engaged in discussions with members of the major Western governments and political organizations both formally and informally. Kashmiris point to the continuing attempts of the Indian government to undermine the success of JKLF, quoting as an example the Brussels affair of 1993. Following the effective lobbying of Kashmiri diaspora activists, the British MPs through the European Parliament Socialist Group organized in October 1993 a three-day conference in Brussels on Kashmir. Representatives from Indian, Pakistani and Kashmiri government organizations were invited including Sardar Qayum, Prime Minister of Azad Kashmir, and Farooq Abdullah, the Head of the National Conference and Chief Minister of Indian controlled Kashmir, as well as Amanullah Khan as Chairman of JKLF. At the end of the first day Amanullah Khan while driving with George Stevenson, the British MP, was arrested by the Belgian anti-terrorism police acting under Interpol instruction following a request from the Indian government. He was incarcerated until his trial in Brussels in December 1993 where again he was exonerated of all charges of terrorism but still deported. This treatment of the Kashmiri leadership with all its undertones of Indian intervention angers Kashmiris across the world and increases the difficulties for diaspora activists organizing legitimate political events in Western countries. Since the 1980s the Azad Kashmir People's Party, the Muslim Conference and Jamaat Islami have also organized official support amongst the British diaspora but with the focus on the development of Azad Kashmir.

Political activity in the Kashmiri diaspora has three different although at times related arenas:
• the first is in Azad Kashmir internal politics focused on the district of origin with the usual vehicle of influence being the *biraderi;*

- the second is in liberation politics mainly but not exclusively through support of the JKLF where the focus is on common beliefs about the reunification of Kashmir rather than *biraderi* or particular districts of origin;
- the third is in mainstream politics of United Kingdom[29] at the local and national levels where mobilization may use *biraderi* but is primarily focused on the area of settlement.

Those active in liberation politics in the diaspora may also use the first and particularly the third arena to exert influence to further the political aims of their cause. Involving the active support of mainstream politicians is an important part of the strategy for influencing the international as well as the national powers.

Basic involvement with the activities of liberation politics amongst the diaspora takes several forms:
- attendance at meetings within the locality of settlement;
- donation of money to support particular events, or in general for the cause;
- participation in rallies both local and national;
- organization of events locally or nationally;
- lobbying of local and national politicians through the signing of petitions, meetings and through letters written to the press (ethnic and mainstream).

The level of awareness of the politics of Kashmir is relatively high even amongst the generation of Kashmiris born in the West and many Kashmiri families are involved in one or more ways with the political work. Research amongst the British Kashmiri diaspora shows that Kashmiri identity is still intimately bound with the territory of Kashmir and that this is likely to remain strong as long as the territory is disputed.[30]

The activities of the leading members of the JKLF involve: development of strategy in the West; organization of events within the diaspora; lobbying of national and international politicians and organization of sympathetic influential groupings in mainstream political arenas; meetings at all levels from local to international; close liaison with JKLF in the subcontinent including organization of worldwide actions such as the symbolic crossing of the border in 1992 where the international publicity coverage was organized from the United Kingdom with some members of the diaspora participating in the crossing itself.

JKLF has first and foremost tapped into a common sentiment strongly held by Kashmiris in the subcontinent and in the diaspora and that is the desire for reunification of Kashmir and secondly into the belief that Kashmiris should have the main say in the future of divided Kashmir. All the interviewees in the fieldwork in Azad Kashmir from President to villagers expressed an overriding belief in the injustice and unacceptability of the present split. Reunification of Kashmir was the agreed goal. It is the JKLF that has put up independence for the reunified country on the political agenda; this is not acceptable to the Pakistani government nor therefore to the Azad Kashmir government. Given the official government policy it was not surprising that the independence option was dismissed in interviews with members of the Azad Kashmir political establishment. However, other interviewees were split over support for this position, but believed strongly that all Kashmiris should have a voice in future decision making. The question of identity as to who the Kashmiris are has important implications for the role of the diaspora in political events.

In relation to the diaspora, all interviewees saw its members as important in bringing up the Kashmir situation on the international political agenda. Many including Sardar Ibrahim and Sardar Qayum gave examples such as the effective influence of the British Labour Party's official position on the Kashmir situation to illustrate the importance of the activities of the diaspora. In August 1995 Robin Cook addressing Indian councillors in Brent, North London, in his role as Shadow Foreign Secretary stated that 'the position of the Labour Party is that Kashmir is part of the Indian State.' The Kashmiri diaspora reacted very speedily along with those in the subcontinent aided by the globalization of the telecommunications networks.[31]

This resulted in a clear policy position at the October Labour Party conference which satisfied the Kashmiri diaspora and which was subsequently followed up in visits by Robin Cook to both parts of Kashmir and talks with Pakistani and Indian leaders as well as with leaders of Kashmiri organizations including the JKLF. Rashid Turabi also used this example and added the comment that British Kashmiris had achieved what the High Commission of Pakistan had failed to manage. Raja Zulqarain Khan highlighted the way in which British Kashmiris had acquired a voice in the British parliament through the formation of the Kashmir Parliamentary Group as well as by bringing the Kashmir issue into the European Union. Several comments were made about the worldwide significance of the British media, in particular the BBC, and the way in which British Kashmiris had managed to achieve coverage of the issue in the media. Justice Gilani[32] voiced the sentiments of several interviewees when he observed that the diaspora had played a much more important role than the people of Azad Kashmir in sustaining Kashmir as an issue. Amanullah Khan too saw the British Kashmiris as significant in keeping the idea of battle alive when it was almost dead in Kashmir. He explained that this was due to the hustle bustle of Pakistani politics in Azad Kashmir and Indian politics in the 'Indian Occupied Kashmir', with 'liberation' taking a back seat to Pakistani and Indian politics. The parties in power gain a lot of advantages and money for their members and so Kashmiris were sucked into this. However, the British Kashmiris were not affected by Pakistani politics and therefore concentrated on liberation politics.

Gilani was also critical of the efforts of the Pakistani government citing the fact that they had put themselves out for Afghanistan with which they have no direct link but were not doing half as much for Kashmir for which they have a responsibility. He was also critical of the way in which the West had begun to respond, since 1980 over the issue of human rights violations while 'they do not see the underlying political rights.' Along with most other interviewees, he saw the situation as one that the British had created and for which they were now morally responsible. However, he recognized that morality is not part of international politics and as 'Kashmir has only beauty and no other resources' he believed that the Kashmiris in both Azad Kashmir and in the Indian-controlled part were dependent on the power of the British Kashmiris for opinion making.

The diaspora including the offspring of the migrants were regarded as Kashmiris by all interviewees irrespective of whether they had acquired a British passport or not. The word 'citizen' was seen to encompass the diaspora both emotionally and legally. According to Justice Gilani, Kashmiri citizenship was defined in 1858 by the Maharajah as applying to all those who lived in Kashmir at that time and their descendants—including up to two generations—of those living outside Kashmir. This ruling still exists as it has never been revoked and has important implications for any plebiscite run in the future for Kashmiris as it would then legally include most members of the diaspora. Many interviewees believed that the diaspora had the right to a voice in future decision-making because in the first place they were Kashmiris and also in recognition of their 'contribution to the struggle'.

The issue of British responsibility in the Kashmir situation was one that was brought up again and again in interviews from Government ministers to villagers. The Bar Association members in Dadyal, the heartland of Azad Kashmiri emigration, were so vociferous on the culpability of the British in the situation that it was extremely difficult to progress to the main questions of the research. In a meeting with the Bar Association of Kotli this position was also restated with the assertion that ninety percent of the population were of the same opinion. A senior female member of the Education Department in Muzaffarabad felt that there was universal agreement amongst men and women that the British Government bore heavy responsibility for the current situation. She felt that they should therefore act as a third party to bring India and Pakistan to the negotiating table but that unfortunately the British Government was inclined towards India. This belief of British partiality was reiterated in several interviews. All these sentiments were again raised in village interviews. The British Kashmiris were seen as the most appropriate and well-placed to exert influence on the British Government and through them on the Americans as key players in the international arena.

The Impact of the Kashmir Situation Fifty Years on

Throughout Azad Kashmir there are constant reminders of the division of Kashmir and its unresolved nature. The situation has had a direct impact not only on the physical, political and economic structure of Azad Kashmir, but also on the social and emotional life of the population. The feelings are a combination of reactions to the injustices believed to have been committed at the time of partition and to the subsequent events in the Indian-controlled part of Kashmir.

A stark symbol of the situation is the existence of refugee camps. Azad Kashmir has been home to refugees from the Indian-controlled part of Kashmir in 1947, 1965, 1971 and again since 1990. Basic shelter, medical facilities and education are provided by the authorities along with a subsistence level financial allowance. However the future looks bleak for many of the recent refugees. Another reminder of the situation is to be found in the presence of large numbers of military personnel permanently based in Azad Kashmir. Everywhere there is political graffiti on the walls calling for the liberation of Kashmir from Indian control. Many families have relatives in the other part of Kashmir and often property and land that have been abandoned with no chance of compensation or hope of a claim-suit. Also there is the ever present threat of physical danger for those who live close to the border from bullets and rockets fired over the ceasefire line.

The division of Kashmir is felt by most residents of Azad Kashmir whether living in the villages or the towns. People react strongly to the situation and that seems to be just as true for younger as for older people, for men as for women, for the well-educated as for the poorly educated. What differentiates people is the language of articulation rather than the basic sentiments.

Money is given from all sectors of the society to support the 'freedom fighters' and the refugees.

Whatever their situation within the society, people consistently describe in anger the continuing human rights violations in Indian-controlled Kashmir. They are often resentful of the way in which the world appears to be turning its back on this situation. For many the United Kingdom is a particular target of attack because of its involvement in the history of Kashmir as the colonial ruler. People at all levels of the society believe that the United Kingdom has a moral obligation to become actively involved in hammering out a satisfactory solution to the situation.

Consistently Azad Kashmiris wish to see the reunification of Kashmir. They also want a plebiscite to be organized. When questioned as to what the constituency for participation might be, many replied that it should include all Kashmiris and they used the old Dogra state definitions of citizens which are still in use in Azad Kashmir. The impression created from much of the discourse is that accession is largely rhetorical; what matters is reunification although Indian-control in that situation is out of the question. It is clearly a very politicized population and this carries with it potential problems for politicians. Azad Kashmir is economically and politically weak. In their wish to hold onto the real or illusory power, the politicians show pragmatic sense in following political developments in Pakistan: the political culture of Azad Kashmir remains subservient to Pakistani politics. However, with a relatively high level of political awareness in the population and an increasingly educated population, politicians face a difficult situation in the near future in balancing their necessary loyalty to Pakistan on the one hand, and, to the new language in politics which is emerging from the assertion of a nationalist Kashmiri identity.

Kashmir is the bone of contention between the two major powers of India and Pakistan souring potential cooperation in a range of areas and diverting resources to the detriment of the social and economic development of both countries as well as of Kashmir. The differences between the two countries over

Kashmir go back to partition. They are fundamental, and appear to be intractable. As Rose outlines:

> To the Pakistanis... religious community formed the basis for partition. For India the division was territorial rather than communal... To admit the legitimacy of Pakistan's position in the Kashmir dispute, the Indians argue, would undermine the secular state concept, one of the fundamental principles on which the Indian political and legal system is based.[33]

This has to be seen at the same time in the context of competition between the two powers with the situation that 'India's hegemony... has not contributed to progress towards a settlement and indeed may have hardened lines in both countries.'[34] This analysis was made in 1972 and more than twenty-five years later this competitive element is still seen to be fuelling 'perpetual conflict and intense rivalry between India and Pakistan that is completely absent in India's relations with other South Asian neighbours.'[35]

It is clear that in the dynamics of competition, the Kashmiris are the losers. Without some loosening of this situation, the present impasse will continue with increasing political militancy amongst the Kashmiris whether in the subcontinent or in the diaspora. The potential for conflict with the Kashmiris was recognized by Wilcox over twenty years ago: 'the leaders of various Kashmiri factions claim different things but almost all champion more autonomy than either India or Pakistan would allow.'[36] The situation in Indian-controlled Kashmir has deteriorated in the last decade and political militancy has spread across the Kashmiri population. In her analysis of India's democratic federalism, Jalal identifies the cause of the worsening crisis: 'regional dissidence was more in the way of an anti-systemic reaction to a constitutional framework patterned on the patron-client model than on an equitable partnership between the centre and the state.'[37] As she goes on to point out

> it is the repeated denial of the political as well as the economic and social rights of citizenship combined with the inversion of

secularism to promote a crude form of Hindu communalism that has led [the Kashmiris] to agitate for complete independence from India.[38]

Many of the Kashmiris in Indian-controlled Kashmir want freedom from the rule of India and many in Azad Kashmir want the reunification of Kashmir whilst all Kashmiris want an end to the suffering. What is open to discussion is where the Kashmiris wish to go. Perhaps fifty years on from partition is the time to find out what the Kashmiris want to do and where they want to go. It is time to move forward from the positions held by India and Pakistan at partition time. One of the greatest contributions that could be made to the subcontinent at this time would be for some outstanding statesperson to succeed in this negotiation and bring peace to South Asia thus unlocking the human and economic potential of this part of the globe.

NOTES

1. D. Judd, *Empire: The British Imperial Experience from 1765 to the Present* (London, Harper Collins, 1996), 341.
2. A. Jalal, *Democracy and Authoritarianism in South Asia: A Comparative and Historical Perspective* (Cambridge, Cambridge University Press, 1995), 158.
3. Studies have tended to focus on the impact of the initial division and the subsequent events in that area in relation to India's development and also on Indian-Pakistani relations and wider international relations implications rather than on the territory itself.
4. This is the main thrust for instance of the recent volume by the former Indian Minister for External Affairs Salman Khurshid, *Beyond Terrorism: New Hope for Kashmir* (New Delhi, UBSPD, 1994). As Jalal comments in *Democracy and Authoritarianism*, 176, 'it would be an exercise in historical fatuity to maintain that New Delhi's recent nightmare in Kashmir is entirely a Pakistani concoction. Seeing India's troubles as a gift from abroad is a standard line of defence.'
5. For detailed discussion of this point see N. Ali, P. Ellis and Z. Khan, 'The 1990s: A Time to Separate British Punjabi and British Kashmiri Identity', in G. Singh and I. Talbot (eds), *Punjabi Identity: Continuity and Change* (New Delhi, Manohar, 1996).

6. The University of Luton has supported for the past five years a research programme looking at British Kashmiri identity and political activities. The main fieldwork in Azad Kashmir was undertaken in May and June 1996 and funded through the Nuffield Foundation Social Sciences Small Grants Scheme. Data collection methods in the United Kingdom have included group and individual interviews of Kashmiris supplemented in some cases by questionnaires and participant and non-participant observation in social and political activities in the Kashmiri community. In Azad Kashmir, group and individual interviews were held with leading politicians, academics and administrators as well as with members of town and village communities with a connection with the British Kashmiris.

7. I. Talbot, *Freedom's Cry: The Popular Dimension in the Pakistan Movement and Partition Experience in North-west India* (Karachi, Oxford University Press, 1996), 16.

8. M.Y. Saraf, *Kashmiris Fight for Freedom, Vol 2 1947-1978* (Lahore, Ferozsons, 1979), 731.

9. W. Zingl et al. (eds), *Pakistan in the 80s* (Lahore: Vanguard, 1985).

10. I. Malik, *The Continuing Conflict in Kashmir: Regional Detente in Jeopardy,* Conflict Studies 259, (Cardiff, Research Institute for the Study of Conflict and Terrorism, 1993), 6.

11. Saraf, *Kashmiris Fight for Freedom,* 735.

12. M. Y. Saraf had been a student political worker for the Muslim Conference whilst at Aligarh. In 1947 he moved to Azad Kashmir as a refugee from the Valley. His legal career culminated with his appointment as Chief Justice of Azad Kashmir.

13. A. Lamb, *Birth of a Tragedy: Kashmir 1947* (Hertingfordbury, Roxford Books, 1994), 31-3.

14. Ibid., 34.

15. Wirsing, *India, Pakistan, and the Kashmir Dispute,* 28.

16. Ibid., 29.

17. Saraf, *Kashmiris Fight for Freedom,* 1288-1291.

18. For more detailed discussion see Saraf, *Kashmiris Fight for Freedom,* 1293-94.

19. Ibid., 1349.

20. Ibid., 1309.

21. R. Ballard, 'The Context and Consequences of migration: Jullundur and Mirpur compared', *New Community,* X1, 1-2, (1983), 127.

22. Ibid., 117.

23. Ibid., 126.

24. Ibid., 128

25. He became a Member of the Kashmir Council prior to the change of government in June 1996 and has remained a Member.

26. At the end of June 1996 he became a Member of the Legislative Assembly (MLA).

27. Ballard, 'Context and Consequences of Migration,' 135.

28. It is still named Kashmir House and is currently owned by a JKLF member.

29. Reference is made here to United Kingdom political activity because this is not only where the largest Kashmiri community lives but also because settled migrants from the Commonwealth countries have the right to full participation in the political process of the the country whether they have taken on British citizenship or not. This situation is not the same in other countries in which the diaspora is situated.

30. See Ali, Ellis and Khan, 'The 1990s for detailed discussion of research findings on British Kashmiri identity'.

31. A full discussion of this incident can be found in an unpublished paper by P. Ellis and Z. Khan, 'British Parliamentarians and the Kashmir Issue in the 1990s', presented at the Annual Conference of the British Association of South Asian Studies in September 1995 and available from the authors.

32. A senior member of the Azad Kashmir Supreme Court.

33. L. Rose, 'India', in W. Wilcox, L. Rose and G. Boyd, *Asia and the International System* (USA, Winthrop Inc, 1972), 77.

34. Ibid., 79.

35. S. Muni, 'South Asian Relations, Bilateral and Regional', in L. Rose and E. Gonsalves (eds), *Towards a New World Order: Adjusting India — US Relations* Berkley, USA, University of California, 1992), 46.

36. W. Wilcox, 'Pakistan', in W. Wilcox, L. Rose and G. Boyd, *Asia and the International System* (USA, Winthrop Inc, 1972), 97.

37. A. Jalal, *Democracy and Authoritarianism in South Asia,* 170.

38. Ibid., 180.

Chapter Ten

The Unidentical Punjab Twins: Some Explanations of Comparative Agricultural Performance Since Partition

Shinder S. Thandi

Introduction

The Indian and Pakistani Punjabs, divided by an arbitrary international border amidst painful and bloody partition which uprooted over eight million people in 1947, provide an interesting case study—according to Sims,[1] almost a controlled experiment—in comparative agrarian performance and development. More generally the socio-economic and industrial experiences of the two regions also provide some interesting insights into the nature of centre-state relations within the political systems of the two nation-states in which the regions are located. Both regions have historically been the most developed and continue to be so today. However, the regions play very different roles within the national context. In Pakistan the Punjab province comprising around 26 per cent of the total area and a population of 47.3 million representing 56 per cent of the total population, appears to 'dominate' the political and economic system with other provinces often perceiving themselves as relatively disadvantaged and victims of Punjabi hegemony.[2] In contrast, in the Indian Punjab, comprising only 1.57 per cent of area and a population of 16.8 million in 1981 representing a mere 2.5 per cent of the population, the complaint usually runs the other way, that is, despite Punjab's significant contribution to Indian foodgrain production and procurement (during 1991-2 the percentage share to the central pool in wheat and rice was 71.5 per cent and 46.7 per cent respectively), the state remains at the margin of Indian politics and is perceived by its majority Sikh community as disadvantaged and discriminated against, especially in terms of industrial development. Certainly in terms of rates of urban industrialization, diversification of the economic structure and export performance, the Pakistani Punjab is at a qualitative advantage.[3]

The two Punjabs have pretty much the same climate, both started off with similar agro-ecological and land tenure systems and both share a common culture, language, historical tradition and institutional arrangements.[4] Furthermore, both regions have since the mid-1960s experienced rapid technological change associated with the so-called green revolution technology. Yet, in terms of agricultural and rural development, the Indian Punjab has shown superior performance.[5] For example, over the period 1965-6 and 1981-2, East Punjab recorded agricultural growth rates of 4.5 per cent per annum, whilst West Punjab achieved a more modest 3.5 per cent per annum growth rate. Despite the fact that partition had left West Punjab with 62 per cent of the land, 55 per cent of the population, around 80 per cent of the united Punjab's irrigation facilities, most of its rural electricity and roads, East Punjab quickly overcame these disadvantages and continued on a remarkable path of agrarian performance, totally reversing the experiences of the colonial period. Until the mid 1980s, agricultural growth rates, yields of major crops, rate of mechanization, consumption of power fertilizer, pesticides etc. — traditionally, all indicators of a highly capitalist form of agriculture — were found to be significantly above those of West Punjab. Even today, as will be argued later, data indicates that yields for the major crops of the region are significantly higher for East Punjab helped by heavy applications of chemical fertilizers and intensity of irrigation. The question under discussion would therefore seem to be a fairly straightforward one: why should two fairly similar and predominantly agrarian regions show such remarkable divergence in agricultural and socio-economic performance? In this chapter an attempt is made to provide a cursory review of the major agro-economic based hypothesis offering explanations of differential performance.

Despite its potential as an interesting case study offering vital policy lessons for other developing agrarian regions in Third World countries, there is a dearth of literature on evaluation of the comparative performance of the two regions. In this context Sims' work was long overdue and represented a welcome contribution to the development literature. Using a multi-disciplinary approach, Sims argued that the superior agricultural performance of East Punjab, as demonstrated by almost twice the rate of productivity, owes its origins to the well-established facilities in social infrastructure, higher irrigation intensity of private tubewells, a greater use of fertilizers and insecticides and a more stable price policy towards agriculture in India than in Pakistan. These policies are then traced back to the nature of the political regimes and the consequent role of political leadership in the two countries. The emphasis is naturally on the public policy responses generated by the two political regimes. Given the lack of literature in this area, Sims' laudable work provided a useful benchmark for evaluating divergent performance and in directing future research. Unfortunately, even after the research, the challenge offered by Sims further comparative studies on the Punjabs have not materialized.

There is one major caveat which needs to be borne in mind. It is perhaps important to acknowledge that geographical size matters and thus comparisons between the two regions may remain a meaningless task. This line of reasoning is rejected here on the grounds that it underestimates the degree of common heritage of the region and its high level of economic integration under colonial agrarian policy. It also underplays the potential role for public policy in post-colonial settings. Thus we must seek other explanations for the neglect of analysis of comparative performance. One important reason for lack of literature and research in this field is related to the 'unfriendly' and cold war Indo-Pak relations which ensure that the communication channels and information flows between the two regions (and even the nation-states) remain highly limited and whatever information filters through tends to be distorted by the government owned or regulated electronic media. Furthermore, as Jalal has forcefully argued with reference to general scholarship on partition,

> the few intellectuals who have sought to transcend the limiting constraints of their nation-states are constantly reminded of their national origins in the critiques and counter-critiques that have characterized partition historiography. Even non-partisan scholarship rarely escapes being labelled 'made in India' or 'made in Pakistan.[6]

A further reason for the lack of literature is the non-availability of comparable secondary data of the post-colonial period and hence the gaps have to be filled in by either fieldwork (as was the case with Sims) and/or through inferences and anecdotal evidence. Secondary data on West Punjab in the public domain is particularly scanty, and is often aggregated and qualitatively inferior when compared with East Punjab. East Punjab's annual Statistical Abstract published by the Economic and Statistical Organization, in contrast, is extremely detailed, giving us district-level information on every item conceivable of enumeration. With few exceptions, however, data analysis and interpretation still leaves a lot to be desired.

Share of the Spoils at Partition and its Impact

The partition of Punjab remains unparalleled in terms of the numbers involved and the suddenness of the exchange of populations — over eight million to be transferred within a period of only three months. Furthermore, unlike some other earlier examples of exchange of populations, the minorities forced to leave had no constitutional guarantees to compensate them for the full value of the property that was to be left behind.[7] In the case of East and West Punjab the population was compelled to quit their assets and homes under conditions of communal butchery which claimed from about a half million to a million lives.[8]

The partition of Punjab was conceived as a corollary to the partition of India and the machinery for the division of Punjab was to closely resemble that for the country as a whole. With less than four months before both countries were expected to take over their affairs from the British, a number of hastily conceived committees were convened. The job of recommending the criteria for allocation of resources and setting up the administration for overseeing the partition fell upon the Punjab Partition Committee comprising two representatives from each part of the Punjab. This Committee in turn was guided by seven Expert Committees covering different items/resources to be divided. The division of assets and liabilities was the most contentious issue and after lengthy deliberations ending in an Arbitral Tribunal adjudication, the assets and liabilities of the united Punjab were to be adjusted for the purposes of the financial settlement in the ratio of 60 per cent for West Punjab and 40 per cent for East Punjab. This ratio, used for all future financial adjustments, appeared to be about the right averaging for population, territory and revenue contribution of East and West Punjab.[9]

As a result of forced migration, on balance, the Sikh and Hindu landholders bore the brunt of the losses. According to an early Punjab government source, out of the 18.8 million cultivable acres in West Punjab, about 6.7 million (around 36 per cent of the total) belonged to the non-Muslims who paid about 34 per cent of the land revenue. In contrast the Muslims in East Punjab owned 4.7 million cultivable acres (around 33 per cent) out of a total of 14.2 million acres and paid only 27 per cent of the land revenue. On migration the Sikhs and Hindus had left behind about 2 million acres in excess of what the Muslims had left in East Punjab. Furthermore, East Punjab's share of canal irrigated water amounted to only three million out of a total of over fourteen million acres — a mere 21 per cent. East Punjab, with equity considerations in mind, adopted the sliding-scale formula given in Table 1 for allocating land to the refugees.

Table 1 – Formula for Allotment of Land for Refugees in East Punjab (in standard acres)

Area Abandoned	Area Allotted	% Allotted
10	7.5	75
30	21.0	70
40	27.0	67.5
50	32.5	65.0
60	37.5	62.5
100	51.5	51.5
150	66.5	44.33
200	79.0	39.50
250	89.0	35.60
500	126.0	25.2
1000	176.5	17.65
3000	281.33	9.37
4000	326.5	8.16
5000	376.5	7.53

Source: M. S. Randhawa, *Out of the Ashes*, (1954) p. 99.

The dramatic scaling down of allotted land relative to abandoned land had a profound effect on the political economy of East-Punjab agriculture. Dispossessed of adequate fertile and irrigated land the erstwhile wealthier Canal Colonist refugee farmers began to engage in owner-cultivation and—putting in an extra physical (and financial) effort to eke out subsistence living. If anything their greater level of adversity prompted new forms of risk-taking and adoption of more progressive farming methods unlike pre-partition days when many were content to lease out land on tenancy.

The unevenness of the resource redistribution was also reflected in other spheres as well: for instance the refugees from West Punjab left behind 154,000 houses in towns compared with East Punjabi refugees who only left behind 112,00 houses. In terms of shops and business premises abandoned, refugees from West Punjab left behind 51,000 whereas the East Punjabi Muslims only left behind 17,000. Finally as Table 2 shows, there was also a wide disparity in the occupational skills of people involved in the transfer. As the table indicates, the migration of the skilled and semi-skilled Muslims from East Punjab would have had a crippling effect especially on the garment and hosiery sectors in which they predominated.

Table 2 – Occupational Structure in East and West Punjab (in lakhs)

Hereditary Occupation	Hindus and Sikhs in West Punjab	Muslims in East Punjab
Agriculture	8.2	29.6
Traders	14.01	2.79
Weavers	00.08	3.70
Shoemakers	1.25	1.64
Carpenters	0.56	0.79
Blacksmiths	0.57	N/A
Potters	0.45	1.64
Dyers	0.04	0.41
Bakers and water carriers	0.57	1.84
Barbers	0.17	0.86
Sweepers	2.10	0.07
Washermen	0.05	0.52
Tailors	0.02	0.08
Total	28.07	43.94

Source: *Economy of Pakistan,* (Government Publication, 1958) p. 397.

It has been suggested that the East Punjab region's relative backwardness in terms of industrialization is partly due to its failure to fully recover this loss in the post-partition period. East Punjab still continues to provide unprocessed raw cotton to the textile and garment manufacturers in the Bombay sub-region of Maharashtra.

As a corollary, the newly migrated skilled labour in West Punjab was not able to use those skills since similar factories and workshops or raw materials did not exist despite the high levels of demand for goods they could potentially produce.

In concluding, the unevenness of the distribution of the spoils, it is suggested, had different effects in the two regions. In East Punjab as the resources left behind were greater and the geographical size represented an important constraint, the 'sense of loss' was felt more acutely. Thus the need for more rapid asset accumulation became more imperative. Certainly, as has been argued by Randhawa[10] and Nair[11], the appearance of more intensive forms of agricultural practices and higher motives for savings can partly be explained by the deep sense of economic and psychological loss suffered by uprooted refugees.

Evaluating Comparative Performance

Given that the agricultural sector in both regions still plays a pivotal role in their continued success, in this section the main emphasis is on examining determinants of agrarian performance. Obviously a more comprehensive study would also need to consider the differing patterns of industrial development as the two regions continue to diversify and reduce their dependence on agricultural production.

One possible approach in evaluating comparative economic performance would be to list down a catalogue of causes of *slow* agricultural growth in West Punjab and a list of causes of *high* growth in East Punjab. The strengths of East Punjab would then be the weaknesses of West Punjab and vice versa. Having identified the variables the researcher could then, perhaps, prioritize the causal factors according to the strengths of available empirical evidence, theoretical formulation utilized or simply leave it to the reader to reach his or her conclusions. The above is quite a legitimate and fruitful methodology and is often employed in development studies where the development strategies of two regions or countries are being compared and evaluated. Examples of this include attempts to explain the disparate experiences of the Latin American and East Asian economies, the successful diffusion of the green revolution technology in South Asia relative to Sub-Saharan African countries. Any attempt, however, must identify the *core* causal factors in explaining differentials in performance. What is offered below is a brief outline of what could be considered as *three* fairly broad *core* explanations. No attempt has been made here to provide any 'hard' empirical support to these explanations although the explanations chosen are prominent in the literature evaluating agricultural performance of the two regions and in the few studies evaluating comparative performance. The following can be identified as the *core* explanations:

(a) Differences in the agrarian structure.
(b) Role of national and regional state policies.
(c) Development and quality of human resources.

The three categories identified above are not mutually exclusive. Rather it is strongly argued that it was the unique interaction among these three variables which enabled East Punjab to be transformed from a state which had a 35,000 ton deficit in foodgrains at partition to become the 'granary' of India. West Punjab, too, has maintained its position as the dominant surplus-producing province of Pakistan.

(A) Differences in Agrarian Structure

The structure of landownership is the main component of any agrarian structure. The agrarian structure of East Punjab, it is argued, has proved to be more conducive and adaptable to the development of capitalist agriculture than was the case for West Punjab.[12] Despite numerous attempts at institutional change via land reforms and tenancy legislation, the structure of landownership in West Punjab still remains relatively concentrated and continues to militate against generating a higher growth in output.[13] Furthermore, a large proportion of the cultivated area remains under a tenurial system, mainly sharecropping, in which neither the tenant nor the landlord has any incentive to partake in productivity raising investments.

Admittedly landholdings, especially operational holdings, are also concentrated in East Punjab but the degree of concentration is much higher in West Punjab. Although comparable data is difficult to come by, Table 3 provides some indications of the relative differences in landholding structures in the two regions.

Table 3 : Agrarian Structure 1980-81

East Punjab Number of Operational Holdings		West Punjab Distribution of Land Ownership		
Size (Hectares)	Number %	Size (Hectares)	Owners %	Area %
Upto 2 2-5	38.62 } 38.21 } 76.83	Upto 2.5 2.5-5	68.8 } 19.9 } 88.7	25.8 } 24.1 } 49.9
5-10 10-20	7.8 6.00	5-10 10-20	7.8 2.3	19.2 12.6
20.40 40+	1.06 } 0.13 } 1.19	20-40 40+	0.7 } 0.4 } 1.1	9.1 } 3.6 } 12.7

Source: Statistical Abstract of Punjab, 1993 and Mahmood Hasan Khan, 'The Structural Adjustment Process and Agricultural change in Pakistan in the 1980s and 1990s, *The Pakistan Development Review*, Vol. 33.4 Part 1, Winter 1994, pp. 533-91.

Whereas in West Punjab large landlords, who are often engaged in pre-capitalist economic activity and are often content with being absentee landlords given that land is perceived to be a political rather than a commercial commodity, still dominate the rural scene. The case in East Punjab is that the majority of the area is under owner-cultivation, predominantly in the hands of the middle and rich peasantry. Owner-cultivation and smaller size of holdings, helped by effective land consolidation and land reform policies, have proved to be a vital combination in East Punjab's success. Perhaps the relevant question to ask here is: why do the large landowners in West Punjab, given their superior resource endowments and potential ability to fully exploit economies of scale, not engage on the same scale of agrarian capital accumulation as their East Punjabi counterparts? Do they perhaps have much greater access to alternative investment opportunities offering better rates of return than crop production? Or is it because the West Punjabi landlord has been unable to shake off the remnants of a feudal hangover in which political status and the ability to exercise extra-economic leverage is deemed more important than the goal of capitalist profit maximization?

The major effect of the differences in agrarian structure (as also reflected in the differences in political power structures) have important implications for the manner and intensity of utilization of new technology as and when it became available. In West Punjab a small minority of large landowners controlling a majority of the land and monopolizing the agricultural inputs market, largely appropriated the benefits, whereas in East Punjab, it was both the middle and the rich peasants, managing most of the land, who seized the opportunities for capitalist agriculture. Thus in the former case benefits remained restricted to a small minority whereas in the latter benefits were diffused throughout the peasantry, albeit disproportionately.[14]

(B) National and Regional State Policies

National and regional state policies have undoubtedly been a major factor in explaining the differential performance and especially so when combined with the differences in the prevailing agrarian structures. Although the nature of the nation-state differs markedly — one a parliamentary democracy[15] and the other, for most part of its history an authoritarian state but in recent years trying desperately to consolidate a fragile democracy — policies towards agriculture, especially in terms of price incentives and procurement, have been broadly similar. The green revolution agricultural strategy in both regions was initiated because of the compelling need for both nation-states to feed their population within the context of declining foreign exchange reserves and external pressure.[16] In fact empirical evidence seems to suggest that West Punjabi farmers have had a better deal, especially in terms of price incentives for some major crops. Whilst, the agricultural pricing and procurement policy displays major similarities, the constitutional form of the Indian state gave the East Punjab regional state a greater room to manoeuvre. The Indian constitution gives the central government the power and responsibility to guide economic development, and the union government consequently has authority over a wide variety of areas, including discretion over all major industrial development as well as power to collect revenue via direct and indirect taxes. At the same time, the constitution gives to the regional states alone the power to tax and regulate agriculture.[17] Although, therefore, the constitution gives the central government a bias towards development through industrial and commercial growth and hence urban development, the state governments are more oriented towards agricultural concerns and constituencies. In many ways, the success story of East Punjab appears very much to be the result of this 'relative autonomy' which the regional state enjoys in its policy towards agriculture and rural development.[18] All East Punjab state governments, irrespective of their political configuration or the socio-economic background of their party leaders, have pursued vigorous programmes for rural development with remarkable continuity. The development of agriculture has received the utmost priority of each successive government. In contrast, as has been suggested by Sims and others, in Pakistan the Muslim League appeared to lack mass support in the rural areas. The middle peasantry was numerically small and thus had little political clout. Given that the political institutions were rather weakly developed, landed aristocracy and bureaucrats tended to predominate in public policy decision making. The major thrust of the economic policies was to serve the need of the cities and industrial establishments rather than disturb the prevailing rural power relations. Ironically, this 'urban bias' would partly explain the successes of West Punjab over East Punjab in terms of higher degree of industrialization in the urban centres, economic diversification within the regional economy and superior export performance especially in foodgrains.[19]

Thus given the above constitutional arrangements coupled with the prevailing incentive mechanisms within the agrarian structure, East Punjab was able to undergo a very early, effective and successful programme of land consolidation and irrigation development.[20] Besides these, as has been ably documented by Chadha,[21] the East Punjab government took upon itself the task of building infrastructural facilities such as rural education, power development, co-operative credit, rural link roads, agricultural research and extension services,[22] foodgrain marketing and procurement agencies. The major cost of building these infrastructural facilities was borne by the state government itself although generous per capita central government assistance in the first three Five Year Plans helped in sustaining a high per capita development expenditure with a marked 'rural bias'. Since the mid-1960s, however, East Punjab has been able to maintain its leading position in terms of per capita development expenditure and per capita income growth by relying largely on its own resources.

In summary, the tremendous investment in infrastructural facilities, including education, made by the East Punjab government proved highly effective in the adoption and diffusion of the new high-yielding wheat varieties which became available around 1966-67. The same infrastructure was also able to fully accommodate the diffusion of rice, cotton and sugarcane of high-yield varieties which became more widely available from the early 1970s.

Table 4: Yields per Hectare of Major Agricultural Crops in East and West Punjab

(Kg/Hectare)

Year	Wheat		Rice		Sugarcane		Maize		Gram		Cotton	
	EP	WP	EP	WP	EP	WP	EP	WP	EP	WP	EP	WP
1970-1	2,238	1,189	1,765	1,554	4,117	3,610	1,555	1,111	797	529	399	364
1980-1	2,730	1,643	2,733	1,616	5,526	3,922	1,602	1,262	582	400	329	339
1989-90	3,593	1,825	3,510	1,528	6,312	4,156	1,902	1,367	712	543	591	560
1992-3	3,770	1,946	3,371	1,579	6,141	4,302	2,297	1,357	672	344	591	543

Source: Calculated from Table 6.7, *Statistical Abstract of Punjab*, 1993 and Table 3.5, *Pakistan Statistical Yearbook*, 1994.

Table 5: Consumption of Chemical Fertilizers in
East and West Punjab

	Nitrogen		Phosphate		Potash		Total	
	EP	WP	EP	WP	EP	WP	EP	WP
1985-6	787	1128.2	287	350.3	24	33.2	1098	1511.7
1988-9	796	1325	301	390.4	20	24.4	1117	1739.8
1989-90	818	1467.6	315	382.4	12	40.1	1145	1890.1
1990-1	877	1471.6	328	388.5	15	32.8	1220	1892.9
1992-3	934	1635.3	254	488.2	11	24.1	1199	2147.6

Source: Table 6.23, *Statistical Abstract of Punjab*, 1993 and Table 4.10
Pakistan Statistical Yearbook, 1994.

It is thus the lack of this infrastructural pre-requisite in West
Punjab which largely explains why the agricultural growth rate
in West Punjab lags behind that of East Punjab.

(C) Quality and Development of Human Resources

Over the past couple of decades the role of human resources and
human resource development has come to be seen as an
important variable contributing to and explaining economic
development. The sustained growth experienced by the East
Asian economies, referred to by the World Bank as the
'Economic Miracle', has emphasized the important role that
investments in human capital play in the process of
industrialization.[23] The remarkable success of East Asian
economies, now spreading to South-east Asia, has been
attributed to their governments' determined policies towards
provision of universal primary education, as well as basic needs
including health and public housing. All of these policies are
assumed to directly contribute towards increasing labour

productivity, flexibility and adaptability to change. It is a well-documented fact that East Punjab's improved economic performance is closely related to its superior quality of human capital. This is clearly reflected in differences in the number of medical institutions and literacy rates in the two regions (for details see Tables 6, 7 and 8).

Table 6: Medical Institutions Dispensaries and Beds in East and West Punjab

Year	Hospitals		Dispensaries		Primary Health Centres		Beds in Hospitals & Dispensaries etc.	
	EP	WP	EP	WP	EP	WP	EP	WP
1985	258	246	1790	1138	130	N/A	22,104	25,827
1990	219	257	1473	1168	442	N/A	24,179	32,981
1993	205	288	1462	1405	446	N/A	24,742	38,708

Notes: Figures for Primary Health Centres for East Punjab include Community Health Centres.

N/A = not available separately but included in hospitals as some hospitals and dispensaries have been converted to Rural Health Centre or Units.

Source: Calculated from Tables 19.2 and 19.6, Statistical Abstract of Punjab, 1999 and Tables 13.2 *Pakistan Statistical Yearbook, 1994.*

Table 7: Newspapers and Periodicals in East and West Punjab

Year	East Punjab	West Punjab
1985	651	941
1990	741	2197
1993	690	422

Source: Calculated from Table 32.2 of *Statistical Abstract of Punjab 1993* and Table 15.1 *Pakistan Statistical Yearbook,* 1994.

Table 8: Literacy Ratios in East and West Punjab, 1981 and 1991

	East Punjab (1981)	East Punjab (1991)	West Punjab (1981)	Pakistan (1994 estimate)
Total	40.86	58.51	27.4	37
Urban	55.63	72.08	46.7	58
Rural	35.21	52.77	20.0	28
Male	47.16	65.66	36.8	49
Female	33.69	50.41	16.8	24

Note: Literacy ratios are based on population aged 6 and above for East Punjab and aged 10 ad above for West Punjab. Literacy ratios not available for West Punjab for 1991.

Source: *Statistical Abstract of Punjab*, 1984 and 1992 and Economic Survey 1994, Government of Pakistan, Finance Division.

Although comparable data on education and health expenditures as a proportion of total expenditures for the two regions are not available, certain inferences can be drawn from national statistics. Pakistan's meagre allocation of resources towards education and health, 2.4 per cent and 0.7 per cent of GNP in 1994-5 respectively, represents a dire reflection of its policy towards human resource development, notwithstanding recent initiatives such as 'Basic Education for All', 'Social Action Programme' and 'Programmes for Balanced Social Development'.[24]

Furthermore, many writers have emphasized the important role played by non-economic factors by asserting that there is a close correlation between culture or cultural endowments and economic development.[25] Again translated in terms of the debates on the dynamic Asian economies, there is much talk of the positive role of culture and especially of the neo-Confucian ethical value system in their successful development.[26]

The debate about the role of values in economic development is not new especially as it relates to Asian economies. The debate started with Marx well over a hundred years ago and has been continued by writers such as Max Weber and more recently by Nobel Prize winning economists Arthur Lewis and Gunnar Myrdal. All of them thought that values had the capacity either to facilitate or to impede economic development. Weber for instance thought that the 'Protestant ethic' had been a major factor in the development of capitalism in northern Europe and North America and it was the absence of this in Asia which was likely to impede their rapid economic development. Gunnar Myrdal, in his 2,200-odd page *magnum opus* entitled *Asian Drama* also painted a very gloomy and dispiriting assessment of Asia's economic prospects blaming backwardness on 'irrational attitudes and outmoded institutions'.[27] Although Myrdal's 'institutionalist' approach provided a welcome alternative explanation to the conventional analysis of determinants of economic growth, with hindsight one can argue that he underestimated the potential for internally-generated economic growth, especially in East Asia.

In this final section an attempt is made to identify and highlight some of the 'specific advantages' which East Punjab has enjoyed over West Punjab especially in the post-colonial period. The reader is warned, however, that some of these arguments remain inconclusive and are subject to further rigorous empirical verification. The author is also fully aware that these arguments are also open to charges of exaggeration, cultural relativism and ethnic stereotyping especially as nurtured under colonial rule in Punjab[28] Collectively these arguments emphasize the importance of the human element and experience in agricultural development and performance *within a given set of enabling and conducive structure conditions.* Since the backbone of the agricultural prosperity in East Punjab are largely the Sikhs, most of what follows relates specifically to this ethnic group.

One of the more challenging works to date relating to our area of study is a recent study by Upinder Jit Kaur which focuses on the relationship between Sikh values and economic development. She argues that one of the reasons why scholars such as Max Weber found Hinduism a negative factor in economic development of India was the over-emphasis on 'other-worldly values'. Sikhism, in sharp contrast emphasizes 'this-worldly values' and does not consider poverty as the outcome of the inexorable law of fate as ultimately individuals are masters of their own destiny. She argues that the attitude of the Sikhs towards life, their hard work, mobility, thriftiness and a belief in their own ability to improve their standard of living, have been pivotal in their onward march along material progress.[29]

Upinder Jit Kaur critically examines the Sikh value system in terms of its three basic dimensions, the scriptural value system, institutional framework and operational value system, in order to assess their consistency and compatibility with the idea of economic progress. By examining each of these dimensions she demonstrates clearly the ethos of progress envisioned within each one of them. By taking an integrated view of life, Sikhism aims to improve the human situation via moral, spiritual and economic progress. Thus all those spiritual activities which do not improve the human condition are treated as barren. Material possessions are deemed necessary for sustaining life and the work ethic is treated as being no less important than worship. All of these ethical values are enshrined in the well-known phrase *kirat karo, wand chhako, nam japo* (Work hard; share the fruits of your labour and medtate on the divine name.) popularized in Sikh writings. Thus the Sikh way of life allows and promotes political and social activities in the cause of improving human welfare for both individuals and society as a whole.

An important aspect of the Sikh world view is the ability of the individual to be creative and to harness the forces of nature in order to improve the well-being of fellow individuals. The history of the Sikh people over the past couple of centuries or so has shown their tremendous success in harnessing natural resources. There are plentiful examples illustrating the Sikhs' ability to manoeuvre, to respond to opportunities, to experiment, and to seek out new openings. Below are presented some specific instances which have been cited as being important for the economic prosperity of the Sikh community and the East Punjab region as a whole.

Firstly, historically, the Punjab peasantry, especially the Sikh peasantry, has shown a much greater propensity towards mobility. Sikh migration to other areas of India, both rural and urban and overseas since the late century is too well documented to be repeated here.[30] The important point, however, is that the migrants very rarely severed their links with Punjab.[31] In the post-colonial period, especially as a result of mass migration during the 1950s and 1960s, vast amounts of regular remittances helped to boost and sustain agricultural investments.[32] In contrast, the degree of labour mobility in West Punjab has been relatively more recent and at a relatively lower level.[33] Even after the mass migration to the Gulf States, remittances in general, did not end up in agricultural investments but rather went into purchase of consumer goods, into house construction etc.[34] It would not be an exaggeration to say that of all the different ethnic groups of united Punjab the Sikhs have made the most from the opportunities offered through Punjab's incorporation into the capitalist world economy via colonialism.[35]

Secondly, Sikh army recruitment to the Indian army during the colonial period and even in the post-colonial period has remained very high relative to the Sikhs' overall percentage in the Indian population. Army experience accumulated over several decades was beginning to be reflected in agricultural practices and performance either through use of better methods or techniques or through re-investments into agriculture — it is not uncommon to find numerous ex-army 'gentlemen farmers' in all districts of Punjab. The learning of new skills and adaptation of new techniques and practices by this group had positive and significant demonstration effects on the attitudes of other groups of farmers. West Punjab has also been a significant recruitment ground for the Pakistan army but ex-army personnel appear not to have the same desire or inclination to engage in commercial farming. As Jalal has recently argued it was mainly the Punjabi-dominated military-bureaucratic alliance which was instrumental in frustrating genuine land reform and other rural development policies.[36]

Thirdly, and rather more contentiously, as has already been argued above the Sikh ethical value system places great emphasis on the work ethic and agriculture in fact, has always been regarded as the noblest of all professions. The British administrators, notably Darling, commented consistently on the Sikhs' extraordinary farming skills, their ability to innovate and to take risks. Many Sikhs were, indeed, generously compensated to migrate to the Canal Colonies and help raise colonial crop production necessary for earning export revenue, and as inducement to avert threats of famine elsewhere in India. In more recent times both Randhawa and Kusum Nair have talked in glowing terms about the sheer hard work undertaken by Sikh refugees in East Punjab and other neighbouring states, in the face of severe adversity after partition. Whilst one needs to remain vigilant against the ethnic hype, Sikh settler experiences throughout the globe do demonstrate the tenacity and opportunism inherent within the community.

Perhaps the overall inference being drawn here is that as a result of pre- and post-colonial policies East Punjab possesses an endowment of human resources which have proved to be qualitatively superior to that of West Punjab. The comparative advantage was further boosted by state policies in the post-colonial period which placed special emphasis on rural development especially on improving educational facilities. It is, therefore, not coincidental that West Punjab's literacy rate lags behind East Punjab's, quite conspicuously especially in terms of gender. As Table 8 clearly shows whereas 35.21 per cent of rural population was literate in East Punjab in 1981, the corresponding figure was only 20 per cent for West Punjab with the gap widening since then. Given that the Sikh peasantry has not been burdened by feudal hangovers, it has been able to adapt, and take advantage much more quickly of the opportunities offered by capitalist forms of agriculture. Furthermore, the Sikh peasantry, historically, has shown a much greater responsiveness to price stimuli and has seized and exploited the investment opportunities much more readily.[37]

Conclusion

This chapter has provided a cursory overview of the major debates over the differential agrarian performance in the two Punjabs. This differential performance has then been discussed within the context of three broadly based explanatory variables drawn from the development literature. It is, of course, always dangerous to try to isolate two or three important variables in explaining differentials in economic performance, whilst holding everything else constant. What is suggested here is that it is the interaction of the above three core variables which has been the most significant. For a fuller understanding of the differential performance of the two regions, there can be no substitute for detailed empirical investigation.

NOTES

1. Sims, Holly, *Political Regimes, Public Policy and Economic Development: Agricultural Performance and Rural Change in the Two Punjabs,* (New Delhi, Sage, 1988).
2. For a recent discussion on this perspective see Yunas Samad, 'Pakistan or Punjabiztan: Crisis of National Identity' in, Gurharpal Singh and Ian Talbot (ed.) *Punjabi Identity: Continuity and Change,* (New Delhi: Manohar, 1996). See also his *A Nation in Turmoil: Nationalism and Ethnicity in Pakistan, 1937-1858* (New Delhi, Sage Publications, 1995).
3. See Lincoln Kaye, 'From Raj to Rebellion', in *Far Eastern Economic Review,* 23 June 1988, p. 72-7.
4. Sims, *Political Regimes,* 18.
5. There is still very little research on the comparative performance of the two Punjabs. Besides Sims' and Kaye's rather journalistic piece cited earlier, there was a short piece by H. S. Mavi 'The Punjabs of India and Pakistan' in *The Tribune,* 28 May (Chandigarh, 1992).
6. See Ayesha Jalal, 'Secularists, Subalterns and the Stigma of Communalism: partition Historiography Revisited', *Modern Asian Studies,* 30, 3 July 1996, pp. 681-9.

7. Two previous similar cases that come to mind were firstly the exchange of
    around two million people between Greece and Turkey agreed by the
    Convention of La-Usanna in 1932 and secondly the exchange between
    Bulgaria and Greece agreed by the Convention of Neviely in 1929. In the
    former case the exchange of populations was completed in one year and in
    the latter case the national minorities emigrating were guaranteed full
    compensation for the properties left behind. For details see Stephan P.
    Landas, *The Exchange of Minorities,* (New York, 1932).
8. There is still considerable inconsistency in the number of casualties
    recorded, partly reflecting the partisan partition historiography and partly
    the intensity of the trauma inflicted on the region where the priority for
    body count took second place. The casualty figures tend to vary between a
    minimum of 200,000 to a maximum of around 500,000.
9. For a detailed discussion of the administrative machinery set up leading up
    to and following the partition see Satya M. Rai, *Partition of Punjab,*
    (Delhi, Asia Publishing House, 1966) and Kirpal Singh (ed), *Select
    Documents on Partition of Punjab, 1947,* (New Delhi, National Bookshop,
    1991).
10. M. S. Randhawa was an ICS officer until 1949 when he was appointed as
    the Director General of Rehabilitation in East Punjab. He later became the
    first Vice Chancellor of the Punjab Agricultural University in Ludhiana
    and has written many articles and books on the agrarian successes of East
    Punjab. His experiences and tribulations are recorded in his *Out of Ashes,
    An Account of the Rehabilitation of Refugees from West Pakistan to the
    Rural Areas of East Punjab,* (Chandigarh, Public Relations Department
    1954).
11. See Kusum Nair, *Blossoms in the Dust, the Human Factor in Indian
    Development,* (New York, Praeger, 1961). Having talked to a number of
    uprooted people in rural East Punjab Nair declares that. '...If seized with
    the urge and curiosity, he will not hesitate to walk the universe in search
    of the atom. The characteristic tends to make him more mobile as well as
    more enterprising', p. 104.
12. There is voluminous literature on this dimension for both regions covering
    both the green revolution and post-green revolution periods. For a
    meticulous survey of the East Punjab experiences see G. K. Chadha, *The
    State and Rural Economic Transformation: The Case of Punjab 1950-
    1985,* (Delhi, Sage Publications, 1986). For West Punjab experiences a
    very useful recent survey, among others, is Mahmood Hasan Khan's
    Chapter 8 on 'Agriculture' in William E. James and Subroto Roy (ed),
    Pakistan's Political Economy: Towards an Agenda for the 1990s, (New
    Delhi, Sage Publications, 1992).
13. It is generally acknowledged that land reform has been a failure in West
    Punjab as in Pakistan as a whole. For a discussion of reasons for failure
    see Mahmood Hasan Khan, ibid; Ian Talbot, 'Survey of Agricultural

Development in Western Punjab after 1947', unpublished paper presented at the Conference on Punjab Agriculture, Columbia University, 1 April 1995; and Akmal Hussein, 'Land Reform in Pakistan: A Reconsideration' in Iqbal Khan (ed), *Fresh Perspectives on India and Pakistan*, (London, Bougainvillaea Books, 1985).

14. There has been a lively debate on both sides of Punjab as to the differential benefits of the green revolution technology. Although, even now, opinions remain divided, the social polarization thesis has stronger support in East Punjab given the nature of the agrarian structure. For an elaboration of this view see Akmal Hussain, 'Technical Change and Social Polarization in Rural Punjab' in Karamat Ali (ed) *The Political Economy of Rural Agrarian Structure in Pakistan*, (Lahore, Vanguard Publications, 1982) and Hamza Alavi, 'The rural elite and agricultural development in Pakistan,' in R. D. Stevens, H. Alavi and P. Bertoccci (eds) *Rural Development in Pakistan and Bangladesh*, (Honolulu, Hawaii University Press, 1976).

15. The only exception at the national level was the brief Emergency period in 1977. In Punjab, however, democratic politics have been suspended far more often with the last suspension lasting between 1987-92.

16. There is considerable literature on the historical origins of the green revolution in South Asia. For a discussion of the historical context see F. R. Frankel, *India's Green Revolution: Economic Gains and Political Costs*, (Princeton, Princeton University Press, 1971). For a discussion of the continuities in Indian agricultural policies see Pritam Singh, 'Political Economy of the British Colonial State and the Indian Nationalist State and the agrarian-oriented development pattern in Punjab', *Indo-British Review*, XXI, 1, (Special Issue on Punjab), pp. 97-110.

17. For an elaboration of this perspective see Murray Leaf, *Songs of Hope: The Green Revolution in a Punjab Village* (New Brunswick, Rutgers University Press 1984).

18. The extent of the actual 'relative autonomy' of the East Punjab state is questionable. One could argue that the actual operation of the policy has meant growing centralization of power in the hands of the central government. This centralized power is exercised through the various government appointed Commissions deciding policies on agricultural prices and costs, subsidies, and distribution of power and irrigation resources. For an interesting discussion of some of these relations see Pritam Singh, 'Federal Financial Arrangements in India with Special Reference to Punjab', *Australian Journal of Development Studies*, IX, 3, 1993, pp. 261-78.

19. For a concise summary of the reasons for 'urban bias' in West Punjab economic policies see Talbot, 'Survey of Agricultural Development'. See also Ayesha Jalal, *Democracy and Authoritarianism in South Asia: A*

comparative and historical perspective, Cambridge, Cambridge University Press, 1995).

20. For an informative discussion of the successes of the earlier phase of land consolidation in East Punjab and its impact on investments in tubewells and agricultural productivity, see Gyanesh Kudaisya, 'The Demographic Upheaval of Partition: Refugees and Agricultural Resettlement in India, 1947-67' in *South Asia,* 18, Special Issue (1995), pp. 73-94.

21. G. K. Chadha, *The State and Rural Economic Transformation.* (Delhi, Sage, 1986).

22. In this context the role of the Punjab Agricultural University (Ludhiana), first established in 1962 with M. S. Randhawa as its founder-Vice Chancellor deserves special mention. Since its opening the PAU has been at the forefront in leading agricultural research, teaching and extension education. It has also been recognized as a centre of excellence in terms of agricultural engineering and technology adaption for developing efficient farming methods. The PAU has won a number of national and international awards for its contribution to the prosperity of Punjab and India. Recently it was declared the best agricultural university in the country and was selected for the first Best Institutional Award by the Indian Council of Agricultural Research. For details see, *The Tribune* (Chandigarh), 17 November 1996.

23. For details see *The East Asian Miracle: Economic Growth and Public Policy,* World Bank Policy Research Report, (Washington, OUP for World Bank, 1993).

24. These figures and new social initiatives are taken from the *Pakistan Economic Survey 1994-5,* (Islamabad, 1996).

25. The specialist American journal *Economic Development and Cultural Change,* published by the University of Chicago for the past 45 years, is devoted entirely to considering the interface between economic development and cultural factors. In April 1988 it published a special supplement issue on the theme of human resources and economic development, containing articles by leading specialists in the field.

26. For a critical perspective on the debate on Asian values in Asian Pacific development see Alan Dupont, 'Is there an 'Asian way'?' in *Survival,* 38, 2, (Summer 1996), pp. 13-33.

27. Quote taken from the publisher's jacket cover of Gunnar Myrdal, *Asian Drama: An Inquiry into the Poverty of Nations,* 3 vols., (London, Allen Lane Penguin Press, 1968).

28. The 'Martial races' theory is too well documented to be repeated here. For a recent treatment with respect to army recruitment see David Omissi, *The Sepoy and the Raj,* (London, OUP, 1995). Ethnic stereotyping in the rural economy of Punjab are epitomized in the well known works of Calvert and Darling.

29. See Upinder Jit Kaur, *Sikh religion and Economic Development*, (New Delhi, National Book Organization, 1990).
30. See N. Gerald Barrier and Verne A. Dusenberry (ed), *The Sikh Diaspora: Migration and the Experience Beyond Punjab*, (New Delhi, Chanakya Publications, 1989).
31. For a discussion of these diasporic links see Darshan Tatla (1994) 'Politics of Homeland: ethnic identity and political mobilization among Sikhs in Britain and North America', unpublished Ph.D. thesis, University of Warwick and Shinder S. Thandi (1995) 'Dangerous Liaisons? An insight into economic and social linkages between Diaspora Sikhs and Punjabi Villages', unpublished paper presented at the Conference on Punjab Agriculture, Columbia University, 1 April 1995.
32. For the role played by overseas remittances in East Punjabi villages see Shinder S. Thandi, 'Strengthening Capitalist Agriculture: The Impact of Overseas Remittances in Rural Central Punjab in the 1970s', in *International Journal of Punjab Studies*, 1, 2, (July-December 1994) pp. 239-70; Bruce LaBrack, 'The New Patrons: Sikhs Overseas', in N. Gerald Barrier and Verne A. Dusenberry (ed), *The Sikh Diaspora*; A. W. Helweg, *Sikhs in England: the Development of a Migrant Community*, (Delhi, OUP, 1979).
33. There is considerable evidence of early Muslim migrants from the Punjab region. The ethnographic studies in the diaspora, however, tend to demarcate between Muslim, Hindu and Sikh migrants downplaying their regionalized Punjabi character.
34. There is difference of opinion among scholars on the utilization and hence impact of remittances in rural areas. For West Punjab there is evidence which mainly suggests the consumption-orientation of remittances. See, for instance, R. Ballard, 'The Context and Consequences of Migration: Jullundur and Mirpur Compared', in *New Community, 11, 4, (1983)*; G. Gunatilleke, *The Impact of Labour Migration on Households: A Comparative Study of Seven Asian Countries*, (New York, United Nations Press). A more recent study by Richard H. Adams, Jr., 'Remittances, Inequality, Asset Accumulation: the Case of Rural Pakistan', in David O'Connor (ed), *Development Strategy, Employment and Migration: Country Experiences*, (Paris: OECD, 1996) has argued that external remittances have a significant positive effect on the accumulation of income-generating assets compared with internal remittances.
35. For a recent attempt at periodization of Punjab history see Pritam Singh and Shinder S. Thandi, (eds.,) *Globalization and the Region: Explorations in Punjabi Identity*, (Coventry, Association for Punjab Studies, 1996).
36. Jalal (1995).
37. For an overview of the investment activities of Sikh settlers in the canal colonies during colonial rule see Imran Ali, 'Sikh Settlers in Western

Punjab during British Rule', in Singh and Thandi (1996). For an excellent study of British agrarian policy and its impact see Imran Ali, *Punjab under Imperialism*, (Princeton, Princeton University Press, 1988).

Chapter Eleven

Post-Partition Refugees and the Communists: A Comparative Study of West Bengal and Tripura

H. Bhattacharyya

Introduction

Refugees have remained the offshoot of the nation-state formation, the 'illegitimate children of modernity' and have been marginalized. As a comparative study of the Indian states of West Bengal and Tripura, this chapter highlights the major patterns of communist-led refugee mobilization and its effects on state politics and ethnic relations. The initial communist hesitation towards the refugees immediately after the partition was a hangover of their role in the pre-1947 period. The communists' refugee mobilization in the end was dictated by two objectives: electoral support and political recruitment. But as the process was subjected to all the shifts and turns in communist' politics, the genuine refugee interests were subordinated to the political needs of the communists. This hampered the prospect of real rehabilitation. Comparatively, while West Bengal is a case of a relative success story of refugee mobilization, Tripura, over-whelmed by the refugee influx, offers a paradoxical situation: combination of two diametrically opposed types of rehabilitation, of the Bengali refugees and original tribals. In conclusion, we argue that in this period of globalization, the Indian nation-state seems unlikely to show the same concern for the refugees as before, and hence recommend the launching of the 'life politics' of the refugees for real rehabilitation.

Refugees, who have been a problem from the earliest periods of human history,[1] assumed a global character particularly after the Second World War. Eric Hobsbawn calls it the 'global human catastrophe which, as unleashed by the Second World War', is almost certainly the largest in human history.'[2] By May 1945, there were some 40.5 million refugees in Europe alone.[3] Today there are an estimated 18 million refugees in the world.[4] Defining refugees has always been beset by a host of problems, and has been subject to changes.[5] The current UN definition of refugees is quite broad-based: persons who are outside their homeland owing to a well-founded fear of persecution on the basis of race, religion, nationality, membership in a social group or political opinion.[6] The post-partition refugees that the states of West Bengal and Tripura received can be said to be covered within this definition, as a combination of religion and nationality had been the most powerful factor in driving millions of Bengali Hindus of East Bengal out of their homeland.

Sociological definitions[7] of refugees, including those based on the study of refugees in northern India, do not highlight the appropriate broader historical processes within which the refugee problem should be located. Lucian Pye highlighted the problem as 'uprooting whole populations of unsuspecting and often politically unawakened people and casting them into new identities.'[8] Keller defined refugees as 'the epitome of the transitional man, a man whose roots have been torn out of the soil of his traditional life.'[9] Thus, the broader historical processes of decolonization and the specificities of the nation-state formation in the post-colonial societies which constitute the appropriate context of the refugees are neglected. The refugee problem has remained the offshoot of nation-state formation for many post colonial countries. In the case of India (and Pakistan), the refugee problem has directly been linked to their rise as nation-states in 1947. In this sense, the problem is 'modernity's own creation', to put in a post-modernist fashion. Since the refugees, in many such cases, have been the unwanted children of the nation-states, they can be said to be the 'illegitimate children' of modernity, and are marginalized.

The basic objective of this chapter is the analysis of the patterns and significance of refugee mobilization by the communists and their effects on refugee rehabilitation as well as on state politics in West Bengal and Tripura. It is based on the assumption that the post-partition refugees in both West Bengal and Tripura played a determining role, in the wake of their rehabilitation, in reshaping the contours of state politics.

Refugees and the Communists: West Bengal

The people of West Bengal could have witnessed the rise of a Left Front Government (LFG) in the state in 1952 rather than in 1977 had the communists successfully mobilized some 4 million refugees who had crossed borders. The state of West Bengal could have become the first democratically elected Marxist government in the world had the state communists followed the appropriate policy and method of refugee mobilization after the partition of India in 1947. The 1951 Census Report of India, recorded as many as 3.5 million East Bengal refugees in the total population of West Bengal, In 1951, one in every four persons in Calcutta was a refugee.[10] In contrast to the CPI, nationally, its Bengal unit during 1947-50 was said to be most unified.[11] And yet, the state communists failed to mobilize refugees when it was most appropriate. This failure was conceptual, political and historical.

History as a Block

A number of historical factors militated against the communists' initial mobilization. Two factors, as we will presently see below, served to explain communists' isolation from, and their self-imposed anonymity in, the national and state politics.

The factors that in the 1940s were most actively responsible for the CPI's growing isolation from the national politics, have received adequate scholarly treatment in the existing writings on Indian communism.[12] They were: the People's War line (1941), and the Adhikari thesis on 'Pakistan and National Unity' (1942). The CPI General Secretary P. C. Joshi wrote of the 'War Policy of the CPI (1942) as:

The Soviet entry into the war isolated fascism as the main enemy of mankind. It flung the non-fascist imperialists into the people's camp. By creating the basis for the international front against fascism, and for freedom... we opposed imperialist war for all we are worth ... we must go into the People's War for all we are worth. *We have nothing to lose and everything to gain by going into the People's War* (Emphasis added)[13].

Ironically, the party gained little and lost a lot by going into the People's War. The Marxist historian Sumit Sarkar believed the 'People's War line has certainly isolated and discredited the CPI'.[14]

The CPI's support for the Pakistan demand in terms of the 'Adhikari thesis' (1942) added insult to injury. In his pamphlet 'Pakistan and National Unity' (1942), Adhikari wrote: 'The demand for Pakistan, if we look at its progressive essence, is, in reality, the demand for self-determination and separation of the areas of the Muslim nationalities of the Punjab, Pathans, Sind, Baluchistan and of the eastern provinces of Bengal.'[15] The party reiterated the same in its Memorandum to the Cabinet Mission.[16] The CPI mentor, R. P. Dutt (CPGB), had theoretically ruled out a definition of the nation on the basis of religion,[17] but could write about the CPI's approach to the Pakistan demand: 'This should not, however, blind us to the genuine national content concealed behind the Pakistan demand.'[18] Such a 'curious' thesis at the heyday of India's freedom struggle added to the further isolation of the party from the mainstream of Indian politics.

Due to the above, the party unit in West Bengal failed to provide leadership to the refugees. The CPI accepted readily the partition and thought rather strangely, that the latter would remove communalism from India, and pave the way for communism, but it failed to define any positive role for its members. The party was yet to get rid of the traumatic experiences of the years between the end of the war and the partition. In Indian politics, it was a political outcast suffering from a kind of 'persecution mania'.[19] Any clear definition of the party's attitude to the refugees was singularly lacking. No Marxist analysis of this new phenomenon was attempted. If the party workers participated in the works of the distribution of relief among the refugees, it was done on humanitarian grounds, and by sheer force of habit.

In 1947-8, 'Joshism' i.e., the political line of P.C. Joshi which extended all support to the Nehru government was another factor which explained the party's indifference to the refugees. As a result the *People's Age,* the official communist weekly, made no comprehensive account of the refugees in 1947-8 despite the request often made by some leaders.[20] Joshism in the above period was tailing behind the so-called 'progressive camp' led by Nehru. This served to immobilize the organization *vis-a-vis* the refugees.

There were other limiting factors too. The refugees, many of whom were followers of Bose, were generally anti-communist and pro-Congress. As Chakrabarti wrote: 'It was fear as well as hope that transformed them suddenly into staunch supporters of the Congress as soon as they reached West Bengal.'[21]

Pre-1950 Phase of Communist Mobilization

The initial approach of the communists to refugees should better be termed 'infiltration' rather than 'mobilization'. In fact the party initially did not want to mobilize the refugees. All that the party wanted was to neutralize the pro-Congress and anti-Communist edge of the refugees. Thus Bijoy Majumdar who, as party member, was assigned the job of infiltration, with the aim of blunting the anti-communism of the refugees. However, with his and his associates' dedication, honesty and complete zeal, within five years they became the recognized leaders of the millions of refugees who began shifting from their anti-communism to a hatred for the establishment.[22]

Capture of Colony Committees

Camp or Colony Committees were the mainspring of the manifold activities of the refugees. They were the governing bodies elected by every adult member of the community. These committees were the organizational form of direct democracy. Hundreds of such committees came up, of many which were initially under the leadership of Congressmen. Soon, they would become the springboard for communist penetration.

In order to finally establish control over these committees, Bijoy Majumdar proposed and took the lead in forming a central committee for coordinating the work of all these committees. The control over such committees would enable him to have contact with all the committees and to give them a particular orientation. Thus, the South Calcutta Refugee Council of Action under Majumdar's general secretaryship was established. The Forward Bloc leader, Chitto Basu, was also drafted into the council.

Added to the above was the (communist-dominated) Mahila Atmaraksha Samiti (Women's Self-Defence Committee) which was incorporated to work as a relief organization. It was easy for the Samiti to penetrate the makeshift household, to make contact with the women who were persuaded to talk, unlike their menfolk against the establishment. For Majumder, the Samiti was a Trojan Horse within the enemy territory.

The All Bengal Refugee Council of Action (ABRCA) was formed in September 1948 and it was dominated by Congressmen. But a few communists such as Majumdar and Binory Ray found their place on it, once again masquerading as Congressmen. The minimum space that the communists found within this body was also utilized for giving the organization a leftist direction. The Jaipur Session of AICC (1948) in a way offered the communists a more favourable opportunity. Nehru reacted negatively and termed the refugees 'foreigners'. This led to Anantalal Chatterjee, a relative of Gandhi and a Congressman, to relinquish office because he did not want to be pressed into an agitation against the central government that the *Karma parishad* now wanted. This cleared the deck for Majumder's ascendancy to the organizational hierarchy of the refugee body. The next conference of the (ABRCA) (December 1948) formed a new Executive Committee with Bijoy Majumdar as a joint secretary.

Many CPI and Forward Block (FB) members were also elected to the committee. Mahadeve Bhattacharyya, a Hindu Mahasabha man but dedicated and courageous, was president of the body. Despite the tilt to the left now, Majumdar underscored the need for united political action of the refugees. The communist party as a party was apathetic to the refugees. Before the Ranadive line (Second Congress of the CPI, Calcutta, 1948), the party had no idea about what to do with the refugees. The party then viewed rather carelessly the continuous influx of refugees. Their bitter anti-communism was a threat to the party. The party's policy of neutralization sounded hollow in a disintegrating society. The party woke up to the strength of the refugees only after the 15,000-strong 14 January 1949 refugee demonstration at Brigade Parade Ground, Calcutta which resulted in police firing and arrests of refugee leaders.[23] Thereafter the party sought to utilize the refugees for the implementation of the Ranadive line which called for violent insurrection throughout India. The 14 January movement revealed to the party leadership the latent power of the refugees which it wanted to utilize for implementing its 'revolutionary programme'. But the refugee organizations built by Majumdar were created on cooperative lines as a broad democratic front. The party directives made the refugee communist leadership panicky, and damaged the credibility of the leadership. The refugee communist leadership refused to toe the official line entirely and participated intermittently in violent party activities.

Post-1950 Phase: Rise of CPI Strategy

The Bengal unit of the CPI in its publications echoed the spirit of the political letter of the Assam Provincial Organization Committee of the CPI which had excerpted extensively an article in the theoretical Bolshevik journal *Bolshevik*. The argument of the above article ran like this: the partition of India did not ease in any way the communal situation. On the contrary, it accentuated it. The imperialists and their lackeys were behind the recent spurt in communal violence (1950). They were using the refugees as pawns in this game. The CPI must conduct persistent propaganda among the refugees to expose the ruling class and their allies. Thus separate refugee organization was needed for refugee agitation for rehabilitation.[24]

In the 1950s, however, the Bengal unit of the CPI was not a disciplined party functioning with a single will. It lost its centre. Disagreements, suspicions and mutual character assassinations marked its inner functioning. Furthermore the party lost its bases in the working class and the peasantry. It is argued that the Cominform Editorial of 'For a Lasting Peace, for a People's Democracy' (January 1950) nearly liquidated the party.[25] The party naturally had little to offer to the refugees until it had put its own house in order.

Formation of the United Central Refugee Council (UCRC)

The UCRC as a central body of the refugees was formed on 12 August 1950 to look after the manifold needs of the refugees, to take under its aegis the mushrooming squatter's colonies. A number of factors were responsible for its rise: the communal riots of 1950, the influx of more refugees, the failure of the government to cope with relief and rehabilitation and the colonizing movement. But the most important factor which gave it its particular organizational shape and its political outlook was the CPI's new-found rudimentary theory regarding the refugees.

However, the UCRC was launched in terms of the Cominform guideline. It was to be made a 'broad democratic front'. The rise of the UCRC coincided with the change of the Indian path of revolution to the Chinese path under the leadership of Rajeswar Rao who become CPI General Secretary.[26] In order to be faithful to the above, the UCRC Central Committee was not CPI dominated . The colonizing movement that enngulfed West Bengal from 1950 onwards like a prairie fire was also in accordance with the 'mass line' of the UCRC. Large-scale unauthorized occupation of government and private lands followed in the wake of the burgeoning squatter's colonies.

Inner Party Guidelines in Late 1950s

After the rise of the UCRC, the Bengal unit of the party attempted to define the tasks for the refugees. These were identified in the light of the unit's self-criticisms following its own organizational recovery from long internal crises that had crippled its functioning.

Task 1

(a) With the formation of the UCRC as a central body the foundation for organizing all the refugees under one organization had been laid. Thus far, our failure to make ourselves popular among some 6 million refugees is mainly due to the internal crisis of the party itself. But a Marxist party should not sit idle and be swayed by such a situation. The party must launch with full Bolshevik vigour campaigns for meeting the immediate demands of the refugees. This mass movement must be considered part of the United Front fighting against imperialism for full freedom.

(b) For the party, the UCRC is a mass organization devoted to organizing the refugees. The idea of the United Front must be more firmly rooted among the refugees. We need to establish leadership over it by convincing others involved in it.[28]

Task 2

(a) In the last two years, due to wrong leftist policies, the refugee movement became weakened. In order to bring all the refugees of West Bengal under the fold of a single organization, the Refugee Action Council (RAC) was formed, but due to wrong policies, it failed to operate properly. We have failed to organize it on the wider basis. The mass basis of the UCRC is much greater than its predecessor (RAC). In the near future, we must (re)build it as a part of the anti-imperialist front. We must establish our leadership over the Central Committee of the UCRC.[29]

Task 3

(a) So the movement we launched was mainly defensive. We have not fought for fulfilling the demands of the refugees.

(b) We must organize a general meeting in the colonies in which the realistic problems of the colonies must be highlighted. The forces opposed to us are trying to harp on the class divisions among the refugees which we must resist.

(c) The refugee movement is not something isolated: it is complementary to the anti-feudal and imperialist movement under CPI leadership. The teachings of Marxism–Leninism suggest that we strike at the reactionary force and other agents. Only then will we be able to provide shelters for the refugees.

(d) Alongwith the above, we must try to recover from the internal crisis of the party. We must rebuild the confidence of the refugees. We must form new party units, groups and revive the old ones. That is how we can become the leader of the refugee movement.[30]

The inner party 'evidences' presented above suggest a number of points as far as the CPI approach to the refugees was concerned. First, the party did not recognize the autonomous existence of the refugees but linked them to the party's prevailing strategy. Second, the party thought that socialism under its banner was the panacea for refugee problems. Third, the refugees' organization could only be considered as another mass organization affiliated to the party, and complementary to its 'revolutionary' activities. Last but not the least, the party eschewed a class-based treatment of the refugees. For the party, the refugees were to be organized as a community, and any attempt to highlight class divisions within them resisted. The last point is a little contradictory for a Marxist party. The tenor of the party's approach was 'modernist': it is marked by the objectives of external control, and is manipulative and instrumental. The party wanted to give its 'politics' to the refugees from outside. That refugees, as a particular social group may have had their own politics, was complete anathema to the paradigm of the communists.

Electoral Success

Those contradictions apart, the party, after the formation of the UCRC, began to intertwine the refugee demands with those of the party itself. Thus, the following became the demands of the UCRC:

Recognize the colonies. Down with the policy of evicting the refugees. We want franchise for the refugees. Down with landlordism. Indian Government quit the commonwealth. We don't want war, we want peace. Down with Anglo-American imperialism.[31]

As the 1952 general elections in India approached,the electoral message of the party was more directly conveyed. The UCRC Circular made the following appeal to the refugees:

Friends, the General Elections (1952) are drawing nearer. It has provided us with a unique opportunity for the realization of our demands. We have to make proper use of this opportunity for the realization of our demands. We have to make proper use of this opportunity. It will be suicidal if we fail to take full advantage of this opportunity. A democratic government would have fulfilled our demands. But the present Congress government has paid no heed to our demands and will not do so in future. The coming elections are an opportunity to install a new coalition government of the democratic parties of West Bengal. If the democratic parties win the elections, a coalition of those parties will replace the present government. We can then hope for a fair solution of our problems.

Thus in view of the importance of the present situation, the UCRC calls upon all the refugees and refugee organizations to proceed in the following manner: they should approach each and every candidate of their locality for support; issue statements in all election meetings. They should participate in all election meetings to popularize our demand for rehabilitation. They should mobilize all their forces to ensure the election of the candidates of democratic parties.[32]

Thus, the CPI electorally politicized the refugees. The slogans such as 'all refugees unite; forge unity with the people of West Bengal' paid off for the party in electoral terms. This also gave the refugees a sense of belonging; they became part of the opposition against the establishment. The CPI-UCRC combination ensured electoral victories of many of the left candidates particularly in urban and semi-urban areas. The communist bases among the refugees have subsequently been retained, more or less. The CPI's urban votes increased from 14.4 in 1952, to 35 per cent in 1962.[33] In terms of State Assembly seats, the party gained 28 in 1952, 46 in 1957 and 50 in 1962.[34] Bhabani Sengupta pointed out that until the late 1960s, the Bengali unit of the CPI had 'almost exclusively a middle class base', 'confined mostly to Calcutta metropolitan areas, urban middle classes, and the refugees from East Pakistan who swelled the ranks of Calcutta's lumpen proletariat.'[35] In urban districts like Burdwan, the communists increased their Assembly seats from 2 in 1952, to 10 in 1962.[36] In the post-independent West Bengal Assembly, the CPI retained its position as the second largest party until 1964 when it relinquished the position to the CPI-M which has been the single largest party since 1969 (barring the 1972 elections). In the remaking of Bengal electoral politics, the role of the refugees, therefore, can hardly be underestimated. The refugees, once mobilized, made all the major differences.

Refugees, Communism in West Bengal: A Summary

From the point of view of the left, the West Bengal refugee mobilization is a case of relative success. By the 1960s, the left especially the CPI-M, had established its near complete control over the refugees. By 1959, the CPI monopolized its control over the UCRC. The left's growing success in refugee mobilization reached the point of its crystallization in the general election of 1967. The refugees helped the left in many significant ways. The CPI largely overcame its self-imposed anonymity and isolation, and the refugees also gave the party its much needed mass base. The squatters' colonies thus became the ideal recruiting ground for the CPI and the Marxist left. When various mass fronts of the party were divided, the refugees became the striking arm of the communists. The effectiveness of this constituency was beyond doubt. Marcus Franda wrote:

> ... the threat of organized violence in Calcutta has considerably influenced the willingness of the centre to provide funds for the rehabilitation of Hindu refugees from East Pakistan, and at least in one case, the communists were successful in placing demands before the government which ultimately resulted in a reduction of the tax assessment on property owners.[37]

However, the story of the success of communist strategy in refugee rehabilitation was not without blemishes. The movement suffered from a number of limitations. The communists had to reconcile their goal of refugee rehabilitation, which in most cases meant resettlement on surplus land, to their goal of land distribution among the peasants and workers. Thus, the 'Alternative Proposal' for rehabilitation put forward by the UCRC in August 1959[38] was a proposal for resettlement on surplus land not only of the refugees but also of a large section of the landless people in West Bengal. Since the formation of UCRC, in almost every statement of its policy, there is a refrain of a united movement of refugees, peasants and workers. Chakrabarti believes the so-called joint struggle of the refugees and landless called upon by the UCRC and the Kisan Sabha since the late 1950s has to be seen as a communist attempt at encroaching upon the Congress votebanks in the countryside.[39] This, however, failed to stop many emerging conflicts between the peasants and the refugees in West Bengal not only then, but even subsequently.[40]

That refugees have merged themselves with the communists was demonstrated by the CPI's leadership over UCRC since 1959, but the relations between the two have often been marked by tension. On occasions, the UCRC criticized the party for the latter's failure to offer a definite stand on the refugees. This has often been admitted by the party.[41] The refugee tradition of movement originally was based on consensus without the hegemony of a single party. The refugee organization was originally a composite body of the left democratic parties working through consensus. But by the end of 1958 that tradition was lost due to the CPI's complete control over it.[42]

Refugees and the Communists: Tripura[43]

Tripura in India's northeast is the only tribal state in India which experienced demographic upheavals by receiving the post-partition Hindu refugees from East Pakistan. This ancient state with its predominant tribal population was transformed into one in which the once-majority tribals were reduced to a minority (34.68 per cent in 1951). The post-partition refugee influx thus overturned Tripura's demography, economy, culture and society. The event remains unique in the history of modern India. The refugee influx during 1951-61 was reflected not only in the spectacular growth in the state's population (81.71 per cent increase in 1961) but also in the lower percentage share of the tribals (31.53 per cent in 1961) in the state's population.

Such a disastrous consequence of partition for the land locked hilly Tripura posed a great challenge to the state's mostly tribal based communist movement in the 1950s. Although nationally the CPI somewhat neglected the refugee problem, until the mid-

1950s, locally the Tripura unit, began to take up the issue from the beginning of 1951. But the solution of the question was linked by the unit to fundamental social transformation. In the very first issue of the local communist weekly, its editor and the founder of Tripura communism, Biren Datta, wrote: The task of fundamental transformation of the agrarian structure and that of refugee rehabilitation productively is the same thing.'[44] The CPI–affiliated Gana Mukti Parishad (Tribal Liberation Council, 1948) likewise saw the solution of the refugee problem in the abolition of landlordism and the formation of a democratic government in Tripura.[45] To be sure, that was only to pay lip-service to the burning issue. Marxist jargon apart, no attempts were made to understand the specific problem of the refugees. The Draft Report of the first Tripura Conference of the CPI (1952) devoted only three sentences to the problem when it asked the party cadres 'to form organization among the refugees and to put pressure on the administration to solve their problem.'[46] Building a communist power base among the refugees was a hard task. Despite the local party's concern for the refugees nothing concrete was done until 1952. This lack of organization among the refugees,resented by party veterans, reflected 'the lack of thought among the party leadership on the refugee problem'.[47]

The refugees in Tripura, however, tremendously added to the voters in the state (Table 1).

Table – 1: Growth of the Electorate in Tripura, 1952-67

Year	Voters
1952	2,71,672
1957	4,32,904
1962	4,80,609
1967	6,66,637

Source: Roy, S., ed. *Lokotantrey Tripura* (Tripura Darpan, 1983).

The Congress-administration in fact 'made' more electors than there were refugees by giving false certificates to people residing in the then East Pakistan.[48] This was supplemented by the Congress propaganda that the Tripura communists were 'Bangal Kheda' (Refugee-bashing). This paid off for the Congress, and it improved its electoral fortunes.

The communist mobilization of the refugees in Tripura could hardly ignore the above situation. The pattern of mobilization of the refugees pursued by the communists consisted of the creation of an organization to demand adequate refugee rehabilitation, and the pressure on the administration to achieve this goal.[49] From 1952 onwards, the communists actively mobilized the refugees: they made representations to the government, organized meetings and processions and staged several hunger-strikes in support of their demands. It was a particularly difficult task because the real power to rehabilitate the refugees lay with the Congress. Hence, the communists, tactically, focused on the failure and limitations in refugee rehabilitation and pressurized the administration to perform more satisfactorily. While the local Congress engaged itself in a policy of blatant anti-communist communalism, the communists retorted by locating the refugee problem in a historical perspective.

The battle was not entirely lost. In both 1957 and 1962 Tripura Territorial Council elections, the CPI unit managed to poll 38.4 per cent (and with its ally, a further 4.4 per cent and 44.9 per cent) share of popular votes respectively. In both cases, the communist share of the vote was higher than that of Congress. Congress received considerable support from the refugees-turned-voters in 1957 but the picture began to change from their onwards. After 1957, there were indications of a shift in loyality: 'refugees were moving from Congress to an alternative leadership.'[50] The Tripura Communist Party organization report (1959) applauded its new penetration among the Bengali Hindu refugees.[51] This was well-reflected in the communist electoral performance: 45.1 per cent in 1957 to 51.3 per cent in 1962 in the case of Lok Sabha elections which earned them both the Lok Sabha seats. The fourth general elections of 1967 somewhat reversed the trend: a communist defeat and a Congress victory; but even so, the newly formed CPI-M's 41.74 per cent share of the popular votes in the Lok Sabha elections and about 30 per cent (CPI-M = 21.72 per cent; CPI = 8.3 per cent) in the elections to the Legislative Assembly, was no mean achievement, and suggested the sustaining bases of the communists among the refugees.

Despite all the subsequent shifts and turns, and turmoil in the state communist movement, the communists have continued refugee mobilization which, ironically enough, still remains an unfinished task. While the original bases among the tribals were retained, they were not obviously enough to ensure the communist's repeated electoral victories in the state especially since 1977-8. The support of the Bengalis, who today constitute about 80 per cent of the state's total population, is needed to win elections.

But the success of refugee mobilization in Tripura has remained highly tension-ridden in the sense that in Tripura's specific socio-economic situation it has been very difficult, if not impossible, to achieve rehabilitation of both the refugees and the tribals. The rehabilitation of the latter, a fundamental objective of the state communist movement, meant the restoration of land 'illegally' transferred from the tribals to the refugees, to its original occupants i.e., the tribals. The two types of rehabilitation seemed contradictory. Somewhat inevitably, the communist success in refugee mobilization, which has resulted in the Bengal ascendancy to leadership of the state communist movement and also the Bengali control over the movement, has lessened the prospects for tribal rehabilitation. This has also been deeply resented by the tribal comrades as amply evidenced by the reports of different conferences and memoranda of the GMP since the 1960s.[52]

Interestingly, the Tripura government was quite eager to rehabilitate the refugees. But the motive was political and the means adopted were anything but fair. The Congress-led administration, mostly manned by the Bengali Hindus, sought to rehabilitate the refugees, to resettle them on tribal lands in most cases forcefully evicted. Thus the wide-spread tribal-refugee conflicts followed in the wake of the 'rehabilitation of refugees' in Tripura. The GMP in order to protect tribal interests had to resist such attempts:

> The Tripura administration in collusion with the *jotedars* has evicted 15-16 Mog tribal families from their lands they have been cultivating in Baisnavpur in Subroom. The Mogs have been cultivating such lands for the last 40 years by duly paying rent. Now the *jotedars* have sold out those lands to the refugees keeping the peasants in total darkness. We demand to revert such process. The refugee families resettled on such lands must be shifted elsewhere preferably on other *khas* lands of the *jotedars*'.[53]

Dasarath Dev (Barma), Tripura's only tribal communist Member of Parliament, delivered a speech in the Lok Sabha in 1966 sharply focusing on the same issue. He said: 'The illegal transfer of tribal land to the non-tribals must be treated as coagnizable offence. Such lands must be transferred back to the tribals.'[54]

The GMP had also to take the issue into the state communist movement itself. In the 1960s, the GMP advocated two types of struggle in the state communist movement: the nationality struggle for the tribals, and class struggle for the Bengalis. This was done as a shield for the interests of the tribals against the non-tribal Bengalis. The GMP raised the bogey of tribal nationalism against the kind of refugee rehabilitation being done in the state:

> The urge among different tribals in Tripura to fully develop as nations is very strong. This urge will simply be killed if the tribal compactness is diluted, if the tribals are evicted from their land and non-tribals are rehabilitated there instead. I have the following to say against those opposed to the idea of tribal reserves: the chauvinism of advanced nationalism does not see the nationalist aspirations of the tribals and explain this away as anti-national and secessionist.[55]

The tenor of the GMP moves was the idea that the refugee rehabilitation in Tripura was standing in the way of the tribal rehabilitation in the state.

Refugees, Tribals, Communists in Tripura
A Summary

Thus, within the specific socio-economic situation in Tripura, the two types of rehabilitation—refugee and tribal, seemed contradictory and delicate. For example, a certain tilt of the Marxist government in Tripura in the late 1970s towards the tribals led to the communal riots in 1980 in which more tribals than Bengalis were killed. Unlike West Bengal, the forcible and illegal occupation of *khas* lands by the refugees in Tripura has not found unconditional support from the state's tribal communists. The post-partition refugees in Tripura and their 'rehabilitation' have become a threat to tribal identity in the state.

In sum despite the apparent success particularly in West Bengal in refugee mobilization by the communists, the refugee issue has been a long-term problem for India. The communist organized pressure tactics brought the refugees some goods and services, plus votes for them in successive elections. The communists recognized refugees as a community but imposed on them, a class perspective. The essence of the communist solution to the refugee problem has been to provide housing and land, both to be privately owned. But Engels, one of the founders of Marxism, would have called this un-socialist. As he criticized Mulberger's solution to the housing question in Germany: ... 'the solution of the housing problem consists in everyone becoming the owner instead of the tenant of his dwelling.'[56] It is known that the rehabilitated well-off sections of the refugees in Burdwan (West Bengal) have been recently turning away from the communists to the BJP.[57] This is the inevitable consequence of an un-socialist solution of the refugee problem by the communists. The great question before the non-rehabilitated refugees in West Bengal and Tripura is: will the nation-state in India, faced with the forces of globalization, be as interested in the refugees as before? It seems unlikely that this will be the case. The post-modern era in India, as elsewhere, will have to co-exist with many of such unsolved problems of the nation-state. The time has now perhaps come for the refugees' true self-assertion and for their initiation into politics of their own which, after Antony Giddens,[58] may be called the 'life politics of the refugees' within a new framework for radical politics.

NOTES

1. *The Oxford Companion to Politics of the World,* entry 'Refugees' (New York, OUP, 1993), 776. See also for detailed knowledge on this global problem, J. Wittenburger, compiler *A Basic Bibliography for Refugee Studies* (Oxford, OUP 1989).
2. E. Hobsbawm, *The Age of Extremes: The Short Twentieth Century 1912-91* (New Delhi, Viking Penguin, 1995, orig. 1994) 52.
3. Ibid., 51.
4. *The Oxford Companion,* 776.
5. Ibid., 776-8.
6. Ibid., 777.
7. For instance, S.L. Keller, *Uprooting and Social Change: The Role of Refugees in Development* (Delhi, Manohar 1975).
8. Introduction to Keller, *Uprooting.*
9. Ibid., Preface.
10. P. Chakrabarti, *The Marginal Men* (Kalyani, Lumiere Books, 1990) 3.
11. S. Sarkar, *The Modern India (1885-1947)* (Delhi, Macmillan, 1983) 47.
12. For an earlier assessment of the issue, G. Overstreet and M. Windmiller, *Communism in India* (Berkeley: CUP 1959), see also G. Singh, *Communism in Punjab* upto 1967 (Delhi, Ajanta, 1993).
13. B. N. Pandey, ed. *The Indian Nationalist Movement 1885-1947: Select Documents* (Delhi, Macmillan, 1997) 164.
14. Sarkar, *Modern India,* 411.
15. Quoted A. R. Desai, *Social Background of India Nationalism* (Bombay, Popular Prakashan, 1976) 425.
16. R. P. Dutta, *India Today* (London, Victor Golacz, 1947) 481.
17. Ibid., 476.
18. Ibid., 477.
19. See, Chakrabarti, *Marginal Men,* 42.
20. Ibid., 42.
21. Ibid., 45.

22. Ibid., 22; 28-46 (for details).
23. Ibid., 55-6.
24. Quoted in Chakrabarti *Marginal Men,* 68.
25. Ibid., 74.
26. V. Fic, *Peaceful Transition to Communism in India* (Bombay, Nachiketa, 1969).
27. See. Chakrabarti, *Marginal Men,* 77-78.
28. 'Provincial Refugee Circular' No. 1 dated 12 November 1950 (meant for party units, members and sympathizers), West Bengal Provincial Organizing Committee, CPI (Unpublished) (in Bengali; translations authors).
29. 'Circular No. 2', Refugee Centre, West Bengal Provincial Organization Committee of the CPI, dated 1 November 1950 (unpub.) (in Bengali; translations mine).
30. 'Circular No. 5 urgent', Provincial Refugee Centre, West Bengal Provincial Organizing Committee of the CPI, dated 26 December 1950 (in Bengali; translation mine) (unpub.).
31. Chakrabarti, *Marginal Men,* 94.
32. Circular No. 11 (1951), UCRC, Quoted in Chakrabarti, *Marginal Men,* 134.
33. See, A. Ray., 'Left in West Bengal' in R. Chatterjee, ed. *Politics in West Bengal* (Calcutta, World Press, 1985), 73. Ray, strangely, failed to explain the increase in communists' urban votes.
34. M. F. Franda, *Political Development and Political Decay in West Bengal* (Calcutta, Firma K L M, 1971) 154.
35. B. Sengupta, *Communism in Indian Politics* (New York, CUP, 1972) 153.
36. Franda, *Political Development.*
37. Ibid., 58.
38. Chakrabarti, *Marginal Men,* 186.
39. Ibid.
40. For instance, the Burdwan District Committee of the CPI-M in its inner party 'Political-organizational Report' of the 14th District Conference (23-26 Nov. 1985) wrote: 'The refugee organizations in the district are more or less active. Our organization is most active among the refugees. However, there is misunderstanding taking place between the peasants and the refugees on the issue of redistribution of lands. In some cases,there has taken place some erosion of our support too. Also, a good proportion of the refugees has been able to improve their economic condition considerably. These sections do not side with us as before'. (unpub. in Bengali, translations mine), 33.
41. Chakrabarti, *Marginal Men,* 141.
42. Ibid., 207.
43. The subject has been discussed at greater length in my Ph.D. on 'Communism in Tripura upto 1965' (unpub. University of London, 1989).

44. *Tripurar Katha* (in Bengali), NO. 1, (March 1951) 1.
45. *Tripurar Katha* (in Bengali), No. 17, (April 1951) 1.
46. S. Chanda, ed. *Two Unpublished Documents of the Party in the Period of its Formation* (in Bengali), Agartala, (Tripura Darpan, 1983) 38.
47. Ibid., 33.
48. J. Chakrabarty, *Tripura Between 1930 and 1980* (in Bengali) (Agartala, 1983) 74.
49. Chanda, *Two Unpublished Documents,* 38.
50. 'Political-organizational Report of the 4th State Conference of the Tripura Unit of the CPI,' (1959) (unpub. in Bengali) 3.
51. Ibid.
52. For instance, the 'Resolutions and Report of the 5th Central Conference of the GMP' (1960) (unpub. in Bengali). The tenor of the GMP conference reports since 1960 is: the refugee rehabilitation in Tripura has been standing in the way of the tribal rehabilitation in the state and hence not the unqualified support to the refugee rehabilitation in Tripura.
53. 'Resolutions and Report' (GMP) 54-5.
54. D. Dev., 'Gana Mukti Parishad in Protecting Tribal Land' (Agartala, GMP, 1965 (unpub. in Bengali) 29.
55. Ibid., 21-2.
56. F. Engels, 'The Housing Question (1872-3)' in *K. Marx and F. Engels: Selected Works* (3 vols), Vol. 2 (Moscow Progress, 1968) 371.
57. 'Political-organizational Report of the 14th Burdwan District Conference of the CPI-M' (23-26 Nov. 1985) (unpub. in Bengali) 33.
58. A. Giddens, *Beyond Left and Right: The Future of Radical Politics* (Cambridge, Polity Press, 1994) Chapters 4, 6, 8.

Chapter Twelve

State, Nation, Identity:
Ideology and Conflict in Bangladesh

Tazeen M. Murshid

Introduction

This chapter aims to demonstrate the contextual nature of the formation of states, nations and identities as an aspect of the reformulation of ideologies by the elite/intelligentsia in their quest for power and legitimacy. In particular, it shows that in the process there has been a significant rise in the influence of the religious right in the social and political scene of Bangladesh. In this context, it examines the role of successive regimes, accounts for the impact of the Taslima Nasrin episode and assesses the implications of the 1996 electoral outcomes. It portrays a gradual shift to the right in the ideological discourse in Bangladesh.

The experience of Bangladesh bears out the arguments of Brass, Eller and Coughlan, for it clearly demonstrates that there is nothing primordial or given about ethnic and national identity.[1] These have been derived through social and political interaction. Elites in competition for political power and economic advantage have constructed and given form and content to national group identity. While the ruling elite has played a decisive role in ensuring state patronage for the promotion of its particular world view, counter elites have risen to challenge its hegemony. Recent examples of the elite conflict have focused on differences regarding the war of liberation of Bangladesh and the role of Islam in social and political life. Death sentences passed by *fatwa* (religious decree) courts on persons accused of atheism have given rise to particularly volatile situations. Among them were nationally eminent figures such as the scholar, Ahmad Sharif and the poet, Shamsur Rahman, as well as the feminist writer, Taslima Nasreen. Alongside others, they reflect a secular challenge to the rising forces of religious extremism at a time when the state appeared to countenance the religious right. The phenomenon is striking when examined in the context of the emergence of Bangladesh as a fledgling secular democracy in 1971.

Religion has periodically played a dominant role in shaping the nature of politics in South Asia.[2] Certain Islamist political groups and parties claim to know the ultimate truth in matters pertaining to religion and demand the right to be the sole interpreters of Islamic law as experts in the field. But it can be argued that there is no essentialist Islam in a world where its interpretation and practice has varied from place to place and where there are four major schools of Islamic jurisprudence, all with equal claims to legimimacy.[3] There is, therefore, potential for conflict at many levels – at the level of interpretation and in the use of *ijtihad* (individual reasoning), as well as in relation to the position of religious minorities and the role of liberal intellectuals in determining the nature of the state.

The religious orthodoxy, using the tools of modern democracy, seeks to forge a nation defined by Islam and a state based on *shariah* laws, notwithstanding the fact that large segments of the diasporic Muslim population belonging to other spatial, cultural and political locales cannot be included within this construct. But this conception of the state and nation is theoretically discriminatory to religious minorities whose status would suffer under *shariah* laws for they could be barred from high office and compelled to pay *jizya,* or protection tax. Hence, the liberal intelligentsia has rejected this view and emphasized other identity markers such as Bengali language and common cultural roots of the Bengali peoples. Their vision of the secular pluralist state acknowledges that a large majority of the subject population share their nationalities with others beyond their political frontiers, – such as the Bengalis of the plains and the Chakmas of the hills. However, those who argue that the *raison d'etre* of a juridical state must lie in its distinctiveness as a nation, are at odds with the position of the liberal intelligentsia, and have engaged themselves in constructing such a distinct nation, described as 'Bangladeshi' after the name of the new state: segments of the army enjoy pride of place among the proponents of this view. Thus, while one can agree with Gellner and Hobsbawm that nationalists aim at a congruence between national and state boundaries, effectively, this is often illusory.[4] Following the arguments of Hugh Setson — Watson as opposed to that of A.D. Smith, I make a distinction between state and nation in that a state is territorially bounded and governed by a set of legal or political institutions through which it maintains order.[5] A nation, on the contrary, may not have such institutional structures, but may nevertheless share a common history, language or other cultural markers of identity, symbolic or otherwise, while being teritorially dispersed.[6] In the conception of neither the religious orthodoxy nor the liberal intelligentsia of Bangladesh is there an exact correspondence between state and national boundaries. However, there is an expectation that the state and nation should be congruous.

Background: the Pakistan Phase – Islam in Danger vs. Jai Bangla

The history of Bangladesh and its search for a national identity is replete with tensions between perceptions based on religious orthodoxy and secular rationalism.[7] Hence, national identity and state ideology remain contested. The national and political boundaries of Bangladesh have been reconstituted several times reflecting the fluid and contextual nature of identity selection. The emergence of Pakistan in 1947 was accompanied by a strong assertion of Muslim nationalism and an emphasis on Islam as the basis of identity and unity, binding together disparate groups. Indian Muslims felt deprived as Muslims *vis-a-vis* the Hindus and hence the emphasis on their religious and communal identity. The emergence of Bangladesh drew support from a rising Bengali ethnic consciousness. The Muslims of East Pakistan felt their relative deprivation as Bengalis *vis-a-vis* the

non-Bengalis of West Pakistan who used religion to control
Bengali aspirations. In both instances, the basic struggle was for
economic emancipation.[8] However, the formulation of new
ideologies and identities served to mobilize popular support and
provide legitimacy for that struggle through which new imagined
nations were emerging. In both cases such reformulations
achieved a fragile unity.

After the creation of the new states, the delicate consensus on
ideology and identity seemed to break down in both Pakistan and
Bangladesh. Secular politicians had rallied Muslim support for
Pakistan with slogans of 'Islam in danger.'[9] In the new state,
created ostensibly to guarantee Muslims the right to live in their
own way, there were several contenders for power challenging
the authority and ideology of the ruling party, the Muslim
League. For example, the Awami Muslim League broke away
from the Muslim League in 1951 because it sought to open up its
membership to all communities, irrespective of religion, and
subsequently dropped the word 'Muslim' from its name. Other
challengers were the Jama'at-i-Islami which demanded an
Islamic state ruled by *shariah* laws; and there was also an
underground communist movement which rejected the partition
of India. Notably, the Muslim League was routed in the first
provincial elections in East Bengal in 1954.

The emergence of Bangladesh in 1971, unlike that of
Pakistan, was sudden – the inevitable aftermath of a genocide
perpetrated by the West Pakistan dominated 'junta' in defence of
its decision not to share power or resources with East Pakistan.
The 1971 debacle was a struggle for sheer survival rather than a
self-conscious attempt to build a secular polity, even though
inspiration was sought in slogans like *'jai Bangla'* (victory to
Bengal) which had no religious connotations whatsoever. Yet,
Bangladesh came to be associated with secular symbols and
ideologies, until the state controlled reversals in the aftermath of
the assassination of the first prime minister of Bangladesh,
Sheikh Mujibur Rahman, in 1975.

The Heritage: State Intervention and Elite Roles in the Process of Identity Construction

Bangladesh has inherited a tradition of state intervention in the process of identity construction from Pakistan, where the state subscribed to Islamic ideology, albeit superficially. For example, in an effort to contain the opposition, the ruling party of Pakistan, the Muslim League, claimed for itself the sole right to interpret 'what Islam is.'[10] It equated itself with the state, Pakistan, and with the religion of the majority, Islam. Henceforth any criticism of the party was interpreted as an attempt to disintegrate Pakistan as well as an attack on Islam itself. The state introduced religion into politics. Even its anti-Indian stance was projected as Islamic. A great deal of effort went into drawing a distinction between the cultures of East and West Bengal. In fact, any stress on cultural similarities between these two regions was interpreted as a desire for unification of the two Bengals. Thus the struggle to establish Bengali as one of the State languages of Pakistan was perceived to be a major threat to the ideology of Pakistan, as Bengali was one of the cultural links between the two parts of Bengal. In contrast, the state took no steps to build an Islamic society or polity.

In such a context, discussion about the identity of Bengali Muslims was fraught with controversy as 'Bengali' and 'Muslim' were presented as incompatible in state parlance, following a tradition from colonial time.[11] For many, this was deeply problematic. *Madrasahs* taught Urdu rather than Bengali. Because it was written in the Arabic script, Urdu enjoyed greater status and was considered an Islamic language by many. The non-Bengali upper classes who dominated politics and the economy as well as sections of the upwardly mobile Bengalis tended to look down upon Bengali language as inferior. It was in this context that experiments were made to write Bengali in the Arabic script.[12] This attitude to Bengali, the mother tongue of the majority, was however resented by the upwardly-mobile, middle classes and the vernacular intelligentsia. Hence a tension ensued between a religious and a secular basis of identity.

The religious basis of identity acquired a special importance because religion was politicized in Pakistan. The pull towards a secular definition was, however, inevitable in East Pakistan not only because of the Bengal Muslims' natural attachment to their local cultural roots, which predate their history of conversion to Islam, but also because of their heritage of eclectic cultural patterns, which arguably carry a secular connotation.[13] Local cultural patterns such as the use of *alpana* (floor decoration with rice paint) at weddings, or wearing colourful *bindi* (cosmetic dots) on the forehead, or making offerings at the shrines of *pirs* or holy persons, also common in the Middle East, were projected by the ruling elite as being essentially Hindu and, as such, opposed to Islamic culture.[14]

Another important factor which contributed to the religious-secular tension was related to the schizophrenic or culturally ambivalent self-image of the intelligentsia. While the intelligentsia idealized *ashraf* ethics and values supposedly derived from the Middle East, the harsh reality was that the majority of them were descended from converts, of peasant stock, spoke Bengali and shared little with the *ashraf* apart from religion.[15] Hence, the fear that Bengali Islam was contaminated by local and un-Islamic practices. The orthodoxy was harsh on those who practised local customs and rituals. They have been referred to as a 'class of fossilized imbeciles and fogies, who live in a cloud of un-Islamic superstition inherited from the local pagan traditions.'[16] The dichotomous self-image was not as devastating for the intelligentsia as it was in 1920, in the 1940s and '50s, when they were still talking in terms of 'choosing' their mother-tongue.[17] Nevertheless, *ashraf* ideals determined cultural and linguistic choices, until groups could break away from the established mould to assert that culture and identity be defined by secular criteria.

In the immediate post-partition period, the Bengali Muslim intelligentsia was acutely aware of the need to define its social, cultural, linguistic and political identity. The concerns of this period had their roots in pre-partition ideologies covering a wide spectrum — the orthodox, pan-Islamist, humanist and communist. Maududi and his Jama'at-i-Islami with its mouthpiece *Al-Islam,* followed the orthodox path of Indian Muslim thought in prescribing a strongly Islamic state. The *New Values* group deeply influenced by humanist thought, envisaged a liberal democratic society where culture belonged to a neutral, or secular sphere. It was an amorphous group of university teachers who contributed to a journal called *New Values,* which was published from Dhaka in the 1950s and 60s. Contributors were influenced by the rationalism of the *Sikha* group of the twenties and thirties. Organizations such as the Yuva League or Youth League, deeply influenced by communist ideas undertook politico-cultural activities with decidedly secular objectives. Other organizations such as the Tamaddun Majlis, which had deep religious orientations nevertheless recognized a secular dimension to questions of language, identity and culture.[18]

Intellectual preoccupations among prose writers in the years after 1947 focused on an anxiety to assess contemporary society in the light of post-independence experiences. One central question was the rightful place of Islam in society. In the ensuing deliberations, the religious ideal was constantly measured against the secular ones of freedom, democracy and humanism.[19]

The multiple and often mutually contradictory identities of Bengali Muslims, have been shifting constantly. These have been affected by a wide range of factors – cultural, religious and political. However, the pulls of symbol manipulation by elites in competition for power have created a range of problems. Some of these relate to the duality in their self-perception, and the need to reconcile the discrepancy between the ideal and the practice, with their social origins, not to mention the trauma of twice forging new states out of old territories, each time involving the need to redefine the nation, nationhood and national boundaries.

The tradition of distinguishing between a Bengali and a Muslim provided grounds for some of the problems of self-perception which confronted Bengali Muslims later on.[20] In Pakistan, this issue appeared to have lost significance at least initially. Research conducted among university students in the mid-1960s indicated that there was no perceived conflict of identities in East Bengal between being a Bengali, a Pakistani, and a Muslim.[21] However, the movement leading to the emergence of Bangladesh in 1971 induced once again the need to define national and group identity. In a sense, 'Bengali' stood for a secular definition emphasizing the ethnic and cultural dimension; whereas, 'Pakistani' had implied a continuing belief in the two-nation theory and an emphasis on Islam as an overall guiding principle. But in fact, the distinction was not as clear-cut as this. Abul Mansur Ahmed, a politician and writer, saw the emergence of Bangladesh as a 'restoration of the Lahore Resolution' which had visualized the emergence of several independent states.[22] His basic faith in the two-nation theory had remained intact. But at the time this was not a widely-held view.

The Secular Phase and the Rise of the Muslim Bengal Movement

Independent Bangladesh came to be associated with a secular ideology because of a number of factors. The autonomy movement of the 1960s which was a sequel to the language movement of the 1950s addressed itself mainly to economic and political issues. The language movement had already created a secular cult and carried the message that culture be allotted a neutral, non-religious and to that extent, a secular zone. The non-communal, eclectic cultural ethos of East Bengal also had a secular dimension to it. Another reason was that the 1972 Constitution enshrined secularism as one of the four pillars of state ideology.

However, there was no absolute national consensus about what secularism meant. The term may be defined in opposition to communalism and theocracy as well as in terms of non-interference of the state in matters of religion, which is treated essentially as a private matter. But some believed secularism to be a form of atheism, or absence of religion.

Mujib faced strong opposition from two fronts: the fragmented left and the Islamic right.[23] Neither recognized the basis of the new state. A 'Muslim Bengal' movement emerged shortly after liberation. Kamal Hossain, the then foreign minister noted in a recent interview that the idea of Muslim Bangla came from a Radio Pakistan Broadcast on 17 December 1971, a day after Pakistan's surrender. In the broadcast, Pakistan welcomed the formation of Muslim Bangla and the restoration of the original spirit of the 1940 Lahore Resolution which envisaged Pakistan as a federation of independent states.[24] Several factions of the pro-Chinese Communist Party continued to describe Bangladesh as 'East Bengal' or 'East Pakistan'.

The relative success of the movement to alter the identity of the new state is evident in the policies adopted since the assassination of Sheikh Mujibur Rahman. That act was one in a series of events which led to the adoption of Islam as an instrument of state policy.

Some scholars have argued that Mujib himself contributed to the process by invoking Islam in state affairs, adopting 'ill-defined secularist goals' and pursuing recognition by Muslim countries which had favoured Pakistan in 1971.[25] While it was imperative for him to diversify his international alliances beyond the Indo-Soviet bloc because of the need for financial assistance to rebuild the war-torn economy, it may be suggested that there was indeed, some discrepancy in the theory and practice of Mujib's secularism. Pre-empting misrepresentation by propagandists he was keen to reassure the populace that he was not encouraging godlessness. Therefore, for example, he replaced a television and radio programme called 'Speaking the Truth' based on secular ethics with one based on citations from the scriptures of Islam, Hinduism, Christianity and Buddhism, thus, allowing equal opportunity to all faiths.[26] This is somewhat more in keeping with the Indian perception of secularism as *sarba dharma bhaba,* or religious tolerance, rather than that inscribed in the 1972 Constitution of Bangladesh as *dharmanirapekshata,* or religious neutrality. Mujib's actions brought religion to the public domain instead of keeping it in the private sphere as was his stated goal.

Zia and the Challenge to Bengali Nationalism

With the military entry in state affairs, the political elite was actively engaged in forging new identities in the hope of gaining new allies and popular legitimacy. The outcome, however, was nationally divisive. Nationality, which was defined in terms of Bengali ethnic, linguistic and cultural identity since independence, was, after the 1975 *coup*, being redefined on the basis of political calculations. Although there were no popular demands for such reformulation, the measure was expected to win over new support bases. The new definition required that a distinction be made between the languages of East and West Bengal, where the former would be distinct from the Sanskritic Bengali of West Bengal. The basis for such an argument had been provided by Abul Mansur Ahmed in the period after partition when he chose to describe the language of East Bengal as Pak Bangla.[27]

In 1978, under President Zia-ur-Rahman's military regime, citizens of Bangladesh were designated 'Bangladeshi', replacing the appellation of 'Bangalee' as stated in the Constitution of 1972. This was a strategic move in that the term specifically demarcated the area and population of the new juridical state. Zia may also have been motivated by an underlying xenophobia which plagued sections of the population, particularly, segments of the religious right, the pro-Chinese left, and factions with the army which had inherited the anti-Indian traditions of the Pakistan army.[28] At one level, Zia's actions were an assertion of sovereignty in relation to India which not only dominated the region geo-politically but also had a sizeable Bengali population. At another level, he was discarding the pro-India sympathies of the previous regime, unpopular among his new following. Instead, he began to woo Pakistan and its supporters in the USA, Saudi Arabia and Libya, which incidentally had resisted the emergence of independent Bangladesh.

Although the preference for 'Bangladeshi' over 'Bangalee' had no strong religious connotation, it was accompanied by another development: 'secularism' was discarded as a principle of state policy through a constitutional amendment in 1977.[29] Aware that a non-secular stance would be regarded as communal or, anti-Hindu, he asserted through the manifesto of his political party, the Bangladesh Nationalist Party, that Bangladeshis had freed themselves from 'the evils of communalism' because of the 'great teachings of Islam.' Zia's actions implied a reassertion of the distinct and separate identity of Bengali Muslims *vis-a-vis* the Bengali Hindus. To this extent, he acknowledged once again the concept of two-nations on which Pakistan had been founded and which had been rejected through the war of liberation in 1971. The basic complexities in the problem of culture and identity which existed during Pakistani rule thus persisted in Bangladesh. His primary motive was to stabilize his rule rather than promote an Islamic upsurge, although this was the long-term result of the strategies he adopted.

Compared to his predecessor, Zia resorted to policies explicitly aimed at giving an 'Islamic' gloss to the state. Hence, the Islamic University Act, 1980 and Islamic Education and Research Act 1980 were enacted.[30] Not only was he seeking to maintain the allegiance of his new allies but was also expecting to obtain approval from the Arab bloc which, thus far, had little regard for the break-away state of Bangladesh because of its great sympathy for Pakistan despite its promise of economic support. In exchange for a religious posture it would be possible to obtain Arab aid. Mujib before him had been lured by similar considerations when attending the Islamic Summit in 1974; but he was less successful than Zia because of his commitment to secularism. Although the amount offered to Zia was not large in global terms, it was politically advantageous for it signified a degree of acceptance by the community of Islamic nations. The Zia period ushered in a new ruling ideology determined primarily by concerns for its own survival rather than any ideological convictions. The new ideology was reflected in the usage of a new political and cultural vocabulary aimed at a shift away from Bengali linguistic nationalism.[31]

Undoubtedly, the rise of the military in politics provoked a legitimacy crisis. In its search for new support bases, the leadership adopted the measures discussed above which may be described as policies of inclusion and exclusion. Clearly, Islamists and the forces opposed to the Bengali language and the liberation of the Bengali people from the control of Pakistan were included. Quite ironically, Zia, the freedom fighter excluded the major force behind the liberation of the new nation, the Awami League, which was also the champion of secularism and inclined favourably towards India. By the same token he excluded Hindus and syncretists. Among the latter were people from literary circles, musicians, artists, dancers and painters, – people who drew their inspiration from the common cultural heritage of Bengal.

Zia thus rejected Bengali nationalism without ever acknowledging the implication of the switch for national politics and international relations. Nationally, the formerly rejected right and left took his policies as signals inviting them to re-enter the political scene and stake their claims. The move was facilitated by the 1976 Political Parties Resolution which lifted the ban on religion-based politics. This was perhaps the most significant development which contributed to the gradual rehabilitation of the 'Islamist' parties, which re-entered politics in 1979. At the international level, a deteriorating relationship with India corresponded with growing overtures of friendship to Pakistan. Pakistani industrialists like the Dawoods and the Isphanis, who had lost their factories in the former East Pakistan as a result of the war, were invited back to run these and were paid compensation. Military rule in Bangladesh signalled a reversal in trends whereby the country quietly headed towards becoming 'Muslim Bangla'. Although Zia's primary objective was to maintain himself in power, effectively, he laid the foundations for the rise of the Islamic right and the forces favourable to closer ties with Pakistan.

The Ershad Years

The Ershad era too was favourable for the Islamic right. Ershad's succession to the Presidency, following the assassination of Zia in

1981, signalled the end of the influence of freedom fighters in politics. Henceforth, repatriated officers from Pakistan, less committed to Bengali nationalism, determined the national agenda. Ershad, a usurper like Zia, lacked the legitimacy enjoyed by him as a freedom fighter. It has been argued that 'the Islamic quantum of state orientation increased with decreasing legitimacy of the ruling elite.'[32] It was no wonder that he pursued Zia's Islamizing policies but with greater vigour. He too identified the Islamic right as a potential ally. In order to woo them Ershad emphasized the Islamic character of the state, led Friday prayers, made periodic attempts to control the norms of social behaviour, dress and manners, and more importantly, initiated policy changes which replicated constitutional measures, adopted in Pakistan.[33] Through the Eighth Amendment of the Constitution, Islam was given the status of state religion in 1988. Women's groups contested it as an infringement on human rights;[34] and secularists feared that the country was sliding towards becoming an Islamic state as in Pakistan, where constitutional change under military rule had cleared the path for the introduction of *shariah* laws in 1979. Protest by the Jama'at-i-Islami and the Muslim League was motivated more by the fear of losing the political initiative than an opposition to the principle, although they claimed that it was a ploy to prevent the establishment of an Islamic Republic based on the principles of the Koran and sunnah (Way of the Prophet). However, various other Islamic organizations such as the Jamiat-i-Ulama, Jamiat-ul-Mudarresin, Sirat Mission, as well as the Pir of Sarsina were pleased with the development.[35]

The Eighth Amendment was a major gain for the Islamists. They were also making gains elsewhere. For example, their augmented influence in the sphere of education was manifest in the number of *madrasahs* and in the recruitment of teachers and students (see Tables 1 and 2). While there has generally been a steady increase in the number of *madrasahs,* student intake, and in the expenditure for such education, periodically there were dramatic fluctuations. During the period of Ershad's rule between 1981 and 1990, as Table 2 shows, there was more than a hundred fold increase in the number of government and affiliated *madrasahs* and nearly 300 per cent increase in the staff and student enrolment. Increased allocation from the education budget and direct financial assistance to these institutions from Saudi Arabia, Kuwait, Libya and Pakistan have contributed to these developments.[36]

Table 1
Student Enrolment in *Madrasahs*
(1970-1 to 1975-6)

Year	Number of Madrasahs #/	Number of Students
1970-1	6,260	716,202
1972-3	6,565	739,163
1973-4	6,807	844,479
1974-5##/	6,471	756,235
1975-6##/	7,971	808,000

#/   Includes all types of *Madrasahs*: Reformed, Old Scheme Senior and Junior, Recognized and Unrecognized.
##/   Includes forquania *madrasahs* as well.
Sources: *Statistical Digest of Bangladesh,* No. 8, 1972, table, 13.1, pp. 252-3; *Statistical Year Book of Bangladesh* (SYB), 1975, table 7.1, p. 177; *SYB,* 1978, pp. 252-3.

Table 2
Students and Teachers in Government and
Affiliated *Madrasahs*
(1977-8 to 1991-2)

Year	Number of Madrasahs ###/	Number of Students	Number of Teachers
1977-8	1,976	375,200	21,579
1981-2	2,864	388,000	29,608
1990-1	5,959	1,028,000	83,761
1991-2	6,025	1,735,000	94,961

###/   From secondary level and above—government and affiliated only
Sources: Bureau of Statistics, *Statistical Pocketbook of Bangladesh,* various issues, based on information obtained from the *Madrasah* Board.

The Electoral Phase: Secular-Rationalists Challenged

The resumption of the democratic process with the end of
military rule revealed the extent of support for the religious right
as exemplified by the Jama'at-i-Islami. During the 1991
elections, the Jama'at won 18 seats and 12 per cent of the votes
cast, while none of the major parties achieved an absolute
majority.[37] The BNP achieved a majority in parliament with the
support of the Jama'at.Thus, for the first time in the history of
the new state Jama'at gained a direct and influential role in
government, whereby it could determine some key cabinet
appointments: there was widespread speculation with some
justification that these were Home, Information and Education.[38]

The alliance was a recognition of the Jama'at's rehabilitation
at the state level. However, the matter was far from resolved in
the streets. The secular forces represented by the literary-
intellectual circles, musicians, dramatists, writers, and bereaved
families of martyred freedom fighters, – who were perhaps
neutralized by the fear of being crushed by military rule, were
jolted into action under the freedom and tolerance permitted in
the relatively democratic atmosphere of the post-election phase.
Their concern was to counter the influence of the religious right
and keep alive the threatened memory of the liberation war.[39] The
selection of Golam Azam, as the *amir* of the Jama'at-i-Islami
provoked a massive protest organized by the newly established
Ekatturer Ghatok Dalal Nirmul Committee (Committee for the
Elimination of the Killers and Collaborators of 1971) which
demanded his trial for war crimes. It was widely believed that
Golam Azam aided and abetted Pakistan's war effort in
Bangladesh, and was guilty of incitement to murder intellectuals
in 1971.[40] Subsequently, a trial was staged to determine the
citizenship status of Golam Azam, to examine whether there was
a constitutional bar to his election as *amir*. In April 1993, the
High Court declared his previous loss of citizenship under the
Mujib government to have been unconstitutional; he was deemed
a citizen by birth under Article 2 of the President's Order
Number 149 of 1972. The court therefore concluded that his

election as *amir* did not contravene the Constitution.[41] The subject of trial for war crimes under a special tribunal was totally fudged.

This outcome gave the Jama'at a new lease of life during which it sought to determine the political agenda. In the next few months it pursued strategies to determine the national political agenda and maintain the initiative. It began a violent counter-offensive against the forces of secularism and Bengali nationalism. The objective now was to divert attention away from Golam Azam and increase the momentum of their campaign for the establishment of an Islamic state based on *shariah* laws. The feminist writer Taslima Nasreen offered them a timely pretext. As a lone woman perceived to have stepped out of acceptable social bounds she was an easy prey. Her anger and frustration in a society which sanctioned injustices against women in the name of religion and her attempt at a rational approach to Koranic liturgy provided fodder to her persecutors. A barrage of propaganda was directed at her from the pulpit and in public platforms. Taslima was accused of subverting the cultural and religious values of society and hence was depicted as a traitor to the state and religion, *rashtradrohi* and *dharmadrohi*. A process of 'psychological manipulation' of the popular psyche was carefully orchestrated. Extracts from her works were presented out of context to portray her as one who insults Islam, hates men and is a woman of loose moral standards. In a leaflet, she is charged with accusing God of being a liar, of making fun of the Day of Judgement, of going against the dictates of religion by insinuating that the birth of a son or daughter has nothing to do with God's will but is determined solely by chromosomes.[42]

The controversy surrounding Taslima Nasreen makes some sense if it is seen in the context of a struggle between the forces of religious extremism and secular liberalism, which are both vying for the hearts and minds of the people in Bangladesh. These forces are engaged in symbol manipulation to secure the social and political order they desire. The main difference however, is that the former is well organized, armed and carrying out a well thought out plan of action much of which had already been tried out in Pakistan.[43] The latter is disorganized, unarmed and believes, perhaps complacently, that Bengalis will not turn into religious fanatics.

But Taslima was only one of the many victims of the vengeance of fanatical forces. She survived because of the publicity, the foreign interest and the support of a few who rose to defend the rule of law. Others were less fortunate: the recent events in Bangladesh include the incident of a woman being stoned to death for alleged adultery whereas, in fact, the lustful gaze of a *mullah* had fallen on her. Another woman was forced to commit suicide to evade the shame of alleged *zina* crimes. Several intellectuals and writers like the poet Shamsur Rahman and the scholar Ahmad Sharif also faced death threats because they subscribe to secular, rationalist, non-communal and democratic values. But they have been spared the same degree of witch-hunting as stalks Taslima, although they too have had to go into hiding periodically.[44] Religious extremists have described them as *deshdrohi, rashtradrohi* and *dharmadrohi,* traitors to the nation, state and religion.[45]

A series of such provocative actions had virtually led to the establishment of a parallel structure of authority in remote areas far from the reaches of officialdom. Various 'front' organizations of the Jama'at supported by their own armed cadre began to impart Islamic justice. They derived their authority from the *fatwas* given by local *mullahs* and not from any court. Not only were the thieves amputated and 'adulterers' stoned, but opposition newspapers lost access to various distributors and their clients.[46] Women were targeted for the most vicious attacks.[47] Many rural women got divorced by *fatwa* for practicing birth control. Such a situation is novel in the history of the region. Some women also lost their marital status for taking bank loans for their small businesses. It was argued that economic independence for women was undesirable because it could give them a status superior to men, which was not part of God's plan.[48] Here, economic competition under conditions of unemployment and poverty cannot be ruled out as a more mundane explanation. Incidentally, the Jama'at itself has set up Islamic banking and loan-giving facilities. Non-government organizations like BRAC and their workers were attacked by *madrasah* students for allegedly spreading Christianity. BRAC schools for girls were burnt in protest against 'westernized' female education. Here coercion was a method of neutralizing the sources of alternative ideologies. Various women's groups and legal bodies gathered evidence and successfully convicted some of the *fatwabaj mullahs*.[49] The trend persisted during Khaleda's period in office, while the police found themselves inadequately armed to face the challenge.[50]

The Strategy and Strength of the Religious Right

The strategy of the religious right was to pursue all means at its disposal, both constitutional and unconstitutional, to achieve its goal of establishing an Islamic state – whether it be through persuasion, intimidation or coercion. One of the constitutional methods adopted, relied on infiltration by members into the lower courts of small towns like Rangpur and Maulavibazaar, and taking advantage of the existing legal system. It involved the following course of action: first, a *mullah* decreed a *fatwa*; subsequently, one of the faithful fielded a case in a lower court where the magistrate was a sympathizer or supporter of the Jama'at-Shibir; next, the magistrate immediately issued a warrant for the arrest of the accused without hearing his defence. Such warrants were issued against the editors of *Janakantha, Bhorer Kagaj, Ajker Kagaj* and *Jai Din* who were accused of hurting the sentiments of Muslims.[51] For example, an issue of *Jai Din* contained a cartoon involving the letter *alif* of the Arabic alphabet. The editor was compelled to obtain bail from three different courts for the same offence.[52] Such persistent harassment hoped to achieve conformity if not consensus.

These developments were accompanied by provocative statements by some members of the religious right in key positions which raise serious questions about their commitment to democracy and the nature of the state and nation envisaged. The Pir of Charmonai declared at a meeting on 29 July 1994 that 'all non-fundamentalists were of illegitimate birth'. At the same meeting, the *khatib* (head) of the Baitul Mukarram Mosque, Maulana Ubaidul Huq stated that Pakistan was divided in 1971 as a result of the *gaddari,* 'treachery of certain western educated individuals' who were currently involved in similarly deceiving the people.[53] Later, in an interview on 4 August, he announced that 'the state should be run by a *fatwa* committee consisting of the *ulama'*[54] thus voicing the thoughts of their spiritual and political leader, Maududi. The statements provoked an outraged protest from teachers, students, freedom fighters, political groups and a large section of the *ulama,* numbering 227. This indicates that there were divisions in the ranks of the *ulama* on the interpretation of history and on state policy.

It would be pertinent to assess the strengths of the Jama'at for these contributed to its increasing assertiveness. An important source of strength for the Jama'at-i-Islami has been its ability to forge alliances with various groups depending on the issues. It built strategic links with the BNP and the Awami League, thus neutralizing them sufficiently to lever open greater political space for itself. It was thus in a position to pursue its own political agenda more openly and contribute to a shift in the national discourse to the right. It also established a broad front with various parties and organizations which had similar objectives, i.e., the establishment of an Islamic state based on *shariah* laws. It successfully brought the Wahabis within its fold and developed a *modus operandi* with the Nizam-e-Islam, Jamiyat-ul-Ulama-islam and Freedom Party and other like-minded bodies. Politically, however, the Jama'at remained the most powerful of the Islamist groups, as is evident from the 1991 election results.

This may be attributed to some extent to its methods of mobilization which have been most successful among the lower middle classes. It followed a strict method of recruitment based on a lengthy initiation process common to the style of communist parties. To maximize gains it worked at various levels, not entirely unlike other parties: it had youth and student organizations such as the Islami Chhatra Shibir which tended to be militant aiming to gain control over university campuses.[55] There were women's branches whose members made door to door contact with sympathizers. Unlike other parties, however, it set up trust funds to support charitable causes such as schools, clinics and hospitals; and opened Islamic banks aimed to support income generating activities.[56]

Notably, Jama'at membership and resources received a boost over recent years despite the setback in the immediate post-liberation period. Based on interviews with an unidentified important party member, U.A.B. Razia Akhter Banu states that between 1981 and 1987, Jama'at full membership rose from 650 to 2,000, associate membership rose from 100,000 to 2 million. In December 1986, the Islamic Chhatra Shibir, its primary source of recruitment, had 300 full members, 6,000 associate members and 40,000 workers, whereas these were 226, 2,000 and 15,000 respectively in 1980. The Jama'at has established 62 trusts, of which 12 are based in Dhaka; and it has founded 200 private schools in Dhaka and outlying areas.[57] The Jama'at admits to receiving indirect assistance from Saudi Arabia although others have charged it with receiving direct monetary assistance. In May 1984 Golam Azam was apparently sent a cheque for US dollars 327,000 from Saudi Arabia which went astray in the mail.[58]

The Jama'at has certainly demonstrated its capacity for survival and potential as a serious political contender. However, its harsh methods of dealing with opponents upholding alternative ideologies do give rise to profound misgivings. In the long run, such a political style is likely to limit its wider appeal. Although a full assessment is beyond the scope of this chapter, in the June 1996 elections, the Jama'at won only 3 out of 300 seats and approximately 8.7 per cent of the votes cast. This was roughly 3.4 per cent less than in 1991 although, numerically, it polled more votes.[59] The Awami League became the majority party after twenty-three years in the opposition, winning 146 seats with 37.5 per cent of the votes polled, gaining 3.8 per cent more votes than in the previous elections contested. The BNP got 116 seats with 33.4 per cent of the votes, an increase of 2.6 per cent. The Jatiya Party made the most significant gains winning 16 per cent of the votes cast, 4 per cent more than before, although it translated into 1 seat only. The remaining 4 seats were won by independents and smaller parties: these were among the 77 other parties which together polled the remaining 4.4 per cent of the votes.[60] The balance of power has thus shifted from the Jama'at to the JP which has pledged its support to the AL. The Jama'at lost much of its support base to the BNP in some areas such as Rajshahi and Chittagong. The main contest was between the two major parties, the BNP and the Awami League, in which voters were keen to use their votes well. The high rate of female participation could not have favoured the Jama'at because of its opposition to the economic emancipation of women and atrocities committed against women in the name of religion as cited earlier.[61] A greater awareness of the negative role of the Jama'at during the war of liberation as a result of the activism of secular forces cannot be ruled out as another explanation for its setback.[62]

Despite the electoral outcome, the party is likely to continue to play an important role because of its numerical strength, organized support base and financial security. Equally important is the changed political climate reflecting an ideological shift to the right wherein parties have refrained from adopting overtly secular and pro-Indian postures, and the majority party has pledged to pursue a policy of national reconciliation and run the country on the basis of a national consensus.[63]

Conclusion

While demonstrating the contextual nature of identity formation, the chapter raises serious questions about the future of a pluralist secular liberal democracy under conditions where the relative autonomy of the state is weak. Bangladesh had become increasingly ungovernable prior to the 1996 elections not only because of the frequent crises besetting the BNP government,[64] but also because its relative autonomy to mediate between various interest and demand groups had been weakened by its centrist appeal. The state had been caught in an ideology trap. While secularists accused the BNP government of pandering to the Jama'at, the latter charged it with not doing enough for Islam. However, in the interest of gaining access to power within a democratic system, political parties have entered into alliances which obfuscate their ideological differences to some extent. The Awami League has worked closely within some of its ideological foes on some issues. It has campaigned with the Jama'at and Jatiya Party on the caretaker government issue and has been offered JP support after the June 1996 elections.[65] However, there can be no room for complacency. The Jatiya Party had allowed privileges to the assassins of the first head of state whereby one assassin, Dalim, was allowed to continue to represent Bangladesh abroad as diplomat, while two others, Farouk and Rashid, were allowed to engage in party politics through the Freedom Party. The Jama'at not only believed in a religious order, but had collaborated with the Pakistan army and conspired to kill Bengali intellectuals. Essentially, whatever its ideological predisposition, a state must guarantee basic human rights – to life, to property and to persuasion; challenge public violations of the legal system, including the authority of *fatwas;* and curtail all forms of violence. It must recognize diversity, help build a non-communal, democratic ethos and propagate the values of civil society. There are only a limited number of options available to the state if it is to achieve these objectives. It can choose to exclude communal and fascist parties from the political process by banning them through constitutional measures as Mujib did after liberation, forcing them underground, eventually risking a backlash. It can render such bodies ineffective by delineating the terms of reference within which these may operate, such as prohibiting the use of religion in politics, which too was once constitutionally guaranteed in 1972 but reversed subsequently under Zia. It can enforce the existing laws of the land to ensure that fundamental human rights are not violated. This was the greatest weakness of the outgoing government and notably, the incoming government has made law and order its first priority. But such measures may be possible only if the power elite itself is not compromising to by partisan interests. It can offer alternative ideologies and value structures based on humanist thought in order to maintain a climate favourable to democratic dialogue. Given the massive poverty and economic hardship facing the country, the state could attempt to separate the ideological from the economic problems, and steer the country towards resolving the latter issues. This could help reformulate a national agenda based on an understanding of the general good. It would be one way of re-establishing the relative autonomy of the state so that it could mediate impartially between the various interest and demand groups.[66]

NOTES

1. Paul R. Brass, *Ethnicity and Nationalism: Theory and Comparison*, (New Delhi: Sage) 1991, pp. 15, 71-2; J. D. Eller and R. M. Coughlan, 'The Poverty of Primordialism: the demystification of ethnic attachments', *Ethnic and Racial Studies*, 16 (2), April 1993, pp. 195-6.

2. Clifford Geertz, *The Interpretations of Cultures*, (New York, Basic Books, 1973) p. 259; Francis Robinson, *Separatism among Indian Muslims, 1860-1923*, (Delhi, Vikas), 1975, p. 13.

3. It is claimed that there are 72 sects among Muslims. See speech by Suhrawardy, *Constituent Assembly of Pakistan, Debates*, 6 March 1948, p. 262. The four schools of Islamic jurisprudence are Hanafi, Maliki, Shafii and Hambali.

4. Ernest Gillner, *Nations and Nationalism*, (Oxford, Blackwell, 1983), pp. 1-6; E. J. Hobsbawm, *Nations and Nationalism since 1979: Programme, Myth, Reality*, (Cambridge, Cambridge University Press, 1990), second edition 1992, p. 9.

5. Hugh Seton-Watson distinguishes thus between states and nations: 'States can exist without a nation, or with several nations among their subjects; and nation can be coterminous with the population of one state, or be included together with other nations within one state, or be divided between several states.' Some states existed before nations and vice versa. Every state is not a nation, and all sovereign states are not national states. 'A state is a legal and political organization with the power to require obedience and loyalty from its citizens. A nation is a community of

370 REGION AND PARTITION

people, whose members are bound together by a sense of solidarity, a common culture, a national consciousness.' See Hugh Seton-Watson, *Nations and States: an Enquiry into the Origins of Nations and the Politics of Nationalism*, (London: Methuen, 1977), p. 1. For an opposite view see Anthony D. Smith, 'The Problem of National Identity: Ancient, Medieval and Modern?' *Ethnic and Racial Studies*, vol 18, 1995, pp. 375-83.

6. Herbert J. Gans, 'Symbolic Ethnicity and Symbolic Religiosity: Towards a Comparison of Ethnic and Religious Acculturation', *Ethnic and Racial Studies*, vol 17, 4 October 1994, pp. 577-92.

7. See Tazeen M. Murshid, *The Sacred and the Secular: Bengal Muslim Discourses, 1871-1977*, (Calcutta, Oxford University Press, 1995).

8. Tazeen M. Murshid, 'A House Divided: the Muslim Intelligentsia of Bengal', in. D. A. Low, *The Political Inheritance of Pakistan*, (Houndmills, MacMillans, 1991), pp. 165-6.

9. Sir Stafford Cripps to Butler, Under-Secretary of State for India, Letter dd. 24 August 1936, in 'Elections in India in 1937. Interference by Public Servants, Bengal', *India Office Records: L/P&J/7/1126.*

10. Speech by Liaquat Ali Khan, Prime Minister of Pakistan, at the first session of the Pakistan Muslim League Council held on 20 February 1949 in Khaliqdina Hall, Karachi, Government of Pakistan Publication (English translation of Urdu speech).

11. For a discussion of colonial perceptions see, Tazeen M. Murshid, 'Race, Ideology and Difference: Identity Formation in Bangladesh', *Nibandhamala*, (Collection of research articles) published by Fakrul Alam, Centre for Advanced Research in Humanities, University of Dhaka, 1994, pp. 225-8. Also see, Badruddin Umar, *Sanskritir sankat*, Dhaka, 1967.

12. *Report of the East Bengal Language Committee, 1940-50*, Government of East Pakistan, (Dhaka, 15958), pp. 6-26; Badruddin Umar, *Bhasa andolan prasanga; katipay dalil*, vol 1, Dacca, 1984, p. 139.

13. Tazeen M. Murshid, *The Sacred and the Secular*, op. cit., Introduction.

14. See Rafiuddin Ahmed, *The Bengal Muslims, 1871-1906: A Quest for Identity*, (Delhi, Oxford University Press, 1981), pp. 67-9.

15. Bengal Muslim society was traditionally divided into *ashraf* or noble born and *atrap* or low born. The former could claim a degree of foreign or upper caste origin and was divided into Syed, Mughal, Pathan and Sheikh; the latter had primarily local roots being descended from local converts. See S.M.N. Karim, *Changing Society in India and Pakistan*, (Dhaka, 1956), p. 12; R. Ahmed, op. cit., pp. 10-12.

16. This was the view of Maulana Maududi, the founder of the Jama'at-i-Islami. See *Al-Islam*, Karachi, 5 December 1961.

17. *Banga Nur*, 1st Year, 3rd No. Magh, 1326 B.S. (1920).

18. Abul Kasem, 'Memoir', *Ekusher Sankalan, 1980 – Smriticharan* (a collection of memoirs), (Dhaka, Bangla Academy, 1980), pp. 2-10.

19. The heart searching is summed up in an article by Syed Sajjad Hussain, 'Contemporary Non-fictional Prose Writing in East Bengal', *New Values,* 7(1), January 1955, p. 22.

20. For an analysis of the consequent culture conflict, see B. Umar, *Sanskritir sankat,* op. cit.

21. Howard Schuman, 'A Note on the Rapid Rise of Mass Bengali Nationalism,' *American Journal of Sociology,* vol. 78, no. 2 (September 1972).

22. Abul Mansur Ahmed, *End of a Betrayal and Restoration of Lahore Resolution* (Dhaka, 1978). The Resolution had envisaged Pakistan as a confederation of states.

23. For a detailed discussion of the role of the left in the Liberation war and in Bangladesh, see T. Maniruzzaman, *The Bangladesh Revolution and its Aftermath* (Dhaka, 1980), pp. 141-53, 169-75, 175-9; Fazl Huq, op. cit., pp. 49-55.

24. Author's interview with Dr. Kamal Hossain, 27 August 1994, Oxford.

25. Syed Anwar Hussain, 1990, op. cit., pp. 141-2, 150.

26. He has therefore been ridiculed for adopting a 'multi-theocracy' model of secularism. See Talukder Maniruzzaman, 'Bangladesh Politics: Secular and Islamic Trends', in Rafiuddin Ahmed (ed.), *Islam in Bangladesh: Society, Culture and Politics,* (Dhaka, Bangladesh Itihas Samiti, 1983), p. 193.

27. Abul Mansur Ahmed, 'Cultural Identity of East Pakistan' *Concept of Pakistan,* 3(1) 1966; also see his *Bangladesher Kalchar,* (Dhaka, 1985). For a discussion of his ideas see Tazeen M. Murshid, 'Bangladesh: the Challenge of Democracy – language, culture and political identity', op. cit., p. 70.

28. Several authors have commented on the strong xenophobia in Bangladesh particularly in relation to India, and fears about national sovereignty against the designs of a big and powerful neighbour. See B. M. Monoar Kabir, 'The Politics of Religion: the Jama'at-i-Islami in Bangladesh' in Rafiuddin Ahmed (ed.), *Religion, Nationalism and Politics in Bangladesh,* (New Delhi: South Asian Publishers, 1990), p. 123; Syed Anwar Husain, 'Islamic Fundamentalism in Bangladesh: Internal Variables and External Inputs' in Rafiuddin Ahmed (ed.) op. cit., pp. 141-2; Taj ul-Islam Hashmi, 1994, op. cit., pp. 105-7.

29. Syed Anwar Husain argues that Zia theoretically Islamized the constitution with this amendment known as the Fifth Amendment. See his Islamic Fundamentalism...' op. cit., p. 150.

30. On his Islamization policies, see Acts No. XXXI, XXXVII, *A Collection of Acts and Ordinance,* 1980, Ministry of Law and Parliamentary Affairs, Government of Bangladesh (Dhaka, 1980).

31. *Eclipse of Secular Bangladesh*, p. 13. Maniruzzaman argues that Mujib himself had begun to use a similar vocabulary based on religious connotations, such as 'Khuda Hafiz' and 'Inshallah' instead of 'Jai Bangla'. But in fact, he always used such language. His famous speech of 7 March 1971 at Suhrawardy Udyan, Dhaka, bears testimony.

32. See Syed Anwar Hussain, 1990, op. cit., p. 149.

33. Afzal Iqbal, *Islamization in Pakistan*, (Lahore, Vanguard, 1986), p. 106. In the years after partition, the political leadership took no chances and kept Maududi at arms length. While religious forces were allowed a social and educational role, they were barred from all political roles until the fall of Ayub Khan. That policy was disregarded by subsequent rulers of Pakistan.

34. *Sangbad* (Bengali Daily), Dhaka, 17 April 1988.

35. Taj-ul-Islam Hashmi, 1994, op. cit., p. 115-17.

36. Syed Anwar Hussain, op. cit., pp. 144-50.

37. The BNP won 140 seats, the Awami League led 8-Part alliance won 100 and Ershad's Jatiya Party obtained 35 seats. BAMNA (Bangladesh Mukto Nirbachan Andolan) ed., *A Report on the Elections to the Fifth National Parliament, 27 February 1991*, (Dhaka, BAMNA, 1991), pp. 62-3.

38. BNP officials admit that the Home Minister was a Jama'at sympathizer and that in return for Jama'at support, it was offered two of the thirty reserved women's seats. Interview with Dr Moeen Khan, Minister of State for Planning, 5 January 1995, Dhaka.

39. Interview with Syed Hassan Imam, Secretary to the Nirmul Committee, London, 25 August 1994.

40. *Eastern Eye*, London, No. 124, (28 April 1992); *Surma*, (Bengali Weekly), London, 17-23 April, 1992.

41. *Bangladesh Observer*, 23 April 1993; also see Tazeen M. Murshid, 'Democracy in Bangladesh: illusion or reality' *Contemporary South Asia*, 4(2), (1995), p. 207.

42. Leaflet, *Dharmadrohi o deshdrohi nastikder rukhe darao*, 26 June 1994, (Dhaka, Oitijhya Sangsad).

43. Jama'at activism in Pakistan had followed a similar pattern, – infiltration into the army, bureaucracy, lower echelons of the judiciary; implementation of *shariah* courts; campaigning for blasphemy laws and declaration of Qadianis as non-Muslims. Some believe that the Jama'at-Shibir Jubo Command have training camps in the border areas of north-east Bangladesh. Kamal Hossain, who was the Foreign Minister of Bangladesh until 1975 and founder of the Gano Forum, a break-away party from the Awami League, said in an interview, that he had requested the Home Ministry to set up a Committee to investigate this, but to no avail. Also see *Leaflet, Elimination Committee*, (Dhaka, 6 June 1992). There is also ample newspaper coverage of the clandestine trafficking in arms in which members of the Jama'at have been involved. Newspapers

have also covered campus violence in Rajshahi, Chittagong, Dhaka and elsewhere extensively where the Shibir have been more successful in inflicting severe casualties on their opponents. See *Bangladesh Observer,* 7 February, 12 May 1993; Sangbad, various issues, March 1991, December 1992, 12 August 1994, p. 6.

44. Recounted by a close friend and associate of Shamsur Rahman, Professor K. S. Murshid, September 1994, London.
45. Leaflet, *Dharmadrahi,* op. cit.
46. An editor of a Bengali weekly thus adversely affected was Shafiq Rahman. See Anis Alamgir, 'Shafiq Rahman Ebong Bichar', Janomot (Bengali weekly), 1-7 July 1994.
47. Ain-O-Shalish Kendra, 'Threats of Violence and Violation of Human Rights by Imams of Mosques and the Religious Right in Bangladesh', a collection of cases compiled for the period 1992-4, unpublished, (Dhaka, 1994.)
48. *Inquilab,* 12 and 19 August 1994.
49. Ain-o-Shalish Kendra, 'Threats of violence and violations of human rights by *imams* of mosques and the religious right in Bangladesh', op. cit.
50. In Chittagong, the police confessed their inability to control the Shibir-Yuva Command because their own weapons were inferior. There was evidence to suggest that arms were coming to specific Shibir members from Pakistan by post among other means. See *Dainik Sangbad,* (Dhaka, Friday, 12 August 1994), p. 6.
51. Anis Alamgir, 'Shafiq Rahman Ebong Bichar,' Janomot, 1-7 July 1994, p. 22. Apart from the editor of *Janakantha,* the others were released on bail.
52. Comment of the Co-editor, Taleya Rahman, Saturday, (London, 17 August, 1994.)
53. *Janomot,* London, 19-25 August 1994; *Saptahik Bichitra,* Dhaka, Year 23, No. 12, Friday 12 August 1994, p. 27.
54. *Saptahik Bichitra,* ibid., pp. 27-33.
55. Politicians tend to regard the control of university campus student politics to be indicative of political strength nationally. As a result, the extent of campus violence has multiplied in the nineties tremendously. As against 7 deaths a year in the eighties there were about 25 such cases annually in the nineties. Ganoforum, *Eto Laash Rakhbo Kothai?* (Dhaka, 1994), p. 30.
56. For a further discussion of the Jama'at's ideology, programme and method of recruitment see, U.A.B. Razia Akhter Banu, 'Jama'at-i-Islami in Bangladesh: Challenges and Prospects', in Hashmi and Mutalib (eds), 1994, op. cit., pp. 83-94.
57. Ibid., pp. 86, 89, 94.
58. See *Bichitra (Bengali weekly),* Dhaka, 1 June 1984; also see Syed Anwar Hussain, op. cit., p. 146.
59. Bharer Kagaj, 14 June 1996, p. 1

60. Re-elections were held in 27 constituencies on 19 June because of violence in 124 to the 60,000 polling centres. A high voter turn-out of 73.61 per cent with a high representation of women went in favour of the primarily rural based AL. 'News', BBC World Service Television, 13-15, 20 June, 1996; *Bharer Kagaj,* 14, 20-21 June 1996, *Sangbad,* 14 June 1996. According to *The Daily Star,* voter turn-out was 73.19 per cent, 14 June 1991, p. 1.

61. The Election Commission has not given an exact figure yet, but both national and international observers of the election comment on this as remarkable. See *The Daily Star,* Dhaka, Friday, 14 June 1996, p. 1

62. Tanwee Akram, 'Is Fundamentalism Still a Problem in South Asia' *South Asia Forum Quarterly,* vol. no. 3, Summer 1996, pp. 24, 29.

63. *The Daily Star,* 14 June 1996, p. 12.

64. Following the Magura by-elections of 1992 when the Awami League lost a safe seat to the ruling party attributed to unfair practices, a lengthy political and constitutional crisis ensured resolved by the formation of a caretaker government in March 1996 and elections in June. It included a lengthy boycott of Parliament followed by the mass resignation of all opposition Members on 28 December 1994 in an attempt to force a constitutional amendment for the provision of caretaker governments empowered to conduct elections, thus enabling a smooth transfer of power. The opposition boycotted the elections held in February 1996 because this demand was not met. In the meantime, the administrative machinery of the country collapsed.

65. JP chairman Mizan Chowdhury offered to support the party which would help obtain Ershad's release from prison, see *Dainik Sangram,* 14 June 1996; *Dainik Inquilab,* 14 June 1996. However, it joined the incumbent AL government led by Sheikh Hasina Wajed, daughter of the late Sheikh Mujib, without any such public assurances, 'News,' *BBC World,* Satellite Television, Mon 24 June 1996.

66. The term 'demand groups' has been coined by the Rudolphs in Lloyd and Susanne Rudolph, *In Pursuit of Lakshmi: the Political Economy of the Indian State,* (Chicago, Chicago University Press 1987), pp. 15, 247, 252. For a discussion of the term also see T.J. Byres, 'A Chicago view of the Indian state: an Oriental grin without an Oriental cat and political economy without classes', *The Journal of Commonwealth and Comparative Politics,* vol. 26 no. 3, 1988, pp. 257-8.

Chapter Thirteen

Reflections on Partition: Pakistan Perspective

Yunas Samad

Introduction

Partition as a concept has re-emerged with the dawning of the new millennium. There is a need to reflect upon and consider whether partition is a long-term resolution to ethnic conflict. The question which needs to be addressed is whether partition simply responds to short-term difficulties and fails to tackle or address long-term issues. The significance of this question is increasing as a global resurgence of ethnic conflicts spiralling into separatist movements, ethnic cleansing, genocide and intractable violence becomes more common. Dramatically the former states of Yugoslavia and the USSR broke up into smaller units and violence continues in Rawanda and Burundi.[1] Partition, however, becomes like a contested and bitter divorce where former partners fight over property, people and even memories of the past and has a lasting negative effect on their progeny. The South Asian experience does throw some light on the long-term trajectories and impact of partition. The sub-continent was partitioned over fifty years ago and that certainly does give us a historical period to reflect upon its ramifications. Has Pakistan resolved the burning issues of pre-independent Indian Muslims? Certainly, Pakistan's history suggests that it has not been a panacea for the problems and difficulties of its people. Its history of five decades is littered with examples of bloody ethnic and separatist conflicts. From Bangladesh to Mohajirstan, the call of separatism, successful in the former and anxiously suspended in the latter has not been quenched by the division of India in 1947.

This chapter does not seek to rake over the embers that led to India's partition. There does not seem to be any benefit in repeating old and worn out arguments of apportioning blame and responsibility for the communal frenzy that led to the division. There is, however, a need to consider and examine the theoretical issues arising from partition and its legacy for contemporary Pakistan. Four theoretical issues straddle the divide and continue to play a vexing and almost intractable role which needs to be examined. The first is the persistence of identity politics and specifically how notions of community are being constantly constructed. While the understanding of what is a community is shifting through the historical period the specific people involved are the same. Prior to 1947, Muslims from the minority-Muslim provinces mobilized around the symbols of religion; today *mohajirs* are mobilizing around ethnicity. What they are asserting is the evolution of their identity across different historical junctures. Theoretically this requires a concept of identity that is flexible, malleable, contingent and contextual which can accommodate multifarious manifestations including nationalism and ethnicity. After all, it is mobilization around notions of community that underpins arguments for partition and separation in the colonial and post-colonial period. The second point considers Gramsci's notion of hegemony.[2] Exclusive hegemonic discourse is a theoretical constant, that runs through from the pre-independence era into contemporary Pakistan. Of course its specificity, location and focus shifts with the emergence of Pakistan but its inability to accommodate difference remains a primary issue. Its exclusive nature significantly provides sustenance and justification for the types of identity politics that have become so prolific and intractable in Pakistan. Next is the question of decentralization of power and its impact upon ethnic mobilization. This issue of decentralization of power is considered to have a major impact upon ethnic mobilization. It is treated as a panacea for ethnic conflict as it allows for the accommodation of difference in the locale. This issue of decentralization of power is again another debate which crosses partition as the demand underpins the politics of the community and for the recognition of difference. While there is significant substance to this point of view it seems that it would be simplistic to consider decentralization on its own to be adequate to resolve ethnic tensions. The final point which I want to raise is the conundrum of the majority versus minority rights: another constant theme that crosses the great divide. Whether it is the rights of Muslims in colonial India or the rights of *mohajirs* in Karachi, the problem continues and I want to explore this issue by interrogating the concepts of social and cultural pluralism. I will look at how different forms of pluralism exacerbate issues relating to minorities.

Identity Politics

Ranger[3] argues that identity is contingent, contextual and not fixed in time or space. He posits a dynamic notion of identity which is plastic and imagined and re-imagined. There is a complex interaction both internal and external in the construction of identity in which structure, agency, and cultural resources play an important part. This approach to social identity allows for a conceptual framework that incorporates different manifestations whether they be nationalism, ethnicity, religious identification or new ethnicity. Imagined identification as a concept is important in understanding the subjective dynamics among demotic groups that are prepared to cross the Rubicon in order to establish discrete notions of community. The significance of this perspective lies in the fact that it explains the behaviour of non-elite participants in identity politics. Rational choice[4] perspectives focus on the instrumentality of elites in how they select icons and idioms and metaphors used for mobilization. Quite often conflicts based on identity have transcendental repercussions that cannot be considered to be rational. In this sense imagining and re-imagining processes of identity politics attempts to address the subjective dimensions which are important in the incorporation of demotic groups in the construction of community. Of course how they are incorporated is subject to internal debate and negotiation, which affects the trajectory of the imagining process that any particular community initiates.

One cannot a priori determine whether any particular ethnicity is progressive or reactionary in effect; there is a constant struggle between different imaginers of ethnic identity; between young and old, men and women, radicals and conservatives, exclusive and inclusive definitions of identity. In this struggle space is sometimes levered open and sometimes foreclosed. Ethnicity is not moral in itself but it constitutes the ground on which fundamental moral debate takes place.[5]

Ranger's framework also accommodates Hall's argument of new ethnicity which enlarges the debate about identification to include class, gender and generation. Pertinently Hall posits the notion of identification rather than identity. 'We know that identities in contemporary society are more flexible, more open, more labile, more fluid, less predictable, more dramaturgical, more dependent on performance less dependent on – as it were – inherited tradition.'[6] New formations of identity politics are emerging which do not fit into classical anthropological notions of ethnicity based on culture. Anthropologists have argued that ethnicity is based on kinship groups, family and culture in its widest sense which incorporates religion, language etc. There are new formations of identity politics that do not fit into these criteria, such as the emergence of black and gender politics. As Benson has argued in the case of Afro-Caribbeans that since they do not demonstrate classical notions of family, language and kinship groupings, anthropological analysis of them becomes a sum of negatives, and therefore, they are denied culture and identity.[7] Clearly though in the arena of politics, there is a black identity, a contested and contingent identification which persistently and intermittently asserts itself. In Pakistan, there are two examples of new ethnicity which do not fit the classical notions of ethnic identity. The emergence of Kashmiri identity among Mirpuris and *mohajir* ethnicity are two examples of this process and I will be focusing on the latter as the issue of Kashmiri identity will take the discussion away from being exclusively on Pakistan.[8]

Three different types of identity politics can be discerned: religious nationalism, linguistic politics, and new ethnicities active among Muslims that eventually became incorporated in Pakistan. Pakistan nationalism was a good example of identity politics mobilized around the cultural markers and religious idioms. This became a counter-hegemonic discourse against Indian nationalism, which established its significance in the mid-1940s. It was, however, a contested identification and in the Muslim-majority provinces of Bengal, Punjab and Sindh strong regional interests juxtaposed with Muslim nationalism. In Sindh and the North-west Frontier Province there were also strong ethnic movements that were in opposition to Pakistan nationalism. Furthermore, within the Muslim League high command there were many contested opinions as to the nature of 'Pakistan.' Jinnah's acceptance of the Cabinet Mission Plan and its acceptance by the Muslim League Working Committee was indicative of the fact that separatism was not inevitable.[9] However, the conflation of exigent circumstances i.e., breakdown of constitutional negotiations, the Civil Disobedience Movement mounted by the League and the accelerated British timetable for departure, coalesced to create conditions for the communal fury that engulfed northern India. It is in this context that opposition among Muslims to Jinnah's project of religious nationalism collapses. Consequently, the failure of India to emerge as a single independent nation was rooted in the inability to accommodate the politics of difference.[10]

In Pakistan, Muslim nationalism became the official ideology; the country was depicted as one united nation bonded by Islam and the Urdu language. This official nationalism was limited to the military-bureaucratic elite which rejected any notions of cultural difference. It was in this context that linguistic politics emerged as a counter-hegemonic discourse. A re-imagining of identification by those previously aligned with Pakistan nationalism took place. Where previously ethnic and religious identifications converged, now those groups that were not represented in the military-bureaucratic elite asserted distinctive identifications articulated through language. The linguistic movements articulated at various times, identify politics around Bengali, Balochi, Sindhi, Pashto and Sirakai languages.

Linguistic politics became the vehicle for counter-hegemonic aspirations and resulted in the confrontations with the state. In the case of East Pakistan inept and brutal handling of the situation by the military junta resulted in the emergence of an independent Bangladesh. No less traumatic however, was the suppression of the movement for Greater Balochistan, Sindhu Desh and Pakhtunistan.[11]

As identifications are contingent, it is not surprising that none of these groups were linguistically homogenous. In the pre-colonial era, the ruling *Ashraf* elites, irrespective of whether they were Bengali, Sindhi, Balochi or Pukhtun used primarily Persian as the official courtly language. Language as a symbol of identity was closely associated with modernity and in this particular context that meant British rule.

The shift to vernacular languages was resisted and was an uneven development. The tendency was for demotic groups in these areas to use vernacular languages while the elite gradually moved to speaking either Urdu or English. In colonial Bengal, the *Ashraf* elite's usage of Persian was replaced by Urdu while the *Ajlaf* demotic groups spoke Bengali. This dichotomy persisted even when the language movement was active in the 1950s in East Pakistan. In the case of Sindh, at the time of independence the language spoken by the elite was English and the vernacular was the language of the people; in the case of the NWFP the National Awami Party which was the champion of Pushto, made Urdu the provincial language when it came to power in the 1970s[12] and in Balochistan the Balochi language was deeply riven with differences of dialects.

The third form of identity politics which has recently emerged is new ethnicity. The mobilization by Mohajirs is not based on language or notions of culture that are recognized by anthropologists to be the basis of ethnicity. The term *mohajir* literally means refugee and was applied to all those who migrated from India. However, its usage has gone through transformation and it first excluded those who migrated from East Punjab to West Punjab and referred to only Urdu speaking migrants. Today *mohajir* as deployed by the MQM[13] includes Urdu and Gujarati speakers. It covers those who migrated from United Provinces, Bihar, Hyderabad Deccan who are Urdu speakers, and Gujarati speaking Memons, Bohras and Khojas. There are at least two distinct linguistic strands and a myriad of regional identifications as well as religious affiliations which are being re-imagined as *mohajir* identity. Urdu speakers are the dominant element in *mohajir* ethnicity; they are bound along with others in a common position *vis a vis* Sindhis, Pakhtuns, Punjabis and Balochis. It is on this basis that among the many demands posited by the MQM is that they are are calling for a separate province and some who are more extreme demand a separate state of Mohajirstan.[14] Again we see that identity politics in its latest manifestation is pushing in a separatist direction challenging state boundaries. Without being premature in making a judgement, it would seem that the chances of a separate independent *mohajir* state are extremely slim.

Identification in the arena of politics is being continuously imagined and re-imagined and is mobilizing demotic groups and challenging the states. In two instances it has resulted in the emergence of full blown nationalism and the emergence of independent states. The movement for Pakistan and the struggle for independence in Bangladesh were initiated originally as identity politics. In the case of Balochistan, the NWFP and Sindh, the trajectory of identity politics was retarded and brutally suppressed by the state. Given this, why is it that politics among Muslims who came to live in Pakistan continues to move in this direction?

Exclusive Hegemonic Discourse

Gramsci's concept of hegemony is used in relation to state and civil society to explain how through ideological processes dominant classes maintain control. In colonial India, British rule was challenged by a counter-hegemonic discourse represented by nationalism that was primarily located in civil society. However, the hegemonic position of the Congress was challenged by another discourse articulated by religious nationalism. What is important to emphasize is that within Indian nationalism, the discourse was exclusive and was not prepared to accommodate religious difference. The consequence was that the processes of exclusion reinforced and intensified the focus on identity politics articulated by the Muslim League.[15]

The initial response of the Muslims to the formation of the Indian National Congress was the fear that majoritarian pluralism combined with democracy would result in the dominance of Hindus. Sayyid Ahmad Khan and Amir Ali argued that western notions of elected representatives represented by the Rippon's Reforms of the 1880s were not appropriate to a society differentiated by 'race and religion and caste and creed'. Muslims were threatened by socially upwardly mobile Hindu middle-class majority which was becoming politically assertive. To counteract this development, Sayyid Ahmad Khan posited the notion of separate electorates and weightages.[16] These features became the touchstone of Muslim politics and formed the basis of the Communal Award of 1932 which was announced at the Second Round Table Conference. Most Muslims were not prepared to surrender to these checks and balances without significant compensation.[17]

On the other hand, the position of Congress concerning Muslims was not so accommodating. The Nehru Report of 1928 proposed a strong unitary structure and recommended the replacement of separate electorates and weightages with joint electorates and reserved seats. These were the maximum concessions possible to Muslims which would keep Hindu communalists on board. As the Congress position hardened after its success in the 1937 elections, its ability and willingness to accommodate the Muslim League decreased. Following Jinnah's adoption of the two-nation theory, Gandhi attempted to bring Muslims back into the fold, but his efforts were rebuffed primarily because he had nothing to offer but good faith. Nehru, whose star was in ascendancy, remained less sympathetic to the Hindu-Muslim question because of his radical and socialist convictions. He believed that religious difference would be displaced by common bonds of social unity. Nehru saw the Hindu-Muslim issue as secondary to independence and hence refused to give it centrality: 'I am afraid I cannot get excited over the communal issue, important as it is temporarily. It's after all a side issue, and it can have no real importance in the larger scheme of things'.[18] Clearly Nehru was dismayed when he was released from prison in 1945 to find this 'side issue' occupying the centre stage. However, partition was not inevitable, as seen by Jinnah's acceptance of the Cabinet Mission Plan on the basis of parity and a weak federal centre. Failure to reach an agreement led to the partition of India, which separated the warring groups.[19]

In Pakistan, the post-colonial state began to construct another exclusive hegemonic discourse. By the early 1950s it became clear that a Punjabi-*mohajir* axis was emerging. This group which had resisted centralization by the Congress now championed centralization of power in Pakistan. Its influence was great because of its pre-eminence in the bureaucracy and military. In contrast, the Bengali political leadership was more interested in a decentralized state structure, even to the extent of decreasing tensions with India and thus obviating the need for a larger military. Its attempts to tighten its grip on the centre through political means were resisted by the emerging military-bureaucratic oligrachy. Later under Ayub Khan's regime, in the 1960s, the resistance went underground. The Awami League[20] resurfaced with vigour in the upsurge for democracy a decade later. Its central demands of decentralization, greater representation in the army and respect for majority decision in the National Assembly, would have reformulated the hegemonic discourse if they had succeeded.

With the break up of Pakistan and the emergence of an independent Bangladesh, Zulfikar Ali Bhutto emerged as the new leader of Pakistan. In this period, he accommodated some of the demands from his native province of Sindh and diffused tension there. In contrast, however, he dealt harshly with the emerging opposition in the Frontier and Balochistan. The crackdown against the opposition, alienated Pakhtuns and

Balochis. This resulted in a full-scale rebellion in Balochistan from 1973. However, with his removal from power in 1977 and execution by General Zia, the hegemonic discourse in Pakistan was reformulated. Zia, due to Pakistan's involvement in the fight against the Russian-backed regime in Afghanistan, incorporated Pakhtuns into the highest level of the ruling hierarchy. For similar reasons he placated the opposition in Balochistan. But this was done at a price. In Sindh, he was confronted by a major rebellion in 1983 and again in 1986. Sindhi participation in the central government had decreased with the fall of Bhutto and the perception gradually developed in the province that it was a colony of Punjab. As a result various strands of ethnic assertions emerged making demands from outright independence to greater autonomy.

In urban Sindh, *mohajirs'* alienation increased, too from Bhutto's time. He had imposed a quota limit on the number of Mohajirs in the Federal Civil Service and in the various departments that came under its control. Also, Bhutto's policy of lateral entry ushered mainly Sindhis and PPP supporters into senior positions while damaging the *mohajir* interest. His nationalization of industry adversely affected business interests which were predominantly owned by *mohajirs*. Under Zia (1977-88) most of these policies remained unchanged and a new Punjabi-Pakhtun alliance was formed which replaced the Punjabi-Mohajir alliance that had emerged with the founding of Pakistan. Pakhtun-Punjabi influence in business, in the higher echelons of the federal government and Karachi administration increased at the expense of *mohajirs*. The shift in the hegemonic discourse in Pakistan now excluded *mohajirs*.[21]

The hegemonic discourse thus went through various manifestations. It excluded, or was perceived to exclude, certain groups and was never truly universal in character. This lack of universality is an issue that spans partition. The Congress was never able to accommodate Muslim demands in the 1940s and this was partly due to the right wing of the party and to Nehru's world view which did not recognize religious difference to be significant. In the case of Pakistan, Punjabis were the dominant partners in the military-bureaucratic oligarchy. Incorporation of one group took place at the expense of another and in the latest manifestation of this hegemonic discourse, Pakhtuns were included resulting in the alienation of *mohajirs*. This is the exclusive characteristic of the hegemonic discourse which becomes one of its structural parameters: drawing opposition of the excluded groups along the road of identity politics.

Decentralization of Power

Several academics have pointed out that the issue of accommodating cultural diversity is associated with the decentralization of power. Rizvi has pointed out that the federalist rationale for larger states has been put on its head. In the case of the United States, the diversity of regions and people necessitated the decentralization of power to curb the central government from becoming too powerful. This logic in post-colonial states and in particular in South Asia has been inverted and it is argued that strong federal governments are necessary to corral and homogenize diverse pluralities into the nation. 'Denial of autonomy to the regional and particularist groups is often a plea for 'internal imperialism.'[22] Rizvi indicates that the key to India's relative success in managing diversity and heterogeneity has been a strategic accommodation. Jalal reiterates this point arguing that India's formal democracy combined with formation of linguistic states. 'Regional political economies and electoral processes' allowed for a greater resilience to central interference. The margins for centre-region negotiations are much greater in the case of India but the greater degree of centralization found in Pakistan leaves far less room for manoeuvre. The options are difficult choices 'of co-operation on the centre's terms or costly anti-state defiance.'[23]

I have argued elsewhere that the issue of decentralization is a historical continuity that spans partition.[24] A common characteristic of identity politics, implicitly or explicitly, was the demand for decentralization of power. The Muslim League was prepared to remain in a weak federation as elaborated in the Cabinet Mission Plan. The Awami League's demands in the 1970s had similar implications; and Pakhtuns and Balochis were only pushed down the road of rebellion when the federal characteristics of the constitution were trampled upon by Bhutto's political intervention. In Sindh, Bhutto's downfall alienated Sindhis and pushed them into making demands for an independent Sindh or for a confederation, or greater autonomy. In urban Sindh, the call for Mohajirstan either as an independent separate state or as a separate province underline the *mohajirs'* desire for greater decentralization of power from a centre which has alienated them.

Clearly decentralization of power is an important factor in accommodating diversity. In reality, however, decentralization is not a simple panacea. The first point that needs to be amplified is the tacit assumption that the democratic processes are prevalent. A stratagem of non-democratic regimes from the colonial period to contemporary Pakistan was to allow for decentralization of power on the local level, while retaining control at the centre. In the colonial period, the Reforms of 1919 and the 1935 India Act were based on the calculation that by allowing for decentralization of power at the provincial level, the authorities would win over support from the nationalist movements. Holding on tight at the centre and allowing flexibility at the provincial level would derail the nationalist projects. This strategy was also employed by the military regime of Ayub Khan with introduction of Basic Democracy which it was hoped could take the wind out of the opposition's demand for parliamentary elections. The trade off was that by allowing some form of democratic processes on the local level, opposition to the regime would be deflated. In both the pre-and post-colonial examples the stratagem failed. The people were not prepared to be bribed by limited democratic processes while being denied a sovereign parliament. The irony is that with a democratically elected government at the centre headed by Benazir Bhutto from 1993-6 there was a reluctance to hold local body elections. The government interest was to manage elections that would ensure a

PPP victory. In the case of Karachi, the central government's nominees were busy gerrymandering a constituency boundary in order to create a PPP majority.[25] The same reluctance to decentralize has also been found in India, where state governments are realizing that empowerment of panchyats is undermining their authority.[26]

The second issue which needs to be considered when reflecting upon decentralization of power is that it can create local hegemonic discourses. In the movements for independent Bangladesh, Greater Balochistan, Pakhunistan, Sindhu Desh and Moharjistan, the assumption has been that they are reflecting homogenous entities. Bangladesh, however, has difficulties in accommodating diversity represented by Biharis, Hindus and tribals in the Chittagong Hill tracts. Balochistan has a substantial population of Pakhtuns, Brauhis, Makrani and Lassis minorities and the NWFP posses a substantial Hindko speaking population. Again in Karachi, we find a heterogeneous population. While *mohajirs* are the largest group, the city has the largest urban concentration of Pakhtun and Baloch in the country and there is also a substantial Punjabi population as well as a significant Sindhi minority.

Decentralization at the local level with respect to Karachi would create a local hegemonic discourse which would exclude non-*mohajirs*. The principle of majoritarian pluralism would result in a simple majority allowing MQM to run the city but would disenfranchise significant elements of the population. Thus decentralization while benefiting the dominant group would be clearly disadvantageous to minorities. The argument for decentralization is that it allows for diversity and difference to be accommodated at the local level. However, the local level itself in many cases is quite heterogeneous and while Mohajirs would gain, minorities would in turn be produced and disenfranchised in the process. Such an outcome would thus contradict the argument in favour of decentralization. The situation in Karachi is emblematic of many regions in Pakistan in that there is great cultural diversity and difference but no mechanism for its recognition.

In sum, decentralization of power in a non-democratic framework is no solution. Within a functioning democracy, decentralization is necessary to accommodate and create the necessary space for cultural diversity. Ironically, decentralization at local levels can, if the principle of first past the post is observed, create local hegemonic discourses which are equally exclusive and disenfranchise various local minorities. This is not an argument for denying the need for decentralization of power; rather it suggests that further mechanisms are necessary before cultural diversity and difference are accommodated.

Cultural Pluralism

To understand how cultural diversity and difference can be incorporated we need to discuss the different notions of cultural pluralism and what that entails. The concept of social and cultural pluralism was formulated by F.S. Furnival[27] with reference to the ethnic segmentation of colonial Indonesia. It was later further examined by M.G. Smith[28] who developed the argument that there were three varieties of pluralism: structural, social and cultural. He argued that structural pluralism was marked by institutional segmentation of cultural and social diversity in society. The differential incorporation of cultural sections was articulated through formal exclusionary policies, for example, as epitomized by the ex-apartheid regime of South Africa or it could be informally instituted through substantial sectional inequalities such as the case of Afro-Americans in pre-civil rights America. Social pluralism he argued is the institutional differentiation of society coinciding with socially sharp demarcation of society into exclusive segments. This form of pluralism was evident in consociational democracies of Switzerland, Belgium and the Netherlands where incorporation of a number of groupings in various spheres including the political realm was based on equivalence. Cultural pluralism consists of variable institutional diversity without corresponding collective segmentation.[29] In Britain and the United States, social differentiation was restricted to the private domain and it had no structural implications for the public sphere. Clearly there are difficulties in trying to adopt the categories of pluralism as elaborated by Smith because they are not necessarily premised on the assumption of equality. Arguments that introduce equality in association with cultural diversity lead the discussion into multiculturalism. Charles Taylor argues for a normative conception of multiculturalism which is about 'stipulating the procedural and substantive principles ordering a multicultural society.' Identity politics are shaped by the recognition, absence, or misrecognition of these principles. Absence of recognition or misrecognition fuels oppression and harm and thus sets the state for identity politics to redress the position.[30]

The ways in which cultural diversity has been recognized institutionally in colonial India and Pakistan have been multifarious. There is evidence for structural pluralism, social and cultural pluralism and also some examples of multicultural practice. In response to Sayyid Ahmad Khan's fears that majoritarian pluralism would lead to the exclusion of Muslims, the colonial authorities introduced separate electorates and weightages from 1906 onwards as a mechanism to incorporate Muslims politically. Later these features were to become central characteristics of the 1932 Communal Award which paved the way for the 1935 Government India Act. By giving institutional recognition to religious diversity within the electoral system, it produced a form of consociational democracy[31] at the provincial level. Muslims did not have to appeal to a wider audience to be elected; they could institute positive discrimination in terms of employment and education. In some instances for example, Punjab, it forced cooperation between different religious groups in order to exploit the political advantages of the decentralization of power.[32]

Recognition of cultural diversity through separate electorates and weightages formed the foundation on which the 1946 Cabinet Mission Plan was based. Within a loose federal framework, there was parity between Muslims and the Congress, combined with majoritarian pluralism. This amalgam of majoritarian pluralism and consociationalism could be considered an inchoate form of multiculturalism. It recognized difference on the basis of equality and simultaneously operated on the first past the post principle.

With the establishment of Pakistan the return to majoritarian pluralism possessed serious implications for the hegemony of the military-bureaucratic oligarchy. The implementation of One Unit which was the centre-piece of the 1956 Constitution, and Ayub's 1962 Constitution reintroduced the notion of equality between East and West Pakistan. Normally such devices are used to give institutional access to disadvantaged groups. In this case it was designed to prevent Bengalis, who were numerically superior in political representation but were socially disadvantaged, from making major inroads into the state structure. This form of consociationalism became redundant when East Pakistan became independent. In post-1971 Pakistan there was a return to majoritarian pluralism and there was also some evidence of structural pluralism and slight evidence of multiculturalism. The quota system Bhutto introduced to limit the numbers of Mohajirs in the federal service was an example of positive discrimination for Sindhis; introduction of reserved seats for women was another. There is also evidence of structural pluralism in the way that non-Muslims are formally excluded by the constitution from high office.

What becomes evident is that recognition of diversity by the state is not necessarily a process of giving access to disadvantaged groups. In certain circumstances the state's recognition is used to maintain hegemonic positions. Mohajir demands, for instance, go back to a combination of colour-blind and structural segregationist approaches. The MQM's Charter of Resolutions, the party's founding document, had the following nine points:

1. Only 'real' Sindhis (*mohajirs* and Sindhis)* would have the right to vote in Sindh;
2. Business licences and permits should not be given to those who do not have the franchise to vote;

3. Stranded Pakistani's (Pakistanis living in Bangladesh–Biharis)* should be allowed to settle and become citizens of Pakistan;
4. Afghans should be restricted to their official refugee camps in the NWFP and Balochistan and not be allowed to buy property or to reside in Sindh;
5. Local bus services should be taken over by the Karachi Municipal Corporation, and bus drivers must be required to be literate before being given driver's licences (directed against the Pathan domination of mass transport)*;
6. Non-Sindhis and non-*mohajirs* should not be allowed to buy property in Sindh;
7. A fresh census should be held in Sindh Province and the *mohajir* share of the federal quota should be revised upwards to reflect the true population of the *mohajirs*;
8. The basis for Sindhi domicile, for purposes of the federal quote should be twenty years continuous residence in the province;
9. Police officers implicated in atrocities against *mohajirs* should be tried before special tribunals (most such officers were Punjabis)*.[33]

To these original demands, the idea that *mohajirs* should be considered a fifth nationality in Pakistan was added. Most of these demands were incorporated into the accord that the MQM signed with the PPP in December 1988. When these demands are examined from the perspective of cultural pluralism what we find is that most of them are designed to institute forms of structural pluralism. The institutional recognition if afforded would effectively exclude competition from other groups and preserve their dominant position or enhance it. The *mohajir* policy is to create institutional barriers to limit competition from other minorities and simultaneously to increase self-representation in areas where they are dominant. So on the one hand, they are asking for an increase in the quota for recruitment into the federal service and this is precisely designed to increase

*Brackets contain the writer's perception or comment.

their position relative to under-represented Sindhis. In areas where *mohajirs* face competition with Punjabi and Pakhtuns for example, in business, and, in the transport industry, they wanted restrictions that would effectively give them a free rein. Moreover, the disenfranchisement of immigrants from upcountry and for the repatriation of Biharis was meant to consolidate their political hold over Karachi.

Lijphart advocates the promotion of a federal consociational democracy combined with proportional represenation, where there would be a coalition on the elite level representing the various ethnic groupings. This recognition of difference would be reinforced by an ethnic veto in the legislative assembly. There would be proportional representation and that would allow ethnic minorities to be proportionately represented in the state institutions. This segmental autonomy would be located in a loose federal system. When we consider this proposition in relation to the demands made by the Mohajirs we find that the problem is that *mohajirs* are not asking for proportionate representation in state institutions, but that their dominance should persist. Of course proportionate representation would also mean that Punjabis would maintain their dominant position by virtue of their number. Another difficulty is that this whole argument is based on the assumption of an elite contract but the demands of the MQM indicate that it would be difficult to reach such an agreement. The 1988 MQM–PPP pact was, for example short-lived. The two main areas of contention were the unwillingness to repatriate Biharis from Bangladesh, and the dissolution of placement bureaux designed to recruit candidates into the civil service. The Prime Minister Benazir Bhutto continued to use placement bureaux to recruit party member (mainly Sindhis) candidates directly into the civil service.[34] The scheme for the repatriation of the Biharis was cancelled primarily due to the opposition provoked among Sindhis. The political reality is such that Sindhis along with Balochis are an under-represented minority in government institutions. The former also make up the home constituency of the PPP leader, whom she cannot afford to alienate.

These problems are seemingly intractable because cultural diversity has been articulated in terms of group rights. The focus on group rights feeds into exclusive forms of identity politics. The majority-minority conundrum from the nineteenth century onwards has been variously expressed as separate electorates, weightages, and then in the twentieth century in terms of parity between the Congress and the Muslim League and in Pakistan it crystallized into the One Unit, the quota system and now the *mohajir* demands. The assumption which runs through this whole argument is that there is homogeneity within groups, that they are not differentiated in terms of class, gender and generation and that whatever advantage that may be achieved would be brought to all equally. But this is clearly not the case. There is thus a need to accept cultural diversity as a human right. It seems that Charles Taylor's argument about absence of recognition being harmful can actually be located in the individual in terms of a human right, rather than a group right. By investing cultural rights in the individual as human rights difference and diversity could be accommodated without going down the road of communalism. The protection of individual human rights would impact on the community without encouraging enclosure and by consequence, group conflicts. Concretely if we take the *mohajir* issue as an example, it is substantively about economic development for socially marginalized groups in the *mohajir* community. The leadership comes from the lower middle-class and middle-class, precisely the groups most affected by competition from Pakhtuns and Punjabis and not the *mohajir* elite. The same point has been made by Ranger who argues that there is a need for a reconfiguration of universalistic values that can accommodate diversity and difference in the wider sense and simultaneously give greater emphasis to development.[35]

Conclusion

Identity politics in their different manifestations have been a recurrent and almost intractable problem for the Pakistan state.

Their origins lie in the formation of Pakistan itself and in particular in the prevalence of the exclusive nature of the hegemonic discourse. It is exclusive in a cultural sense in that it is dominated by a Punjabi-Pakhtun military bureaucratic oligarchy. Without the restructuring of this hegemonic discourse, identity politics will remain an intractable problem. Such a reconstruction would require a major reform of the federal structure which implies that new, more universalistic notions of the nation need to be formed which are more prepared to recognize cultural difference and diversity. It is also important that greater decentralization of power take place and that local institutions become more vigorous. There is, however, the danger that this could lead to local hegemonic discourses. It is, therefore, necessary to introduce multicultural policies which recognize diversity and difference not in the form of group rights but rather on the basis of individual human rights. This implies a need for constitutional reform.

NOTES

1. For the importance of partition as a device for managing ethnic conflict, see John McGarry and Brendon O'Leary 'Introduction: the Macropolitical negotiation of ethnic conflict', in John McGarry and Brendon O'Leary (eds) *The Politics of Ethnic Conflict Regulation* (London, Routledge 1993).

2. Antonio Gramsci, *Selections from Prison Notebooks,* edited and translated by Quintin Hoare and Geoffrey Nowell Smith, (London, Lawrence and Wishart, London, reprinted 1978), pp. 12-3.

3. T. Ranger, Y. Samad, O. Stuart, 'Introduction' Terence Ranger in *Culture, Identity and Politics: Ethnic Minorities in Britain,* Editors, Aldershot: Avebury, 1996).

4. Rational Choice Theory understands ethnicity in terms of the wishes and actions of individual actors interacting with political structures and processes. A rational actor responding to different structures of opportunities at different times. Subrata Mitra cited by Gurharpal Singh in 'What is Happening to the Political Science of Ethnic Conflict,' *International Journal of Punjab Studies,* Vol. 3, No. 2, 1996, pp. 229-42.

5. Terence Ranger 'Introduction' in *Culture, Identity and Politics.*

6. Stuart Hall, 'Politics of Identity', Ibid.

7. Susan Benson 'Asians have Culture, West Indians have Problems: discourses of Race and Ethnicity in and out of Anthropology'.

8. Nasreen Ali, Pat Ellis and Zafar Khan 'The 1990s: A Time to Separate British Punjabi and British Kashmiri Identity' *Punjabi Identity: Continuity and Change*, Edited by Gurharpal Singh and Ian Talbot, in (New Delhi, Manohar, 1996), pp. 229-56.

9. Ayesha Jalal, *Democracy and Authoritarianism in South Asia: A comparative and historical perspective*, Cambridge: Cambridge University Press, 1995. Yunas Samad, *A Nation in Turmoil: Nationalism and Ethnicity in Pakistan, 1937-1958*, (New Delhi, Sage Sage 1995).

10. Gurharpal Singh, 'The Partition of India as State Contraction: Some Unspoken Assumptions', paper given at the *14th European Conference on Modern South Asian Studies, Copenhagen University, 21-24 August 1996*.

11. Yunas Samad 'Pakistan or Punjabistan; Crisis of National Identity, *International Journal of Punjab Studies*, Vol 2, No. 1, 1995, pp. 23-4.

12. Tariq Rahman, 'Language and Politics in a Pakistan Province: The Sindhi Language Movement', *Asian Survey*, Vol XXXV, No. 11, (November 1995). Tariq Rahman, 'The Pashto language and identity-formation in Pakistan', *Contemporary South Asia*, Vol 4, No. 2, (1995).

13. MQM represented a shift for many *Mohajirs* from supporting religious parties to extolling ethnicity. Altaf Hussain was initially a leader of Jamat-i-Islami's student wing. He became disillusioned with the organization due to its domination by Punjabis. In response to this he, along with others in 1978 formed the All-Pakistan Mohajir Student Organization (APMSO) which in 1986 broadened into the MQM.

14. Charles Kennedy, 'The Politics of Ethnicity in Sindh', *Asian Survey*, Vol XXXVI, No. 10, (October 1991). Iftikhar Malik, 'Ethno-Nationalism in Pakistan: A commentary on Mohajir Qaumi Mahaz (MQM) in Sindhi', *South Asia*, Vol XVIII, No. 2, (1995).

15. Gurharpal Singh, 'The Partition of India as State Contraction'.

16. Farzana Shaikh, *Community and Consensus in Islam: Muslim Representation in Colonial India, 1860-1947*, (Cambridge: Cambridge University Press, 1986).

17. Yunas Samad, *A Nation in Turmoil: Nationalism and Ethnicity in Pakistan, 1937-1958*, (New Delhi, Sage 1995).

18. S. Gopal (ed) *Selected Works of Jawaharlal Nehru*, Vol 7, (New Delhi, Orient Longman, 1975).

19. Ayesha Jalal, *Democracy and Authoritarianism in South Asia: A comparative and historical perspective*, (Cambridge, Cambridge University Press, 1995). Samad, *A Nation in Turmoil: Nationalism and Ethnicity in Pakistan, 1937-1958*.

20. The Awami League had been founded by Shaheed Suhrawardy, who had led the last Muslim League government of united Bengal, and had deep roots in East Pakistan. In the late 1950s it was the only political party with

All-Pakistan pretension and the military *coup* was primarily designed to keep it from coming to power.

21. Yunas Samad 'Pakistan or Punjabistan'.
22. Gowher Rizvi, 'Ethnic Conflict and Political Accomodation in Plural Societies: Cyprus and Other Cases', *Journal of Commonwealth and Comparative Politics*, Vol. 31, No. 1 (March 1993.)
23. Jalal, *Democracy and Authoritarianism in South Asia.*
24. Samad, *A Nation in Turmoil.*
25. Farhat Haq, 'Rise of the MQM in Pakistan: Politics of Ethnic Mobilization,' *Asian Survey*, Vol XXXV, No. 11, (November 1995), p. 1001.
26. Krishna Tummala, 'India's Federalism under Stress', *Asian Survey*, Vol. XXXII, No. 6 (June 1992.)
27. J. S. Furnival, *Colonial Policy and Practice: A Comparative Study of Burma, Netherlands and India.* (New York: New York University Press, 1956) pp. 304-5.
28. M.G. Smith, *The Plural Society in the British West Indies.* (Berkeley and Los Angeles, California: University of California Press, reprinted 1994:) pp. 75-91.
29. Leo Kuper and M.G. Smith (ed.) *Pluralism in Africa.* (Berkeley and Los Angeles), California: University of California Press, reprinted 1971:) p. 440, 444.
30. Charles Taylor, 'The Politics of Recognition', David Goldberg, Theo (ed.) *Multiculturalism: A Critical Leader.* (Cambridge Massachusetts: Blackwell 1994), p. 75.
31. Arend Lijphart defined consociational democracy in terms of four principles: 1) Coalition of all ethnic groups in the establishment of the government. (2) An ethnic veto which would allow any group to prevent legislation which it considered inimical to its group interest. (3) Proportional representation to allow ethnic minorities to participate in government. (4) A loose federation or even confederation which would allow for segmental autonomy. Arend Lijphart, 'Conception and Federation: Conceptual and Empirical Links' *Canadian Journal of Political Science*, Vol. XII. No. 3 *(September 1979).*
32. Ian Talbot 'Back to the Future? The Punjab Unionist Model of Consociational Democracy for Contemporary India and Pakistan' *International Journal of Punjab Studies*, 3, 1 (January-June 1996), pp. 65-73.
33. Charles Kennedy, 'The Politics of Ethnicity in Sindh', *Asian Survey*, Vol. XXXI, No. 10, (October 1991.)
34. Ibid.
35. Terence Ranger, 'Introduction' in *Culture, Identity and Politics.*

List of Contributors

Ishtiaq Ahmed is Reader and Associate Professor in the Department of Political Science at Stockholm University. His extensive writings on Modern South Asian Politics include *State, Nation and Ethnicity in Contemporary South Asia* (London and New York, Francis Pinter, 1996).

Harihar Bhattacharyya received his Ph.D. from the University of London and is now a lecturer in the Department of Political Science at the University of Burdwan, West Bengal. His publications include, *Micro Foundations of Bengal Communism* (Delhi, Ajanta Press 1996).

Joya Chatterji was formerly a Fellow at Trinity College, Cambridge. She has published, *Bengal Divided. Hindu Communalism and Partition 1932-1947* (Cambridge, Cambridge University Press, 1994).

Patricia Ellis was formerly Head of the Department of Social Studies at Luton University. She has researched and published on Kashmiris in Britain.

Carol C. Fair is a research student at the University of Chicago.

Taj-ul-Islam Hashmi is a member of the Department of History at the National University of Singapore. His publications include, *Pakistan as a Peasant Utopia: The Communalization of Class Politics in East Bengal, 1920-1974* (Boulder, Westview Press, 1992).

Zafar Khan is a Senior Lecturer in the Department of Social Studies, Luton University. His current research is on Kashmiris in Britain.

Iftikhar H. Malik was formerly a Senior Research Fellow at St. Antony's College, Oxford. He is presently on the faculty at Bath University College. His extensive publications include, *State and Civil Society in Pakistan. Politics of Authority, Ideology and Ethnicity* (London, Macmillan Press, 1997).

Tazeen M. Murshid is an Associate Senior Research Fellow, Modern Asia Research centre, University of Geneva and Senior Lecturer, University of North London. Her publications include, *The Sacred and the Secular: Bengal Muslim Discourses, 1871-1977* (Calcutta, Oxford University Press, 1995).

Yunas Samad is a Lecturer in the Department of Social and Economic Studies, University of Bradford. His publications include, *A Nation in Turmoil: Nationalism and Ethnicity in Pakistan, 1937-1958* (New Delhi, Sage, 1995).

Gurdit Singh is a Research Student at Harvard University.

Gurharpal Singh is a Professor in India Politics at Hull University. He is the author of *Communism in Punjab* (Delhi: Ajanta Press 1994) and jointly edited *Punjabi Identity: Continuity and Change* (New Delhi, Manohar, 1996).

Ian Talbot is a Reader in South Asian Studies at Coventry University. He has written extensively on Punjab politics and the emergence of Pakistan. His publications include *Khizr Tiwana: The Punjab Unionist Party and the Partition of India* (London: Curzon, 1996) and *Freedom's Cry: The Popular Dimension in the Pakistan Movement and Partition Experience in North-West India* (Karachi, Oxford University Press, 1996). He is a member of the editorial board of the *International Journal of Punjab Studies*.

Shinder S. Thandi is a Senior Lecturer in Economics at Coventry University. He has published on the impact of remittances on the Indian Punjab's economy and on counterinsurgency and political violence in Punjab, 1980-94. He is a member of the editorial board of the *International Journal of Punjab Studies.*

Mohammad Waseem is a Senior Research Fellow at St. Antony's College, Oxford and a Professor at the Quaid-e-Azam University, Islamabad. He has written extensively on Pakistan's politics. His publications include, *State and Politics in Pakistan* (Islamabad, Natioal Institute of Historical and Cultural Research, 1994).

Index

Mochi Gate, 70
Moghalpura Workshop, 127, 128
Mohajir Quami Movement (MQM), 45, 216, 221, 380, 381, 387, 390, 391, 392
Moududin, Syed Abul Ala, 53, 54, 55, 162, 353, 365
Mountbatten, Lord 2, 121, 160, 169, 172, 173, 174, 175, 176, 177, 178, 192, 205, 206
Mudie, R.F., 62, 65, 230
Muhammad Justice Din, 122, 149, 158
Muhammad, Bacha, 20
Muhammad, Monglu, 20
Munir, Justice Muhammad, 122, 149, 150, 157
Munshi, Bacha, 20
Munshi, Lal Muhammad, 20
Munshi, Mudassar, 23
Muslim Conference, 275, 278, 287
Muslim League (Bengal) 14, 27, 180
Muslim League 16, 22, 24, 26, 27, 28, 29, 33, 34, 42, 43, 45, 46, 47, 55, 56, 60, 65, 70, 72, 73, 75, 76, 81, 82, 101, 102, 103, 104, 105, 106, 116, 117, 118, 119, 121, 122, 129, 130, 131, 132, 139, 140, 141, 142, 143, 144, 145, 150, 151, 152, 153, 154, 155, 156, 157, 158, 161,. 173, 174, 175, 179, 180, 181, 182, 191, 273, 350, 351, 359, 379, 382, 285, 393
Muslim National Guards, 208
Mussolini, 45
Myrdal, Gunnar, 315

N

Nadavi, Syed Suleman, 55
Nahal, Chaman, 229, 233, 241, 247
Nalit Bari conference, 15
Nami, Dr Mohammad Ismail, 78
Nankana Sabib, 2, 127, 128, 133, 136,

140, 144, 148, 153, 159, 161, 254, 255, 256, 257, 259, 260
Narayan, Tag, 21, 24
Narayar, Rup, 20
Nasrin, Taslima, 347, 348, 362, 363
Nath, Raja Narendra, 77
National Awami Party (NAP), 380
National Socialism, 51
Nationalist Christian Association, 147
Nawab of Mamdot, 72
Naxalite Movement, 13
Nazimuddin, Khawaja, 180
Nazis, 63
Nehru Report, (1928) 382
Nehru, Jawaharlal, 7, 106, 116, 160, 174, 176, 274, 330, 382, 383, 384
Neo-Marxist, 13
New Bengal Association, 182, 183, 184
Nietzsche, Friedrich W., 51, 54
Nietzschean, 54, 57
Nizam of Hyderabad, 62
Non-Cooperation Movement, 7, 8

O

O'Dyer, Michael, 163
One-Unit, 212, 219, 390, 393
Operation Bluestar (1984), 223

P

Pakistan Peoples Party (PPP), 109, 219, 278, 279, 287, 391, 392
Pakistan Resolution (A.K.A. Lahore Resolution), 43, 76, 103, 354, 355
Pakistan Scheduled Castes Federation, 148
Pathan, Ghyasuddin, 34
Pattbhi, Sitaramya, 80
Penny, J.D., 69
Permanent Settlement Act 1793, 8
Pervaiz, Ghulam Ahmad, 54, 55
Phulbari Conference, 15